D0070188

Front Row

Also by Jerry Oppenheimer

Martha Stewart: Just Desserts: The Unauthorized Biography

The Other Mrs. Kennedy: Ethel Skakel Kennedy:
An American Drama of Power, Privilege, and Politics

State of a Union: Inside the Complex Marriage of Bill and Hillary Clinton

Seinfeld: The Making of an American Icon

Barbara Walters: An Unauthorized Biography

Idol, Rock Hudson: The True Story of an American Film Hero

Front Row

Anna Wintour

The Cool Life and Hot Times of
Vogue's Editor in Chief

Jerry Oppenheimer

St. Martin's Press
New York

FRONT ROW. Copyright © 2005 by Jerry Oppenheimer. All rights reserved. Printed in the United States of America. No part of this book may be used or reproduced in any manner whatsoever without written permission except in the case of brief quotations embodied in critical articles or reviews. For information, address St. Martin's Press, 175 Fifth Avenue, New York, N.Y. 10010.

www.stmartins.com

Frontispiece photo of Anna Wintour by Corbis.

Library of Congress Cataloging-in-Publication Data

Oppenheimer, Jerry.
    Front row : Anna Wintour, the cool life and hot times of Vogue's editor in chief / Jerry Oppenheimer.—1st U.S. ed.
        p. cm.
    Includes bibliographical references (p. 361) and index (p. 365).
    ISBN 0-312-32310-7
    EAN 978-0312-32310-3
    1. Wintour, Anna, 1949– 2. Periodical editors—Great Britain—Biography.
3. Fashion editors—Great Britain—Biography. 4. Vogue. I. Title: Anna Wintour, the cool life and hot times of Vogue's editor in chief. II. Title.

PN5123.W585O66 2005
070.5'1'092—dc22
[B]   2004051313

First Edition: February 2005

10 9 8 7 6 5 4 3 2 1

For Caroline, Cukes, and Trix

Contents

Acknowledgments

Some two hundred people on three continents who have known *Vogue* editor in chief Anna Wintour—present and former friends, lovers, colleagues, employees, and associates—agreed to be interviewed for this book. Others kindly opened doors for me, steered me in the right direction, or agreed to verify or back up controversial facts and anecdotes.

The writing of a book such as this is a collaborative effort, and I could not have succeeded, inasmuch as I did, without their candid insights, observations, and critical assessments.

Wintour, the daughter of a prominent British journalist, refused to be interviewed for this book and declined in any way to help. Moreover, she instructed others not to cooperate. Some abided by her directive, others didn't.

Wintour's response was odd, since over the years she has offered up numerous, though mostly self-serving, interviews and even permitted a British television crew to follow her, in a limited way, for a documentary. At the same time she has been quoted as saying she resents the press. It was clear she did not want a book over which she had no control written about her life.

Most everyone I contacted agreed to talk on the record and without any ground rules. A minority, for personal, professional, or financial reasons— their livelihoods depend on Wintour—requested and were granted anonymity. Not everyone was willing to put his or her career on the line, or to jeopardize relationships. You know who you are.

My goal from the beginning was to portray Wintour in the truest and most objective light, and I believe my sources aided me in fulfilling that end. I'd like to offer my heartfelt thanks to all those who took the time to answer my many questions:

Patti Gilkyson Agnew, Shig Akida, Moriah Allen, Judy Bachrach, Curt Bass, Julie Baumgold, Dianne Benson, Frances Bentley, A. Scott Berg, Robin Blackburn, Chris Blackwell, Andrea Blanche, Peter Bloch, Isabella Blow, Stephen Bobroff, Patricia Bosworth, Sheila Botein, Catherine Jay Boyd, Jimmy Bradshaw, Peter Braunstein, Joe Brooks, Stephanie Brush, Gay Bryant, Paul Callan, Jeremy Campbell, Jenny Capitain, Carol Carson, Anne Carter, George Carter, Maureen Cleave, Alex Cockburn, Nik Cohn, Dana Cowan, Toni Cunliffe, Elen Curran, Judith Daniels, Marie Davis, Emma de Bendern Galitizen, Jacques Dehornois, Nigel Dempster, Joanna Dingemann, Byron Dobell, Susan Duff, Susan Edmiston, Tony Elliott, Richard Ely, Edward Jay Epstein, Michel Esteban, Diane Lokey Farb, Nigel Farndale, Clay Felker, Carol Felsenthal, Willie Fielding, Stephanie Fierz, Zandy Forbes, Phillip Frazer, Kathleen Fury, David Gilbert, Eliza Gilkyson, Nancy Gilkyson, Robin Givhan, Adair Gockley, Elaine Greene, Sarah Griffiths, Barbara Griggs, Michael Gross, Liz Groves, Valerie Grove, Catherine Guinness, Chris Hall, Sophie Hicks, Felicity Green Hill, Pat Hill, Ian Hislop, Jade Hobson, Jennifer Hocking, Shelby Hodge, Annabel Hodin, Min Hogg, Georgina Howell, Barbara Hulanicki, Richard Ingrams, Helen Irwin, Leslie Jay, Liz Jobey, Laurie Jones, Anne Kampman, Mary Kenny, Philip Kingsley, Marilyn Kirschner, Elsa Klensch, Nora Lee Knight, Gini Kopecky, Willie Landels, Jack Langguth, Vivienne Lasky, Guy Le Baube, Stacy Schneer Lee, Zazel Loven, Earle Mack, Dan Matthews, Anthony Mazzola, Joanie McDonell, Angus McGill, Peter McKay, Nancy McKeon, Barbara McKibben, Quita McMath, Richard Meier, Polly Mellen, Sheila Metzner, Carol Mithers, Valerie Monroe, Alma Moore, Jimmy Moore, Alida Morgan, William Mostyn-Owen, Bryan Moynahan, Karen Mullarkey, Jillie Murphy, Tohru Nakamura, Mary Beth Naye, Richard Neville, Nancy Slade Newlove, Helmut Newton, Charlotte Noel, Edna O'Brien, Denise Otis, Patricia O'Toole, Jean Pagliuso, Laura Pank, Betsy Parish, Helen Jay Pennant, Lisa Petersen, Carolyn Pfeiffer, Tom Pocock, Jeffrey Podolski, Virgina Pratt, John Pringle, Dermot Purgave, Jean Rafferty, Piers Paul Read, Barbara Reilly, Brian Rendall, Susie Rich, Glenys Roberts, Frenelle Rogers, Uli Rose, Pat Rotter, Leslie

Russell, Jordan Schaps, Laurie Schechter, Susanna Schindler, Arthur M. Schlesinger Jr., Marian Schlesinger, Joan Schnitzer-Levy, Gaia Servadio, Mort Sheinman, Barbara Shoemaker, Drusilla Beyfus Shulman, Milton Shulman, Paul Sinclaire, Jerold Smokler, Lady Valerie Solti, Davis Sprinkle, Winston Stona, Susan Summers, Dan Taylor, Sara Taylor, Elizabeth "Neal" Gilkyson Stewart Thorpe, Becca Cason Thrash, Ann Trehearne, Elizabeth Tretter, Deborah Turbeville, Jean Vallely, Helen Vanam, Rosemary Vanamee, Nanette Varian, Claire Victor, Brian Vine, Alexander Walker, Liz Walker, Beverly Wardale, Marilyn Warnick, James Wedge, Carol Wheeler, Cristina Zilkha.

Those hundreds of hours of interviews and the huge amount of research that go into a biography of this sort could not have been accomplished without the assistance of seasoned researchers.

I owe a special debt of gratitude to author and journalist Judy Oppenheimer, whose probing, careful interviewing style, and devotion to fairness and objectivity helped make this book possible, as did Caroline Walton Howe's brilliant investigative work and sharp eye for detail.

In London, Elizabeth Fay and Jessica Barrington did important legwork and research. There are many more who assisted on both sides of the Atlantic, and I hold you in great esteem.

An author cannot make it through the many pitfalls of the publishing world without men (and women) who are made of steel: the literary agent. I have been blessed with having the crème de la crème—Dan Strone and Robert Gottlieb of Trident Media Group. A special thanks to Dan's assistant, Hilary Rubin.

At St. Martin's, I'd like to thank Jennifer Weis, Stefanie Lindskog, Sally Richardson, John Murphy, and the rest of the team for making it all happen.

Prologue

Though the Manhattan sidewalks were coated with grimy slush and patches of ice, the thirty-something woman wore strappy Jimmy Choos and was bare-legged, something even Carrie Bradshaw wouldn't have done for Mr. Big at his weirdest. But an exception had to be made in this case, despite the wintry weather, for what was to be a memorable moment. This was the woman's big day—her first and final job interview with the goddess of the world's fashion bible, Anna Wintour.

A ranking candidate for a six-figure-a-year-with-perks features editor job, the woman had been well-briefed by a friend, a Voguette already safely ensconced in the elite fold, as to the toe-cleavage shoes *sans* stockings. Anna, the bosom buddy had warned the job seeker, dictates *everything* that goes into the magazine, along with the behavior and attitude in its hallowed halls, from how subordinates should act on the elevators when she's aboard—subdued, respectful, no eye contact—to how they are supposed to dress if they want to work there, or continue working there.

Thus, naked legs and open-toed stilettos in the bitter New York winter were requirements of the famed and feared editrix's unwritten dress code. It's known among the fashion world cognoscenti that Anna is prone to hire based on dress and looks, let alone spike stories if someone is not photogenic enough for her. "If we're talking about fashion editors, on the whole it's important to me that they have a sense of style," she's intoned. "And on the editorial side"—where the candidate in question hoped to work—"after a few months they will end up looking like *Vogue*. It just rubs off that way." As a *Vogue* editor who knows and abides by Anna's rules notes, "People who work here have to look a certain way. If somebody hasn't changed their appearance within six months . . . something isn't going right."

Besides the bare legs and towering heels, the *Vogue* wannabe has been advised by her friend to wear little makeup and a coat with a matching dress. To pass Anna's muster, she's told, one must strictly comply. And she was finally instructed not to be fashionably late; Anna fumes when she's made to wait.

The candidate arrived at the appointed hour, confident in securing the job she had always dreamed of. She'd already passed muster with flying colors in interviews with *Vogue*'s managing editor who does screening and with Condé Nast's human resources department. Her résumé—and pedigree—have been thoroughly checked. In her mind, the job's in the bag; in her case a four-figure Hermès Birkin for which her name had sat on a waiting list at Bergdorf's for more than a year.

She also has gilt-edged credentials and a solid reputation for writing about fashion and boldfaced names—celebrities, artists, designers, society types—and possesses a dynamite chic red leather Filofax brimming with all the *right* names *and* private numbers. She knows all the dirt and how to dish it—also prerequisites for getting the nod from the editor in chief.

Besides all of that, she's a fashionista par excellence—all in all, a perfect *Vogue* candidate.

Last step, the final interview with Anna of the dominatrix power bob.

But things do not go well from the moment the boss woman's assistant—one in a relatively long and harried line—summons her to enter the royal chamber in the Condé Nast palace that towers high above Times Square.

The first thing that strikes her is the immensity of Anna's office and the long, *long* approach from the door to where the editor once dubbed "nuclear Wintour" is holding court behind her enormous, sleek, and devoid-of-any-semblance-of-work prototype Buchsbaum desk; the distance seems to the interviewee like the seemingly endless runway at the Versace shows in Milan. The office itself is stark and cold, much like the pin-thin, famously glacial woman who inhabits it. Anna, in a little Chanel number and her signature sunglasses—which make eye contact all but impossible—never rises to greet the candidate, just briskly commands, "Sit, please."

"I really thought I was going to get the job *until* I met her," says the *Vogue* aspirant, well known and respected in fashion and celebrity media. "Anna was very, very cool and contradicted *everything* I said. She would ask me questions and I would answer in the most intelligent way I could, and then she would contradict me. For instance, she said, 'What would you do in the music section?' I said something about 'going very upscale.' And she said, 'We're a *populist* magazine.' She asked me what I'd do with another section, and I told her I thought that deserved a populist view. She said, 'We're an *upscale* magazine.' She just didn't want me to win. She's *very* scary. And I've *never* been scared in journalism.

"I've gotten almost every job I've interviewed for because I'm really good on interviews," continues the *Vogue* hopeful, "but I knew within just a few minutes that I would never get that job because I felt she was *looking* for me to fail, there was something almost *sadistic* about what was going on.

"I thought, 'What's my best mode of behavior here? I truly *cannot* contradict her. I don't want to get into a battle, or competitive mode with her.' I wasn't intimidated, but I wouldn't allow her to *make* me contradict myself. I wasn't going to be spineless, so I tried to stick to my guns. I thought, 'Why let her fuck with my head?'"

After twenty minutes, Anna, looking bored, brusquely concluded the interview.

It's the last time the woman heard from *Vogue*.

Afterward, her friend and others at the magazine told her she was better off because "everyone at *Vogue* is miserable, and everyone's terrified of Anna."

The woman, who went on to other desirable media jobs and a book deal, observes, "A lot of people around Anna, and this is true at every fashion magazine, are gay men, and they're the *only* ones at *Vogue* who are not terrorized by her. The thing is, she doesn't really *like* women, which is certainly curious for the editor of the world's most influential fashion magazine *for* women. I've always wondered, what's with her? Why is she like that? What makes her tick? What's her story?"

People want to read about
fashion and controversy and gossip.
If *Vogue* can't give it to them, who can?

—ANNA WINTOUR,
The New York Times, October 31, 1988

Front Row

one

Family Roots

Born on November 3, 1949, Anna was a healthy tot with a mop of straight, shiny dark brown hair and intelligent, dreamy grayish-green eyes set in a beautiful, tiny oval face. She was late to talk, and when she did, she spoke very little and was thought by her parents to be a shy and distant flower. Anna had come into the world at an ironic moment in time; only weeks before her birth, years of clothing rationing had ended in war-torn Britain—and clothing and fashion would become her passion.

As the first daughter in what was then a family of two sons whose father came from a line of military men and who had become a steely, ambitious newspaperman, the dainty girl would have much to live up to. She was the second of Charles Vere Wintour and Eleanor Trego Baker Wintour's children who were born in London after the Nazi bombs and rockets had stopped raining death and destruction. The other postwar child was James Charles, a gentle, easy-to-handle tyke who was born two and a half years before Anna.

But the Wintours' first, Gerald Jackson, born almost a decade before Anna, was the parents' true pride and joy, the one the others would be compared to.

Charles Wintour felt certain that Gerald would follow in his footsteps as a journalist. For his eighth birthday, the father had given the fair-haired son a toy printing kit from Harrods, complete with various faces of little rubber type with wooden blocks to set them in, a messy black ink pad, and a sheaf of blank newsprint. It was his favorite gift of all. On his own, Gerald produced a little newspaper, a diary about his small world, and proudly presented the first edition of the *Wintour Daily* to his father, a memento Charles Wintour would treasure his entire life.

Eleanor Baker, an American, who was nicknamed Nonie, met Wintour at Cambridge University in England in the fall of 1939. The petite, bright, bespectacled, and extremely plain-looking twenty-two-year-old Bostonian, who had a prettier sister named Jean, had gone to a fancy girls' boarding school in Connecticut called Westover and was just out of Radcliffe.

She had initially tried to get to England as a correspondent for a small weekly newspaper, *The Daily Republican,* in Phoenixville, Pennsylvania, owned by close relatives, but when that failed, she enrolled at Newnham College, one of the two schools for women at Cambridge. "It was just something to do—Nonie had no particular ties to England," notes an American cousin, Elizabeth Gilkyson Stewart Thorpe, known as "Neal," who became a prominent women's magazine editor in New York. Always known for her sharp tongue, critical manner, and liberal politics, Nonie Baker had dreams of becoming a writer or journalist. Instead, she would marry one and become a dedicated social worker.

Playing Cupid for Nonie and Charles was a mutual friend and Peterhouse College, Cambridge, classmate of Wintour's, Arthur M. Schlesinger Jr., who saw him as "a pleasant-looking young man with glasses, a somewhat saturnine expression, and an impressive air of professional efficiency."

Nonie Baker and Schlesinger had known each other from his student days at Harvard, where her father, Ralph Baker, was a distinguished professor at the Harvard Law School and where Schlesinger's father was a famous historian. During the war, Baker also was cocounsel for the U.S. office that confiscated alien property. Her parents, who had met at Swarthmore College, and "thee and thou'd" each other in a Quaker wedding ceremony, were well-to-do. Baker had made a bundle as a corporate attorney in Philadephia representing clients like the Pennsylvania Railroad before moving to Harvard to teach. His wife, Anna Gilkyson Baker, for whom Anna Wintour was named, was a charming, matronly, somewhat ditzy society girl from Philadelphia's Main Line who was known to leave her children in the park and not realize it until she got home.

Like his father, Schlesinger would go on to become an eminent Pulitzer Prize–winning historian, author, and, moreover, a trusted adviser to Jack and Bobby Kennedy in the sixties, while his very best friend, Charles Wintour, would become one of Fleet Street's most powerful, creative, respected, and feared newspaper editors.

Neal Thorpe maintains that in Boston, Schlesinger "was very much in love with Nonie" at one point "and wanted to marry her." This is something that Schlesinger denies years later. "I was fond of her," he acknowledges, "but she did not attract me physically." Schlesinger remembers Nonie from those early days in Boston and London as "bright, witty, and critical. She had a sharp eye for the weaknesses of others; she took a generally critical stance toward the world."

Looking back, he feels that Nonie was critical as a form of "self-protection because I think she was extremely vulnerable. But she also was great fun to be with so long as one wasn't the target."

While Charles Wintour initially appeared to Schlesinger to be "a quintessential Britisher," he had actually spent the previous summer hitchhiking through the United States and was considered "an Americanophile."

When they met, Wintour was editor of an undergraduate Cambridge weekly called *Granta,* which was a mix of the Harvard *Crimson* and the *Lampoon.* Schlesinger critiqued the magazine. Wintour accepted his comments with "brisk but somewhat enigmatic courtesy" and invited Schlesinger to write articles and attend editorial board meetings. The two later invented a false byline, A. G. Case—A. Glandular Case—that appeared every so often on stories that were critical of other campus publications.

Wintour was quite the operator and took Schlesinger under his wing, introducing him to everyone who counted. Schlesinger got to know "more campus big shots" because of his chum than he ever knew at Harvard. To Schlesinger, Wintour was "a man after my own heart—inquiring, skeptical, sensitive to relationships among people, and politically adept at influencing them, flexible, vigorous."

Wintour, who had a sly and bad-boyish quality about him, took Schlesinger to meet his family in Dorset. While there, he gave his friend a tour of some of the more interesting local landmarks, such as the Cerne Abbas. Carved out of a hillside, it was the figure of a nude male with a twenty-six-foot erection, which Wintour put on the itinerary because he enjoyed getting a rise out of his guests.

Schlesinger thoroughly enjoyed Wintour and repaid his friendship by introducing him to Nonie Baker, and the two "hit it off at once."

Recalls Schlesinger, "They became a couple two or three months after they first met. Charles found Nonie very entertaining, certainly stylish, and she had a kind of patrician manner about her and seemed to represent a good, healthy American girl. Charles had great charm and wit, too, but also a sense of control. I wouldn't say he was terribly handsome, though. He wasn't a Ronald Coleman." Schlesinger was no godsend in the looks department, either, so the two also had that in common.

At the same time Wintour and the Baker girl started dating, Schlesinger began seeing a friend of Wintour's, Anne Mortimer Whyte, the daughter of a member of Parliament and private secretary to Winston Churchill. Wintour always made it his business to know all the right people.

The two couples—Charles and Nonie, and Schlesinger and Whyte—double-dated often. When Schlesinger directed a college production of Shakespeare's *As You Like It,* he cast Wintour and Whyte in starring roles.

With war looming, the two couples enjoyed their last days at school, taking motor trips in Wintour's convertible with the top down.

It was, as Schlesinger recalled, a "careless, glorious" time.

Charles and Nonie, madly in love, got married in the little parish church of St. Mary the Less near the university on March 13, 1940, a simple ceremony performed by a university chaplain. Wintour's father, crisp and stern retired Major General Fitzgerald Wintour, a career military man, served as their witness. When the happy couple settled in a local hotel after they tied the knot, Gerald Jackson Wintour was conceived. It was a wartime love affair and marriage; Charles Wintour had already enlisted and was in uniform. There was no time to dilly-dally.

Little more than a month before she was due, the very independent Mrs. Wintour kissed her husband, a second lieutenant in the Royal Norfolk Regiment, good-bye and departed London for Boston, to be with her family and have the baby. With the war raging, the young parents-to-be felt it would be safer if the child was in America, out of harm's way, as London was being blitzed by German rockets and bombs.

On November 20, eight months and a week after the Wintours' nuptials, Nonie gave birth in New England Baptist Hospital to the healthy boy they named Gerald.

She took the baby back to her family's apartment in the Barrington Court on fashionable Memorial Drive on the Charles River, where she breast-fed him.

Baby Gerald would grow into a sturdy, independent, rough-and-tumble boy, despite extremely difficult odds.

For the first four years of his life he didn't know who his real parents were.

With London in flames, and with her groom in the middle of the Battle of Britain, Nonie Wintour decided to leave Gerald with her parents and return to England to be close to her husband and do whatever she could to help in the war effort over there—a real-life Mrs. Miniver.

"She left the baby because she was so much in love with Charles," recalls Nonie's first cousin, Patti Gilkyson Agnew, whose father was Anna Baker's brother. "Aunt Anna and Uncle Ralph raised Gerald until he was something like four years old."

In what Agnew and other American relatives felt was an emotionally difficult situation, the Bakers became Gerald Wintour's surrogate parents for the duration. As often as she could, Nonie mailed home photographs of herself and her husband, which the Bakers would show to little Gerald, gently telling the toddler that those strangers in the shapshots were his real mommy and daddy so that he would recognize them when they came to retrieve him in the waning days of the war.

It was a highly emotional scene when that moment arrived, recalls Patti Agnew. "Ralph and Anna nearly died, were devastated, when Nonie and Charles came to claim Gerald. They felt as if he was *their* baby." Her sister, Neal Thorpe, observes, "It was a real strain on everyone involved."

Wintour survived the war, having spent most of his time in intelligence, and ending up at General Dwight Eisenhower's headquarters in Paris. He saw little if any combat but was awarded the American Bronze Star and the French Croix de Guerre, usually pinned on men who had actually seen action. A longtime friend and newspaper colleague maintains that Wintour got the medals "for administrative work." Years later, Schlesinger, who had also served in Europe and had even spent some time with his friend as fellow officers, was surprised to learn that Wintour had received such high military honors. "He never told me."

Back in London, with the war over, the Wintours bought a pleasant contemporary-style home on Cochrane Street in the upper-middle-class London area of St. Johns Wood.

Wintour had gotten a job in 1946 on London's *Evening Standard,* starting as a secretary of sorts for one of the world's most powerful, shrewd, domineering, and dictatorial press barons, Max Aitken, better known as Lord Beaverbrook. Wintour was a young journalist on the way up and would soon become one of Beaverbrook's extremely loyal and creative fair-haired boys.

For the Wintours, the future looked exceedingly bright. In fairly quick succession, Charles and Nonie had James, and then Anna, the future editor in chief of *Vogue.*

But eighteen months after she was born, a tragedy struck the family that would have long-term emotional implications for Anna, her siblings, and particularly her parents.

Tuesday, July 3, 1951, was a pleasant day in London. With no rain expected, Nonie Wintour had allowed ten-year-old Gerald to ride his two-wheeler to the Hall School, a private preparatory school for boys in Hampstead, where he was a student. The boy had been riding a two-wheeler since he was five. His father had "complete confidence in his ability" and allowed him "to choose his own route" to and from school because "he was an extremely cautious driver." Gerald left home with his book bag and wearing the school uniform, a pink blazer and cap. He never returned.

Pedaling home in the afternoon on Avenue Road, a wide street lined with trees and large homes, the boy was hit by a car. He was thrown into the air, landed on the hood with such impact that he smashed the windshield, and fell unconscious onto the asphalt. "I was not in a hurry, I did not see the boy until I was a few yards away," testified the driver at the inquest. "I went to pass and did not blow my horn. I did not think he was going to turn. I did not see him put his arm out." Witnesses said the boy didn't know what hit him.

After getting the call, Nonie Wintour rushed to New End Hospital in nearby Hampstead, but she was too late. Gerald had died twenty minutes after he arrived in the emergency room of a fractured skull and other injuries. His death was later ruled accidental.

His mother was hysterical. She got on the pay phone and tried to reach her husband, who on that hellish day was meeting with Beaverbrook at Cherkley Court, his enormous, secluded nineteenth-century gray stone mansion with some thirty bedrooms, near the town of Leatherhead in Surrey, about two hours in those days from London.

What happened next, and there are a number of versions, became part of the whispered Fleet Street legend surrounding Charles Wintour's life and was one of the reasons why he was thought of by many as an editor with ice water running through his veins.

Paul Callan, a respected veteran London journalist who had started his career working under Wintour, is one of the many who heard what he believes is a credible account of what happened that tragic day.

"At the time Charles was Lord Beaverbrook's secretary, and he was taking dictation from him when the butler came in and asked to speak to Charles," recounts Callan. "Charles went outside with the butler, who told him his little boy had been killed. Charles went back in, never said anything to Lord Beaverbrook, and resumed taking dictation. Nobody ever knew what made him do it. Charles wasn't a monster, but he could be a bit cold-blooded."

Alexander Walker, who would become a noted film critic at the London *Evening Standard,* the paper Beaverbrook eventually gave Wintour to run, heard that he had actually telephoned Nonie after getting the urgent message about Gerald. "But Charles had decided to finish his work with Beaverbrook before returning home," Walker says. "He told his proprietor what had happened to his son, and Beaverbrook was impressed at how bravely and businesslike Charles had taken the news, and that he was able to go on working. It made Charles's reputation with Beaverbrook."

Milton Shulman, who had started in journalism with Wintour immediately after the war and later worked under him as the *Evening Standard*'s esteemed theater critic, says years later, "There's no question that the death of the child put Charles into the arms of Beaverbrook."

Whichever way it happened, whether Wintour rushed to be with his distraught wife or stayed at his boss's side, the death of their firstborn was devastating, and the events surrounding the tragedy left a permanent dark cloud over the Wintour family.

As Callan notes, "Charles's behavior when the son was killed split the marriage."

Walker, who was close to both Charles Wintour and especially Nonie, asserts, "The great tragedy of Charles's life was he, like a lot of Beaverbrook's editors, was a creature of his proprietor. The boy's death *absolutely* destroyed the Wintour marriage, changed Charles forever, and he became a very chilly, withdrawn figure. It's a terribly, terribly sad story."

Furious with her husband, despondent over her son's death, Nonie Wintour gathered up little Anna and James and left England for Boston to be with her family, to be consoled. Some thought the marriage was over.

While his wife was gone, Wintour and Beaverbrook bonded. The two met frequently because at the time Beaverbrook needed bright, young editors for his newspaper chain. So he put Wintour to the test, inculcated him with his various conservative philosophies, had him write editorials to see if he was able to present them with Beaverbrook's point of view, and promised to put him on the gravy train by giving him an editorship someday.

At the end of that terrible summer of 1951, Nonie Wintour returned to London with Anna and James. She and her husband had a chilly rapprochement, but their marriage never was the same.

It was in that horribly depressed and icy atmosphere that Anna grew up.

With hopes that a larger family might warm the frigid air, Nonie Wintour had two more children in quick succession in the wake of Gerald's death. Less than a year after the tragedy, she became pregnant, and on February 3, 1953, Anna got a sister, Nora Hilary, with whom she'd never be close because they were so different: Anna would grow into a beauty and a fashionista, thought of as frivolous by the rest of the family, while Nora was plain looking like their mother, academically inclined, and a political activist.

A year later, Nonie got pregnant again, and two days before Anna's fifth birthday, on November 1, 1954, she gave birth to another son, Patrick Walter.

But it was Anna who replaced Gerald as the fair-haired child in Charles Wintour's eye. Though he loved all his children, Anna became and would always be his favorite. And Anna was the one of the four surviving Wintour children who would turn out to be the most like him—driven, ambitious, creative, icy, with her eye always on the prize.

Anna would become the most famous of the Wintour brood, far surpassing her father as a powerful editor. Of the other three, only Patrick became a journalist. Like their mother, James and Nora became societal do-gooders and lived rather quiet and stable lives. James worked in public housing in Scotland, and Nora married a Red Cross worker in Switzerland.

Besides the animosity Nonie felt toward Charles regarding his response, or lack thereof, to their firstborn's death, she came to despise her husband for working for Beaverbrook, whose political and social views she vehemently disagreed with.

"Nonie was very left-wing," says Milton Shulman, "and she always despised Charles's compromises working for Beaverbrook, compromises which you have to make if you're going to become editor of a right-wing newspaper."

Like Beaverbrook, Shulman was a Canadian, so the publisher had a fondness for him beyond his being a bright young journalist. In the early fifties, Shulman says, he was asked by Beaverbrook to become deputy editor of the Manchester *Daily Express,* one of the papers in the Daily Express chain, where Beaverbrook tried out young editors for bigger jobs. But Shulman, who had been involved with the Socialist Party in Canada, turned down the job on the grounds that he didn't share Beaverbrook's political views. "I told him I would have to compromise either my work on the paper or my own political views. I didn't want to do that. That was my one test to be editor, and he never asked me again."

But when Beaverbrook asked Charles Wintour to take the job in Manchester, he accepted without reservation, but to his wife's chagrin. "Nonie never moved up there with Charles," says Shulman. "She stayed in London with the children."

Shulman's wife, the journalist Drusilla Beyfus Shulman, who socialized with the Wintours, observes that Nonie "was very disappointed in Charles's loyalty to the Beaverbrook line, which was very much contrary to her own instincts and beliefs. She wasn't sympathetic to Beaverbrook's values and was quite naggy to Charles about them. Nonie and Charles weren't particularly interested in each other's views."

Wintour impressed Beaverbrook, and in 1954, when Anna was five, her father was made deputy editor of the *Evening Standard,* and in 1959, at forty-two, he was appointed editor in chief. He turned the paper around with his extraordinary eye for spotting talented editors, writers, and columnists.

He also earned the sobriquet "Chilly Charlie" because of how stern, aloof, and demanding he was. As his power grew, he also became a womanizer, which added to the marital turmoil in the Wintour home, especially impacting young Anna.

During the 1950s, Nonie Wintour became a devoted, some say obsessively so, social worker; they attributed her intense involvement in the sad plight of others to her liberal Quaker background. Her first job involved dealing with people who were determined by the government to be mentally incompetent. Later, she worked with foster children and adoptive parents. For a time in the early fifties, the writer in her came out and she tried her hand at freelance film criticism for an intellectual and political British magazine called *Time and Tide,* whose contributors over the years had included Virginia Woolf, D. H. Lawrence, and Emma Goldman. She could be vicious. One film she called a "preposterous story," another a "lachrymose tale of love," and a third "an airy French trifle . . . a stale bit of sponge cake." In the dozen or so reviews she wrote, she rarely gave two thumbs-up.

In a home filled with so much angst, Anna turned inward, became even more shy and withdrawn, and had no known close friends. At the North Bridge House School in Hampstead she was quiet as a church mouse, a loner who did not stand out from the crowd. It was clear she was horribly affected by her parents' turmoil. Along with the curtain of gloom that had descended in the wake of her brother's death, her father, whom she dearly loved, was rarely around, busy devoting his life to Beaverbrook and his success as an editor.

At the age of eleven, in September 1960, Anna was enrolled at London's exclusive Queens College, which wasn't a college at all but rather a fancy middle and high school that catered to such wealthy young heiresses as Christina Onassis, girls who arrived each morning in chauffeur-driven cars. It was a school that at the time, according to one of Anna's classmates, "prepared women to be educated wives."

Though Queens College had quite a lot of cachet and was very chichi, Anna despised it, hated putting up with the very intense discipline. Under the rules, students were not permitted to talk in certain parts of the building and were required to stand and stop speaking when a teacher entered the room. The school was kept so cold—warmth was considered bad for discipline—that a classmate developed a mild case of frostbite on her feet.

Anna also hated the school uniform—a pinafore with a long-sleeved white shirt, striped tie, and cardigan sweater, which she thought was ugly and dated.

With all of the discipline and regimentation, Anna was viewed as "willful, resentful, and very complex," according to a classmate. "Anna didn't seem to have a need for a lot of girlfriends. She didn't have any really close friends, and if she did, she didn't appear to keep any."

Susan Summers, who went to Queens and later worked for the *Evening Standard,* was once told, "When you meet Charles Wintour, you'll be put off by his rather glacial exterior, but when you get to know him better you realize it's only the tip of the iceberg." She says, "There's clearly a lot in common between Anna and her father in that they're both cold. . . . The difference is, he was actually loved by his staff, and she was *not* a popular leader. She had a pretty screwed-up childhood, and she became a very icy woman."

Anna remained at Queens College until July 1963, when the Wintours, tired of her complaints about how dreadful life was for her at the school, transferred her to another fancy all-girls' school, the century-old North London Collegiate, where she was admitted on September 18, and where the students were known as "North London Clever Girls."

two

A Teenage Bond

At North London Collegiate, Anna bonded with another new student with whom she would have a seemingly loving and enduring friendship, albeit one marked by sporadic petty jealousy and Machiavellian cattiness. Anna's relationship with Vivienne Lasky, her first and only true teenage soul mate, would eventually end years later, suddenly, sharply, and bizarrely, like a number of Anna's subsequent adult female friendships and professional associations.

Anna never was, and never would be, a girls' girl, would have few close female friends over the years, and didn't appear to like or enjoy the company of other women—curious for someone who one day would control fashion magazines that catered to women's styles and taste.

But back then, from the moment Anna and Lasky met in the dreary, frigid halls of North London Collegiate, about to turn fourteen, they became as close and dependent on each other as those four mop-heads called the Beatles who were about to launch the first British invasion of America. In the next decade, Anna would be among those at the forefront of a second—an encroachment upon the American shores of a brigade of British journalists, writers, and editors dubbed the "Briterati."

"We were the two new girls at North London," says Lasky. "Being the new girls was not easy. No one else would talk to us. We felt very left out. Anna would ask me, 'Do you know where we're meant to go?' We arrived totally unprepared and no one said, 'Go here, go there.' Nothing was made clear to us. It was not a warm and nurturing place. We used to have discussions, 'How long are we going to be the new girls?'

"I liked her immediately. I could see she was smart, pretty, didn't *seem* stuck up. We were just drawn together and became best friends. Anna was half American, and I was half American. We were both living in Britain, and our fathers were in journalism. We fit easily into each other's lives. We were as close friends as girls could be. It was just the two of us."

Like Charles Wintour, Vivienne Lasky's father was a prominent journalist and editor. Melvin J. Lasky, a New Yorker, was cofounder and editor of *Encounter,* an influential intellectual monthly. During the 1950s and 1960s, the best and the brightest wrote for the journal: Bertrand Russell, Vladimir Nabokov, W. H. Auden, among other literary intelligentsia. Under Lasky, *Encounter* held what the British author and filmmaker Frances Stonor Saunders once called "a central position in postwar intellectual history. It could be as lively and bitchy as a literary cocktail party." The magazine also became the center of a controversy when it was revealed that it received clandestine funding from the U.S. Central Intelligence Agency.

There were other similarities between the two fathers. Like "Chilly Charlie," Lasky had a reputation for being cold and tough. "Charles and my father, they were *very* critical," Lasky states. "They edited in their own lives as well as in their work. If I said to Charles at Sunday lunch, 'I'm reading a most marvelous book,' he'd say, 'What a bunch of slop!'"

Wintour and Lasky both were womanizers, and the Laskys' marriage was also troubled. Both Anna and Vivienne shared the emotional upheavals ignited by their parents' travails.

Lasky's coeditor at *Encounter* was Sir Stephen Spender, the literary and art critic, journalist, and social commentator. Unlike Lasky, who had an eye for beautiful women, Spender was bisexual. His daughter, Lizzie Spender, had grown up with Vivienne Lasky and had attended North London Collegiate, where she got to know Anna. After a giddy and madcap life, the tall, elegant blonde, who was an actress and a friend of Prince Charles, settled down, and became the fourth wife of Barry Humphries, better known as the drag queen talk-show host and stage performer "Dame Edna Everage."

Despite all of those intrigues, none of it seemed daunting or of concern to Anna. As she told Lasky, "We're the daughters of celebrities. So be it."

While the one subject at NLC that interested Anna was history, the most contemporary event taught was the Boer War, which Anna instantly dubbed "the Bore War." Academic studies were of little interest to her. Anna loathed *everything* about school, especially the classroom couture. She thought the uniform "looked liked shit," Lasky asserts. "It was the same color."

In fall and winter, young Anna, who one day would rule the fashion world draped in Chanel, standing confidently in Manolos, was required to wear a brown felt blazer that had the feel of a horse blanket, the jacket worn over a stiff, scratchy tan poplin blouse, and a pleated brown skirt that was too large because the elderly spinster educators who ran the school wanted her to grow into it. Anna complained that it made her look pregnant. Moreover, the skirt was made of a synthetic fabric that once actually melted when Anna leaned against a classroom radiator to try to warm herself. The powers at North London Collegiate, like those at Queens College, kept the heat in the bitter and damp midwinter at a minimum, thinking it would inspire the students to work harder.

For a time, when she was at Queens, Anna had been a runner, the only extracurricular activity in which she is known to have participated during her school years. "When she was ten she was amazingly fleet of foot," her father once observed. "Some sports instructor indicated that if she really worked at it she could probably become a sprinter of Olympic standard. That finished it. Anna said, 'How frightful! What on earth will happen to my legs?' and stopped running."

By the time she got to North London, the teachers had to force her to run. "She hated that," Lasky recalls. "She'd hide in the toilet." Manolo Blahnik was years away from designing *Sex and the City* shoes, but somehow adolescent Anna foresaw that one day her legs would be a part of her signature look, so they needed to be slender and shapely, not thick and muscled.

Besides the impact she thought running would have on her legs, Anna avoided gym by either cutting the class or claiming she was ill because she was physically sickened by the suit she was required to wear—scratchy brown culottes with a culotte skirt studded with dozens of little buttons on each side that made getting in and out of the outfit a formidable task. All of this was set off by a light blue preppyish polo shirt, brown and blue being the school colors.

Another reason she always tried to skip gym was that she had to participate in bare feet, a school rule based on some obscure turn-of-the-century health theory. Anna feared picking up a skin irritation, such as the highly infectious virus called verrucae, a wart on the sole spread through athletic activity, which her friend had caught. "Actually, Anna thought it was terrific because I just got to sit on the bench," Lasky recalls.

But more, Anna feared that the barefooted gymnastics might disfigure her slender feet.

Anna liked to show off her good legs and was at the forefront of the miniskirt revolution, the decade's defining fashion statement then hitting London like a German V2 rocket during the Blitz.

While the school skirt's length was set by the headmistress and was meant to cover the crease behind the knee, Anna rebelled by wearing a belt to hitch up the waist or by rolling up the hem, which got her into hot water. A number of times Miss Dobson, the scary math teacher, caught her shortening her skirt.

If "old Dobbie" caught Anna leaning out the window with her skirt rolled up and saw the back of her legs, she'd jab her hard with the chewed metal end of a pencil that once held the eraser and severely reprimand her. Other times, as Anna marched in line to morning prayers—the Church of England and Catholic girls prayed in the east gym, the Jewish girls in the west—she'd be spotted for shortening her skirt. The eagle-eyed teacher sneaked up behind Anna and pulled her sweater up over her head. Disoriented and frightened, Anna was yelled at and berated for breaking the rule. Anna was "scared shitless," Lasky remembers, but believes she continually broke the rule in order to "get a rise out of them. The short skirt thing happened time and time again."

Anna's stubborn decision to wear minis, to defy the rules, would eventually lead to serious problems at school.

Most of the North London Collegiate teachers—all women—were unmarried, and some had lost husbands or fiancés in the First World War. Anna scoffed at them, whispered about them, joked that they were so doddering she was absolutely certain their men had been killed in the Boer War. Anna had already developed a thing about age and would later use it as both a creative tool and a weapon when she became a fashion editor.

North London's uniform changed slightly in the spring, when students were required to wear long gingham dresses in various shades of the ubiquitous brown. "It was like a Donna Reed dress hanging on Anna Wintour," recalls Lasky, giggling at the vision of her defiant, fashion-forward friend looking like the wholesome character on the golden-age TV sitcom *The Donna Reed Show.*

Outside of school, Anna was required to wear a brown beret and a knitted scarf that displayed the school colors. The beret was mandatory through all seasons, and North London girls wore it to and from school. However, at four o'clock, when classes ended, Anna and Lasky, on the way to the underground station, doffed their school covers and stuffed them into their book bags. Enough with uniforms! Enough with regimentation! All of which got Anna into more trouble on a number of occasions.

Riding home on the subway one late afternoon, Anna and Lasky were spotted sans berets by a proud alumna and reported. "Some woman called the school," Lasky recalls, "and said, 'I've just seen two North Londoners *not* wearing their berets!' We were the only two girls who lived downtown, so they knew it was us. We got caught a few times. We got called in to the head-mistress's office and Anna would just sort of bullshit them. 'You mean I can't take my hat off?' she asked innocently."

A stern lecture, one of many she received during her school days, ensued. "Your uniform stands for something. It shows where you're from," the head-mistress intoned. "You must *always* wear your beret *proudly.* You, Anna Wintour, have to live up to your uniform!"

With wrist slapped, Anna left, stifling a giggle. She didn't care about the school's dress rules. "It's a stupid hat. I hate it!" And she continued not to wear it if she thought she could get away with it.

Years later, after she became head of American *Vogue,* the beret was still on her "out" list. She called it that "awful brown beret" and suggested that the required school uniform might have been one of the reasons why she became interested in fashion in the first place.

Not until she was swathed in Chanel and standing on stilettos at the helm of the world's fashion bible would Anna fully live up to her uniform.

Eating in public was another issue that school authorities seriously frowned upon. Unfortunately, Anna once again was a violator, caught gulping down an occasional biscuit, hungry for a quick sugar rush because she rarely ate at all. Each time she got caught, her parents were called. "What do you mean she was eating biscuits?" demanded a furious Charles Wintour of the headmistress. "I would think my daughter was hungry!" Arguing in Anna's defense, he swiftly and pointedly ended the discussion. "What," he asked, "is this idiocy?"

At fourteen, stick-thin Anna watched her diet obsessively, mostly by not eating. Her school lunch usually consisted of a Granny Smith apple. Lasky's mother, a former model, was worried about Anna's health and thought she was too bony, though Anna felt she was fashionably emaciated like the premier model of the swinging sixties, Twiggy, whom Anna thought looked fab.

"Anna only ate if it was something special," says Lasky. "She always has had *terrific* self-control."

Anna was sickened even contemplating the school menu, which consisted of dishes such as "bubble and squeak," so named because of the sounds that were emitted during cooking. It consisted of bland boiled potatoes and soggy green cabbage mashed together. Or a pudding with the saucy name "spotted dick," which a British grocery chain wanted to change to "spotted richard," because customers were too embarrassed to ask for it. At home, Nonie Wintour served a mousse called "housemaid's knee," which also disgusted Anna, who would bring leftovers to her friend, who ate it on the subway after school. Moreover, Anna didn't feel that the atmosphere at school was conducive to a relaxed meal, what with one of the teachers seated primly at the end of the long table, carefully watching her deportment and manners.

"The place was so stiff-necked," Lasky asserts. "There was no warmth."

Only on special occasions did Anna gorge herself, such as when she and her friend cut into their formidable allowances and splurged on lunch at the posh four-star Caprice in Mayfair, which later became one of Princess Diana's favorite Italian restaurants, or at the delectable Fortnum & Mason, just west of Piccadilly, for tea and a quick bite. Anna kept on top of restaurant, pub, and club ratings in trendy magazines and guides. "She always liked the best of everything," Lasky says.

Bored with school, Anna and Lasky played hooky, forging their parents' signatures on official-sounding notes they typed, asking to be excused from classes because of an urgent doctor's appointment or a great-aunt's funeral.

"We went to the ladies' room in Trafalgar Square and changed into regular clothes. We'd go to museums. We'd go shopping. We'd go out to tea. We'd go to the movies. Anna loved the old romances, the black-and-white classics—*Rebecca*. We would walk miles to see them over and over again."

Ferris Bueller had nothing on Anna Wintour.

three

Swinging London

Nineteen sixty-three, the year Anna matriculated at North London Collegiate, an explosion of enormous proportions rocked Britain. It was dubbed a youth quake, a psychedelic nuclear blast of fashion, style, and music that quickly resounded around the world. And Anna came of age in that momentous time, infusing her with an extreme interest in fashion.

"That moment in time that Anna and I were growing up in London," Vivienne Lasky reminisces, "was just not to be replicated."

The hair—the sexy, sometimes fetishy but always timeless bob—became an integral part of *the* look in the swinging London scene. Always on top of trends, Anna rushed to get her lush, thick, straight brown hair cut and styled in the new fashion, which became a key component of her chic image, the cut she still wore in her mid-fifties, a cut that not so coincidentally has been favored and popularized by the British dominatrix, as Anna, the editrix, would later be described by some submissive and mistreated underlings.

The bob had been around for ages, first given public attention in the 1920s when the actress Louise Brooks wore it as the character Lulu. Also a model, Brooks appeared occasionally in fashion ads exposing the bob to the masses, which helped define the flapper look. Now it would define trendy London birds in the revolutionary and exuberant sixties.

Among those whose look inspired Anna to get the bob was Maureen Cleave, one of Charles Wintour's talented favorites on the *Evening Standard* staff.

"Charles simply adored Maureen," says journalist Valerie Grove, one of Cleave's close friends and a colleague on the paper. "She was petite, dark, brisk, brilliant, clever, sharp, and very articulate—adorable in every way. And Charles was absolutely enthralled with her. Maureen had the bob, and it became sort of her trademark. Everybody on the paper thought that Anna copied Maureen's hairstyle and that is the origin of the Anna Wintour look. People thought Charles was expressing his adoration of Anna, and his ambitions for Anna, through his keenness for Maureen. It was really some kind of dynamic there."

In fact, Alex Walker believes that Anna's decision to copy Cleave's hairstyle was, indeed, psychologically complex—more than just her desire to be in fashion. "Charles revered Maureen, Charles was Maureen's mentor, and Anna desperately wanted Charles to cherish *her*, too," he maintains. "It's quite complicated, but I'm sure Anna wanted to be able to say, 'Look at me, Daddy. I *look* like Maureen.' Anna always desperately—*desperately*—sought Mr. Wintour's love and attention, and he wasn't always there to give it."

Wintour wanted a hipper, younger readership, and twenty-three-year-old Cleave, an Oxford graduate with a degree in art, was given the youth page beat—the same with-it demographic that Anna later targeted, likely on her father's advice, when she first became a fashion editor.

"Charles ran many of his ideas for me through Anna because she was keeping her eye on [trendy] things," Cleave says, looking back. "She was a hip kid, so to speak. I got in trouble once for not knowing the difference between 'hip' and 'hep.' Anna obviously told her father about that. I'd written the wrong word and Charles said it should be the other word. I knew he'd gotten the correct one from Anna."

Cleave had virtual free rein to cover the smashing rise of swinging London. The nonpareil Maureen Cleave interview became dinner table and cocktail party conversation.

Her biggest score came when she got a tip from a friend in Liverpool. "She said to me, 'I hope you realize there's a lot going on here. There's this group called the Beatles.'" The quartet had recently cut their first single, "Love Me Do," and had signed a five-year contract with a manager named Brian Epstein.

Cleave ran the Beatles story idea by Wintour, who asked Anna whether she had ever heard of them. Of course, she told her father, they're fab. The next day Cleave headed north, thinking she had an exclusive, but was disappointed when she arrived to find a competitor on the scene from the *Daily Mail*, who had also gotten the word to check out John, Paul, George, and Ringo—known as "the Fab Four"—and this new Mersey Beat.

The gentleman from the *Mail* didn't have a chance, though. Lennon preferred Cleave as their interviewer, which she attributes to her bob. "I had a fringe like the Beatles. They liked me from the start because of my hair. I guess they felt we could relate."

Beginning on Thursday, October 17, 1963, and continuing for three days, the first major interview with the Beatles ran in Charles Wintour's *Evening Standard*. That same day the Beatles were at the Abbey Road Studios recording what would quickly become their first American number one hit, "I Want to Hold Your Hand."

Cleave's series, pushed by Anna's highly competitive editor father, who ran the story idea by his with-it teenage daughter who kept her eye on who and what was in and out, had helped to catapult the most successful singing group in music history.

Anna's bob had helped, too. If Cleave hadn't been wearing it, the Beatles might not have been so friendly and open, and she might not have gotten their story. In any case, it didn't hurt.

In its 1963 incarnation, the bob was the brainchild of Vidal Sassoon, who had a shop in posh and fashionable Mayfair that had catered for centuries to London's upper classes and royalty. Sassoon's guinea pig was the fashion designer and sometimes model Mary Quant, the epitome of the with-it, miniskirted swinging London chick. She was thrilled with the cut and decided to have all of her models given the bob by Sassoon. A British *Vogue* editor, attending Quant's show, was overwhelmed. "At last," she wrote, "hair is going to look like hair again."

Other trendy haircutters soon jumped on the bob bandwagon, such as Leonard of Mayfair, where Leslie Russell gave Anna her very first bob. "Anna was about fourteen, fifteen when she came in. She had hair way past her shoulders, like Jean Shrimpton's. She said she saw photos in [British] *Vogue* of some cuts that I did, and I remember she came in with a picture she'd torn from *Vogue*. And so I cut her hair, and it was *the* haircut of the time, which *everyone* was getting—the straight hair, the long fringe, the same bob she has today."

Mainly, Anna chose Leonard of Mayfair over Sassoon because two of her idols got their bobs there—Maureen Cleave, and a kicky nineteen-year-old former ten-pound-a-week secretary named Cathy McGowan, who overnight jumped to the forefront of the British pop revolution as the trendy host of a top-rated music television program *Ready, Steady, Go!*, Britain's version of *American Bandstand*. Virtually every teen from London to Liverpool—and Anna was no exception—tuned in early on Friday evenings, 6:07 P.M., to be precise, before they went out clubbing. The show's energized motto was "The Weekend Starts Here!"

Teenage Anna adored Cathy McGowan, who wore the trendiest boutique fashions and the latest makeup styles, and featured the jargon, the attitude, and the sensibility of mid-sixties happening London. Anna would come away from the TV each week knowing what to buy, where to buy it, and how to wear it.

"Cathy was a client of mine," Leslie Russell says. "She had the bob, and Anna had read in a magazine or a newspaper that I'd cut Cathy's hair, and that was another reason for her coming to me. It suited Anna *perfectly*. And still does. She's got those nice cheekbones, which looked perfect for that look of the time. Certainly in those days she had perfect, shiny, thick light brown hair, very good hair to hang straight, with a bit of blow drying to turn the hair under a bit. Anna was *very* sixties looking."

Scores of super birds and dollies passed through Leonard of Mayfair in those days, but Russell never forgot Anna's look: short, *short* miniskirts; low-heeled, pointed shoes; tight tank tops; and very little makeup—"some eye shadow and mascara, but that was about it. She was *not* red lips and caked up. She didn't need it."

Besides going to Leslie Russell to have her hair cut, Anna paid particular attention to the health of her tresses and began getting scalp treatments and buying special-formula hair products from a bespectacled man named Philip Kingsley, who took hair quite seriously. He originally planned to become a doctor, but visits to his uncle's hair salon got him interested in hair care. Instead of medical school, he became certified as a trichologist, an expert in hair and scalp problems. In the early sixties, he opened a one-man practice in London.

"Charles Wintour originally came to see me as a client because his hair was thinning," Kingsley says. "And he saw me throughout his life. He told Anna, 'You should start taking care of your hair when you're young.' When Anna first came to me as a teenager, she didn't have very much wrong, but I started treating her, too. I get people's hair in the best possible condition, and then they can do what they like with it. It's *like* going to a doctor."

Over the years, Anna dutifully used Kingsley's shampoo, containing a formula based on the texture of her own hair, along with his exclusive hair tonics and conditioners. Kingsley also recommended that she take a lot of yeast tablets, but they caused constipation.

After Anna moved to New York in the mid-1970s to begin her climb to the summit, she continued seeing Kingsley, who had opened a practice there. Kingsley believes that stress is bad for hair, and as Anna rose in the high-pressure fashion magazine field, jumping from one anxiety-ridden fashion editor's job to another, her stress built up and she required his help.

"How often I saw her depended on how stressed she became," Kingsley reveals. "Her hair didn't behave as it ought to have done when she was under stress, and sometimes Anna was under more stress than others." Kingsley made a chart for Anna's good and bad hair days, and every so often reassessed the health of her hair, depending on the highs and lows of her anxiety.

Anna was among Kingsley's first clients—a celebrity list that grew to include Cher, Jerry Hall, Mick Jagger, Ivana Trump, Sigourney Weaver, Kate Winslet, Candice Bergen, and Barbra Streisand, among others.

Besides her hair, teenaged Anna worked hard at maintaining her skin. She read voraciously about ways to fight pimples, acne, and blotches—and how to deal with other teenage girl problems—in her gospel, the American magazine *Seventeen,* copies of which she borrowed from Vivienne Lasky, who had a subscription. Convinced she was going to have bad skin, and obsessed with keeping it clear, she went weekly to an exclusive salon on Baker Street, fancier than Elizabeth Arden, to get facials and was no doubt their youngest client.

"Her skin was fine," Lasky points out, "but she went to the salon every week for *prevention*."

While Anna was sleek and chic, she was harshly critical and sarcastic, and spiritedly made fun of people who weren't. "Anna *really* cared about appearance. She would point out another girl and say, 'My God, look how fat *she* is . . . look at *her* face . . . look at *that* girl's horrible, curly hair,'" recalls Lasky, who had curly hair and became at times the target of her best friend's biting tongue. Although both wore glasses—Anna's were expensive tortoiseshell granny glasses—she ridiculed Lasky's poor eyesight. "Anna didn't wear her glasses all the time," Lasky says. "She could manage very well without them, although sometimes she'd ask me who somebody was across a crowded room. But she'd be very critical of me and bitchy when we'd go horseback riding or play tennis because my eyesight was so bad. I had trouble seeing the ball. I couldn't ride as fast as her. She could be mean like that."

From the time she was a teen, Anna was brusque and snarky—traits she inherited mostly from her father but also from her mother, who was known for her critical and sarcastic manner.

Anna's nastiness appeared calculated and was offensive, which made Lasky and others who were her targets feel terrible.

"If I disliked anything about Anna when we were kids," Lasky offers, "it was her rudeness on the telephone. Her entire family did it—they never said good-bye. They'd just hang up on you. With Anna, I knew it was coming. 'Well, I'll see you.' Click. No good-byes.

"My mother would say, 'It's the rudest thing, no civility.' And my mother *loved* Anna. I confronted her. 'What is it with this not saying good-bye?' And she said, 'Well, there's no point, is there, really? We're finished talking. How can you feel bad about that?' And I said, 'Nobody else does that. If you want to make friends with people, they're going to think it's odd. You're the *only* person I know who does that.' She didn't care."

There were even worse slights that left Lasky hurt and with a sour taste, both about herself and their friendship. Unlike Anna, Lasky was an eater, and Anna gloated over the fact that she always stayed thin. For instance, Anna bought little gifts of clothing for Lasky. But there was always one major hitch. Everything was thoughtlessly too small, including a custom-made

Regency ball gown with lavender and white stripes that Lasky could barely squeeze into.

"My mother noticed these things. She always used to say, 'How could your best friend buy you something and it's always a size too small?' That dress Anna bought me, I couldn't get into the damn thing because the arms were so tight." Another time, Anna bought Vivienne an expensive patchwork quilt skirt at Liberty's, one of the grandes dames of London department stores. "Like everything else, it didn't fit," she says, "I think I squeezed into it once."

Lasky's mother was a Prussian former ballet dancer and model, an exotic cross, according to her daughter, between Audrey Hepburn and Greta Garbo. Brigitte Lasky, who converted to Judaism for her Jewish husband and became a U.S. citizen, was a fashion plate with whom Anna bonded, spending almost more time with Mrs. Lasky than with her own plain-Jane mother, who was preoccupied with her social work. "Anna was especially crazy about my mother," offers Lasky. "She thought she was the cat's meow and saw her as a role model."

Nevertheless, Brigitte Lasky felt that Anna bought the small sizes purposefully and maliciously to tease and taunt her daughter. Unlike Vivienne Lasky, who was a tad plump, Anna was skinny, but she was big-boned and usually had to buy larger sizes for herself and have them taken in. While Lasky thought Anna looked "great" in certain things, such as later in Chanel, she felt she looked "awful" in evening dresses then and now, "because her elbows, wrists, and knees are too big. She's like Calista Flockhart and Lara Flynn Boyle. It can look *painful.*"

Anna knew that juicy, thick lamb chops were her pal's favorite. She even taught herself to cook them to Lasky's taste, so she could gloat while she watched her clean her plate. "Anna would make my favorite food. Then she would just sit there and watch *me* eat. She wouldn't eat, or she would just pick, and she'd point out that I was 'pleasantly plump.' I said, 'Well, Anna, I don't want to be a model,' and she said, wagging her finger, 'You know, Vivienne, *we* don't want to get *too* pudgy.' My mother says I would always come home from those dinners feeling a lack of self-esteem. She said I didn't come back confident and smiling."

Anna hurt her friend's feelings by making fun of her weight and putting her on the spot by demanding, "Why don't you have more self-control?"

Lasky's meek response was, " 'Life is too short . . . dieting all the time makes me crotchety.' Well, that sends a message. I wasn't so stupid. My mother always said, 'Anna invites you to dinner, makes your favorite food, buys your favorite cheesecake, and she's flitting about, but did she eat anything?' I said, 'Mom, you *know* she didn't.' My mother thought she was malicious. I'd say, 'I don't believe that of her. She loves me. She's my best friend.' "

As one of Charles and Nonie Wintour's favorites on the *Evening Standard*'s staff, Alex Walker often socialized with his editor. He was invited to their cocktail and dinner parties—Charles specialized in mixing a martini that left guests reeling—and was an overnight guest at their country place in West Farleigh, a village in Kent. And he got to know teenage Anna, who, he noted, was an "absolute monster" who "didn't mind insisting on [her] own views on whatever anyone else said, particularly in that family."

Walker thought Anna would do or say things just to be mean. He says he thought of her as a complex amalgam of such wicked film characters as *The Bad Seed*'s Rhoda Penmark, *Mildred Pierce*'s Vida Pierce, and *All About Eve*'s Eve Harrington. As a movie critic and a serious biographer of Hollywood greats, Walker enjoyed film analogies, even if possibly exaggerated.

"I'd stay with Charles and Nonie for the weekend," he recalls. "I suppose Anna was fourteen, fifteen, and she had a horse. I'd hold the long harness while I delicately led her around, rather than galloping around, the paddock. When she was through riding, she'd say, 'I think I've had quite enough of this, Mr. Walker. Now help me down.' I was struck by the fact that she was very, very mature—far more mature than her age. The future editrix was in the blood there, that's for certain."

Anna was crazy about riding at that time, and she made a serious pitch to her father to quit his powerful job at the *Evening Standard* and take over editorship of the local *Kent Messenger* so that she could enroll at the local stables with thoughts of becoming a chic, miniskirted veterinarian.

"Even as a child she had her father's coldness," continues Walker. "She was very much like her father. Anna had a self-possession that was beyond her years. She was in fact *more* than self-possessed. She was patrician. She was not a playful child. Her behavior manifested itself in quite small ways back then—simply in being stiffly polite but not taking very much notice of you. What she did, she did with purpose."

But Anna had no tolerance for rude behavior that intruded upon her life and was especially upset with people who were tardy. "Anna could be very impatient," Vivienne Lasky emphasizes. "She was actually a perfectionist. In that way she was sort of a Martha Stewart–ish person, always in control. To Anna, the thought of anyone being late was terribly rude, and she cut off people if they didn't arrive at precisely the specified time—at least not anyone terribly important to her. 'Well, we're *not* going to meet them again, that's that,' she'd say with finality. 'They're not reliable. We'll just go on our own. What's the point of meeting people if they show up late.' "

four

A Growing Independence

Around the time Anna turned fifteen, in 1964, the Wintours decided to move from their bland contemporary town house in St. Johns Wood. The uninteresting house no longer fit the regal image of the editor of a serious London newspaper.

Anna especially hated her tiny bedroom, though all of the rooms in the house were small. She felt hers was babyish-looking, and just prior to the family's purchase of the new house she redid her room in an elegant green, faintly striped wallpaper.

In general, the house held bad memories because of the death of the Wintours' firstborn.

Vivienne Lasky had always found it odd that all of the windows in Anna's room and those of her siblings had bars on them, which in those days was a rare addition in most British homes. One afternoon, sitting with Anna, she asked her about the guarded atmosphere, and Anna's response surprised her. "My mother's paranoid," she stated, "that one of us is going to fall out."

When Lasky asked her why, Anna revealed the sad story of her brother's death and said that her mother still feared that the worst could happen to another of her children. "Anna said Nonie was edgy, nervous about the children's safety, that one of them might stand on a footstool or a chair and fall out"—thus the prisonlike bars. "Anna never talked about him again, and I never heard anything about the dead brother from other members of the family. But neither Anna nor any of the other children were permitted to ride or had bikes."

The Wintours moved to an elegant late-nineteenth-century four-story white stucco home at 9 Phillimore Gardens, in fashionable Kensington, close to the area's fancy department stores and antiques shops, a neighborhood "still stuffily grand at that point in time," observes Valerie Grove. "Grandeur and wealth was the keynote." It was a fine family house for entertaining, with a large garden, immediately adjacent to bucolic Holland Park. Compared to their previous home, the Wintours' new house was enormous: nine bedrooms, four bathrooms (one en suite), three reception rooms, many fireplaces (the mantels of which were stolen during the renovation), a kitchen and breakfast room, and a cloakroom, all high-ceilinged with beautiful moldings. The facade had eight windows that faced the street, flooding the front rooms with light.

It was, as Grove notes, "an appropriate house for an editor of a newspaper in those days, and for an American heiress. The first thing anyone said about Nonie when one first arrived [on staff] at the *Evening Standard* was 'Charles Wintour has a rich American wife.' It was understood that, however well-heeled his army family was, it was Nonie's money that had enabled them to buy the house in Kensington."

Alex Walker believes that Beaverbrook may also have had a role in helping Wintour with the purchase, by giving him a loan, the kind of special perk he offered favored high-level employees. (Years later, Anna would also have a powerful and enamored media king for a boss, Condé Nast's S. I. Newhouse Jr., who is said to have assisted her, too—one of his favorite editors—in buying a town house in Greenwich Village with an interest-free $1.64 million mortgage on the property from Condé Nast.)

Back then, though, teenage Anna didn't care how her parents got their financing. She adored the fact that they now lived in a classier neighborhood, closer to the action, with powerful and well-to-do neighbors, and fancy shopping steps away. But most of all, she was enthralled with the lower level of the house, where there were servants' quarters—a staff flat, consisting of a living room, kitchen, and bath, with a private entrance.

Anna believed she was old enough to have her own place, even though it was just a stairway away from the rest of the family. She asked, and her par-

ents readily agreed. The permissive Wintours viewed Anna as mature and responsible enough to live somewhat independently from the rest of the family
and felt that she deserved her privacy. They were ahead of their time—by the
nineties homes would be built with separate teenager suites.

"So, at fifteen, Anna had her very own flat and total privacy to come and
go as she wished," says Vivienne Lasky. "Once she had her flat, she didn't really participate upstairs at her house unless it was Sunday lunch, which was
sort of sacrosanct in the Wintour household. She was very precocious, very
adult, and was playing at being an adult."

Discerning and opinionated about what she wanted, Anna furnished most
of her flat at Habitat, the decor lifestyle store that brought designer Sir Terence Conran to prominence, a store that sparked a design revolution in the
middle-class British home. To Anna, the shop was known as "Shabitat" because everything was relatively inexpensive—her parents footed the decorating costs, of course—but had a chic look. Habitat was the Ikea of its day,
only classier.

Anna's bedroom was all blue and white, but spare, and not very girly-girl.
Against one wall was a fabric-covered kidney-shaped dressing table. The duvet on the queen-sized bed had matching fabric. (Conran asserted later that
his introduction of the duvet had a positive impact on the supposedly boring
British sex life because the cover made it so easy to make the bed and hide the
evidence after a quick romp, and it also had a sexy, Swedish overtone.) Anna's
living room had floor-to-ceiling shelves, a wall filled with her parents'
books—she enjoyed Doris Lessing and Agatha Christie. In the bathroom she
had a large framed purple poster promoting a New Year's Eve party she had
attended at a hotel discotheque in Zurmatt, Switzerland, during a ten-day
Christmas vacation with Lasky and Anna's younger brother, Patrick. The flat
opened through French doors onto the pretty landscaped garden that included a little pond with a water-spouting frog. The garden backed on to the
greenery and flowers of Holland Park. It was a suite fit for a princess.

But, surprisingly, the parents of the woman who one day would be noted
for her sense of style and be appointed editor of the venerable *House & Garden* magazine had little if any taste of their own.

Aside from Anna's room, the rest of the enormous Wintour house was, observers maintain, horribly decorated in a glitzy contemporary American style. "Charles had very little visual sense of his surroundings," notes Valerie Grove. "He was a cerebral person but was not into decorating a house in an appropriate style. I don't think he particularly minded what backdrop he had as long as it was neat and tidy and businesslike. I never ever thought of Charles and Nonie as having a cozy or comfortable or warmly welcoming atmosphere."

By her midteens, having her own flat and lots of independence, the world of dating and night-clubbing opened up for Anna.

Swinging sixties London was at her pretty feet, and men, young and old alike, were mesmerized by her appealing face, her ivory skin, her chic shiny bob that gave her an exotic with-it look, those skinny legs in the shortest of minis, and a Lolita-like come-hither shyness—an enigmatic quality that excited men all the more. All in all, Anna Wintour at fifteen was an alluring package and quite a catch. Another component of her aura was her father, a powerful figure in journalism and a lure for some of the up-and-coming scribes who pursued her. And Anna was immensely attracted to writers and journalists, and the older, the better. Over the years she would be drawn to father-figure types, surrogates, in a sense, for the absentee Charles Wintour, whose primary family was his newspaper.

As one armchair psychologist who worked on Fleet Street in those days, and who squired Anna briefly, notes, "I always felt she was chasing the daddy figure who was never around. She was like a needy, shy little girl, and I think that was all a bit of an act to get your full and undivided attention, which she never got from old Charles."

The first in a relatively long queue of older men whom Anna dated was the future best-selling and critically acclaimed author Piers Paul Read, who at twenty-four was a year or two out of St. John's College, Cambridge, where he had studied history. Fifteen-year-old Anna met Read, aptly enough, at a wedding—the nuptials of her first cousin on her father's side, Oliver James, a future professor of geriatric medicine, and Roseanna Foster, one of Read's closest childhood friends from his hometown of Yorkshire.

Among the conservative guests at the wedding party, Anna stood out, a chic and seductive vision to Read, who was instantly smitten with this sensual teen in a pink miniskirt and heels, flirtatiously hiding behind the long bangs of her bob, giving her an air of mystery.

"Here was Anna, this sexy and pretty teenager, at fifteen, and I was this depraved twenty-four-year-old," says Read, half jokingly. "She was very young, very pretty, very sophisticated, very sort of culturally up-to-date, and just slightly timid."

Though to Read she exuded extreme poise and confidence, model-thin Anna was unnecessarily consumed with, and obsessed about, her weight and didn't think she was attractive, despite the way she lorded the poundage issue over Vivienne Lasky. "She hated the photographs that were taken of her at Oliver's wedding," recalls Lasky. "When she saw those pictures, she said, 'God, do I look terrible.' She thought she was chubby. She thought her legs looked awful. She thought she was not photogenic. She looked at the wedding pictures and said, '*Good God!* Is that how people see me?' I said, 'You look fine.' She said, 'But just look at my knees! They're *ugly*.' I mean, she was just a kid, but she was *so* involved with how she looked. She said, 'Your knees don't look like mine. Mine look *bigger*,' and she actually took out a ruler and measured her knees, and then measured my knees. Her knee bone was wider than mine. She was *so* upset."

Anna was a firm believer in Mary Quant's adage that "a woman is as young as her knees."

The width of Anna's knees notwithstanding, Read was hooked and so was Anna, though each had his or her own agenda. He appealed to her elitist tastes, was an intellectual of sorts, and already was being talked about as having a great future as a writer; therefore, she was fired up to go out with him, a trophy kind of guy, plus—and this was a big plus—he was older. Her interest in men of letters, as it were, was passed on to her by her father, who thrived on the excitement generated by being among journalists, of discovering new writing and editing talent, especially of gaining access to and being among celebrities, a taste Wintour had inherited from Beaverbrook and that he handed down to Anna, a taste she would cultivate throughout her life.

"Piers was very talented, very British," observes Lasky. "He was older, sort of funny-looking. But his smile was devastating. For Anna, it wasn't so much a man's looks as [his] brain."

Read was commuting between Yorkshire and London and working on his first novel when he and Anna began dating—inexpensive dinners, the cinema, visits with the Wintours. He couldn't afford much more, which wasn't the way to win Anna's heart. "If you were to take Anna out on a date," recounts Lasky, "she expected it to be as fancy and well planned as any she would arrange for herself. She had very high expectations."

Nevertheless, Anna had a major crush on Read, which wasn't quite reciprocated. Aside from her sexiness, Read states, "Anna wasn't particularly interesting. She was a curiosity as much as a sexual desire."

But through Anna, the ambitious Read hoped for access to a higher stratum of society, which was *his* main agenda. "I felt that I could sort of get to know London and the influential people in the big city," he acknowledges, "by sort of chatting up the daughters, as it were."

It was an eye-opening experience for this young man from the north of England who had never known a girl quite like Anna, especially such a young one, who had her own flat, free to come and go as she liked and to entertain friends there. Read also was surprised that the Wintours didn't mind that Anna was dating a man nine years her senior, though he was certainly respectable.

"I was and am a Roman Catholic, so their kind of liberal take on things wasn't quite mine," he notes. "They had different values. They were fairly antireligious. And Anna's parents had a very sort of liberal attitude towards sex. I was sort of horrified and fascinated at the same time by their sexual permissiveness. I'd been brought up with sort of rather straight, Catholic views. When I visited Phillimore Gardens it was with a combination of fascination and horror. I don't want to give the impression that I was priggish or disapproving, but I was a Catholic country boy from Yorkshire, sort of an incredibly muddled young man at the time, and I had the feeling I was in Sodom and Gomorrah. But you know, it was the sexual revolution, so I didn't mind cashing in on that."

But he says he didn't get past third base.

"Nothing irrevocable happened between us," he claims. "I was quite young and inexperienced. We held hands, kissed occasionally. I don't know for certain, but I don't think Anna had lost her virginity when I went out with her. She certainly didn't give me the impression that she'd been to bed with anyone, but I could be wrong."

To Anna's shock, horror, and dismay, Read suddenly and with finality ended the relationship—stopped seeing her, stopped calling her, disappeared off the scope, as it were, after telling her he didn't think their relationship had much of a future.

As Lasky recalls, "Anna was more keen on him than he was on her. But she wasn't ready to give him up."

Anna had difficulty dealing with the young writer's rejection and did not take kindly to having someone else decide what course her life would take. More appalled than confused that she'd been the one to get the heave-ho, Anna demanded answers. But rather than confront Read herself, Anna enlisted her best friend as her intermediary.

Anna told Lasky she didn't want to meet with Read because "she was afraid she might become clingy" and believed her friend could be more objective in confronting him.

Anna Wintour clingy?

Indeed, Anna's handling of the matter underscored a growing neediness involving men that would become even more apparent in later years—a shocker to female colleagues who viewed her as a strong and independent ice queen.

"Clearly, Anna didn't believe Piers's explanation, which was that Anna was too young for him. She said to me, 'I want you to call up Piers and see if you can meet him for lunch.' She wanted me to ask him basically why he dumped her," Lasky says. "Piers was very British, and I guess he hadn't made it terribly clear. So I was meant to plead Anna's case, to find out what the hell was going on, because Anna didn't want the relationship over. She was my best friend, so I agreed to do it. I had to schlep way across town.

"I said to Piers, 'She's not really quite clear on what's going on. She doesn't want to lose your friendship. Anna feels the story is unfinished'—all that sort of crap you say. I said, 'She's my best friend. I'm here for her. She doesn't quite understand the situation. Talking to me is easier than talking to her because there aren't those feelings.'

"And he just said, 'I'm much older than she is. I don't think the relationship is going anywhere. I don't have those feelings. She's too young.'"

Read also indicated that there might be someone else in the wings.

Back in her flat, Anna anxiously awaited Lasky's report. "The first thing she asked me was, 'Well, did you plead my case?' I told her it was a nice lunch, not very awkward, and I guess he realized he hadn't handled it very well with her. I told her what he said, and I said, 'I don't think you have a chance with him.' I was honest. I said, 'It's clear, whatever it is, he does not want to pursue it with you. It's not like there was a misunderstanding, or you did anything wrong, or disappointed him. It just wasn't to be.' She said, 'Well, did you *really* try hard enough? Did you *really* put my case forward? Because I think *he* won *you* over. He *did* win you over.' She didn't show anger or emotion—that's not Anna. But the later Anna, the Anna of today, would have held it against me that I hadn't completed the task and gotten him back for her."

As it turned out, there was another girl who had captured Read's interest, and she was just a year older than Anna; his future wife, sixteen-year-old Emily, a student at the French Elysée in London.

Over the years, Anna and Read would continue to have contact: Emily Read became a contributor to *Vogue,* and one of the Reads' children became an executive in London for Condé Nast.

Anna's enduring friendship with Read is not an anomaly. Many of the men she was involved with over the years have remained loyal to her, even ones on whom she cheated.

Around the time the romance with Read ended, Anna dated the only young man known to have been in her age group, a quintessential good-looking British preppy from a good family—well brought up—who took her to the races at Ascot.

five

London Party Girl

More in line with the kind of men Anna was drawn to was a hustling, ambitious charmer of a Fleet Street "hack" named Nigel Dempster, almost a decade her senior. When Dempster began seeing sixteen-year-old Anna, he was digging up dirt at parties for London's *Daily Express* gossip column.

Anna was attracted to Dempster's good looks and debonair manner, and especially his growing circle of fancy friends and the posh riffraff he attracted. Vivienne Lasky, however, came away feeling he was "smarmy and slimy." And Charles Wintour's blood boiled when he discovered that his daughter was seeing "a gossip hack." For the most part, Anna's father was rather sanguine about the men she dated; Dempster was a glaring exception.

There were other facets about Dempster that were appealing to Anna, such as his purported lineage: He claimed he was a member of one of the two families who founded the powerful Elder Dempster Lines, a shipping company that controlled West African trade beginning in the late nineteenth century and were on a par with the Cunards. There was even a glossy in circulation of Dempster at the age of twenty in white tie and tails, which he asserted was a family society shot.

Whatever the truth, Anna was intrigued, and Dempster, always on the make, saw both journalistic and romantic possibilities with her. The two became an item. They had much in common, sharing similar interests and values: power, wealth, and celebrity. Journalist Paul Callan, who would later have his innings with Dempster, notes, "A lot of guys wanted to go out with Anna because they wanted to curry favor with Charles Wintour—and that included Dempster."

Through Anna, Dempster had fantasies of becoming Charles Wintour's big gun: His goal was to be the best-known, highest-paid gossip columnist of his time. The latter would come to be, but without the help of Anna's father, who thought he was a cretin.

Years later, Lasky still couldn't see what Anna saw in Dempster. "He was so quintessentially British, backstabbing, and bitchy," she says. "I didn't think he had a moral fiber in his body . . . charming to your face, then 'that slut.' "

Through Dempster, who was beginning to hobnob with the highbrow and lowlife of British society and celebrityhood, Anna became a fixture of sorts on the London party and club circuit, not quite the Anglo version of a Hilton sister but considered hot stuff and recognizable to the cognoscenti (Fleet Street reporters who also made the scene and who knew who her father was).

Friday evening before going out, Anna watched *Ready, Steady, Go!* And first thing Saturday morning she was at either Biba or Mary Quant, two of the hippest boutiques, shopping for the kind of kicky, sexy outfit Cathy McGowan had worn on the tube the night before. Saturday nights, she trucked off to the Laskys' palatial duplex apartment overlooking Hyde Park for dinner, with eight o'clock set aside to watch *The Forsyte Saga.*

At eleven—never, *ever* earlier because it wasn't fashionable—she'd trot off to the clubs, usually starting her rounds at midnight at Dempster's main hangout, Annabel's, filled with an assortment of aristocrats, real and self-styled, and a slightly louche gambling crowd. Anna loved the attention of the men, consumed the bitchy gossip, and kept a sharp eye on the women—what they were wearing, how they wore it, what was in and what was out.

She always made a showing at the Ad Lib, near Leicester Square, which had a reputation as being a hangout for the hottest dollies in London, a club where virtually everybody in the balcony overlooking the dance floor was toking up.

Anna didn't do drugs, even though marijuana, cocaine, LSD, and everything else one could snort, inhale, or shoot to get recreationally high was all around her, everywhere she went.

"Anna was always too much in control to be interested in drugs," Lasky maintains. "She was *hideously* healthy." She says Anna didn't even drink at the clubs, but nursed Coca-Colas, though she wouldn't turn down Veuve Cliquot if offered by a gentleman.

Anna often went off to Dolly's, on Jermyn Street, which drew a hip crowd of journalists and rockers, and she was a regular at the very exclusive London discotheque called Sibylla's, on Swallow Street near Piccadilly Circus, which became known as the Beatles' disco because George Harrison owned a small percentage of the place. The club's private preopening night was unforgettable, with an elite boldface list of celebs: all of the Beatles, the Stones, Cathy McGowan, Julie Christie, Mary Quant, among other London fixtures. It was the kind of place where the owner felt it was successful only if you *couldn't* get in, making it Anna's kind of place, and she was there with Nigel Dempster for the premier.

"At fifteen, sixteen, Anna had this downtown London life," Lasky says. "London was a hotbed of clubs, concerts, and endless parties. She went where it was fashionable to be seen and to see people. She didn't need much sleep. She had enormous energy.

"She liked clubs and clubbing and dancing more than she liked the Beatles or the Stones. Anna didn't go to rock concerts and didn't go gaga over anyone in pop music."

But Anna did once become mad for a sexy star in his late fifties, more her speed—the actor Laurence Olivier, whom she saw in Shakespeare's *Henry V* at least a dozen times. While most girls Anna's age were chasing Mick and Keith, she began pursuing Olivier. She often skipped school, bringing a satchel of clothing with her, changing out of her ugly North London Collegiate uniform and into something sexy in the ladies' room of the underground station near the office building where Olivier had his production company. She'd stake out the lobby and wait for hours in hopes of meeting him. This went on sporadically for months, but she never was successful, and she finally gave up her quest.

Nothing seemed too risqué for sixteen-year-old Anna, who became delicious arm candy for Dempster, who once boasted that his nubile girlfriend's breasts were "large" and "quite delectable." When the London Playboy Club

and Casino, the five-story swingers' paradise, had its star-studded opening
night party, overseen by Woody Allen as a favor to Hugh Hefner, on July 1,
1966, Anna partied the night away with Dempster and hundreds of other
sybarites, hedonists, and celebrities who had turned out for the festivities. As
Vivienne Lasky notes wryly, "She'd go to the opening of an envelope." In
this case, though, it was a celebration of half-naked Bunnies spinning
roulette wheels and turning cards for oil-rich Arabs, British playboys and
their birds, and the usual turnout of Euro trash. The wild goings-on continued through the night at the Playmate Bar, in the disco, and at intimate gatherings in members' rented private rooms.

An *Evening Standard* photographer was there to cover the event and shot
photos of Anna shaking hands with pajama-clad Hugh Hefner. The next day
a gloating photo editor showed the pictures to Anna's father. "It did not go
over well," recalled Dempster.

Charles Wintour didn't mind Anna having her independence, but he did
mind her going out with Dempster. Brian Vine, a onetime New York bureau chief of the London *Daily Express,* saw Anna and Dempster together at
the Playboy Club opening. A few days later, Dempster told him that
Charles Wintour exploded when he called for his daughter at Phillimore
Gardens.

"Nigel said Charles was very angry, so I think Nigel had to always hide the
fact that they were seeing each other," recounts Vine. "Charles Wintour was
a rather conservative chap and a powerful editor, and he couldn't think of his
daughter going out with this sort of a scurrilous gossip hack. Nigel wasn't acceptable to the Wintour family."

Nevertheless, Anna was enthralled with the glitzy world Dempster opened
to her, and their relationship continued on and off, Dempster claimed, for
seven years.

"Dempster likes to *suggest* that he had [a relationship] with Anna," asserts
London *Daily Mail* gossip writer Peter McKay. "Dempster tells a story of
how he was on a sofa in the drawing room of the Wintour house with Anna
one evening when he looked up to see this very unnerving sight of these two
scuffed suede shoes beneath the set of doors to the room. Charles [Wintour]
had come home unexpectedly, didn't come in the room, but was standing

quietly outside eavesdropping. Dempster says he had to hide it [the romance] from Wintour, who was in a position to get him fired."

Brian Vine heard a similar tale from Dempster, with the details tweaked a bit. In that scenario, Dempster said he had to duck into a closet because Anna feared that her father would storm into the room and discover them together.

Those who know Dempster feel certain that the relationship was not intimate. "Dempster would be frightened because he wanted a career as a journalist," observes Vine.

Dempster's first wife from the early 1970s, Emma de Bendern, who came from a titled background, says, "Anna was very young and Nigel thought she was terribly beautiful. I'm sure it was a dating thing," she maintains. "Before I married Nigel, he brought Anna to Spain where my mother had a little house on Majorca and I was living there. She came to stay with Nigel for a long weekend. She wouldn't go in the sun because she had the most wonderful translucent skin and sat under an umbrella so as not to get any light. She was sort of a porcelain doll, absolutely perfectly manicured, very quiet and very unassuming, hiding behind the fringe of her very immaculate bob, and her body incredibly skinny—but with extraordinary, lurking determination.

"She didn't seem to have *any* personality, and I didn't feel there was *any* sexuality about her. I just remember Nigel being rather protective, acting like a father towards her. I didn't feel there was any romance. But perhaps I was just being fooled, perhaps that was a clever ruse to not arouse my suspicions. But if he was having an affair with her, there was no vibe. It didn't *feel* like it."

If anything intimate was going on, one would have expected Anna to confess all to her best friend. But she remained mum. "Anna *never* talked about sex or relationships, *ever*," says Vivienne Lasky. "We were not *Sex and the City* girls. And Anna's very British, very private, and she's not touchy-feely. She'd never talk about what happened between her and a man."

By 1971, Dempster had moved from lowly legman at the *Daily Express* to second in command under Paul Callan, who hired him to work on his new *Daily Mail* "Diary" column. Callan quickly realized he had made a major mistake hiring Dempster, who tried to steal his job. According to one report, "Dempster knifed him. It was classic stuff. He kept all his decent stories until Callan was away, then produced them in a way that made Callan look second rate."

Whatever Callan might have thought about Dempster's career manipulations, Anna is said to have respected his cutthroat methods. They shared a similar philosophy: "Get to the top any way you can," a journalist who knew them both says.

six

Shopgirl Dropout

If there is a singular, defining moment for young Anna Wintour, it might have been the day her father summoned the *Evening Standard*'s fashion editor, Barbara Griggs, into his office and said, "I wonder if you could do me a great personal kindness?" Griggs, who had been covering fashion for years and had once worked at British *Vogue,* said, "Charles, I'd be delighted. What can I do?"

Sounding a bit uneasy, he said, "Well, my daughter Anna *thinks* she wants something to do in the fashion world. I wonder if you could take her out to lunch and give her some advice. I'll pay for the lunch, of course."

Looking back on that moment years later, Griggs remarks, "I don't think that Charles was big on fashion, and I don't think he wanted that for his favorite daughter. He hoped for more for Anna at that point."

Griggs invited Anna to lunch and found herself sitting opposite "this incredibly self-possessed child—*extreme* self-possession, which is unusual in someone of her age." She found Anna *very* focused and came away from their meeting thinking that this girl would go far. "It appeared to me that she needed absolutely *no* advice from *anyone,* and she'd carve her own path fairly smoothly."

The next day, still following through on her editor's request, Griggs telephoned Barbara Hulanicki, the owner of Biba, one of the hottest boutiques in London, and asked her whether she had any part-time openings for a very savvy and confident schoolgirl whose father happened to be the powerful editor of the *Evening Standard*. Anna was a regular customer and wore the styles Hulanicki promoted—knee-high boots, tight tops, and miniskirts—and Vivienne Lasky firmly believes that Anna's obsession with clothing was strongly influenced by Biba and its fashions.

The boutique became a glittering star in London's sixties fashion firmament, influencing the way girls in the street dressed. Hulanicki paid particular attention to the cut of her clothes, giving them a couture look, so every girl who wore her designs was made to look thin. Overnight, Biba's customer base cut through the class system and changed from strictly working-class girls to include pop stars, actresses, aristocrats, and all the young fashionistas like Anna who wanted the "look." An expert at promotion, Hulanicki shrewdly designed outfits specifically for influential trendsetters like Cathy McGowan and for the very visible pop singer Cilla Black. Julie Christie wore Biba for her role in *Darling*. And iconic model Twiggy's reed-thin frame was always draped in Biba designs.

Biba's hot mail-order catalog used photographers like Helmut Newton—a favorite of Anna's when she became a fashion editor—to produce shots that juxtaposed innocence and knowingness, which, in fact, was the image Anna possessed in the eyes of men during the sixties and seventies.

As Hulanicki remembers the call from her fashion editor friend at the *Evening Standard*, Barbara Griggs asked, "Oh, could the daughter of Charles Wintour come and have a holiday job? You know, just to learn about working in a boutique." Hulanicki said yes immediately—a prominent editor's daughter as a shopgirl couldn't hurt business—and hired her to help out on Saturdays and holidays in her Kensington Church Street shop and also at a Biba branch in touristy Brighton on the English Channel. Hulanicki often escorted Anna and few other girls on the one-hour train ride. They spent the day working in the shop, returning that night.

"Anna would have been about fifteen, sixteen," Hulanicki recalls, "and was *very* young, *very* sweet, *very* pretty, and *very, very* quiet, but I had a feeling her intellect was definitely a little bit higher than fashion. Anna came from an educated family and most of the Biba girls didn't. She was not typical. But she became one of the girls who were learning the boutique business."

Hulanicki was intrigued with Anna and kept a close watch on her. While Anna appeared shy and timid, "I could see she was taking *everything* in," Hulanicki says. "Anna was interested in fashion, but also Biba was *the* place to be. Boutiques were the most important places in those days . . . all the girls wanted to work in them."

Hulanicki remembers Anna, who was paid about fifteen dollars a day, as being "quite chubby" compared to the other Biba girls, who looked even skinnier than Twiggy. But that may have been because of eating disorders or, worse still, drugs. And most of them were older than Anna, at least eighteen. A number of them lived extremely wild lives: Some became addicts or alcoholics, and others died tragically in a series of auto accidents, probably intoxicated or stoned, victims of the excesses of swinging London.

Biba was a scene, to say the least.

Beautiful, tall, very skinny Joanna Dingemann, Anna's age and also a "Saturday girl," later a Biba manager, a Paris model, and a fashion school teacher, says that even then Anna stood out from the beautiful crowd—an elegant and, she notes, very furry vision. "She used to wear fur—a full-length fox coat—at a time when it was just becoming *unfashionable* to wear fur . . . it was just sort of going out of favor, not in a political sense like today, but just in terms of style. But there she was draped in it. Anna went her own way."

While Charles Wintour used his good name and influence to get Anna her boutique gig—and it would not be the last time her father's power would help her up the ladder—his hope then was that Anna wasn't really serious about fashion as a career.

"Charles and Nonie thought it was just a phase," observes Vivienne Lasky. "It was what she expected them to say. Her parents didn't understand it, but Anna had latched on to fashion with a passion that would endure. By sixteen she was fashion, fashion, fashion all the way."

The London fashion revolution had encompassed her. Years later, remembering that time, Anna said, "You would have had to have been living up in Scotland underground to not have been affected by it."

Brigitte Lasky gave Anna the kind of encouragement for her fashion passion that she didn't get at home. Lasky, who wore couture, and Anna talked constantly about clothes and style, the kind of conversations Anna never had with her own mother.

As a social worker, Nonie Wintour wore thick glasses, shunned makeup, and dressed conservatively—"like a working person, Talbot-*sy*," says Vivienne Lasky. "Nonie was more like Hillary [Clinton] . . . can't be bothered, I'll wear the next navy blue suit. Nonie wore navy a lot." Later, when she got into fashion magazines, Anna would buy clothes for her mother to make her appearance smarter.

Unlike Anna, none of the other Wintours had a sense of style, and all dressed plainly. "Anna *hated* badly dressed people," recalls Lasky. "We'd sit on Bond Street having tea at some trendy place and she'd comment on all the people. She was very judgmental. *Everybody* had to be perfect. She criticized their clothes. 'How can people go out like that? Don't they ever look in the mirror?' "

Anna once bought an expensive Dior dress shirt for her brother Jim, who wore it incorrectly, letting it hang out of his trousers. Anna just shook her head and rolled her eyes.

"For Anna to have come out of that family is amazing," states Drusilla Beyfus Shulman, a onetime editor at British *Vogue* and a Wintour family friend. "They were all terribly badly dressed. They were *laughable*. Nora's clothes were pathetic—they were *all* pathetic. Nora's a rather plain girl and suffered dreadfully from being a plain girl in Anna's shadow. She was always the plain sister and Anna was incredibly pretty, always looked wonderful.

"Right from the age of twelve, it seems, Anna was *convinced* of the almost psychic power of clothes. When she went off with her boyfriends, age thirteen or whatever, she always looked just dreamy. I remember seeing her in a very shiny white coat and boots, vinyl I guess, and she was going off to spend a holiday in Switzerland. She must have been about fourteen, and she just looked *marvelous*."

Shulman says that Anna's parents never understood her early obsession with fashion. She compares their response to parents who are stunned to discover their son or daughter is a music prodigy. "Where did it come from? Who knows? Why do these amazing qualities emerge? They just do. It came from no one in the Wintour family, that's for certain. Her secret is natural talent."

Because of their close relationship, Anna took Brigitte Lasky into her confidence, one of the few women who ever entered that charmed circle. Shockingly, Anna complained that her mother seemed more concerned about, and loving toward, the foster and adoptive children in her case files than about Anna herself. Anna saw her as a mother figure, but not to her own flesh-and-blood children. Anna referred bitterly to the children in her mother's case files as "Nonie's kids." While Anna rarely showed any form of emotion, she clearly felt some resentment toward her mother because she wasn't more of her focus.

"It made Anna feel second fiddle," says Vivienne Lasky.

Lasky, who remained friends with Anna's mother for years, believes that Nonie Wintour felt absolutely fulfilled because of her social work with children. "Maybe by throwing herself in and saving other people's children, Nonie was compensating for the loss of her first child whom she couldn't save."

Anna had the same hunger for Charles Wintour's attention—a father figure and mentor to his staffers at the newspaper but not often there for his own daughter.

Years later she acknowledged, "When I was a child I was never alone with my father. There were just too many of us. He was the one we were frightened of, but he wasn't judgmental. He's discreet and charming in that way, but he notices everything and you know what he thinks all the same." He was even more tied to his work than his wife. Anna said she didn't see much of him because of his newspaper and remembered "interrupted holidays" whenever wars broke out or people got killed. Anna complained that her parents were usually out and that she spent a lot of time as a child with nannies and au pairs.

"Nonie had a work ethic, and Charles had an *incredible* work ethic," says Lasky. "They had the same passions for what they were doing and stayed with those passions. Anna has it, too—an *extraordinary* work ethic."

But when Anna did see her father when he was home from the office, or taking time from social engagements, he generated excitement, telling her which celebrity or famous politician had come into the office that day or the big story the paper was working on. He passed on to her the same rush of adrenaline that made him rub his hands together and shout "Hah!" in the

Evening Standard newsroom when exciting stories like the John Profumo–Christine Keeler sex scandal came thick and fast as they did in the sixties. He made Anna feel empowered, he made her feel like an insider. She thought it was wonderful getting to know firsthand something that would make headlines the next day.

"Nonie and Charles really did like their children, and they were much admired by them. But there never was a particularly cozy family feeling because Charles's mind was always inevitably elsewhere. You can't edit a paper like the *Evening Standard* and have your mind focused on whatever Anna wants to do in the afternoon. That didn't exist," observes Drusilla Beyfus Shulman. "I won't say Charles was an absentee father, because he was certainly concerned about his children, but he was at his desk very early in the morning, was there all day, dining out with people in the evening. He didn't have a lot of time left over for Anna."

Anna found a surrogate of sorts in Vivienne Lasky's autocratic father, the esteemed Melvin Lasky, who wasn't an easy man to spend time with because he could be horribly caustic and cutting.

But Anna? Anna was tops in Lasky's book. He used all of his charm around her, probably because Anna was reverential and worshipful—she naturally knew how to handle men and their egos—and appeared captivated and enchanted with his stories about the celebrities he knew and the instantly recognizable writers like Mailer and Eliot and Auden and other big names whose pieces he edited and corrected. Anna'd sit at the table seemingly spellbound but sometimes peppering him with questions. Did he know this person? Had he met that person? Do famous writers *ever* object to your correcting them? Anna knew that her own father's style was to keep hands off his reporters' copy unless absolutely necessary. "Some will ask, 'Did you change anything?'" Lasky told her. "Anna, you have to make them feel that that's the way *they* wrote it."

While the Wintours gave Anna an extraordinary amount of independence—her own apartment, freedom to date older men, clubbing until all hours—Charles and Nonie's prime concern was over her disinterest in school as underscored by her attitude at North London Collegiate. Charles, from Cambridge, and Nonie, from Radcliffe, were educational elitists and wanted her to graduate and go on to a proper university. The Wintours had planned for Nora, Patrick, and James—all academic high achievers—to receive Oxbridge educations and had started putting the pressure on Anna. "I remember them discussing it with Anna, telling her, 'You'll be the first not to go.' Of course they expected her to follow in their footsteps," Vivienne Lasky says.

"Charles was the great brain of the family," notes Drusilla Beyfus Shulman, "and Anna was, well, *pretty*. As the great brain of the family, Charles always took a rather skeptical view of Anna's intellectual capacities."

In 1966, the Wintours' tug-of-war with Anna over her schooling became a moot point. About to turn seventeen, Anna had had it with North London Collegiate. It would be a piece of clothing—the miniskirt—that helped bring down the curtain on her formal education.

When Anna was nabbed for small infractions during her three years at North London, she usually got off the hook, mostly because the headmistress, Dame Kitty Anderson, was a friend of Charles Wintour's brother-in-law, Lord James of Rusholme, a noted educator. Because of Dame Kitty's ties to the Wintours, Anna felt a sense of entitlement. But all that changed when the headmistress retired in July 1965 and was replaced by Madeleine McLauchlan, who proceeded to make life miserable for Anna. "She was cold and hard," recalls Lasky, "and acted like she had a stick up her ass. The whole school changed. It became very tense. Tests were given that no one passed. Everybody felt insecure."

Like the stories surrounding Charles Wintour's handling of the tragic news of his first child's death, there are variations to the story of the sudden demise of Anna's school career. The only thing that's documented is a simple notation in the records of North London Collegiate School. According to the archivist, Elen Curran, Anna "was here from 1963 to 1966." Nothing in the records speaks of her graduating. While she is one of the most famous and successful women to have attended North London Collegiate, she left barely a trace of herself. As Curran states, "Sadly, we do not have any further information of Anna Wintour in our archive."

Anna entered the hallowed halls of North London Collegiate for the last time one day in July 1966, age sixteen, wearing a skirt way above her knees. She was spotted by McLauchlan, who decided to make an example of her.

"Anna was always six months ahead of fashion," Charles Wintour once said in discussing the end of his daughter's schooling. "At North London Collegiate she was getting on famously until a new headmistress arrived and spotted Anna's miniskirt. She stood Anna on a table and ripped her hems down. Then Anna had to go home on the tube in a torn skirt, and quite seriously, it finished her interest in academic life."

As Drusilla Beyfus Shulman recalls the incident, it not only ended Anna's "interest" in schooling but caused her actually to quit North London Collegiate a year early. "Anna didn't graduate from anywhere." According to her version of the events, "Anna cut her gym skirt so that it was above the knee—I mean *well* above the knee, which was a very prophetic thing to do in terms of fashion. Those *very* short skirts had only just kind of kicked in. Anyway, her French mistress lifted Anna up onto the desk and said, 'Look at this girl! She's not worthy of this great school, and she's just obsessed with clothes. She can go home!' And so Anna left North London Collegiate and never went back.

"Anna's rather proud of the story. It is entirely—*entirely*—consistent with her character—*very* self-possessed and also with this sort of sense that she was doing the right thing."

Whichever way it happened, Anna had permanently finished her formal schooling at sixteen, leaving in a snit over having to play by the rules. Her last day was July 27, 1966.

"She was rebellious and clearly had had it with school," states Lasky.

Anna's parents' worst fear had been that she wouldn't go to college; they never expected her to be a high school dropout.

"I guess I went the other way," Anna acknowledged many years later. "My sister always had this joke when she left a message on my answering machine. She asked if I was at the hairdresser's or the dry cleaner's. So I was always the bimbo."

Now the Wintours were concerned about Anna's future and had come to the realization that her preternatural preoccupation with fashion wasn't just a phase as they first thought. Her father's dreams of her following in his footsteps were also dashed because she wasn't interested in working in the newspaper business, in getting her delicate hands soiled with printer's ink. As Anna has stated, she never tried to "prove anything" to her parents. Her interest in fashion was all-consuming, but what she would do with that interest was still undefined and unfocused.

"I'm not a very introspective person," she once said, reminiscing about that period. "So I didn't have a great game plan for life."

seven

Finding Love at Harrods

In the fall of 1967, Anna's class at North London Collegiate was completing its final semester. Following in Nonie Wintour's footsteps, Vivienne Lasky had been accepted at Radcliffe. But Anna had no interest in the traditional markers of young adulthood, like going to college or moving out of the family home. In the Wintours' downstairs flat she played at being grown up.

Instead of pursuing academics, Anna, with help from her father, was accepted into a training program at Harrods, where she worked in every department with the goal of becoming a buyer. At one point, she was assigned to learn all facets of the jewelry business; at another she sold scarves and accessories in the Knightsbridge emporium's groovy teen boutique, her favorite department in the store.

Since it was a work-study program, Anna also took courses at a middling Trafalgar Square–area fashion school at the behest of her parents, who thought that even in fashion she should have some sort of formal schooling. Anna almost torched the place during a classroom experiment that apparently had gone awry. The way Anna later recounted the incident to Vivienne Lasky, she mixed and matched a couple of fabrics with some chemicals, put a match to them—and *whoosh*. Anna's matriculation didn't last very long; she soon lost interest in what the school had to offer—you either know fashion or you don't, she protested when she dropped out.

Next to fashion, Anna's major passion was men—attractive, older achievers.

"She had many boyfriends," her father once said. "She was once literally chased around the house by Indian statesman Krishna Menon." Wintour never stated whether he thought the fatal heart attack Krishna Menon suffered at the age of seventy-seven in 1974 was brought on by his supposed hot pursuit of his comely daughter. He also never mentioned he and Krishna Menon had been students at Cambridge together and that the story, which he told to a London newspaper, might have been a fabrication.

"I'd see Anna around and I'd think, 'What is it these guys see in her?'" Paul Callan remembers. "There was this mystery about Anna, hiding behind her hair, peering out, appearing so shy. Of course nobody knew that behind all that was this fierce girl very much like her father, very Wintourian, purposeful, everything planned, very clever."

While working at Harrods, Anna met and began dating Peter Gitterman, who was thought to be the stepson of the brilliant conductor Georg Solti, music director of London's Royal Opera House and later principal director of the London Philharmonic Orchestra, which gave the young man entrée into London society.

"He wasn't particularly good-looking, but he was interesting and smart," says Lasky. "He clearly adored Anna and had this mad crush on her."

For her part, Anna was especially intrigued by Gitterman's circle of celebrity friends, a rarefied crowd that included Rudolf Nureyev and members of the royal family, such as Princess Margaret's husband, the fashion photographer Antony Armstrong-Jones, better known as Lord Snowdon. Through Gitterman, Anna met Peter Sellers, Vidal Sassoon, Mary Quant, among others. Anna's interest, however, posed a dilemma. While she was enthralled with him, she couldn't have cared less about his great passions—the symphony, opera, and ballet.

In a quandary, she approached Lasky for guidance. "Anna didn't know anything about any of those things, so she felt rather insecure. I said to her, 'He really likes you, he'll probably like teaching you, but you should read up.'" Anna took Vivienne's advice and crammed as if she were preparing for the Oxbridge exams, so as to not embarrass herself. "Because she liked and dated this guy, she learned opera fast, and ballet, too. The next thing I knew, she told me, 'I'm going to the opera! What shall I wear?'"

Eventually the romance faded, and so did Gitterman, who disappeared from the scene. Around the same time Anna quit the Harrods training program.

For a time she dated a good-looking left-wing figure named Robin Blackburn, who gave lectures at the London School of Economics focusing on the Cuban revolution and wrote for the *New Left Review*. Charles Wintour once described Anna's preparations to go to an anti–Vietnam War rally with Blackburn. "Having spent two hours wondering what you wore to a demonstration," her father recounted, "I heard her patter down the steps, turn and run up again. I opened the door and she said, 'Daddy, am I for or against Cambodia?'"

While Wintour made light of his daughter, and had long ago come to the realization that she wasn't destined for rocket science, Blackburn says he didn't think she was as much of an airhead as her father made her out to be.

"I suppose compared with Anna's later development, or with Charles Wintour's own then-politics, he found this bit a cause for remark," says Blackburn years later. "Her father's implying Anna didn't know anything about politics isn't my memory of the matter." Blackburn, who went on to become a professor of sociology at the University of Essex, says that besides accompanying him to the demonstration, Anna had made a short visit to the United States and returned with a gift of several books about the war in Vietnam, which he found quite useful, although he acknowledges that Anna may have bought the books based "on someone else's advice." But, he adds, "She seemed to have some knowledge of political life."

After their romance ended, Anna and Blackburn remained friends. In the seventies, he became part of her social circle that included Patrick Wintour and up-and-coming literary darlings like the novelist Martin Amis and the hard-drinking journalist and later American TV talking head and *Vanity Fair* scribe Christopher Hitchens, who early in his career wrote editorials under Charles Wintour at the *Evening Standard*.

Anna had bought the Vietnam books for Blackburn in New York City during a monthlong stay with her mother's favorite first cousin, Elizabeth "Neal" Gilkyson Stewart Thorpe—the Stewart and Thorpe signifying her first and second husbands—who was then an articles editor at *Ladies' Home Journal*, where she handled personality pieces and cover stories, and conducted interviews with celebrities and politicians, ranging from Carol Burnett to a chief justice of the Supreme Court. She also had worked at *Redbook* as a fiction editor.

Anna, who had dual citizenship because of her mother, had decided on the New York visit, her first such trip on her own, to scope out the possibility of jobs on Seventh Avenue and to look into possibly attending fashion schools. Thorpe hardly knew Anna—a first cousin once removed—and had met her on only a couple of occasions when she was just a child.

Thorpe looked forward to Anna's visit. With her two sons from her first marriage away at boarding school, she gave Anna one of their bedrooms and settled in for a fun time with hopes of getting to know her better.

She was stunned by Anna's maturity, sophistication, and style. "My God, I was so impressed by how she dressed, how she carried herself, how pretty she was." But she also felt that her cousin's daughter showed little intellectual depth and thought her interest in fashion was shallow. As it turned out, the magazine editor and the future magazine editor didn't bond.

"We had no connections over the fact of magazines," she says. "Anna's interest was solely fashion, and I was totally uninterested in fashion, so we really did not have a lot in common. I was interested in literature, writing, she was interested in clothing. It was fashion that eventually led Anna to magazines, *not* an interest in magazines."

Thorpe tried her best to entertain Anna, but she was repaid with an unfriendly, cold attitude, and things quickly went downhill.

Anna's departure left a bad taste in Thorpe's mouth. Her sister, Patti Gilkyson Agnew, Nonie Wintour's other favorite first cousin, who lived in New Mexico, says Anna's lack of gratitude for her stay left Neal feeling hurt and used. "Neal can never forget that Anna never said as much as 'thank you for letting me live with you for a month and eat dinner with you.'"

The visit underscored the frigid relationship Anna has always had with her mother's American relatives. Some of that was almost certainly due to the ocean of distance between them. But even after Anna settled permanently in New York, she made no effort to bond with any of them. "She never even got in touch with me," Thorpe says.

The only other time Anna spent with the American side of her family—an interesting and creative lot—was in the early sixties, just before she enrolled at North London Collegiate. Nonie, along with her sister, Jean Read, an editor for New American Library, brought Anna, James, Patrick, and Nora to a reunion of the Gilkysons and Bakers at a beautiful wildlife area in central New Hampshire called Squam Lake. There, the Gilkysons had rented a group of summer cottages; besides Nonie and her brood, family members came from New Mexico, California, and Pennsylvania.

Anna met a number of her cousins, two who arrived with their parents from Hollywood, where their father, Hamilton H. "Terry" Gilkyson III, was a well-known musician and composer. One of them, Nancy Gilkyson, Anna's second cousin, who later had a career as an executive at Warner Bros. Records, recalls, "Nonie and my parents that summer had a wonderful time and laughed all the time. After that summer, I wrote to Anna and she wrote to me for about a year, then we lost touch."

Gilkyson's sister, Eliza, about a year younger than Anna, remembers Anna at the reunion as being "*so* beautiful, beautiful and remote. She was not warm, not friendly. That was the only time our paths crossed. I never met or saw her again." She later became a singer of her own compositions dealing with sex, drug addiction, and death. Eliza and Nancy's father's songs were recorded by the likes of Johnny Cash and Tony Bennett. With his group, Terry Gilkyson and the Easy Riders, he cowrote such hits as "Marianne" and "Memories Are Made of This."

Few, if any, in Anna's circle ever knew she had such interesting American relatives. She never talked about them and acted as if they didn't exist. It was as if she was ashamed of, or denied, her mother's American heritage. Anna considered herself British through and through, at least back then.

eight

Live-in Model

Vivienne Lasky had only just arrived home from her freshman year at Radcliffe, in the summer of 1969, when Anna rang her up. "Oh, you're back. Good. I have this new boyfriend. We're fixing up this place. I'm at his parents' house. You *must* come over this very moment."

Thinking "typical Anna—*bossy*," Lasky nevertheless was thunderstruck. New boyfriend? His parents' house? She'd received many letters during the school year from Anna on everything that was going on in her life but, curiously, not a scintilla of news about a new man. Anna, who enjoyed playing head games with Lasky, was savoring the juiciest for last.

It was warmer than usual that summer in London, and Lasky found Anna ensconced poolside on the beautifully manicured grounds of her boyfriend's parents' Georgian revival mansion in the estate area of fashionable Highgate. Lasky was shocked to learn that Anna and Steve Bobroff, a tall, handsome, dark-haired, *veddy* British, trendy and talented freelance fashion photographer about five years her senior, were living together. And Bobroff appeared to be quite a catch—the scion of a wealthy Jewish family who made their money in real estate development and furniture.

"Anna," says Lasky, "was quite smitten with him. This was a whole new world to her. It was very serious, and it all seemed so natural. There were *many* crushes. This was clearly a different step for her."

At nineteen, Anna had moved out of her basement flat in the Wintour home and into Bobroff's charming carriage house–studio, the first of a number of live-in relationships for her. Their place was located near the historic Vale of Heath—where people fled during London's cholera epidemic in the late eighteenth century—in Hampstead Village, a hip area of London favored by artists, writers, and the rich and famous.

"Clearly, she thought that with both their talents they could conquer the world," Lasky believes. "They seemed really close. They thought they had it all. Not that I didn't think he had talent, but he was all bought and paid for by his parents. He had to prove himself. I had misgivings."

Anna and Bobroff's place was a knockout. On the ground level was his starkly modern, all-white photographic studio, furnished with contemporary Italian chairs in primary colors, all top-of-the-line, a kitchen, and changing rooms for models.

Carpeted stairs up led to a minstrel gallery surrounded by leaded-glass bay windows where Anna and Bobroff lived—all taupe and gray, with beautiful flower settings everywhere and a wonderful window seat. "I thought, 'Wow! Just the most unusual space,'" Lasky recalls. "It was *so* clever what Anna did—sort of a mixture of living room–dining room, with a big oak refectory table, and a bedroom. It was *minute* but exquisite. She was always fussing with the candlesticks—'Do you think these pewter ones are right for the period, Vivienne? Well, do you?'"

Anna was worried about what her parents would think about how she had decorated the place and what she served them for dinner when they visited. But she wasn't concerned with what they thought about her living arrangement. "Knowing Nonie and Charles as I knew them," says Lasky, "they said, let her try, let her fall on her face. The Wintours were never critical of what she did—that was their thing. Why fight it? It would only make it worse. And he was a charming fellow with some talent."

That summer of '69, Lasky worked at Charles Wintour's *Evening Standard* as an assistant on the "Londoner's Diary" gossip column. While Anna idolized her father, she never wanted to work for him.

Anna, meanwhile, was playing Miss Homemaker for the first time, while Bobroff was downstairs in his studio with models prancing around him whom he shot for fashion layouts in newspapers and magazines such as the trendy *Harpers & Queen*. "Stephen loved being surrounded by the party scene," asserts Lasky. "He loved the glamour, the celebrity, being around gorgeous women."

The whole scene was like the setting for Antonioni's 1966 film *Blow-Up*, in which David Hemmings portrayed a hip British playboy photographer, and the milieu gave Anna an insider's view of that wild, mod sixties London fashion zeitgeist.

And at one point, Anna jumped at the opportunity to be one of Bobroff's models. For him, she had let her bob grow so her hair, for the last time ever, was shoulder length, thick, and brown, with the ends modishly flipped up. She posed in a variety of cute outfits, including very short and skimpy skating skirts. "She looked really lovely, at her best, the waiflike look, which was very in," says Lasky. "I remember the photos vividly because they appeared in a black-and-white fashion spread in one of the London newspapers." It was the second time Anna is known to have modeled for a fashion layout that was published. A year earlier, she and Lasky posed in the teenybopper magazine *Petticoat*, edited by Audrey Slaughter, the woman who would become Charles Wintour's second wife. Anna and Lasky appeared in a two-page spread, wearing fashionably skimpy dresses and shoes that were far too big; the stylist had to stuff tissue paper in them so the girls could stand comfortably.

Anna's live-in relationship with Bobroff lasted less than a year. They were still together when Lasky returned to America for her sophomore year at Radcliffe in September 1969, but by the time she came home to London at Christmas, it was over, and Anna had returned to her bachelorette digs at Phillimore Gardens. She never spelled out for Lasky why the love affair had ended.

Some years later, the gossipy magazine *Private Eye*, which would go after the Wintours vigorously through the 1970s, described Bobroff as one of Charles Wintour's "putative son-in-laws."

Bobroff, who was said to have gotten out of photography, remains mum on the subject of his relationship with Anna Wintour. "I would prefer not to say anything about that time, not to talk at all about her," he states. "It's easier that way."

At a party in the latter part of 1969, Anna met and fell for Richard Neville, a twenty-four-year-old shaggy-haired, tall, thin, good-looking, and bright

Australian underground journalist. Down under he had started a successful hippie newspaper, and his goal now was to establish the first such rag in London, called *Oz*, and shake up the Establishment. In the process, he would become both famous and infamous, with friends and supporters the likes of John and Yoko.

By the time Anna set her sights on Neville, he was being fawned over by rich liberals, trendy media types, and chic poseurs. Neville had become more than just an underground newspaper editor on the make; he was considered *the* expert on London's counterculture and was a regular on BBC television panels, so he was no stranger to tuned-in Anna.

One could practically hear the twang of Cupid's bow when their eyes met, the way Neville tells it. "I was struck by her egg-white skin. Hailing from the country of bronzed Anzacs, she was a rare sight. Anna was unusual. She had that fringe that just made her slightly alluring, like a silent-film star. She was almost mute, but she had an entrancing quality."

It also didn't hurt, Neville freely acknowledges, that her father was the editor of the *Evening Standard*. The newspaper published the first stories about his arrival in London and his publishing plans, and later supported *Oz* and its founder when they got into trouble with the authorities.

When they met at that party, Anna, twenty, was on the arm of a friend, the older, more traditional journalist Anthony Haden-Guest, a member of Nigel Dempster's dazzling, hard-drinking crowd. "Anthony was one of those people with a great sense of social curiosity," observes Neville. "He would turn up at upper-class things, but he loved to slum it with the counterculture."

Anna and Neville met a few times by chance after their introduction. "She would arrive at various parties, where there were the more trendy, groovy journalists, the ones always at the right soirees," says Neville. Unlike other women he knew, Anna acted and looked different, always chic and elegant. "She didn't dress like radical counterculture people," he notes, "and she didn't dress like Mrs. Main Street, either. She wore high heels, stockings, smart little jackets. I wasn't at all interested or knowledgeable about fashion, but she always had a look."

Like the other men she'd been involved with, Neville found Anna shy, and he noted that she had few friends, most of them men.

"I think of her as in the singular. She wasn't a powerful, gregarious woman by any means," he observes. "She was more introverted. I'm a very noisy person and she was a very quiet person, and often noisy people think that quiet people have more going on inside—you get attracted to what you imagine might be depth." However, he soon discovered, "she didn't have great depth but was kind of street sharp." And he couldn't get a take on her values. "She was still cruising around, unformed. A lot of what happened to her later on [with her career] took me by surprise."

They became fast friends and then lovers, he says, using the bedroom of her flat at Phillimore Gardens, sometimes after having dined with the Wintour family upstairs. There was a hitch, however, to going public with their relationship, a big hitch. Neville was living with his beautiful longtime girlfriend in a basement flat with a double mattress in the corner of the front room, in a funky section of Notting Hill, within walking distance of Anna's. As Neville acknowledged, "My girlfriend and I loved each other, [but] I was more in love with making a splash than with trying to make a relationship work."

He says Anna was aware of his live-in relationship but was most willing to share the spoils.

"We had a very clandestine, discreet affair," reveals Neville. "Looking back it was just a strange relationship, going back to her house because I couldn't really have her in my house for obvious reasons. Anna's place was a safe abode."

Occasionally, when his live-in girlfriend wasn't around, Anna arrived at the sometimes cannabis-beclouded *Oz* office late at night in her trendy Mini with darkly tinted windows to watch Neville and his cohorts put together the next issue. Besides sleeping with Neville, Anna had a burgeoning love affair with what she saw as the creativity of the underground press. "I'm not sure whether Anna knew what her media destiny was going to be, or even what her ambitions were, but anybody with a bit of curiosity about what youth was saying gravitated towards the underground press, and Anna did that," says Neville. "She had a curiosity about the direction of youth culture." At the *Oz* office, she flipped through stories and sometimes played editor, making astute critical comments about overdramatic writing or finding a badly written, repetitive piece. "You've used the word 'empirical' twenty-five times. You should fix it." Neville respected her opinions.

He became a frequent dinner guest of Anna's at Phillimore Gardens, where he saw the family dynamics up close and personal. Her parents were aware of their intimate relationship. Often after dinner the two adjourned to her basement flat for lovemaking. "Anna was given her privacy and her parents were discreet." Unlike Piers Paul Read, Richard Neville felt that the permissive atmosphere at the Wintours' was way cool.

But like so many others, Neville noted the chasm that existed between Charles and Nonie Wintour. "Like oil and water," he recalls. "I never imagined them as a sort of fusion. Nonie was kind of very informed and alert, but I just think Charles was bored by it all. There was a certain deadness between them, emotionally. And that's just at the table."

At one dinner party, the talk centered on the legacy of colonialism in Latin America. Anna was bored to death. Among the guests was Charles's much-admired Maureen Cleave, who had gone off staff at the *Evening Standard* and was just back from Peru with her husband. Also present was Anna's sister, Nora, whom Neville described as "a dour and fervent Marxist, Marxist and very serious. She wanted to talk about Gronsky and Marx, and the labor movement in Chile, and Anna just wasn't interested. Anna was pop oriented. Intellectually and physically, Anna and Nora were opposites."

Involved with Neville and the psychedelic counterculture scene, Anna decided at her hairdresser friend Leslie Russell's suggestion to experiment with her classic bob. "Around that time, we started to do a lot of crazy colors, like Elton John had pink hair and green hair. People were getting extraordinarily bright blue colors and greens and pinks," says Russell, who also began cutting Neville's hair. "Anna was always looking for new ideas and new fashions, and she had a really good eye for it. I gave her this sort of two-dimensional haircut, like two bobs in one. It was actually easier to use two different colors to get the same effect, but Anna kept her own color. She loved the cut, was always ready to have something new."

The intimate part of Anna and Neville's affair was short-lived, lasting less than a year, says Neville, who later told a confidant, "Anna and I, we were not the hottest thing in London. There was a moment of intensity, like an exploding firecracker, and then we became friends."

In 1971, after a highly publicized investigation and trial, Neville and a few of his cohorts were convicted of publishing obscenity in *Oz*. He was sentenced to fifteen months in prison, spent some time behind bars, but his conviction was quickly reversed on appeal. At one point John Lennon came to his aid, telling Anna's father's paper, "Yoko and I have proposed marriage to Richard Neville so he can't be deported." Throughout the case, the *Evening Standard* stood behind Neville, and Anna was active in rousing support for him. Their friendship continued for years.

nine

Making the Masthead

The education of Anna Wintour as fashion magazine editor began with the dawn of the glitter, glam, and disco seventies at *Harper's Bazaar,* once Britain's premier couture monthly. It was in the process of becoming hipper by merging with a magazine called *Queen,* which had become *the* irreverent, witty, and trendy fashion must-read of swinging London.

With the deal in the works, the word had gone out: The combined magazine was looking for new hires, especially a fashion assistant, the lowest-paid job in the business. But Anna didn't need or care about the paycheck. She was far more intrigued with being around hot fashion, cool people, and a hip environment.

In early January 1970, she arrived at the magazine's offices for an interview with the editor, Jennifer Hocking, a former model who was a bit in the dark about the identity of this fabulous-looking fashionista, sporting Missoni, with the fringe over her eyes.

"When I took her on I had no idea who she was," recalls Hocking, who, because Anna looked so young, thought she was about seventeen. "She said something about her father being a journalist, and as I can never remember anybody's name, it didn't connect with me that he was *the* Charles Wintour." Hocking also wasn't aware that it was Wintour, working behind the scenes, who got Anna in the door.

But she was satisfied that this new girl could work out. Anna struck her as quite reserved, had an extraordinary look, and, unlike other girls she'd recently interviewed, had neither asked nor cared about company benefits. She didn't know at the time that Anna—unlike Hocking herself, who made most of her own clothes—had family money.

"We weren't looking for anyone sensational," Hocking continues, "just someone who would work well with other people and get on with it."

Besides, the fashion department was a very small part of the magazine, which was more generalized in those days. The department took up a very small area at the end of the office, with a closet for clothing and other accoutrements. As Laura Pank, one of the editors, notes, "Fashion was kind of a bit that we had to tolerate. The editorial was much more important."

And so Hocking hired Anna, who had even beaten out an applicant with more experience from British *Vogue*.

Years later, Anna said her start in the fashion world was virtually predestined. "I think being Charles Wintour's daughter probably got me my first interview and my first job." She also boasted that she had bluffed her way through the interview—something Hocking hadn't caught—by claiming she could handle fashion shoots, though she had no prior fashion magazine experience. Well, she did have a little. Having lived with Stephen Bobroff, who had shot for *Queen,* and having modeled twice before, and having posed as a trendy bird in London's hottest clubs since she was a teen as part of her nightlife world, Anna probably knew a bit more about what was required in a shoot than the next girl in line.

Modestly, she later asserted that she didn't see a future for herself in the world of *Harpers & Queen.* "I just sort of fell into magazines," she maintained. "So much of what happened to me has happened by chance. There was no master plan. . . . This was a time when the fashion magazines were widely regarded by one's mothers as finishing schools for girls of a certain background and a certain name. One had fun there, but one dabbled in the business in anticipation of marriage and, all being well, a large house somewhere in the English countryside."

But that's not the way Jennifer Hocking viewed what she quickly saw as her "very clever, incredibly organized, so together, quietly driven, sometimes terrifying" new hire.

Anna's name first appeared far down on the masthead as one of three fashion assistants in the March 1970 issue, whose cover featured "The Anne Boleyn face, a summer tanned image of Elizabethan beauty."

She had landed on her feet her very first day on the job and never stopped running and never looked back to see whom she left in her dust.

The Wintour girl didn't strike Hocking as a dilettante, as were some of the others on staff. From the beginning, she saw someone "driven, determined, and ambitious." Anna's coworkers endured her—some with awe, others with contempt, and still others with fear and alarm.

"She had this incredible brain, and I used to think it would be amazing to meet her when she was thirty-five, because she was too mature for her age," observes Hocking. "She was *so* organized. She would make business appointments for lunch when the rest of us were sort of sitting around twiddling our thumbs. She was just *so* together. With most young people, it's, 'Oh, I forgot this, I forgot that.' There was none of that nonsense. She was very quick at picking up things. If you said something to her, you knew she'd taken it in because next time she was talking about something, she'd say, oh, such and so, and I'd remember, I told *you* that. Just extraordinary."

Willie Landels, a creative, perceptive, and gentle man who had been promoted to editor but handled the duties of art director at the same time, felt from the first day he was introduced to Anna that her ambition was obvious, that she was very determined to succeed. "There were other girls," he notes, "who were more talented, who had amazing taste and were chic, but didn't have that *incredible* drive that Anna had—like a businessman who is really successful, who only looks in one direction and goes for it. Anna had that— this *total* conviction that she was aiming for the top job."

But Landels had his qualms about her, too. "She had very precise ideas about clothes, a very good sense of quality, but nothing adventurous, always rather conventional. I didn't see her as being very original, but was very much in the mainstream, which made her right later for *Vogue*, which was hardly revolutionary. Her intelligence? Well, obviously she's no fool. People like Anna who are so beamed at something have an intelligence that is highly developed in one direction. The whole energy goes into one thing. In her case it was succeeding."

At the same time, the editor found her to be a poor communicator in a business where communication is key. "It was very difficult when she did a feature story to get out of her *why* she did it, *why* she would do one story over another, because she was *not* very articulate."

He also was concerned about her being a team player, because "she was rather cool, didn't smile, wasn't very open, wasn't very friendly."

Nevertheless, it was not long before Anna began to accompany Hocking on photo shoots and to the collections, where the fashion editor privately began calling her young assistant the "bacon slicer" because of her cutting and critical manner.

"I sat next to her at some of the shows in Italy, in Paris, and the terrible things she used to say about people—nasty things—and no expression would alter her face. She wouldn't sort of indicate she was saying these extraordinarily cutting and caustic things. She was just *so* pin sharp and *so* cruel."

On one occasion Anna, to Hocking, quietly lit into Ernestine Carter, a doyenne of fashion journalism in Britain who had worked for *Harper's Bazaar* and had written several books on high fashion with introductions by Diana Vreeland, the legendary and influential American fashion editor of *Harper's Bazaar* and later editor in chief of what would become Anna's *Vogue.*

"Ernestine was at one of the shows with some famous American journalist, and they were both very tiny women whose feet never touched the ground, and Anna made very cutting comments about them," Hocking says. "I had never come across anyone, and I don't think I've met anyone since, who was so bitchy and sharply critical."

Anna's attitude also caused problems for the magazine with more than one design house. Still a neophyte, but a neophyte with fangs, she'd flounce into some of the lesser-known houses looking for clothing to feature, flip through the racks, and then declare, "There's *nothing* here." Her caustic visits sparked irate calls to Hocking from vociferously complaining designers with deflated and bruised egos.

"Somebody might have been brave enough to tell her to be a little more politic," says Hocking, who was afraid to confront Anna, fearful of her wrath. "I was the fashion editor and this was something I wouldn't do, even if I hated the clothes. You sort of say, 'Oh, we're not doing blue this year.'"

Later, Anna would toss out one very devastating word—"rubbish"—to describe something she didn't like, and strong men and thick-skinned women would fall like lumps of clay. "She was very much to the point," notes Hocking, "and very clear thinking. I'm sure she didn't then, and doesn't care now [what people think of her], because she would not have been able to do what she managed to do with her career. She's so single-minded, and basically she's probably right all the time as well."

Anna was part of a team of several fashion assistants, one of whom she regarded with seemingly irrational and utter contempt. The young woman was the daughter of a well-placed London publicist and a friend of Jennifer Hocking's. "Anna certainly, basically, destroyed this girl, who felt very inefficient by comparison," declares Hocking. "Anna was being Anna, just being cleverer than anyone else, and defeated this one girl. I think somehow she puts the evil spell on people."

Another of the fashion assistants on the team, Jillie Murphy, who had come to *Harper's Bazaar* before Anna with some experience as a stylist for photographers like Richard Avedon, remembers clearly how Anna made the other girl's life "a living hell." "It was a conflict of personalities," explains Murphy, who had been assigned by Hocking early on to take Anna under her wing and show her the ropes. "Anna found the other girl to be a weaker personality, and I wouldn't have thought Anna liked that. Occasionally someone comes into your party that you don't get on with, and that obviously happened with Anna and [the other girl]. From day one, they didn't get on."

Anna made nasty comments to the girl, put her down in front of her colleagues, and claimed she was incompetent. Anna made the poor young woman's life miserable—and for no apparent reason except she enjoyed bullying those who couldn't fight back.

Because of the infighting, Hocking had to take out time from her relevant duties to trim Anna's sharp claws.

"Jennifer would have to take Anna for lunch to have a talk, and then she would have to take [the other girl] and her mother to lunch, to kind of make things sweeter, to make the relationship work, because we were a team," declares Murphy. "I liked Anna. I liked her firmness. But some people were terrified of her. She was quite cutting. But she wasn't as tough as what she grew into, as what she became later."

Landels says the other girl was "sweet," but that Anna "absolutely" beat her down and literally drove her out of the magazine. Anna didn't fear competition from her but rather was disgusted by her weakness, which brought out the bully in her.

Unlike the defeated and victimized girl, Murphy was a fighter who stood up for herself and therefore wasn't going to let Anna get to her. "It made Jillie basically investigate the enemy," notes Hocking. "She wanted to know what made Anna tick. She even managed to get Anna to invite her to stay overnight at her house. She got in under the radar, and I've always been absolutely amazed by that, because no way would I have been brave enough to do that with Anna. There was no way Jillie was going to be destroyed like the other girl."

While there were enormous differences in their lifestyles, Anna and Murphy bonded, or at least Murphy thought they had, though Anna never let her hair down. But she acted friendly. When Murphy was hospitalized for a brief time, Anna trekked to the blue-collar London suburbs to visit her. Afterwards, Murphy wondered about Anna's motives.

Because she couldn't afford private care, Murphy was treated in one of Britain's National Health hospitals, the kind of public institution someone of Anna's social standing would never have seen the inside of. "She was curious, not only to see how I was, but to see what a National Health hospital was like," says Murphy. "I'll never forget. She said, 'It's like *real* life.' I didn't think she had that human element."

On another occasion, Murphy had a chum whose boyfriend was in prison. She made mention of it in passing to Anna, whose eyes lit up. "She was interested to know what the inside of a prison looked like, so she actually went to visit him. I didn't even go. But that's what her curiosity was like."

As she got to know Anna, Murphy was surprised to find that she had very few close women friends. "And as her career took off," she adds, "her circle of friends took off as well." Back then, Anna's posse consisted of Murphy and another very ambitious young woman named Joan Juliet Buck, who years later became editor of French *Vogue* and a contributing writer to American *Vogue*, under Anna, where the two had an up-and-down relationship. "We were like the Three Musketeers," Murphy recalls fondly. "Joan's an American and I met her through Anna, and then we just all hung out together, liked the same hip things, looking for things that were new."

Still, Vivienne Lasky remained Anna's closest friend, but she was in the United States pursuing her undergraduate degree at Radcliffe while Anna was getting her real-life degree on the job.

Murphy didn't come from money, was kind of a free spirit, and was a couple of years older than Anna. Like Anna, though, she had not gone to college, and they were both size eight. If they were going to a party, Anna often lent Murphy some of the expensive designer clothing from her vast and always updated wardrobe. "Anna used to have all the Missonis, all the designer things, so I got all the leftovers. If she got fed up with something, as she often did, she'd give it to me."

Another beneficiary of Anna's largesse was Liz Walker, Willie Landels's young deputy art director, who thought of Anna as a fairy godmother. Though she saw her as "distant, frozen-faced, private, and rather determined," she also felt that Anna was "incredibly generous in a quiet sort of way" by giving away outdated pieces—usually no more than six months old—from her wardrobe. "We were all paid virtually nothing," Walker says, "and Anna was probably the only person on our block who had a private income. And every season she would get rid of her clothes, and she'd have worn some of these things maybe once.

"She used to have a really amazing figure, really great boobs and quite a tiny waist, and we were sort of the same size and about the same height, about five foot five, a classic size eight to ten, with a very slight-looking frame," continues Walker, who had an eye for such detail, going on to become executive fashion and beauty editor at British *Marie Claire*. "Anna would pass on her clothes, but she'd do it in a really charming way, not in the I-am-the-rich-girl-giving-my-clothes-to-you. She would choose things she thought you might like, or would suit you. It was really done in a very gracious way."

Giving away her castoffs became part of Anna's modus operandi, something she'd do throughout her life. Some, with a cynical point of view, thought it was her way of securing loyalty or buying friendship from the beneficiaries of her generosity. Whatever the motive, it was also a quick and easy way to make room in her closets for the new lines.

"None of us were paid much, but Anna had her own money, family money," notes Hocking. "We used to go to the shows in Italy, and Anna would be the only one of us who would then actually buy clothes from the designers. Here's this young girl going to Milan and Paris, and that could be a bit of a shock for anyone else—but not to Anna. Nothing fazed her because she was used to going to the best places and meeting top people in her personal life. Nothing would impress, unless it was *really* good, but I don't remember ever seeing her *really* impressed. She wasn't the sort of person who would say, 'Gosh, that's amazing!' She was always on one level, but taking everything in."

Despite Anna's contention that she had no master plan for herself in the fashion mag game, she expressed a major goal less than two years after she joined *Harpers & Queen*. In the fall of 1971, the staff began planning features for the Christmas issue. "All of us, Anna, myself, and Jennifer, had to do a page—our ideal Christmas present," recalls Murphy. "Mine was a trip to a desert island. But Anna's goal was to be appointed editor of *Vogue*. That's what *her* dream was."

Since *Vogue* was a competitor, Landels didn't see fit to mention Anna's fantasy in his magazine. Instead, she appeared in the late November issue of *Harpers & Queen*—a bimonthly at the time—with five of her colleagues under a headline that read, "6 *H&Q* employees describe their ideal Christmas presents, illustrated by models' photos."

And there she was, smashing, in her third modeling assignment. The copy read: "Anna Wintour, fashion assistant, 21, would like to taste St. Moritz living next year and hopes to escape from the Underground (quilt-trousered Japanese work woman division) wearing this ankle-length white fox coat, £1,950 from Harrods, SW1, and diamond feather brooch from Collingwood, 46 Conduit St. W1 (also the diamond band ring), and leading this large Pyrenean mountain dog from Harrods. The cane chair is £29 from Biba, 124 Kensington High St. W8. Hair by Herts at Vidal Sassoon."

Back then, being a fashion editor involved very little writing, just a simple intro to a layout now and then, if that. "The problem was, Anna couldn't write," asserts Landels, which he thought was odd for the daughter of a newspaper editor. But neither could Jennifer Hocking write, which would eventually result in her dismissal by Landels and a bitchy battle for her job involving

Anna. But that was still down the road. "We never wrote words," acknowledges Hocking. "We weren't asked to write. We'd write down the facts—'blue shoes.' We were fashion editors. We selected clothes. We didn't write about them."

Moreover, Anna had problems getting across what *needed* to be written. "Anna couldn't express her thoughts about fashion," adds Landels. "We had a subeditor who said to me, 'That fucking Anna Wintour! She's given me this folder and I don't know what to write because she doesn't tell me anything.' And I said, 'Don't be unkind about Anna. One day she will be our boss.'"

During Anna's tenure, most of her writing was done by Laura Pank, who had to devise kicky sentences for "the ridiculous fashion sets" and headlines "for these weird things that Anna told me were 'wonderful,' so I just believed it, really, and wrote it that way." Anna briefed Pank in a voice that still echoed in her ears years later. "She sounded like sandpaper, really grating, like a door that needs oiling, a floorboard, something really painful. Otherwise, she tried to be mysterious behind the glasses, honing her persona." Of all of the people working on fashion news, Anna "certainly dressed as she shot," notes Pank. "She actually lived fashion, wore her dark glasses all the time, in and out, was immensely stylish, and pin-thin. I think she existed on lettuce leaves."

Pank was convinced, and people gossiped, that Anna was restricting her diet. "That's her personality," she asserts. "She's a control freak, always had to be in control of herself and everyone else."

The most difficult aspect of the job, whether one was a junior like Anna or a senior like Hocking, was learning to work smoothly with prima donna photographers who wanted only one thing—their creative freedom. The fashion editor's job was to keep control of the shoot.

Anna seemed to have a preternatural ability. She worked well with some of the best of them back then—Alex Chatelaine, in Paris, and talented neophyte James Wedge in London, whom Anna knew, so no problem there. He was part of the group of cool older men in her social sphere, a player in the London boutique scene where Anna had first met him.

Wedge had just started shooting professionally when Anna began giving him assignments. Before long, they became romantically involved. She was in good company. Among his girlfriends was the model Pat Booth, who became a popular novelist, and after Anna the actress Helen Mirren, with whom he had a long, tempestuous relationship.

"Anna hired me as a photographer, and that's how we met, and then we became lovers," acknowledges Wedge, who says he succeeded Richard Neville. "When I met her she was still with Richard and they were sort of splitting up."

Anna and Wedge, a decade older, were together for about eighteen months. Since Wedge considered himself "a loner" and Anna had few female friends, he described their relationship as a "very private affair." When he first met Anna, he thought of her as a *Vogue* type. "Though she was working for *Harpers*," he observes, "she had that *Vogue* attitude—very snooty about fashion, seemed to know it all."

In fact, much of their relationship revolved around fashion, as had her involvement with Stephen Bobroff. "We were lovers, we went out together, and we worked together at the same time," says Wedge, "and most of our time together was spent talking about fashion and never seemed to depart from that. It was always—*always*—the same subject." Wedge knew Bobroff professionally. Unlike Bobroff, though, Wedge and Anna didn't set up housekeeping together. He had an enchanting cottage in a forest in the Gloucester countryside where they spent weekends together, and Anna had an elegant apartment near Earl's Court, in the city.

"Anna was very determined, ambitious—it was pretty obvious in the way she acted—and she had very strong views on fashion and the work we were doing together," he says. "Often you can be employed by a fashion editor because they like your work and leave all the decisions up to you, but she had a lot to say on how my work—the photos—was to be achieved. But I was quite a young photographer in the sense that I hadn't been working very long, so it was nice to work with someone like Anna who was *so* strong-minded."

Anna took Wedge to Phillimore Gardens and introduced her new beau to her father, who he found "very frosty." After several visits, Wedge came away thinking, "It runs through the family."

Even though Wedge fancied Anna, there were aspects of her personality that he found irritating or just plain odd. The first had to do with her eating habits: "She'd order coffee," he remembers clearly, "and have cream put on the top and then she would just eat the cream off with a spoon and never touch the coffee. And when the food came, she'd just pick at it, never eat it."

The other issue that he found odd had to do with Anna's relationship with her colleagues at the magazine, which was underscored for Wedge during a weeklong shoot in Greece. "Normally on those sort of occasions the crew gets up early, has breakfast together, do the day's shoot, and then you all meet up for dinner in the evening. But with Anna, it was different. She *never* had dinner with us, had her meals sent to her room and ate alone. It always struck me how aloof she was. It's sort of a sign, not to eat with everyone in the evenings. It's unusual."

Like all couples, they had tiffs. It might have been over something Wedge had said that ticked off Anna, but when she got angry, she didn't explode. "She went the opposite way. She became cold, did *not* speak." Their relationship eventually bottomed out. "We just went our separate ways," he says. "Nothing special happened to end it. It was the seventies, you know—if you remember [what happened], you weren't really there."

Wedge left London, moved to the country, and began painting. Sometime in the early to midnineties, Anna showed up unexpectedly at his London studio during the Christmas holiday to say hello, looking "slightly older, but her style was the same—the bob, still very slim, but a little bit more aloof, a little crisper." They hadn't spoken for many years, and he was pleasantly surprised to see her. But it wasn't until long after she left that he discovered she had gotten married and had children, none of which she told him during her visit, which didn't surprise Wedge, who always felt she was secretive.

"Despite spending quite some time with her as her boyfriend, I knew very little about her," he notes. "It's amazing. With Anna you look back and think how little you know of her."

Jennifer Hocking recalls that Wedge was "very keen" on Anna, and she knows of at least one other photographer, a Frenchman, with whom Anna was involved while working at *Harpers & Queen*. "When we used to go to Paris she would see him. She had a busy life, but on the surface she never came in looking as if she'd spent a night out, but always looked calm, collected. You couldn't read her life by talking to her. She certainly attracted interesting guys, intelligent ones, but she did it quietly, didn't boast, didn't say I'm doing this or that. A lot of the shoots Anna did, she did with James Wedge. She used to get things out of photographers nobody else could, so maybe she had her own methods—I don't know. Men obviously liked her . . . and that is why she always got these amazing photos."

Manipulating men has always been one of Anna's great strengths. With the photographers, she flirted, complimented, ego-stroked, and slyly directed in order to get the best out of them. Moreover, as she became more experienced as an editor, she was savvy enough to take *their* advice, to use the shots *they* recommended, the photos *they* determined were their best from a particular shoot, rather than making her own personal choice. That way, in most instances, she could do no wrong.

Hocking, who knew a thing or two about handling men, was amazed that such a young thing like Anna could do it as she did and make it appear so easy. A valise, as it turns out, underscored it all for her. "We'd go to the shows and she'd always be able to get men to carry her suitcase," she said, remembering those moments years later. "I'm tall and no one would ever carry my suitcase. I used to say, 'My God, in my next life I'm going to look like Anna Wintour.' She looked frail, she looked fragile, and obviously that appeals to a lot of men. Men loved her. Anna would stand there with the fringe hanging down over her eyes, looking very sort of helpless, a waiflike look, but far from being a waif, and the men would line up."

From the beginning of her career, Anna had an eye for interesting locations. One memorable and magical shoot for *Harpers & Queen* that she oversaw was for a collection of clothing by Japanese designers, a favorite of Anna's through the seventies and eighties. The magazine wouldn't spring for an expensive and time-consuming location shoot in Asia, so Anna, working with Wedge, found a farm that grew watercress in the English countryside that had from a distance the look of a rice paddy, and that's where she posed the models, wearing peasant hats and Japanese fashions. "It was fantastic," recalls Hocking. "She could organize, she would make sure people sent in the props and clothing she wanted, and she got very good work out of the photographers. Her mind was always sharp and crystal clear. I don't think I've ever met anyone as clever as her."

Years later, Anna looked back on her work at *Harpers & Queen* and noted that she considered the fashion shoots to be "amateurish affairs." She recalled being sent to India for a weeklong assignment with nothing more than twenty pounds, which in those days was less than fifty dollars. "When I asked my editor, 'How am I supposed to pay for everything?' He said, 'Oh, just find a maharajah with a palace.' And I think I did."

ten

Family Affairs

From the age of fifteen, Anna had begun hearing well-founded rumors that her father was a womanizer. Later, gossip items alluding to his extracurricular affairs began appearing in the "Grovel" gossip column of London's bitchy satirical magazine *Private Eye*.

The column linked him to a married woman and made light by calling him "Sir Charles" because he never received knighthood, which he felt he deserved.

Arthur Schlesinger Jr., who had been introduced to the woman by Wintour, says, "It was evident to an old friend his interest in her had a certain sexual tinge. She was very vivacious, sexy, and bright, and Charles was a powerful editor by this time. Womanizing was not the central theme of his life, but he liked intelligent, pretty women, and I suppose went to bed with them. Charles had a British reserve about things and was not given to confessionalism."

Wintour once showed up with the beauty at the *Evening Standard*'s Washington, D.C., bureau, staying with her at the Madison Hotel, according to the paper's then-correspondent in the nation's capital, Jeremy Campbell, who had long heard the stories about his boss's affairs. But Wintour attempted to dispel the rumors. "Charles said to me, 'Whatever you hear, she's my traveling companion, and nothing more.'"

Campbell's reaction? "I suspended belief."

Alex Walker, who had become close to Nonie Wintour before, during, and after her marriage, believes that the tensions that had long existed between her and her husband had reached their zenith in the late sixties and early seventies. "The children were growing up. Nonie was deeply involved in her social work. Charles consequently became more involved in the feminine comforts that a number of women offered him.

"Charles would have absolutely never talked about any of this. He would have thought that that would have been a breach of faith in marriage. If he had any real confidantes, they were probably the other women that he was with. He became the kind of husband who relaxes with a mistress to get rid of the tensions of home life."

Besides the boldface names with whom he had liaisons, Wintour "riffled through secretaries at the paper, one after another, and poor old Nonie was at home," recounts a female former *Evening Standard* reporter. "He was very frigid and horrible to her. They gave wonderful cocktail parties, but they were very unhappy together."

Anna knew of her father's wanderings from what she saw and heard firsthand at home, from *Private Eye,* and from the whispering in the circle in which she ran. Always very private, she never talked about the gossip items.

"She was very reserved that way," notes Jennifer Hocking. "She wouldn't have discussed it, and Anna was not a gossipy person who you could sit around and have a good dish with."

Her father's philandering was difficult for her to deal with, or to comprehend intelligently, says Vivienne Lasky. "Anna thought that some of the women reporters who worked at the *Standard* weren't just protégées. Anna sensed something. One was invited along to the country, was included in a lot of things even with Nonie there, and often he would take her to parties if Nonie didn't want to go.

"Anna couldn't go to her mother, or her father, and say, 'What's this all about?' She's so terribly British," observes Lasky. "We had many conversations about our fathers being womanizers. She knew of his infidelities, was aware he had protégées, and she forgave him everything. Early on, when *Private Eye* first started reporting the gossip, she tended to side privately with her father. It was tough, but we both loved and idolized our fathers and didn't quite know what to do with our feelings. I don't even know if it was anger. It was just sort of like, what does this all mean?"

In a childish and naive way, Anna seemed to understand her father's philandering more than she could Melvin Lasky's, mainly because Brigitte Lasky was chic and beautiful as opposed to her own frumpy mother. "I remember Anna wondering, 'Why would your father go any further than *your* mother? Why would he, if he's got *the* most beautiful woman?' "

Anna seemed to have the mind-set of a *Cosmo* Girl—that it all had to do with a sexy look and sex, with little understanding that relationships were far more complex.

"I adored Charles, he was charismatic and flirtatious," Lasky says. "And I knew his flaws. I don't want to put any blame on Nonie—she didn't deserve that kind of treatment—but once in a while she could have gone out with her husband. Nonie never went anywhere with him. Charles would buy Nonie jewelry for her birthday, but she'd say she didn't want it. It's as if he didn't really know her."

On September 4, 1970, nine months after Anna had joined *Harpers & Queen*, Nonie received an urgent transatlantic call from her sister Jean in New York. Their mother, Anna Gilkyson Baker, had died at the age of eighty-one. The matriarch had been widowed for almost four years, ever since pneumonia claimed the life of her renowned Harvard corporate law professor husband, Ralph Jackson Baker, at seventy-eight. Hospitalized for a week, Baker died on November 5, 1966, two days after his granddaughter Anna's seventeenth birthday.

Anna's grandmother had been found dead in the Bakers' Boston apartment where Nonie had spent her formative years. The cause of her mother's death, though, was kept secret from other family members on the American side.

Unlike Ralph Baker, who had long suffered from heart disease and chronic bronchitis, which were the cause of his death, Anna Baker did not die a natural death or from illness. Apparently long depressed, Anna's grandmother committed suicide, taking an overdose of the barbiturate Nembutal.

Anna's maternal grandfather had invested his money wisely and left an impressive estate of $2,279,578.62 (in 1966 dollars), of which Anna was a beneficiary. Her grandmother when she died had a personal worth— excluding her husband's sizable trust for her—of $204,162.93, of which Anna also was an heir.

On November 3, 1970, two months after her grandmother's death, Anna celebrated her twenty-first birthday at a party thrown by her parents at the posh Savoy Hotel. She now had substantial income at her disposal from the family trusts, the kind of money that would allow her to take low-paying fashion magazine jobs, such as the one at *Harpers & Queen*, and still live the high life: have chic apartments, wear beautiful clothes, drive a trendy car, spend nights on the town, and date outrageous men.

eleven

Creative Energy

Anna's first discovery of a new face and potential cover girl at *Harpers & Queen* was a debutante on the London social scene named Annabel Hodin, who had been a year behind Anna at North London Collegiate. They rode the same underground line, passed in the hall on the way to classes in their drab brown uniforms, nodded at one another, but didn't mix because of the slight age difference. But both were intrigued.

"I knew of Anna because I liked pretty people, and she was pretty," says Hodin. By the time Anna was promoted to assistant fashion editor in late 1971 under Jennifer Hocking, Hodin was just breaking into the modeling game. She had quite a timely look—her bright orange bob was cut by Sassoon and she wore microminiskirts. She was the real deal. Anna was hooked. "Like attracts like," Hodin observes. "She discovered me as a model, liked my look, took me under her wing, and gave me my first job."

Anna had created a story called "London Originals" and had booked Hodin for the layout with hopes of getting her on the cover against stiff competition— the stunner Charlotte Rampling, of television's *The Avengers* fame. Rampling made the cover of the February 1973 issue, but Hodin was one of the featured London beauties, and from there her career took off.

Anna had pulled together quite a team for the shoot, including the South African photographer Barry McKinley, who was hot at the time, and the innovative Barbara Daly, who handled the extraordinary makeup for Stanley

Kubrick's 1971 terrifying sci-fi classic *A Clockwork Orange* and his 1975 *Barry Lyndon*. The period photos of the models with crimped hair and marcelled waves were shot in the dramatic art nouveau–style apartment of the renowned Chinese art director and designer Barney Wan, whom Anna knew.

She was quickly building a reputation of being able to round up the best people and locations, mainly because of her connections through her father, pals like Nigel Dempster, and other well-placed types with whom she networked socially.

"Her shoots were always very high style, very classy," notes Hodin. "Anna would have the best of the new designers, top makeup. She had *the* most immaculate eye. She never chose mediocrity in any form, and when you get a good team, you get a great shot."

After "London Originals," Anna booked Hodin for a shoot in Corsica, with her lover James Wedge as the photographer, with fashions by Missoni and jewelry from the posh London shop Emeline—everything in coral, ebony, and ivory. Such location shoots usually took about a week. "Afterwards, the jeweler gave everyone marvelous bracelets," recalls Hodin, "and then we'd go off to San Lorenzo [an expensive celebrity restaurant in Knightsbridge] where we'd all have lunch."

Rigid in so many ways, such as with her bob, which she kept for a lifetime, and her signature sunglasses, Anna also never digressed from her luncheon regimen. "It was so odd, because she had the same meal every day at a little Italian restaurant around the corner from the magazine," says Liz Walker. "It was smoked salmon and scrambled eggs—*every single day*. She would eat nothing else. She was practicing the high-protein thing even then. We all had at least a glass of wine, but if she did, she drank the tiniest amount."

Besides kick-starting the careers of models like Hodin, Anna launched up-and-coming photographers in her early days at *Harpers & Queen*. One was Eric Boman, whom Landels describes as a "very beautiful, wonderfully blond, and charming" college boy who had done some "very lovely" drawings that had caught his keen art director's eye. Anna had planned to do a feature on lingerie, and Landels, looking for a different slant on what he thought was a boring and cliché subject, asked her to get Boman to sketch the models.

A few days later, the pair appeared at Landels's desk with spectacular photographs of a beautiful girl in underwear, sitting at a dressing table in a luxurious room at the Savoy. "Anna took a room and they went there and those photos were shot," says Landels. "So Anna made Eric, an artist, into a photographer. I thought, 'What vision on her.' It was very perceptive of her to know he would be good. I adored the photographs. Maybe Eric said, 'Let me shoot pictures.' But the fact that she let him, and took the risk of me saying, 'What the hell are you doing?' said something about her."

As much as any woman could bond with Anna in those days, Annabel Hodin did. It was a time of constant partying, with many champagne-filled evenings spent at the Clermont, a posh gambling club on Berkeley Square, or at Annabel's, or at any of the other chic nightspots where rich and powerful men and beautiful young women on the make gathered in the glitzy, disco seventies. Very briefly during this period, Anna dated, among others, Tony Elliott, who, just out of college in 1968, had founded the very successful weekly events listing magazine *Time Out,* and impresario Michael White, who produced the first London stage performance of *The Rocky Horror Show.*

"Everybody wanted to go out with Anna," says Hodin. "She was very beautiful, and any powerful man with any aspirations would want to be with her."

There was an endless line of high rollers who adored Anna and competed for her affections. Two among them were friends, part of a hard-drinking, playboy rat pack of sorts. One was a powerful British advertising executive twice her age, the other a freelance American journalist a dozen years her senior.

"Anna was attracted to older men, and thank God for that! Otherwise I wouldn't have had a hope," states dashing John Pringle, who at the time was nearly fifty and had been the chairman of the European branch of the powerful American advertising agency Doyle Dane Bernbach. "Oh, God, Anna was much younger, but that never hindered me. I always rather fancied a young woman."

By the time Anna met Pringle, the ad business was in a recession, DDB had lost some big clients, and he had been appointed director of tourism for Jamaica, based in London, with offices worldwide. He was quite successful in putting the island on the map, vacationwise. He had big-time family connections there. An ancestor, Sir John Pringle, had arrived in Jamaica, then still part of the British Empire, in the early 1900s as supervisor of the lunatic asylum in Kingston. He later made a killing by buying up abandoned sugar plantations and planting bananas.

Pringle fit Anna's profile. "Anna only liked men who were stimulating and exciting, and she would fall in love with that," notes Hodin. "Anything else would be just a sex thing."

The moneyed Pringle had just ended a long marriage and was playing the field when he was introduced to Anna by a mutual pal at one of the clubs. "Because of the divorce I was terribly unhappy," he says. "I'd been married for a number of years and did all sorts of stupid things. Anna came into my life during that period, and she was very exciting."

A charming raconteur and good-looking man-about-town—the type who calls both male and female friends "dahling"—Pringle was utterly smitten with the chic young assistant fashion editor. "I found her extremely attractive, she flirted with me, and I had a big crush on her," he acknowledges. "I saw quite a lot of Anna, took her to Annabel's, the usual places. She was just so sexy and funny and amusing and attractive, but at the same time she was a tough little bird."

As he got to know her, he found downsides to what he considered to be Anna's intriguing persona. For one, he came to the conclusion, after numerous attempts to seduce her, that she was a tease. "Anna was cold in a very sexy sort of way, if one can cope with that sort of strange statement. She flirted. I stuck my tongue in her mouth, and she rather liked that. But I never got to bed with her."

He also was put off a bit by her vanity and imperiousness. "She always struck me as being *incredibly* spoiled, *very* flirtatious and slightly naughty, and *enormously* secretive. She isn't one of those people who disclose their innards to anyone. She never told you anything about her feelings, about what she was going to do or not going to do. She just did it."

And one of the things Anna did was to fall in love with Pringle's best friend, an American freelance writer named Jon Bradshaw. "I was very fond of Bradshaw, I *loved* Bradshaw. He was a complete rascal, and he was magic to women, who fell in love with him all over the place. And Bradshaw came along and had a crush on Anna, and I had a crush on her, but Bradshaw started fucking her."

twelve

Meeting Mr. Wrong

Anna and Jon Bradshaw—everyone called him Bradshaw, never Jon—were introduced in 1972 by their mutual friend Nigel Dempster, who had known Bradshaw since his arrival in London from New York City in the early sixties when he went to work as a freelance for *Queen* magazine.

Giving a gossip item ring to how he played Cupid, Dempster says, "I introduced them, and Bradshaw said to me, 'Anna's a wonderful girl,' and went off with her to Tramp," the hot, celebrity-studded nightclub in posh Mayfair. "Afterwards, he told me, 'Anna's the girl for me.'" Bradshaw's attraction was that he "was a discoverer, an interesting character who came to our city and showed us things we'd never seen before," says Dempster, extolling his friend's virtues.

A dozen years Anna's senior and recently divorced from a wealthy Englishwoman after less than a year's marriage—the two actually had a well-publicized London divorce party—Bradshaw was a devilish rogue with enormous appetites: of liquor, Johnny Walker Black being his favorite, but anything would do as long as someone else was picking up the tab; of recreational highs—a toke here, a snort there; of nicotine—at least three packs of unfiltered British Rothmans a day; and of rich foods. He also was a gambler who played high-stakes backgammon and wrote a book about it called *The Cruelest Game* during the halcyon days of the backgammon boom in the seventies.

The writer Nik Cohn, a close friend of Bradshaw's who penned the *New*

York magazine story that became *Saturday Night Fever* starring John Travolta, had an apt description of the man for whom Anna fell hard: "His calling cards were wit and charm, a world-class talent for gossip, and good looks of an almost Hollywood order. A louche, more dissolute version of James Garner, he carried himself with conscious roguery, a Rothman's perpetually dangling from one corner of his mouth and that lopsided shark's grin plastering the other. He sported Turnbull and Asser silk shirts and Gucci loafers, flashed gold lighters and a Piaget watch; slathered himself with Vetiver cologne; tended to speak in mock-abusive italics: 'the *awful* Mailer, the *dreadful* Elaine, the *unspeakable* Timothy Leary.' The insults were his style of showing admiration. Awfulness, if married to flair, was golden. . . . His devouring passion was for action."

Men, straight and gay, as well as women loved and fawned over him. In the new millennium he'd be typed a "metrosexual."

Anna found everything about Bradshaw incredibly fascinating and attractive, especially his family background.

In New York, Bradshaw's mother, Annis Murphy, a drinker, a smoker, "strong and domineering," had been a copy editor at *Vogue* and was a close friend of Beatrix Miller, the longtime editor of British *Vogue* whom Anna would replace in the mideighties. She also was a chum of Anne Trehearne, the clever, longtime fashion editor at *Queen* with whom Bradshaw stayed when he first hit London and who was his entrée to start freelancing for the magazine. Bradshaw's father had abandoned the family early on, so besides his mother, he was raised by an uncle, an executive at the Vanguard Press in New York who helped oversee publication of the 1954 best-selling novel *The Bridge on the River Kwai.* Bradshaw grew up in a book-filled apartment in a genteel building overlooking the East River at Seventy-second Street, where family friends included the writer and Renaissance man George Plimpton and the famed Tiffany's window dresser Gene Moore. Bradshaw had gone to a prep school in Pennsylvania and later attended writing classes at Columbia University, and tried to sell pieces to the *New York Herald Tribune* before splitting for London.

Despite Dempster's assertion of having brought Anna and Bradshaw together as lovers in 1972, there are some who believe they had actually gotten to know each other much earlier—when Anna was in her club-hopping midteens.

A journalist who had worked for the *Evening Standard* in the early sixties and later had an "on-and-off romance with Bradshaw" recalls seeing him in Charles Wintour's newsroom—"sprawled all over the 'Londoner's Diary' desk, making personal transatlantic calls to New York"—as early as 1963, when Anna was just fourteen. Moreover, she recalls seeing him around that same time at the Wintour house.

"I just have this picture in my mind's eye of being in the house in Phillimore Gardens and seeing Bradshaw and Anna going downstairs to her flat and somebody saying to me, 'Are they living together down there?' It was extraordinary because her father was a stern father figure to everybody at the *Evening Standard*. He was quite possessive, so why he would allow his favorite daughter to be with this charming guy who never earned a penny is a mystery. Bradshaw might have just been bumming a bed off her down there then because he never seemed to have a place of his own."

Since Dempster was already a friend of Bradshaw's, and Dempster was seeing Anna when she was in her mid- to late teens, it's likely Anna had met Bradshaw in Dempster's circle, which included the likes of John Pringle long before they became romantically involved publicly.

How and when they met, and whether Charles Wintour took kindly to his daughter's latest suitor, became a moot point because Anna and Bradshaw quickly became an item and moved in together, renting a partly furnished quaint town house in trendy Chelsea.

"Anna had done a lot of decorating, with all very warm touches," recalls Vivienne Lasky. "She had *such* style. What were hers I could pick out—the books, and the way they were stacked, the Provençal fabrics, and Bradshaw had a lot of his very tasteful memorabilia on display."

Anna's lover's possessions included a series of stamps that he and his buddy, the photographer Patrick Lichfield, the queen's first cousin once removed, had produced as a publicity stunt. On a lark, the pair had started a private postal service—Rickshaw Limited—using six couriers on Honda motor scooters in January 1971, during a postal strike in central London. "Back comes royal mail—posted by the Queen's cousin," declared a headline in the *Daily Express*. The story was illustrated with two photos, one of Lichfield, looking amazingly like a Las Vegas Elvis impersonator, with coiffed hair and sunglasses, and one of "Lord Lichfield's postman Jon Bradshaw," straddling a Honda, wearing a hippie-style leather-brimmed hat, loafers, and velvet slacks. He was shown handing over mail to a long-legged and slender beauty in a microminiskirt and boots at her shop in Chelsea, who was described as "one of their satisfied customers."

Lasky first saw Anna and Bradshaw as a couple when she returned to England in June 1972 to attend graduate school at Cambridge's New Hall College. She found him handsome and charming.

"Anna wanted to pick up where we left off when I went away to Radcliffe. She would say, 'Oh, come to dinner. We're all going. I want you to come and meet my friends. They're all interesting. You haven't got anything else to do.' Anna was forceful. She was always with a group of men, never other women."

Besides Bradshaw, Anna's posse consisted of Anthony Haden-Guest, whom Vivienne found "amusing and effete"; Dempster, who she describes as "weaselly"; and Lichfield, whom she thought of as bright, good-looking, and well-bred.

"Maybe Anna wanted another girl there because it was all sort of guy camaraderie. If they talked about sports, we would talk in the corner. She would say, 'We can talk while we eat and at least we'll get to be together.'"

Lasky looked and felt like a college kid compared to her glamorous assistant fashion editor best friend who, during London's cold and rainy months, went about town wearing a dramatic floor-length coat made of the fur of a white wolf.

Of all of the men in Anna's circle, Lasky adored Bradshaw. "He had a teddy bearish quality to him. He was genuine, the only one who would say hi and give me a hug, the only one who had an ounce of warmth, and I thought she needed a warm person in her life. I knew Bradshaw was older, but it wasn't a Pygmalion relationship. He wasn't trying to make her over into someone else. Anna was very well versed, lovely looking, well-spoken, had read everything, seen everything, and traveled a lot. What man wouldn't want to spend time with her?"

In fact, it was Anna who apparently tried to change Bradshaw, or at least encourage him, cheer him on in terms of his writing. She knew he had aspirations to write the great American novel, or screenplay, but was too much of a layabout ever to succeed. He needed, she believed, her guidance. Her goal became apparent in intimate letters she wrote to him, which Bradshaw saw fit to share with his friend A. J. "Jack" Langguth, a Vietnam war correspondent for *The New York Times*, author, and much later a professor of journalism at the University of Southern California's Annenberg School for Communications.

Langguth, who had had many uproarious adventures with Bradshaw over the years and loved him dearly, was surprised that his friend revealed the intimate and private correspondence to him. "He would read them not with a malicious attitude," emphasizes Langguth, "but to let me know that Anna was crazy about him. Anna was seeing herself as Bradshaw's muse who would inspire him to new heights, cheering him on as a young lady would write to Lord Byron, somehow influencing his life and production. And I knew Bradshaw would play the wounded artiste to the hilt. I'd say, 'Come on, Bradshaw, this young woman really has been taken in by this.' He'd say, 'Oh, Langguth, I'm a very sensitive person. You don't give me credit for that.'"

From the letters, Langguth came to the conclusion that Anna was sincere, "a nice young woman" who he thought "was too good" for Bradshaw.

But Anna and Bradshaw's relationship was far more complex than Langguth had perceived from letters. Others in closer proximity saw Bradshaw as a father figure to Anna, both emotionally and professionally. They felt she played a needy little girl role with him, and Bradshaw was always a sucker for people in need. Because of his many connections, he would be able to help her get in the door for jobs and meet the right people after she arrived in New York.

As John Pringle notes, "Bradshaw was a terribly generous man, and if he liked you—and he *loved* Anna—he would do anything to help her."

Anna, friends of the couple observe, would come to be the dominant figure in their tumultuous relationship.

It was a wild and crazy time, those early to midseventies years of the Wintour-Bradshaw romance.

But Annabel Hodin, who was a part of the scene, observes that despite all of the partying, Anna was "quite solitary. You'd always think of Anna being *apart* in the group—not *needing* to be liked, *very* self-contained."

Besides wild nights in the trendy London clubs, Anna and Bradshaw were frequent hangers-on at Shugborough Hall, Patrick Lichfield's magnificent two-hundred-acre, seventeenth-century ancestral home in Staffordshire. For Bradshaw, it was a platinum card freeload—lots of marvelous food, drink, fascinating men, beautiful women, and servants at his beck and call.

For Anna, it was a wonderful environment in which to network. Lichfield, who had snapped his first photo when he was six, was an influential friend to have if, like Anna, you were trying to make it in the fashion magazine world. He hung out with the new breed of fashion photographers, such as David Bailey, whom he once described as "strongly hetero East End kids," as opposed to what had been a mostly gay elite of shooters.

But of greater interest to Anna was the fact that Lichfield had developed a close relationship with Diana Vreeland, the doyenne of fashion editors, and had shot fashion for five years under her at American *Vogue*. His fellow photographers included the greats like Richard Avedon and Irving Penn, who also shot for *Vogue*. He was close to designers like Oscar de la Renta, with whom Anna later became friends. Most important, Lichfield was a respected friend of Alex Liberman, the all-powerful editorial director of Condé Nast who ran the show at *Vogue* and down the road would become Anna's guru, mentor, and Svengali.

Long before she came to America, Anna's name was known to many of the key players in the upper echelons of the fashion magazine world because of the contacts she made for herself during those fun weekends at Shugborough Hall.

For her, working at *Harpers & Queen* was like a power pitcher working his way up through the minors, but with George Steinbrenner keeping a keen eye on his record.

Sometimes Anna and Bradshaw went to Lichfield's with Annabel Hodin and her boyfriend, Robert Wade, who managed the British rock group The Kinks. Ironically, the group had put down as obnoxious and pretentious the whole London fashion scene, including fashionistas like Anna, in a rant of a single called "Dedicated Follower of Fashion."

"We did lovely things," reminisces Hodin of the weekends spent with Anna and Bradshaw at Lichfield's country estate. "Chauffeurs would take us to the woods and we'd all be given a gun so we could shoot at helium balloons. Then the butlers would lay out the picnic. There'd be movie shows in the evening. We'd stay all night, and in the morning the women would have their breakfast on silver trays, and then the men would go to the breakfast room where you pulled the doors back and the scrambled eggs and sausage and everything were. And then the men would read their newspapers. It sounds all very *Gosford Park*, but *Gosford Park* was about an industrialist, and Patrick was an *aristocrat*. It's *very* different. Then we'd all play tennis and run around on the lawns. He had funny cars for us to ride in and motorbikes. We could do anything we wanted."

But sometimes it all became too much for the lord of the manor, especially if someone like Bradshaw took advantage of the good life the earl offered to his friends and hangers-on.

John Pringle remembers one particular weekend when "that shit Lichfield was in one of his peevish, bitchy moods, and Bradshaw had tummy problems. He was not feeling well and he'd been staying at that rather grand house for what seemed like weeks and he knew all the servants. I was sitting at the table, and he said to one of the butlers, 'I can't eat very much. Can you make me a bowl of soup?' And Lichfield, at the other end of the table—and there were eighteen people at the table—said, 'Bradshaw, this is *not* a fucking hotel!' I got up and left the table and left the house that very afternoon because he was so rude to Bradshaw."

Bradshaw never forgot the embarrassing incident. After a very raunchy bachelor party thrown for Lichfield just prior to his marriage to Lady Leonora Grosvenor, daughter of the fifth Duke of Westminster, Bradshaw got his revenge. "There were a few girls here and there," says Bradshaw's Jamaican artist pal Willie Fielding, one of the revelers. "Bradshaw went and wrote about the whole thing in *Private Eye,* which came out the day before the wedding. He shat on Patrick, and none of us really wanted to talk to him for a while."

By 1974, Anna and Bradshaw had been together for some two years. Friends thought they seemed happy, despite the kind of lives they led.

"He was always very tender with her," observes the writer Glenys Roberts, a onetime *Evening Standard* reporter whom Bradshaw was seeing along with other women on the side. "It was almost a sort of paternal relationship with Anna, perhaps because her father was very cold and Bradshaw very warm. It might have been as simple as that."

Anna was proving herself at *Harpers & Queen,* where colleagues saw her as becoming increasingly driven and restless for more power. Bradshaw was often on the road, supposedly working on stories and book ideas, but was mainly living the high life with his pals and bedding down with other women.

"I had sort of an on-and-off platonic romance with Bradshaw, and he would pass out on my couch regularly," discloses Roberts, who had once been the girlfriend of *Monty Python*'s Terry Gilliam and later was married to a well-to-do London tailor. "I knew Bradshaw was supposed to be living with Anna, but he never rang her up and said, 'I won't be home tonight, darling.' He'd collapse on *everybody's* floor, so I don't think he was a very good bet for any woman, really. The one thing Bradshaw could do for Anna would be to introduce her to people, because he knew everybody."

Anna may have caught on to Bradshaw's womanizing, or been stung by it, or just come to the conclusion that they had an open relationship, because in 1974 she had an affair with one of his compatriots.

It all transpired like a scene out of a Jackie Collins novel.

Anna and Bradshaw had set sail on the *Queen Elizabeth 2,* Anna said to be working on a fashion assignment for *Harpers & Queen,* Bradshaw hustling money by participating in a shipboard backgammon tournament sponsored by Dunhill. Also taking part was a pal of Bradshaw's, a tough competitor by the name of Claude Beer, the 1974 world backgammon champion.

Like Bradshaw, Beer was a rascal and a rogue, a darkly handsome Paris-born playboy and gambler who had been spoiled by his mother who mostly supported him with her second husband's American oil money. "Claude was more fun than anyone could ever imagine," exclaims a female Palm Beach pal. Especially when he drank, and Beer loved the bubbly. He and his buddy Nigel Dempster had once gotten into a fight at Castel's, the fancy Paris nightspot, over a bottle of champagne. Beer won—then promptly passed out.

Beer also was a womanizer who had "a million girlfriends—a *million*," says his Florida chum. On that *QE2* cruise he romanced Anna, who was a dozen years his junior.

Dempster noted the shipboard romance in his *Daily Mail* gossip column—not once, but twice—a number of years after it happened. On November 29, 2000, in an item about Anna and Shelby Bryan, the multimillionaire for whom Anna left her husband and the father of their two children in the late nineties, Dempster dredged up the quarter-century-old affair: "During Anna's romance with Bradshaw, she ran off on the *QE2* with noted Palm Beach drunk and backgammon gambler Claude Beer . . ." In a second column, dated September 16, 2001, mourning the death of "my old friend" Beer, who had died of alcohol-related illnesses at the age of sixty-three in Palm Beach on the same day as the terrorist attacks in the United States, Dempster reminded his readers, "Back in 1974 on a Dunhill *QE2* backgammon jolly, he fell in love with American *Vogue* editor Anna Wintour, but that's another story."

After the ship reached port, Anna continued to see Beer. According to friends, Bradshaw was furious and, as he made it seem, broken hearted. They didn't immediately resume cohabitating. It was only after a while that he took her back, but things were never the same.

"Claude was hot, very exciting, and naughty," says Hodin, who knew him when he was with Anna. "He was around with her for a while. She would never be in love with someone like Claude. I don't know exactly what happened between them because Anna was very private like that. We'd talk about boyfriends but never go into detail. It was always, 'Oh, we had great fun.' Nothing more.

"Bradshaw, of course, knew about Anna and Claude, and that was why it was so exciting for Anna, because she was hiding and rushing in and out— two-timing a bit. Bradshaw was a bit vulnerable there. He was just about able to cope because Anna wasn't being *too* naughty. But Bradshaw played it quite well, let her go as long as necessary. He knew Anna was a different caliber of woman—you *had* to be jealous of her."

Bradshaw's ego had been badly bruised and his macho image tarnished. Word of the Anna-Beer romance had spread quickly around Bradshaw's wide circle of fellow ladies' men in London. And he himself carried the tale to New York, where he bemoaned what had happened to a friend, the up-and-coming novelist and poetry editor Joanie McDonell, whom he had met in the early seventies when she was working as assistant to another Bradshaw pal, Lewis Lapham, then the managing editor of *Harper's* magazine. "One day this guy with a big cape blew into the office, handsome as possibly could be, larger than life, looking for work," she recalls, "and within five minutes three people were saying, 'Bradshaw, you owe me money.'"

Bradshaw quickly became one of McDonell's "most dearest and intimate friends." And so she listened with utter horror and overwhelming sympathy when he described how crushed he was by Anna's actions.

Bradshaw, however, was the only source from whom she ever heard the story. And she was aware that Bradshaw was something of a hype artist, and that he hadn't always been faithful to Anna. "He was a bit of a rake," she acknowledges. Nevertheless, she bought his story of how Anna's behavior on the high seas had devastated him. He told her that there was no problem in their relationship prior to the shipboard event. And he admitted to her that when Anna left him for Beer, he got drunk and stayed drunk rather than confront his adversary.

"Bradshaw was humiliated and horrified and devastated," she says, still angry and emotional about it years later. "It was a hideous thing for Anna to do."

From the way Bradshaw described what had happened, his feelings, and the aftermath, McDonell saw "the boat incident," as she refers to it, as "a pivotal moment" in their relationship, and she was one of those convinced that things "were never the same" for them.

McDonell, who got to know Bradshaw and Anna as a couple in New York, points out, "He took her back because he loved her—and she did love him—but it hurt. The truth is that Anna was the love of his life. That was clear. But it was the end of the relationship as a romantic relationship. In terms of love, as I saw it, it was over."

A year after the *QE2* incident Bradshaw's first book was published. *Fast Company* profiled professional gamblers. The dedication page reads: "For Anna."

The two would have an all-consuming and tumultuous relationship, one that spanned two continents and simmered and boiled, on and off into the eighties.

thirteen
_____

Playing Hardball

Things were changing in the British fashion magazine world by the mid-seventies. Top editors wanted fashion people who could actually write, not just pick clothes. In 1974, Willie Landels decided that Jennifer Hocking would have to be replaced with someone who had genuine journalism experience, someone who could write and edit and express on paper her thoughts about fashion. It was a difficult decision for him to make because they were close friends. He'd known Hocking for ages, since she was a young model, and he wanted to be fair and square with her, so he decided to ease her out.

Somehow word leaked—magazines, especially fashion magazines, being gossipy, competitive, and bitchy places—that Hocking was going to be replaced and that Landels had begun a search for a new fashion editor.

That's when Anna, twenty-four, with no proper university schooling, with no writing ability, and with only four years of experience under her Gucci belt, let it be known through the two most important men in her life—Jon Bradshaw and Charles Wintour—that she was the brightest, the most creative, the most ambitious fashion person on staff and therefore deserved and should be handed on a Tiffany platter the most powerful fashion position on the staff of one of the hippest established magazines in all of Great Britain.

Landels wasn't shocked that Anna wanted the top job. He always knew how hungry she was for power and was aware of her dream to become editor of *Vogue.* But he was surprised by how she went about it. She never discussed the job with him directly. Anna's campaign began in an elegant private club in Mayfair over a fine meal.

"She was determined to be made the fashion editor, so she and Bradshaw took me to lunch, a very fancy place, and he did all the talking," Landels recalls vividly. " 'Willie, Jennifer's leaving,' Bradshaw said. 'I think you should make Anna the fashion editor.'

"I said, 'Bradshaw, I don't tell you how to write, so don't tell me how to run my magazine.' It was perfectly amicable, but I could see Anna wasn't happy. Anna just sat there behind her fringe, poker-faced. She had a way, when she wasn't happy about something, to look rather sulky."

When the luncheon ploy failed, Anna brought out her other big gun: her famous and powerful father. It was either a letter or a telephone call or both, from him, recalls Landels. Charles Wintour had made a case for his favorite daughter's promotion, but without success.

Though Landels certainly had come to know over the past several years that Anna was clever and creative, he felt she was too young, too inexperienced, too lacking in writing skills, and too unpopular with other staffers because of her icy, unfriendly demeanor to be promoted to the magazine's top fashion job.

Instead, he hired Min Hogg, who for a time had worked for *Queen* and for the Sunday *Times,* had been a photographer's representative, and was doing freelance writing.

From the start, Anna resented Min Hogg with a passion. Not only was she seething that she didn't get the top fashion job, she also felt Hogg didn't know fashion and wasn't cutting edge. "Anna considered that Min wasn't a fashionista," says Landels. "But Min was very intelligent and very articulate, and I was delighted to talk to a fashion editor who could actually speak *and* write."

It didn't take long for Min Hogg to feel the resentment emanating from Anna. "We didn't get on, she didn't approve of me getting the job. She wanted it herself and was absolutely furious when she didn't get it," says Hogg years later, not enjoying dredging up the bad memories of that time. "She had a degree of ambition that must eat away at her heart all the time. Fashion was her absolute world, and she did know more about it than me, so she just didn't know how to deal with having someone like me over her. Fashion, that's all she thought about, and she didn't like anyone who didn't—in other words, *me*. She didn't respect me for my work as a fashion editor at all, at all, at all, and despised my professional standing."

Anna's contempt for her new boss exploded openly in Paris at the winter collections shortly after Hogg's arrival at the magazine. Hoping to bond with her deputy, Hogg took Anna along but quickly discovered that she was trying to undermine her. From day one, Anna let her contempt be known. "I got a seat on the front row and she didn't," Hogg recalls. "She loathed that. She didn't need to say anything. It was perfectly obvious."

Anna's behavior became so intolerable that Hogg was forced to make an emergency phone call to Willie Landels, who was enjoying a vacation in Italy. She told him that Anna was essentially sabotaging the important assignment. "If she can," says Hogg, recalling that time, "she will ride over anyone."

Says Landels, "I was on holiday and I had to leave to go to Paris to sort things out. Min called and said, 'Anna's making things rather difficult for me—you'd better come to Paris. She's making trouble. She's telling people not to listen to me.' Anna was absolutely trying to undermine Min. It was like two mad dogs. It was all a bit naughty of Anna. I had to stay there the whole week like a policeman."

During the shows in Paris, Hogg also saw the seductive side of Anna's persona. "She puts on a sort of femininity, pushes her hair about a bit, and men do go for her on sight," Hogg observes. "There was an American journalist at the collections who never stopped photographing Anna: Anna coming in, Anna sitting down, just nonstop. If she was there he couldn't take his eyes off her, and she knew it. It was a complicit thing." The photographer, who has shot literally hundreds of photos of Anna over the years, was Bill Cunningham, who later shot brilliant street fashions for *The New York Times*.

After Paris, the chill emanating from Anna toward Hogg was palpable throughout the office. "Anna and I talked about it," recalls Vivienne Lasky. "There was a feeling at the magazine that Anna was sort of a ballbuster, and she definitely knew that. She *was* [a ballbuster], but she felt if she were a man, it would be admired. It wasn't the first time Anna felt her career had been derailed over the years by controlling people."

Not long after the Paris shows, Anna quit, while Min Hogg stayed on until 1979.

All Anna has ever said about her tenure at *Harpers & Queen* was that her rise by gradual degrees from fashion assistant to Min Hogg's number two was not meteoric—a tidbit of irony she gloatingly tossed to a journalist when she was appointed editor in chief of British *Vogue* in the mideighties.

"During that time [at *Harpers & Queen*], my father would pick me up for lunch and we would each talk about our problems and I guess I got a feeling of what it was like to be an editor," she observed. "Then they fired the fashion editor and appointed another one over my head." No mention of what happened in Paris, *ever*. "I got straight on a plane for New York. At the time it seemed the place with the most pull—partly because I had a boyfriend [Bradshaw] there, partly because I love American society. You're not placed by your surname and accent as you are in London."

Anna left the magazine in March 1975, though her name last appeared on the masthead in the May issue.

As Anna was abandoning London to begin a new life in New York, and with her relationship with Bradshaw on rocky ground, her parents' marriage of more than three decades was on its last legs.

Friends of the Wintours, like Drusilla Beyfus Shulman, think the reasons for the breakup were obvious. "For years, Charles was hardly ever at home. He had an intense family life that was entirely the responsibility of Nonie. She didn't sympathize with what he was doing on the paper and despised Beaverbrook. He was flirtatious with other women. And, of course, their adored son had died. She'd have had to have been a saint."

There had been several attempts to salvage the marriage, one of which was a vacation, because both enjoyed traveling. "They took a trip by automobile through Afghanistan, and I always interpreted that in view of what happened later as an attempt to save the marriage," says Arthur Schlesinger. "I doubt, though, whether either of them said to me it was a last-ditch effort, but that's a fair appraisal."

Charles Wintour had all but left his wife for the talented woman's magazine editor Audrey Slaughter, otherwise known as the "flame-haired temptress," who was about a decade his junior. Their affair had become public, thanks to *Private Eye,* which published the juicy details through the mid- to late seventies. "I wasn't even very red-haired," Slaughter protested feebly years later, "and I always wanted to be dark and mysterious."

Wintour had been introduced to Slaughter at a dinner party by her friend Shirley Conran, a journalist, onetime wife of the designer Terence Conran, and later author of a string of best sellers. Unlike some of Wintour's other female companions, Slaughter was not glamorous and didn't have anything like Nonie's Boston society background or Ivy League education. But Slaughter captivated Anna's father. "Audrey's a very brilliant editor, very finger-on-the-pulse, an energetic businesswoman always launching new magazines, and that's what attracted Charles," says Valerie Grove, who had known Slaughter since the late sixties. "They had something in common, which he didn't have anymore with Nonie. Audrey was a great contrast to Nonie—much warmer, amusing, self-deprecating, clearly happy to be on Charles's arm. Charles was captivated by her."

And Wintour adored being idolized, something he hadn't gotten from Nonie in years. "Charles missed the sort of adoration that Audrey brought," notes Drusilla Beyfus Shulman. "She *worshipped* Charles, and he could do no wrong. She didn't have any of the kind of intellectual judgments about him that Nonie had. She just really adored him."

With their marriage in tatters, the Wintours had sold off their wonderful house in Phillimore Gardens, where Anna had spent her swinging sixties teenage years, and moved into what Grove describes as a "ghastly, soulless apartment" on Southampton Row, steps from a subway station and a blue-collar tourist hotel.

Attempts at putting on a good front for friends were disastrous, such as the time Wintour tossed a Sunday brunch at the new apartment, inviting some of his favorite *Evening Standard* staffers. Nonie had taken to her bed, claiming she was sick, and everyone brought flowers to try to cheer her up after being warned by Charles.

"I think actually she'd said, 'Oh, to hell with your staff. . . . I'm going to bed. I'm not feeling well,' and she was ill," recalls Grove, one of the guests. "We went into the bedroom where she was sitting up in bed feeling just grumpy, gave her flowers, and then went on with our lunch."

Grove felt the Wintour apartment "had the aura of a marriage falling apart."

A string of sometimes hilarious gossip items about the Wintours' marital travails and his affair with Slaughter appeared in the "Grovel" column of *Private Eye*. The source of most, if not all, of it most likely was Nigel Dempster, who some believe was still angry that Wintour thought he wasn't good enough for his daughter or for his newspaper.

In a profile of Dempster that was published in *Harpers & Queen* in 1974 under the headline "The Scum Also Rises," Jon Bradshaw wrote that Dempster had made a deal in 1973 with his employer, the *Daily Mail*, to secretly write the "Grovel" column as long as he didn't include any *Daily Mail* dirty laundry. According to Bradshaw, this allowed Dempster "to attack his targets with greater impunity. . . . As a result of his rude assaults, Dempster has been banned from various London clubs . . . he has made powerful enemies within his own profession and more than a few of his victims have seriously considered sending heavies round."

Meanwhile, Anna would hold Audrey Slaughter in utter contempt for years, blaming her for destroying her parents' marriage, her animosity intensifying after her father married Slaughter. It would take almost two decades, until her father's death, for Anna to have a semblance of a rapprochement with Slaughter.

fourteen

Axed American Style

Twenty-five-year-old Anna landed in New York City in the long, hot summer of 1975, just in time for the Big Apple's era of decadence.

Anna's world was Manhattan's high life and nightlife: the trendy Upper East Side, where she again established a shaky live-in relationship with Bradshaw, whom she had followed to New York; the chic *Saturday Night Fever* scene at Studio 54, with its Andy Warhol–beautiful people set; the downtown scene where other recent British expatriates—journalists and fashion people—lived in funky artists' lofts, ran trendy new boutiques, and opened exclusive boîtes. Though the city was almost bankrupt, there was nowhere in the world more hip and open than New York in the mid- to late seventies. It was a freewheeling era of artistic creativity.

Anna's arrival in the far-out seventies, however, was greeted by a fashion scene that wasn't very far-out, and fashion magazines of the day had little of her kind of pizzazz, which may have been part of her master plan for coming to America—even though she denied having one—or merely a stroke of luck.

Women's wear was nowhere, with more focus on the personality of who was wearing the clothes than the clothes themselves. Men wore polyester leisure suits and loud shirts with big collars and gold chains around their necks à la Tony Manero. Women's fashion was very laid back, relaxed, and chic because of its simplicity—spurred by designs from Calvin Klein, Bill

Blass, Diane von Furstenberg, and Ralph Lauren. Sparked by the feminist movement and sexual freedom, women were declaring their individuality.

The miniskirt and bell-bottoms from the sixties remained in vogue, but seventies skirts were in two other lengths, midi and maxi. Jeans paired with tight white T-shirts, which became a favorite of Anna's—who also wore hot pants—was a chic and popular look. On the high end of the fashion food chain were designs by Givenchy, Norell, and Oscar de la Renta. And then came Woody Allen's *Annie Hall*. Diane Keaton's la-di-da look—a tie, a waistcoat, a man's shirt, thirties-style wide pants, designed and styled by Ralph Lauren—became de rigueur overnight.

Anna felt that fashion, and especially fashion magazines, in midseventies America needed a major fix of direction and focus, and a creative eye—something she was confident she had plenty of, so she began job hunting. As she once stated, "It wasn't until I came to the United States that I became more disciplined and more focused."

By late 1975 she had caught the eye of Carrie Donovan, the flamboyant and eccentric fashion editor at *Harper's Bazaar*, which was going through some rough times under editor in chief Tony Mazzola. Creative and managerial turmoil had become a way of life at the magazine. Donovan, a good two decades older than Anna, had come to *Bazaar* from *Vogue*, where her mentor, Diana Vreeland, once told her that in fashion she had "the common touch," which was a compliment.

Donovan and Anna had much in common. Both had bobs and both had become fashionistas at a young age: When Donovan was ten, she sent Jane Wyman sketches for a wardrobe and received a treasured thank-you note. And like Anna, Donovan had her first taste of fashion in a low-level spot in a department store, Anna at Harrods, Donovan in the hat department at Saks Fifth Avenue under the wife of *Vogue*'s Alexander Liberman. Donovan, though, had a formal education, having graduated from the Parsons School of Design.

With a reputation for discovering and nurturing new talent, Donovan liked what she saw in Anna and hired her as a junior editor. The fact that Anna had worked for *Harpers & Queen* also helped—the two magazines had Hearst corporate ties; Mazzola, in New York, was on the masthead of *Harpers & Queen* as editorial director, a position having to do with *Bazaar*'s editions in countries around the world.

Anna started on the bottom rung again as a twelve-thousand-dollar-a-year junior fashion editor. She appeared for the first time on the masthead in January 1976. She didn't have an easy go. Her British frost and in-your-face ambition turned off her American colleagues and bosses, and her edgy concepts didn't go over in what then was a conservative and tumultuous environment. But Anna had become part of *Bazaar*'s grand tradition, America's first fashion magazine, a graphics leader that debuted in 1867 and over the decades had the world's most famous fashion editors at the top—Vreeland, Carmel Snow—and brilliant photographers like Avedon and Man Ray.

But when Anna was hired, the magazine was having severe problems because management wanted to keep the outdated look. As a result, advertisers and subscribers were abandoning the old girl in droves. One of the reasons Donovan hired Anna was that *Bazaar* needed an infusion of new blood, a younger approach, something kicky and contemporary that would appeal to advertisers and readers.

Anna, one of four young fashion editors under Donovan, was assigned to a tiny office that she shared with another chic and engaging editor, Alida Morgan, who had previously worked under Vreeland and had been at *Bazaar* for little more than a year. Morgan, a society girl, was immediately impressed with the new hire's demeanor—very dry, kind of deadpan—and her style. Unlike the other girls who came to work looking like "slobs," surprising at a fashion magazine, Anna was usually wrapped in designer clothing and wore very little makeup, and every hair was perfectly in place, though she changed the length and direction of the fringe slightly from time to time.

Marilyn Kirschner, another glamorous and with-it fashion editor, who had been at the magazine for five years and whose name was above Anna's on the masthead, believes the only thing that stood out about Anna was the Missoni and Kenzo that she wore and her upper-class British accent. "Otherwise, she was very aloof."

Morgan was of interest to Anna. Besides being striking, she had a blue-ribbon pedigree—she was a granddaughter of Averell Harriman, a presidential adviser and multimillionaire, which appealed to Anna's elitist side. Morgan perceived Anna as risqué and mischievous. "One night," she recalls, "I was having dinner with my dad and Anna was in the same restaurant and she sent over a bottle of expensive champagne, and my father said, 'Uh-oh, she's trouble, schoolgirl trouble.' And I said, 'Yeah, yeah, yeah, she is.' "

It wasn't long, though, before Morgan and others in the office saw through Anna's schoolgirl guise, always a great come-on to men, and became aware of her enormous ambition and incredible discipline, her marvelous visual sense, and her intense interest in *everything* to do with fashion and style. And Morgan suddenly realized that *Harper's Bazaar* was just a way station.

"Anna *always* wanted *Vogue*," she states. "I knew that from the jump. *Everybody* knew it. She wanted to run *Vogue*, and the *Vogue* to run is American *Vogue*. That was the plan. She absolutely knew from the jump that that's what she wanted, and that's why she came to America. Her plan was to come here, get a better job, and start moving up."

To prove it, staffers remember Anna's unconscious doodling on *Bazaar* scratch pads—the word she kept writing over and over was "Vogue."

Not long after Anna got down to business, the magazine promoted some of its chic and glamorous staff in a two-page spread in the March 1976 issue, headlined "*Bazaar*'s SINGLE WOMEN," with the caption "The new young spirit of *Harper's Bazaar*. Here are some of *Bazaar*'s single women who help keep that spirit going in every issue." The layout was part of a special issue devoted to America's bachelorettes. Photographed by Bill King, the double truck showed eleven coiffed and gorgeous staffers.

"Bill was making us all jump up and down to get into the spirit," recalls Kirschner. "He wanted us to look very happy."

In King's shot, Anna is where she would always be in the fashion mag world—front row center. She's wearing a modified bob, her fringe boyishly brushed to the side. The other staffers appear officious and career-girlish, smiling broadly, sporting long-sleeved black T-shirts emblazoned with the word "BAZAAR" in white.

Except, that is, for Anna.

While the others have their hands planted on their hips or behind their backs, Anna's are crossed, blocking the word "BAZAAR," and she's the only one wearing something over the company T-shirt—a chic Kenzo vest.

Looking back years later, and knowing the heights to which Anna subsequently rose, Kirschner believes the photograph is telling. "Completely covering the *Bazaar* T-shirt with a Kenzo vest is so symbolic," she observes, armchair analyst–like. "It was Anna clearly asserting herself."

As another member of the fashion team, Zazel Loven, notes, "Anna was a little bit disdainful of the lack of sophistication in the American fashion magazine scene, and she didn't fit in with Hearst corporate. That was her attitude. She certainly wasn't staring down her nose at everyone—she was one of the players—but she just had a stronger vision, a stronger personality. She was very independent and had her own sense of taste, had her own way of doing things, and that didn't jibe with Tony Mazzola's way."

Anna quickly butted heads with Mazzola, who colleagues assert had major problems with Anna's independence, ego, ambition, and edgy fashion point of view. At the same time, Anna felt that he didn't understand her creativity, particularly the very stylized photographs that were coming back from the shoots she was assigned. She was ordered by Mazzola on a number of occasions to go back to reshoot.

At a certain point, Anna adamantly refused to turn in all of the film as required, editing it with the photographers and turning in only the shots she thought should be used. Mazzola had never encountered such a stubborn and independent neophyte editor, so Anna quickly rose to the top of his shit list. (Years later, as head of *Vogue,* Anna would do a one-eighty and make life a living hell for staffers and photographers who didn't turn in every single frame of a shoot.)

At the same time, Anna was hiring photographers like James Moore, who was considered more experimental, which also infuriated Mazzola. In fact, Moore's highly sexual and erotic work was inspired by *Bazaar's* legendary art director Alexei Brodovitch, who ran the magazine at its creative height, from the thirties to the end of the fifties with fashion editor Carmel Snow. Moore began shooting for *Bazaar* in the early sixties under Marvin Israel, Brodovitch's remarkable successor. But after Mazzola came on board, Moore was being used less, until Anna, who loved his work and working with him, began giving him assignments.

"Mazzola made Anna reshoot with Jimmy four times on a couple of assignments," recalls Morgan. "Anna would pick five shots and say, 'This is it.' She picked three and gave him two backups."

Anna had begun handling beauty stories, along with fashion, with Moore.

They worked so closely, and spent so much time together, that rumors began to fly at the magazine.

"Anna was a little naughty with the men," observes Morgan. "She had a flirty quality about her. Bradshaw was the love of her life, but she was tempted by a lot of other things, and she was saying he was getting too possessive and too demanding. His life took him away a great deal, and her life was taking her away a great deal, on shooting trips, and that's difficult. It was a tempting world out there, and Anna's a very physical and passionate woman."

Anna began asking girls in the office to cover for her. "She was always hysterical about that," says Morgan. "She'd call up from wherever and say, 'God, if Bradshaw calls, you've got to say . . . ' She had that bad-girl component."

Years later, nervously laughing when asked about the gossip, Moore says, "I'm taking the Fifth," refusing to confirm or deny an intimate relationship with Anna. "We had a working relationship, and we had a friendship," he concedes. "It wasn't love. We weren't living with each other. Anna and I worked together very well. When people have romances, after the romance they're out of each other's life, but Anna and I worked together for a long while."

But Morgan, Anna's closest acquaintance at *Bazaar,* says, "If she had a flirtation, it was usually because of something like that extraordinary thing of having been stuck with Jimmy Moore in the studio for months. That was whom we lied to Bradshaw about. When she picked someone it would be on the side, very discreet, and it was passion—and it was usually a photographer in those days. Like with Jimmy, they spent so much time together in the studio. He's very bright and their sensibilities locked so well. We covered for her like mad. We lied through our teeth to Bradshaw.

"Bradshaw, who was very macho and very jealous, was wildly suspicious. He was very obsessive and used to call all the time, which is why we all had to invent cover stories for her. But Anna invented them for us, too: 'She's working late at the studio,' 'They're on location and can't be reached,' 'We're all going out to dinner.' It would have been hard to explain to Bradshaw what happened when you're in that creative setting—so intense, minds merging, senses merging. If you find each other at all attractive, it's pretty difficult not to, at some point, let it happen. It's almost a step in the creative process. They were so tightly put together, exposed together because there's a lot of trust in a photo shoot. They [the magazine] kept Anna working with Jimmy, and then they got pissed off when the pictures started looking a little more erotic. Well, what did they expect?"

While Anna was seemingly playing the field, she and Bradshaw were living together in a small, lovely apartment in a brownstone on the Upper East Side in the seventies, according to Vivienne Lasky, who was working on another graduate degree, this time at Columbia University, and living in upper Manhattan with the man who would become her husband.

During this period, Anna and Lasky had pleasant lunches and shopped. During one of those excursions, as they breezed through Henri Bendel, Anna made a prediction about the future of the American woman that she firmly believed would materialize. "She felt that the 'new woman' was going to be so career oriented and busy that this leisurely shopping we were doing would become a thing of the past. Anna truly believed that these new career women, women like herself, would have personal shoppers working for them."

Anna occasionally visited Lasky's apartment for dinner, but always without Bradshaw, which Vivienne thought odd.

Lasky also visited Anna and Bradshaw's flat, and what stood out most to her was their bedroom. "It was monastic, white and spare," she says.

Lasky perceived that their relationship was on increasingly unsteady ground. "They stayed together amicably, long after things were over," she says. "Anna should have moved out when she knew it was over, but she was comfortable. They stayed on decent terms, but they'd grown apart. There was a real difference from how they were in London, and even how they were when they first came to New York—but it went on and on and on. They were going in different directions. I could see it, did see it, and she admitted to me that they were growing apart. It didn't make her feel good. It was a loss. But Anna was always philosophical and never whined."

Besides her friendship with Moore, Anna had fallen for someone most unlikely: a dreadlocked, ganja-smoking, black Rastafarian, albeit a famous one—the first third world superstar.

As it turned out, it was Bradshaw who helped turn Anna on. One of his close friends, a member of his rat pack, was the creative record producer and multimillionaire businessman Chris Blackwell, founder of Island Records, who brought reggae into the mainstream in the midseventies with one of his major discoveries, Bob Marley & the Wailers. During Anna's tenure at *Bazaar,* the Wailers had a big concert in New York, and through Blackwell, Bradshaw had arranged for a backstage pass for Anna at the Beacon Theater.

She virtually disappeared for a week.

As Alida Morgan succinctly put it, "Anna met God!"

Bob Marley took her off the scope during the Wailers Manhattan gig. "She went every night and stood backstage," recounts Morgan, still dumbstruck years later at the memory of Anna at a reggae concert, let alone making the scene with the legendary Marley, who had a reputation as a womanizer.

"Anna was riveted, and she'd go out every night after the concerts with the band to have dinner, go on the town. When she came back we said, 'Anna, you look exhausted.' She had these purple circles under her eyes. She says she didn't have an affair, but she had this revelation and felt she had a mystical experience. I said, 'How come I'm not being invited?' But when Anna found something *that* good, she wanted to keep it to herself. I don't think anything moved her as much as Bob Marley."

Anna's hard playing along with trying to stay on top of her game in a difficult work situation required enormous physical and emotional stamina. To handle this anxiety-filled load, she had a daily regimen that included the same high-protein lunch of scrambled eggs and bacon or basted eggs and shirred chicken livers at the tatty Women's Exchange, where, with Morgan, she'd "invent cover stories for Bradshaw and complain about Tony Mazzola."

Anna also took an hour a day for an expensive and tough physical training workout at Lotte Berk's. Just as Philip Kingsley was Anna's hair guru, Berk became her body's Svengali. Berk was a ballet dancer, a free spirit who had escaped Hitler's Germany and had become one of London's swinging sixties icons who practically terrorized her clients into shape.

As corpulent Ms. Middle America worked out dancing to the oldies with perky Richard Simmons on VHS at home, stick-thin Anna—obsessed with keeping her trim body looking like a lean, mean, and sculpted fighting machine—did her exercises to pop music at Berk's chic brownstone studio in Manhattan. The routines of the Lotte Berk Method had been given bizarre and sexually explicit names: "Fucking a Bidet," "The Prostitute," "The Peeing Dog," "The Love-Making Position," and "The French Lavatory." Therefore, men were never permitted into her studio.

At *Bazaar,* Jimmy Moore viewed Anna as a phenomenal young editor who supported his work and didn't try to control his ideas or creativity. "She was gifted," he declares. "She was growing, she was ambitious—not just to get ahead, but to do good work. She was one of the best editors I ever worked with. Anna had style, intelligence, and was a take-charge person. I could never see her as an assistant to anyone."

Like others, Moore feels that Mazzola, and a shortsighted and conservative corporate mentality, was a hindrance to Anna's creativity. "Tony," he says, "had his own ideas."

As Morgan points out, "We didn't get any support from the ruling brass, so it was very difficult, and it was a cheap place that cut corners in every direction. The art department was impossible, putting type right over a model's face."

All of this incensed Anna. Even more maddening to her was the model situation. Mazzola, according to staffers, had a list of half a dozen or so approved cover-girl types that Anna and the other fashion editors were supposed to use.

"It was Cheryl Tiegs, Cheryl Tiegs, Cheryl Tiegs," recalls Morgan. "We used to get letters asking, 'Who's in love with Cheryl Tiegs there?'" When Anna tried to use new girls, Mazzola balked. Not to be denied, Anna and others convinced Donovan, who supported change, to bring on a models editor responsible for recruiting new faces. Hired was Morgan's close friend Wendy Goodman, sister of Tonne Goodman, who later became a top lieutenant of Anna's at *Vogue,* her fashion director. "We had to fight every step of the way," says Morgan, "and the fights Anna had were real knock-down, drag-out."

Elsa Klensch, the fashion doyenne, was then a senior editor at *Bazaar.* She perceived Anna as "very conscientious. She had to learn her way around the city, learn her way around manufacturers, but she was so methodical and tried very hard to please. But Tony was a very difficult man who ran a tight ship and was a control freak who really didn't want anybody's ideas. So it was impossible for someone like Anna to succeed there. He was so insane about cutting costs that he used to sit in his office and go through all the messenger slips and then send memos saying, why was this sent? And Anna had her own vision of where she wanted to go."

A perfectionist, Anna made it clear that she thought of Mazzola as "the Hearst button man" who watched every nickel—when Morgan asked for a small raise, Mazzola told her to "get married, or ask your family"—and was opposed to doing anything innovative.

Thus, Anna's end came quickly.

She has maintained over the years that she was fired because the powers that be didn't think she had a grasp of the U.S. fashion market. "They fired me after about a year and a half for being too European, I was screamed at all the time," she told the London *Guardian* years later when she took over British *Vogue*. "They didn't feel I understood the American woman—maybe they had a point."

Actually, Anna had shaded the truth a bit about her time spent at the magazine. The fact is that she was axed after about nine months, not eighteen, or even a year as she states in some interviews. She last appeared on *Bazaar's* masthead in September 1976. And no one who worked closely with her recalls her being screamed at; the fights were a two-way street.

The real reason Anna was given her walking papers was a dispute with Mazzola over a series of very moody Jimmy Moore black-and-white photographs taken of a sultry model during a lingerie shoot.

"Tony thought the photos were too sexual," says Morgan. "They had this huge fight about it"—with Anna intensely defending *her* work on the shoot—"and he fired her. We all knew what was going on and we were really upset and angry. Anna was very upset, but she came into our office and said, 'It's okay. I'll be fine.' And she was."

"Anna's coming to *Bazaar* was a nonevent," recalls Marilyn Kirschner, "and her leaving was a nonevent. It was less than a year, just a drop in the bucket. When one reads her profiles, Anna kind of slides over it. She certainly didn't leave her mark on the magazine, and I don't think she was really allowed to or given a chance to develop."

After the firing, Zazel Loven came to the conclusion that Anna might have appeared upset but really didn't care. "She's always had a strong sense of self and felt that getting fired was their problem, not hers, that she'd just take her vision elsewhere and refine it."

Years later, Mazzola denies firing Anna and claims it was Carrie Donovan who wielded the ax. He asserts that he ran a creative fashion magazine. "Carrie, who was the huge star who came from *Vogue*, was the one who con-

structed the department and was responsible for who came in and who left,"
he says. "Carrie Donovan decided she wanted to make a change, and that's
what she did. It was her right to say, 'I think we need to make a change.' People can think what they like, but I didn't fire Anna Wintour.

"I remember one sitting with Anna. I happened to be in Paris for the collections, and she was the editor in charge. Anna was very professional, and I
remember she did a great job with those pages. We published everything she
worked on. If anything, I tried to encourage the editors to do unusual, interesting things."

Anna also remembered that shoot in Paris. "It was for the couture," she
said, "and the editor in chief had a breakdown because I had used models
with dreadlocks. You know, it just wasn't a blonde American look."

fifteen

A Curious Betrayal

Just as Anna and Bradshaw were growing apart, it was clear to Vivienne Lasky that Anna was severing their bond of many years—the closest female friendship Anna ever had up until then.

Their fun shopping expeditions and the lunches and dinners in Anna's favorite hole-in-the-wall Italian restaurants were becoming few and far between. The girly chats about fashion and Anna's sporadic gossip about her love life while still with Bradshaw were winding down.

When, in November 1975, Lasky had a fancy engagement party in Boston, Anna ignored the invitation and was a no-show, which hurt Lasky terribly.

Looking back years later, she came to the conclusion that Anna—focused solely on success—was actually envious, if not altogether jealous, that Lasky was in love and about to get married and start a family. Anna had even made snide and catty remarks about the "conventional route" Lasky's life was taking—graduating from Columbia on May 12, 1976, and getting hitched on May 16.

"She was surprised that I was actually going to be married," says Lasky.

And when Lasky told her that she and her fiancé were planning to leave New York to begin their careers and raise children in a sedate New England city, Anna smirked, making it clear that she felt that Lasky's life was boring and mundane.

Although Anna had missed Lasky's engagement bash, she did show up, alone, at her wedding at New York's Central Synagogue, looking smashing in a black-and-white Dior suit. Lasky was happy that Anna had honored her nuptials with her presence, though she barely spoke a word to the bride.

Some weeks before the wedding, Anna had asked Lasky out of the blue what her fiancé's middle name was. She didn't explain why, just acted secretive, and Lasky assumed that Anna was going to have something engraved or monogrammed.

Weeks after the nuptials, Anna made a surprise visit to the newlyweds in their Manhattan apartment, bearing her wedding gift, albeit a curious one. "It was bizarre beyond belief," says Lasky. "It was simple engraved stationery. It was brown"—like their despised uniforms at North London Collegiate. "It was ugly, but it was from Bendel's, which sort of linked us back to a time twelve years earlier."

During a visit to the States in the midsixties, Lasky had picked up a little gift for Anna at Bendel's, a stack of cool notepads in different colors, which Anna adored because there was nothing like them available in London.

Lasky viewed Anna's offering as bizarre for a couple of reasons. For one, Lasky expected something a bit classier from someone like Anna, with whom she had been so close for so many years and who certainly could afford better. "She was raised better than that," Lasky points out. What would it have taken for Anna to have gone to Cartier or Tiffany, for a present more appropriate for her best friend and her groom? For another, Lasky had made it absolutely clear to Anna that she wasn't going to use her married name—after all, this was the midseventies, the era of the feminist. Lasky felt as independent as Anna, marriage notwithstanding. Moreover, she and her brother were the last of the Laskys, and she was proud of her family name, all of which Anna knew.

And all of which Anna ignored.

The stationery she gave Lasky was engraved "Vivienne Lasky Elliot Freeman." Besides everything else, Anna had gotten Lasky's husband's name wrong. "His name was Robert Elliot Freeman, so I had gobs of stupid-looking stationery and had to cut off the Elliot Freeman part. It was idiotic, but I didn't have the heart to tell her. She knew his name and she had specifically asked me what his middle name was. It was the goofiest thing."

To Lasky, it was clear that Anna had given the off-the-wall and inappropriate gift spitefully and on purpose, a bitchy message that she didn't like the idea that she had gotten married, either first or at all. "Anna's competitive," notes Lasky. "My husband, who liked Anna, used to say to me, 'Well, you got married first. I see a competition you're not engaging in.' He said, 'You're just oblivious to these things.' "

After Anna bestowed the stationery, she told Lasky she had another gift, just for her, but it wasn't ready yet. "I said, 'That's sweet. It isn't necessary.' And I thought, 'Oh, God, what now?' "

A couple of months later, Anna called and asked Lasky to stop by the *Harper's Bazaar* office to catch up because they were seeing less and less of each other and to pick up the gift she'd promised. But when Lasky arrived at the hour designated by Anna, she found she'd been stood up. "Someone in the office said, 'Oh, you must be Vivienne. Anna's left a parcel for you.' It was like I was a messenger. She could have left a message for me, but there was nothing."

Lasky took the package outside, sat on a bench, and unwrapped the white tissue paper, thinking, "What the hell is this?" Inside, she found a wool Missoni shawl in muted colors of gray, red, and orange—possibly one used in a recent *Bazaar* shoot, freebies being one of the perks of fashion magazine editors.

Neither Lasky nor Anna ever made mention of the gift.

Lasky clung to what remained of their friendship, but the stage was set for what would be the very strange and emotional penultimate act of Anna and Lasky's intense relationship.

The bucolic setting was the Cornwall Bridge, Connecticut, country home of Anna's aunt Jean, the book editor, and her American Cancer Society executive husband, Cliff Read. It was a lovely place in the Litchfield Hills, filled with elegant furnishings, rugs draped on beams, books, and art, including a valuable de Kooning.

Anna's brother Jim, who remained close to Lasky, was visiting from England and had asked his aunt to invite Anna and Lasky and her husband to spend what he hoped would be a pleasant summer weekend. Lasky had been there many times, hiking on the nearby Appalachian Trail and helping Jean Read tend her lovely garden. "Jim said, 'Please, will you come down, it'll be so much fun,'" recalls Lasky, who readily agreed, eager to see Anna, who had not kept in touch after Lasky's marriage. But when Anna heard that Lasky was going to be there, she made an excuse to come on another weekend. Jim and his aunt pleaded with her, and she eventually relented. Lasky had brought a present for Anna, but the way things turned out, she never gave it to her.

"Anna was thinner than I'd ever seen her, and she was all in black leather," says Lasky, who was dressed New England preppy–style and was taken aback by Anna's gaunt, avant-garde look and manner. "She'd been delivered in a limo and she behaved like a twelve-year-old. She didn't say hello to me. It was like I was invisible. She refused to come to lunch, refused to help out, and sat in a chair sulking. I heard Jean, who was furious, saying to her, 'You're so un-believably rude. What's the matter with you?' She refused to interact with anyone. She seemed to be ticked off that they had guilt-tripped her into com-ing because it was the correct thing to do so we could all be together. She just didn't want to be there. She wasn't happy to see me, and she didn't talk to me about anything. I'd never seen her like that in my life. You could cut the ten-sion with a knife."

At one point during the hellish weekend, Anna made a call to New York. A couple of hours later a limousine arrived with a mysterious-looking fellow also in leather. Anna and the man huddled for a time, and then he left. He was never properly introduced. It was all very awkward for everyone. (He was a French record producer by the name of Michel Esteban, with whom Anna was starting a relationship.)

"I was very hurt," says Lasky. "I said to my husband, 'I want to go home.' But he said, 'No, we have to stay. We don't have to go down to her level. Just ignore her.' Jim took over and asked me to go for a walk with him, and we walked for several hours. I told him I was very uncomfortable, and he said, 'I don't know why she's being so bloody rude. I don't know what's gotten in to her. She's like a child. Don't take it personally.'"

That night, Lasky cried herself to sleep.

The next day, Sunday, was sunny and glorious, and everyone sat in the Reads' wild garden, an idyllic spot. Anna opened up a bit to Lasky, telling her that she planned to move to a new apartment; her long relationship with Bradshaw was nearing its demise. "She said she would give me her address and I turned to her and said, 'There's not much point to that, is there?' I've never done that before, and she looked shocked. That weekend I knew Anna and I had lost something. We had been so much a part of each other's lives, our families so intertwined, so much love and affection. I've never understood what happened."

sixteen

An Embarrassing Position

Anna's firing from *Harper's Bazaar* had come so swiftly and so unexpectedly that she was in a state of shock. Out of work for several months, with nothing lined up, she was getting desperate. Money wasn't the issue, but getting back on her career track was. Her primary concern was her climb to the summit, to get to the Holy Grail, *Vogue.* That's when she turned to Jon Bradshaw, who would always be there for her no matter how troubled the state of their relationship.

As Bradshaw's writer friend Nik Cohn notes, "He was very protective of Anna. There was a very fatherly way about him toward her."

Bradshaw had media connections all over Manhattan, and one of them was Beverly Wardale, an advertising executive at Bob Guccione's *Penthouse* magazine. Wardale, a Brit, was married to Bradshaw and Nigel Dempster's chum Brian Vine, the New York bureau chief of London's *Daily Express.* Bradshaw and Anna had met Wardale and Vine for drinks at the King Cole Bar at the St. Regis Hotel, and Bradshaw mentioned that Anna was looking for a job in fashion. Wardale said she'd see what she could do, thinking there might be an opening at *Penthouse*'s sister publication, *Viva.*

Acting on the tip, Bradshaw put in a call to another acquaintance, Peter Bloch, an articles editor at *Penthouse,* then *Playboy*'s major competitor in the mainstream girlie magazine field. "He said he had a girlfriend who was looking for a fashion gig in New York and that she had lots of experience in London, and was there any chance *Viva* would be interested in talking with her. There was no mention of her recent firing."

Both Wardale and Bloch mentioned Anna's availability. As luck would have it, Alma Moore, the editor of *Viva,* was looking for a new fashion editor.

The last fashionista had just been axed in another Friday night massacre—the place was a revolving door—by Guccione's significant other, Kathy Keeton.

A thirty-something ballerina turned exotic dancer who had polio as a child, Keeton had conceived and launched *Viva*—the "International Magazine for Women"—with Guccione's money in October 1973, with pieces by Joyce Carol Oates, Norman Mailer, and Tom Wicker. She ran the monthly with a halter top, tight pants, fuck-me heels, and an iron hand in a velvet glove from an enormous office filled with white wicker furniture and a desk guarded by two ferocious-looking Rhodesian ridgebacks. But Keeton, a South African whom Guccione had met in London, only dressed like a bimbo. She was bright and ambitious and was now hoping to have *Viva,* which was her baby, compete for readers against such higher-end magazines as *Vogue, Cosmopolitan,* and *Glamour.*

Viva attracted strong, literate, creative women's lib editors such as Patricia Bosworth, who, like Anna, had worked for *Harper's Bazaar,* and later went on to write well-received biographies. There was Dawn Steel, who had worked as a secretary and in promotions developing X-rated products for *Penthouse,* who became a powerhouse in Hollywood as head of Columbia Pictures. André Leon Talley, the flamboyant black fashionista who would become Anna's creative sidekick years later, did some time there. Keeton recruited top-notch editors from magazines like *Esquire* and Gloria Steinem's *Ms.*

Ironically, all of this high-toned editorial activity was happening just across a divider from where *Penthouse's* shaved and pink gynecological-like shots were being laid out and where the world-famous raunchy "Dear Penthouse" letters were penned.

Based on Wardale and Bloch's suggestion, Alma Moore interviewed Anna and was impressed. "I explained what I wanted to do, and she knew what she wanted to do, and we were in agreement. One knew she had ambitions."

In late 1976, twenty-seven-year-old Anna was brought on as the editor in charge of *Viva's* fashion department, which consisted at that moment of

Anna. It was the most powerful position she had held up to that point. The month she started, the magazine featured an article called "How to throw fabulous parties, create new faces, wear silk stockings, have sexy fantasies and perfect orgasms."

Word of her hiring was instantly communicated to London—probably by Bradshaw or one of her British compatriots in New York—where *Private Eye* duly reported that the "pulchritudinous daughter of Sir Charles . . . is working on a porn magazine."

The Wintours, about to get a permanent separation and soon a divorce, did have one thing in common: mortification about where their daughter was working.

The cloud that had always hung over *Viva*—mainly because of its X-rated sister publication—was, indeed, an embarrassment to Anna. The reminders were always there. To get to her office, she had to walk down a hall lined with photos of shapely female legs and other body parts, and pass offices where former *Penthouse* Pets worked and were on display—young, shapely babes with "big hair, lots of makeup, and enormous boobs," as one former *Viva* staffer recalls. While there was no mixing of staff, *Viva* and *Penthouse* did share the art department and copyediting.

Over the years, Anna has ignored, downplayed, and even blatantly fibbed about the time she spent at *Viva*, and was known to take circuitous routes later to avoid people who worked with her there, apparently not wanting to be reminded.

In March 1998, in a profile in the *London Daily Telegraph*, for instance, she tweaked the truth to suit her *Vogue* image. She was quoted as saying, "Once I got over being fired [at *Harper's Bazaar*] I did a little freelance again before getting a job on *New York* magazine."

The truth of the matter is that Anna spent two aggressive years on the staff of *Viva* and had three years of other personal and professional adventures before *New York* agreed to hire her. It was, in fact, quite a chunk of résumé time that she had brushed off as "a little freelance."

Moore felt that Anna's aloofness in the office, which surfaced on her first day on the job, and the fact that at *Viva* she always hid behind what became her trademark sunglasses, had to do with her discomfiture. "There was embarrassment on her part, and maybe her family said, 'Are you sure you want to be working at a place like that?' "

Still in touch with Anna, Vivienne Lasky was horrified. "She told me she was working for that awful Bob Guccione. I said, 'I wouldn't trust him as far as I could throw him.' But she said, 'Well, one needs a job. Work is work.' Anna said she had complete editorial control, that she was being given carte blanche. I said, 'Good for you, but is it two pages of fashion, or five?' And I remember her giving me this look like, you're giving me the third degree just like your father used to give me. I know she felt awkward there."

As it turned out, Anna had an incredibly good situation for someone who had just been pink-slipped from one of the world's leading fashion magazines. Her department was hidden away in a corner of the *Viva* office where she was left on her own, reporting only to Moore and Keeton, with whom she pitched story ideas. "I gave her pretty much control, and that's very unusual," acknowledges Moore. "She was very sure of herself, decisive, a young woman to be reckoned with. We both saw fashion and beauty the same way and agreed that what *Viva* did had to be distinctive, had to stand out from other magazines, and she managed to do that. She realized she could call the shots and could go far."

Unlike the plain-Jane feminist story and copy editors at *Viva* who wore jeans or conservative business suits, or the *Penthouse* secretaries in stilettos, tight skirts, and lots of cleavage à la Kathy Keeton, Anna showed up for work in dramatic style. For a time, her outfit of choice was jodhpurs worn with riding boots, missing only the crop. "She looked smashing," recalls Moore. "I used to tease her. 'Anna, when you become fashion editor at *Vogue* you'll end up wearing Chanel suits.' And she scoffed and said, 'I will always dress the way *I* want to dress.' "

Anna also sported another glamorous look—a chic and expensive outfit consisting of tight white T-shirts over Yves St. Laurent peasant skirts and leather boots, all of which made her look like a skinny Cossack. In spring and summer she sported Alice in Wonderland straw hats over her bob, and in winter she kept it warm with a fur hat with the furry tails of little animals hanging from it, a gift from Bradshaw. One colleague remembers thinking,

"That is the mother of all hats, and if you aren't Anna Wintour, don't try this at home."

Not long after Anna came aboard she hired a young woman in her early twenties as an assistant, the first in a long line over the years. As her first foray into the fashion and magazine world, she initially viewed Anna as "very creative." Hoping to learn from her, the assistant watched her boss closely but soon was shocked to discover that "most of her work was looking for ideas in foreign fashion magazines."

She says that one of her most important roles was making excuses to Anna's many suitors when she was off with someone else. "She was having affairs left and right. . . . She was dating married men and she had no qualms," the woman maintains. "She'd enlist me to cover for her, which put me in a very awkward position. If the person she was involved with called up and I knew where Anna was, I couldn't let on. I'd just have to keep it vague. Anna knew I knew who she was involved with, but we wouldn't talk about it. She was involved with two and three persons at the same time sometimes, and not all were photographers. Some were very prominent men."

Anna often borrowed clothes from designers or retailers. That's how the job of fashion editor gets done. Anna got credit for the spread and the fashion trade people got their names in print. It was one happy, productive, and close relationship for all.

However, the assistant soon came to realize that Anna was wearing some of the clothes she borrowed. "She would take clothes home and wear them, bring them back to the office, and have me return them for her," she claims.

The relationship between Anna and the assistant deteriorated and she was gone in less than a year. Looking back on the experience, she says, "Anna has to have it her way. She's extremely manipulative of assistants and of everyone. Anna Wintour is definitely a trip."

Another assistant was described as "a sharp cookie," but they apparently didn't get along. She lasted just a few months before being given the hatchet.

Anna's next assistant was a whole different story, and they would become involved in a long-running love-hate relationship.

Paul Sinclaire, a fashionista friend of Anna's, walked into Yves St. Laurent in Manhattan one afternoon to browse—he and Anna often shopped there together—and spotted an interesting-looking young woman. With her wild hair and red, red lips she reminded him not of a saleswoman but rather Louise Brooks's Lulu character—glamorous and eccentric and right out of fiction. "I thought, 'Wow!'" As it turned out, Sinclaire and the young woman, a Brit named Georgia Gunn, had a mutual friend. They became pals, and Sinclaire introduced her to Anna, who "absolutely adored Georgia."

But when Sinclaire, who was affiliated with the chic Manhattan boutique Dianne B., tried to hire Gunn, Anna freaked out. She stepped in and hired her as her own girl Friday and, as many saw it, her whipping girl. Most of the stories over the years about Anna's shoddy treatment of assistants started at *Viva* with talk about her behavior toward Georgia Gunn.

"Anna didn't get along with her," Alma Moore recalls. "They traveled together on everything, and Anna treated her badly. She blamed her for a fiasco of a sitting, which cost a lot of money because it was shot on some exotic island, and poor Georgia took all the heat."

Colleagues remember Anna acting like a wild-eyed diva, verbally flagellating Gunn if anything, even the most minor detail, didn't go according to Anna's perfectionist plan. "As cool and aloof and in control as Anna was," recalls *Viva* and *Penthouse* female staff photographer Pat Hill, "Georgia seemed to be kind of a bumbler—but she wasn't. It was a strange balance between them and very interesting to watch."

Stephanie Brush, a twenty-two-year-old Northwestern University Drama School dropout but a talented writer who joined the staff around the same time as Anna, saw Anna as glacial and Georgia as down-to-earth. "If you were to cast them in a film, Anna would play Princess Diana because Di and Anna both managed to cultivate a mystique, and Georgia would have been the Fergie character. Georgia got the brunt of whatever pressure there was to do the fashion job right," maintains Brush. "Anna would have the ideas and think, 'Oh, it would be great if we did such and such.' But Georgia was the one who did all the work—and took all of Anna's BS that she was spewing out that particular week. I know Georgia got frustrated, and Anna was a fairly frustrating person to work for because she had pretty strong ideas about things and was not known for her tact. It would not occur to Anna to sort of soften the blow. She didn't have the time or energy or inclination. She had the attitude without the power. Eventually, she got both."

Coworkers winced years later when they thought of Anna and Gunn's stormy relationship, described as one of master and slave. Beverly Wardale, who thought Gunn was terrific, recalls Anna having her ironing clothes and sending her to the other side of Manhattan to pick up a pair of gloves because she decided at the last minute that the ones Gunn had originally chosen just weren't quite right—and Anna wanted the new ones ASAP.

"There were explosions with Anna, who had terrible temper tantrums, and you could hear her *screaming* at Georgia," asserts Susan Duff, who had come on staff as beauty editor shortly after Anna and worked very closely with her. "It was very unpleasant for Georgia—and for everyone. We were all sort of creeping around and walking on eggshells trying to stay out of Anna's way because she could get really mean and didn't care about people's feelings. She was one of those perfectionists who couldn't tolerate mere mortals.

"There was something about the way Anna worked—her *singlemindedness,*" continues Duff. "You couldn't imagine she had any life outside of being a fashion editor. One never had any intimation she had a friend or a family.

"It appeared to me she never thought of anything *except* fashion, and doing those shoots, and getting those photographers together with those designers, and dreaming of layouts. It was almost her whole being. The rest of us were sort of having a good time—we traveled a lot, were well paid, and had long martini lunches—but she was a workaholic on a mission, which was kind of a mystery until you got to see that what she was about was discovering designers and putting together the most fabulous photographers available. No one was doing stuff like that back then.

"But in doing it she intimidated everyone. It wasn't just Georgia, but *anyone* who got in her way. You could hear her screaming on the phone to whomever—someone not doing what she wanted them to do. Anna was *so* intense. She couldn't tolerate any mistakes or incompetence. To her, all of this was life-and-death stuff, which is probably common among people who do just one thing and it's all they ever think about and it's got to be done their way."

Anna quickly gained a reputation at *Viva* as the editor from hell, a reputation that would stick and come to haunt her as she moved up in the fashion magazine business. Years later, people who had worked with her compared her to another imperious diva, the convicted felon and queen of domesticity, Martha Stewart.

There were times, though, when Anna was happy with Gunn's work. She was given the title of accessories editor, and on rare instances, Anna would join Gunn and Duff for drinks—rare because Anna had made few if any friends at the magazine and didn't appear to care. On one of those nice Anna moments, when she was in a good mood and getting along, Duff asked her for some fashion tips, what to wear, how to make what she had in her closet look great. Anna glared hard at her for a long moment, looked her up and down, and then flippantly replied, "You'd have to throw out *everything* you own." Anna wasn't being cute with her criticism; she was being harshly honest, which was her style.

"You couldn't enter her realm," observes Duff. "She was alone in that, and that didn't bother her either, as far I could tell. She felt superior to everyone in kind of a class way."

While virtually everyone at the magazine respected Anna's fashion sense and her eye for what was new and hot, it was widely known and joked about that she couldn't put any of her styling talent into words on paper—a criticism she had faced back in her *Harpers & Queen* days.

"Anna was known for not having any particular verbal or writing skills," notes Stephanie Brush, one of the few on staff whom Anna took a liking to. "She wasn't articulate like a Tina Brown. Anna wasn't someone who would sit and talk about complicated ideas. She would just say, 'Oh, that's *fabulous*.' She didn't seem to have a lot of complicated ideas in her head. Maybe that's why she liked me, because I was a writer. She liked people who were good with words, and I was known on the grapevine as this up-and-coming writer, so that didn't escape her notice."

After Anna settled in, Duff was assigned to write all of her fashion copy. "She never had anything to do with any kind of description of what she was doing," says Duff. "I would get these layouts from her with these absolutely wild Helmut Newton photographs and I would just write fiction. I would write a little short story. Sometimes I'd create the story after I went to the shoots and interviewed the models and the photographer. Even at the shoots, I'd have very little interaction with her. Anna had no input on the copy and wasn't interested in having any. I always thought of her as an exalted stylist because she never had anything to do with any of the written description."

Anna's failure to communicate in words what she had her stable of high-priced and big-name photographers communicate in pictures infuriated Rowan Johnson, *Viva*'s very talented and off-the-wall South African art director. To punish her, he often put the gorgeous layouts that she had obsessively conceived and developed into the magazine without giving her credit in the form of a byline. Instead, the story would say, photographs by Helmut Newton, text by Susan Duff, even though the text was usually modest compared to Anna's electric spreads. All of which infuriated Anna and was embarrassing to Duff, because she knew how hard Anna had worked.

Though their work relationship was stormy at times, Anna and Johnson "adored each other, although Anna was rather eclipsed by Rowan," says then-*Penthouse* art director Joe Brooks, one of Johnson's close friends. In fact, there was considerable gossip that Johnson hoped for more with Anna. "There was talk," acknowledges *Penthouse* editor Peter Bloch. "But in those days there was talk about everyone [at the two magazines]."

Beverly Wardale got a call one night from Johnson who was on a shoot with Anna in Montauk, in the Hamptons. "I'll never forget that call. He asked me, 'Do you think I should jump Anna tonight?' He would try anything if he got scotch in him. He would have quite fancied being involved with Anna. He was Peck's Bad Boy, extremely creative and terribly attractive."

Like Bradshaw, Claude Beer, and some of the other rogues Anna had known, Rowan Johnson fit the profile—an intriguing bad boy, the son of a judge and the brother of a Rhodes scholar. When the film *Arthur*, starring Dudley Moore as a ne'er-do-well lush, was released, everyone who knew Johnson said he was Arthur Bach. "Everything in that movie, Rowan had done, from the drinking to the Rolls-Royce to the hookers," says Brooks. "We all phoned each other and said, 'Jesus Christ, they've made a movie about him.'"

The other thing about Johnson was that he was a user of hard drugs. When the door to Johnson's office was shut, everyone figured he was shooting up. "He basically took every drug in the world," says Brooks. "The drugs and the drinking made him difficult to take." One night, at Brooks's apartment, Johnson crawled out onto the ledge fifteen stories above Fifty-fifth Street. "As much as you loved him, he became tremendously hard to tolerate, so I shut the window on him, sort of left him out there, high above the street, screeching. I said, 'Make up your mind, in or out.' Eventually, I let him back in."

Johnson's drug habit became so severe at one point that Guccione and Keeton sent him to an expensive rehab clinic and picked up the tab.

Johnson's favorite watering hole was P.J. Clarke's, the *Penthouse-Viva* hangout, across from the office on Third Avenue at Fifty-fifth Street. He was sometimes spotted with Anna cozying at his side, though she was probably there more for political reasons, because Clarke's wasn't her kind of place. "She'd be there wearing her dark glasses with Rowan, who considered himself the Mozart of art directors," recalls Peter Bloch. "I can see him and Anna sitting over in Clarke's endlessly, as we all did in those days. I was awestruck by Anna being in Clarke's with her dark glasses on because the place was dark as a cave. I don't know how she even managed to find her table with those glasses on."

Johnson and Duff weren't the only staffers who had difficulty getting information out of Anna for scheduled stories. Photographers such as Pat Hill, a female and the only shooter and photo editor on staff, faced a similar dilemma.

Hill straddled the very different worlds of *Viva* and *Penthouse,* snapping *Penthouse* Pet pictorials for Guccione and artsy portraiture for Keeton. When Anna came aboard, Hill kept a close eye on her work, which was always shot by her stable of mostly male freelance photographers, and was duly impressed. "She produced some wonderful pages," she says. But when they passed in the hall, Anna looked down her sunglasses at her. "It was like I was not important enough to talk to because I was a staff photographer," notes Hill. "I'm a pretty friendly person. I would say hi to everybody, but I don't go out of my way to get smacked down. She was just very icy from the start. I really kind of kept away from her because I got such negative vibes."

On one occasion, though, Hill was assigned by Johnson to work with Anna. He probably foresaw what would happen if the two collaborated and

wanted a vicarious high when their claws were bared. He was on the mark—
the assignment quickly deteriorated into a catfight. The only information Hill
was given by Johnson was that the feature involved a dancer from the American Ballet Theatre. "I never had a clue what was really going on," she says
years later.

An intense and creative photographer who took all of her assignments seriously, Hill immediately put in a call to Anna to find out what she needed.
And Hill called and called and called. "I must have called her at least three or
four times a day for three weeks, or whatever the lead time was. She was always unavailable. I'd call her, and if I caught her, which was rare, she'd say,
'I'll call you back,' and never did. I'd call Georgia, and she'd say, 'She'll get
back to you, she hasn't gone over that yet.' But she never did call back. The
day before the shoot I called Anna's office and said, 'I'm shooting, starting at
eight o'clock.'"

One of the reasons Hill had a hard time reaching Anna was that Anna
made her own hours, unlike the other editors. Anna didn't tie herself to her
desk and was often off doing other things—no one knew what—so she was
hard to pin down.

"Anna pretty much showed up when she felt like," recalls Stephanie
Brush, who had been promoted from editorial assistant to an associate editor
spot after one of Kathy Keeton's many editorial shakeups. "There wasn't any
nine-to-five for her. It was just understood she showed up when she wanted
to show up. I never got the sense of her working *for* anybody. She sort of had
her own little fiefdom. Anna popped in, made phone calls, and left. I don't
think she ever really moved into her office. It was kind of a place where she
kept a phone, tacked up some photos that she liked, and had some clothes
she liked sort of lying around, which are what fashion editor offices look like.
She didn't turn her office into a little home away from home, because she
didn't really have a homey kind of personality."

Every so often Anna would breeze in and out of an editorial meeting when
the peons were deciding what to put in the magazine. Stopping for a moment
during one such brainstorming session, Anna volunteered her magic formula.
"A magazine," she proclaimed, "should be like a perfect dinner party. The
two essentials are a politician and a pretty girl." As she scooted out, jaws

dropped. And if by chance she sat in on a meeting, she usually remained mute. "She kept her opinions to herself, and not to say anything at all, or contribute vaguely, seemed almost insolent," recalls an editor.

Not to be stymied by Anna's failure to return her calls, Pat Hill went ahead and prepared for the shoot with the vague information she was given. She rented Merce Cunningham's downtown dance studio for the day, determined her lighting needs, and stayed up late for several nights dyeing bolts of fabric in various shades of plums and pinks and reds, which she thought might be used as backdrops to match ballet skirts, after doing research on Degas's paintings of ballet dancers.

"On the day of the shoot, I got there at the crack of dawn and set up and everything all fell in line, and then in trails Anna with her hair and makeup people, looks around at the setup and says, 'Just what do you think you're doing? Don't you know this is just a service feature. It's just dance positions one, two, and three.'"

Hill couldn't believe what she was hearing. "I said, 'Well, I couldn't get a hold of you and I've taken all this trouble and I'm just going to have to shoot it like this with the background.' And she just gave me that Anna look. She was not nice about it. She was a bitch. She said, 'Well, shoot it the way you want, but then you're just going to have to reshoot it, aren't you, because I'm telling you to.' I was going to shoot it my way at that point because I never could get any answer out of her. It was a really horrible, ugly scene."

As Hill learned at that moment, the shoot was tied to a new 1977 film about the ballet world called *The Turning Point*, starring Shirley MacLaine, Anne Bancroft, and Mikhail Baryshnikov. The dancer Hill was assigned to photograph was Leslie Browne, a star with the American Ballet Theatre, who played Baryshnikov's love interest.

Meanwhile, at the dance studio, battle lines had been drawn. "Anna stayed on one side of the studio, and I was on the other side," Hill says. "They would dress the dancer and put her makeup on, and then send her over to my side and I would do what I needed to do. Anna was never next to me the entire day."

Around noon, Hill, trying to restore some semblance of propriety, asked her assistant to take lunch orders, this still being the days before such assignments became Hollywood-style catered affairs. The lunch break brought the morning's work to a halt. Everyone placed his or her order, including Anna, and then she sat around looking sullen as everyone waited for the assistant to return with the grub. An hour passed, then two. All the while Hill was running out of natural light. When the assistant finally returned with brown bags, Hill was livid.

"I said, 'You took so long. What did everybody order?'

"He said, 'Well, Anna wanted quiche, caviar, and champagne.'

"I couldn't believe what I was hearing. First of all, we didn't have the budget for that, and the location was in a dead zone. He had to run blocks and blocks but couldn't find what she wanted, so he made a decision. He got her a tuna fish on rye. I was like, 'Good for you!' You can't get away with not giving me the information I needed for the shoot and then come in and act like a queen."

After the shoot, Hill went to Johnson and demanded, "'What the hell's going on with her?' He just said, 'Pat, it's Anna's baby. But I'm going to give you an opening spread so that we don't have to waste those photos.' He wasn't going to confront her but was making amends to me for all that aggravation from Anna. But that was it between me and Anna. We never worked together again. I really kept away from her; there was just this sense of negativity, and life's too short to deal with it."

Hill was convinced that Anna's lack of communication from the start was "intentional" because Anna wanted Hill to look bad and not get another assignment at *Viva*. Anna's motivation, Hill firmly believes, was paranoia that all photography might be turned in-house and away from Anna's freelance photographers, which would diminish her power.

Years later, the memory of the incident still riles Hill, who says, "It's probably the ugliest experience I've ever had in dealing with an editor, and it affected me for a long time."

Jean Pagliuso, another female fashion photographer, who started shooting for Anna at *Viva* and became a member of her "little family of photographers" that worked with her over the years, saw Anna as very methodical, very determined, very demanding and self-possessed.

"She brought the fear of God into everybody, and I felt it on *every* shoot," Pagliuso says. "Nobody seemed to ever tell her what to do because she really was quite good, and her choices of designers and photographers were made intellectually. She had it all together, and it was always top of the line. She had a gift."

After working with her for a time, Pagliuso perceived that Anna had a number of eccentricities, one of which was to tune out while overseeing a shoot. "Anna had a very low boredom threshold, and once the shot was set up, and once Anna liked it, she was not there anymore in her head," the photographer says. "It's very hard to shoot when you know somebody's doing that, when you know they've tuned out, because you're both supposed to be working toward something. But she'd be standing next to me, and suddenly she wasn't there anymore. That's not giving me creative freedom. That's like saying, 'I'm no longer interested,' that I was boring her. Other fashion editors stay with it. Not Anna."

After a time, Pagliuso became part of Anna's social circle, but then was suddenly and inexplicably dumped for no discernible reason. "It was over," she says. "That was it."

As others have noted, women aren't Anna's cup of tea, and she therefore preferred working with male photographers and gave them more freedom and less attitude. The ones she chose to be part of her stable were imaginative, creative, and good-looking types like the Frenchman Guy Le Baube. As a young photographer, Le Baube, at the recommendation of Helmut Newton, was the first to put a new model named Jerry Hall in the camera's lens for a L'Oréal calendar, and his pictures caught the eye of *Vogue*'s Alex Liberman, who hired him and gave him his start in America in 1976.

At *Viva*, Anna began using Le Baube. But even though they had some wild and fun times on location together, he says, she was not very pleasant to work with. "Anna was *very* straightforward. She didn't go for the phony, nicey-nicey fashion bullshit, and the relationship could be rough, and sometimes we wrestled. She'd say, 'I don't agree with you . . . it should be done this way . . . *my* way . . . this is *rubbish* . . . this is *ghastly*,' with a very British manner. I'm French, and naturally the British and the French have this enmity. With Americans it's always, 'Ah, you're *so* French.' But with the British it's just, 'Fuck you!' We don't play together."

Like others who were loyal members of her crew, he eventually got dropped when she got the big job at *Vogue*.

"Anna picked people to work with who were on the top at the time in the marketplace," he explains. "She chose people who were up and in, and she didn't take much risk. She wasn't experimenting."

He also notes that that once he completed a shoot with her, Anna would permit him to pick the best five or six photos, and then she would decide which ones would make it into the magazine, the kind of freedom she didn't usually offer to female photographers. For Le Baube, and any photographer, that was a wonderful situation, because it gave him a great deal of creative control.

"She was quite loose about letting you be free to shoot your way," he maintains. "She gave you an immense space of freedom, and she was very trusting," he notes, compared to Grace Mirabella, then editor of *Vogue,* or top *Vogue* fashion editors like Jade Hobson and Polly Mellen, with whom he often worked. "I would end up having the shittiest photograph of the series being picked and published by them, and I would have no say about it. With Anna, she gave you the say. The result was what counted with her."

He felt that her style of giving the photographer freedom was more "old Europe" than the American fashion editors with whom he worked who demanded more control. Later, all of that would change with Anna, but for now she thought it in her best interest to allow the pros to judge which photos were the best. Their trained eye and experience would make her look good in the end, and she could take much of the credit.

Despite their little battles, Le Baube did find Anna desirable. "She's very attractive and extremely discreet." He maintains that nothing ever happened between them, "though I do believe it would have been possible if it was pushed. I think she needed to be attractive to a man. She was more attracted to me than I was to her . . . there was a lot of frustration.

"I felt it was no good to have a sexual relationship, or a sentimental one, or both with someone like Anna, who I wrestled with professionally. We had some tête-à-tête dinners and lunches, but she was not very compassionate and extremely selfish. To have lunch or dinner with Anna, you don't do ha-ha."

Because Guccione and Keeton were willing to spend money, Anna was able to travel the world on location shoots—from islands in the Caribbean to Japan. She hired cutting-edge photographers like Helmut Newton, Deborah Turbeville, Patrick Demarchelier, André Carrara, and Shig Ikida. And she discovered and presented to readers new and edgy designers like Issey Miyake.

At *Viva,* savvy staffers glimpsed Anna as a demanding and creative editor, a take-no-prisoners executive, and a Fashionista with a capital F—gifts that would eventually catapult her to the top of the fashion magazine world and make her a legend in her own time.

Along with being possessed of a rare and unerring creative eye, she was a singular wizard at delegating work to highly creative people, which many consider one of her greatest attributes. Like her father, she hired the best and the brightest, demanded absolute loyalty, and gave them a free hand—to a point.

"A lot of Anna's success at *Viva* was because of Rowan Johnson, who had a wonderful sense of design and was very creative," observes Stephanie Brush, who after leaving *Viva* went on to write a best-selling humor book and had a syndicated newspaper column. "Someone once said that Anna doesn't really know what she likes, but if it's the right designer, she'll like it. If she hears the name of the designer, she'll say, 'Oh, that's good.' It was fashion if Anna said it was fashion. She had that kind of definitiveness about her. She was this strange and exotic and distant creature who looked cutting edge, was *out* there, with a mysterious way about her, this aura. And she obviously knew it."

seventeen

Complex Persona

Outside of the office, the domina of *Viva's* fashion pages exhibited an entirely different persona. In the office, Anna was the aloof ice queen whom everyone found a bit scary and gave a wide berth. But in the company of Bradshaw socially, she played her long-running little girl role to the hilt.

Friends of Bradshaw's, such as Byron Dobell, found her game intriguing if not totally off-the-wall. He was never really quite sure what was what with her. A perceptive editor at *Esquire* and at *New York,* where he gave Bradshaw plum assignments, Dobell, and his equally astute *Redbook* editor wife, Elizabeth Rodger, were dumbstruck and mystified by Anna's manner when they socialized with her in their East Sixty-ninth Street apartment.

"She would sit totally silent, her legs tucked under her in a catlike position, wearing these beautifully pleated wool skirts, and she would practically put her thumb in her mouth," Dobell recalls vividly. "I will not swear that she put her thumb in her mouth, but my impression was she was about to. She was like a baby doll. She was very childlike, incredibly passive, and I didn't know what was going on. I had no strong sense that she had *any* career. That's why it always amazed me that she blossomed into this successful editor."

Elizabeth Rodger, a beauty who had a reputation as an insightful and sharp editor, watched Anna closely and came to the conclusion that "she was a zed, just a blank," says Dobell. "Her assessment was, Anna was a passive being. That's how she saw her, and how we saw her. Now whether she was willingly passive, or whether Bradshaw did something that intimidated or over-whelmed her so that she didn't speak up around him, I had no way of know-ing because I never met her alone. All I can say is that in the presence of Bradshaw, she was quiet as a mouse."

The other aspect of the relationship that stuck out was Bradshaw's attitude toward Anna, which was extreme impatience, or at least that's the way it struck Dobell. He remembers Bradshaw describing Anna as "childish, too clinging, too dependent, and annoying. Anna was obviously very attractive and they obviously had something going," he says. "But he did express to me his annoyances with her. Now, whether he was covering up for her becoming annoyed with him, who knows."

The seemingly passive Lolita-like character that the Dobells saw, and the shrew many of the *Viva* people witnessed, had still another face. With men in her life, past and present, Anna played curious head games.

In one, she appeared to pit her onetime London hippie boyfriend, Richard Neville, against her current live-in, Bradshaw.

By the midseventies, Neville, the once-controversial *Oz* editor, had moved to New York City like so many other Brits and Australians to get a toehold on American journalism.

Neville, trying to freelance, was then living in a loft on the Lower East Side with his future wife, a beauty named Julie Clarke, who was the U.S. cor-respondent for the high-circulation magazine *Australian Women's Weekly,* with an office in the *Newsweek* building on Madison Avenue.

Neville contacted Anna at *Viva,* and the two renewed their friendship. "My God, I thought, here's that quiet little girl, Anna Wintour, who I re-member in London was not even sure of what she was doing, and here she is now, in New York, working for Bob Guccione," he notes. "This was the *new* Anna." Anna also became friendly with Julie Clarke, who was young and kicky and covered fashion and style and recognized in Anna, as Neville puts it, "a person of great aesthetic confidence."

Right after Neville called, Anna arranged to have lunch with him at the fashionable Russian Tea Room to catch up on old times, but he was surprised when she arrived with Bradshaw, whom Neville had never met but had heard about. Did Anna hope to see a duel over her? To see her guys duke it out? Winner take all? It seemed all so sophisticated and bitchy, like something

Samantha might have dreamed up years later on *Sex and the City*. If Anna's reason for bringing them together was simply to put them on the hot seat and see what would happen, she was relatively successful. Neville felt extremely uncomfortable, while Bradshaw eyed Anna's ex-lover with icy suspicion.

"I found it very strange that Anna had lunch with the both of us. My guess was that she was pitting us and we were both supposed to dislike each other," Neville clearly recalls. "It was all rather odd."

But as it happened, Anna's mind game backfired. "Bradshaw and I got on much better than he with Anna, or me with Anna. Instead of disliking each other, Bradshaw and I eventually became friends. I was so enchanted. He occupied a world with which I was not familiar," says Neville.

From their initial lunchtime chatter and subsequent mano a mano conversations, Neville got the distinct impression that Bradshaw could well have preceded him as Anna's boyfriend in London, as others have suggested, which would have put Bradshaw with Anna when she was in her midteens.

While Bradshaw had complained to Byron Dobell about Anna's neediness and childlike behavior, Neville says Bradshaw teased her about her "facileness and her superficiality. We both used to joke about Anna. Bradshaw was very mocking of her—not in a cruel way, but in an amusing way. With jocular comments, he teased and made fun of her opinions and attitudes. He was older than her, and more worldly, and there was that daddy complex going on between them, and his criticism struck me as slightly paternal, although some might call it condescending. I thought it was, in a way, affectionate. And I don't think she minded being teased; she seemed to rather enjoy it. I saw them as an odd couple. He was this tall George Raftian guy with a great love of words who'd been to Vietnam, and she [was] the ingenue on the lower end of journalism. The irony is that little was he to know that she would become a superstar."

Anna's relationship with Kathy Keeton, the associate publisher and editor of *Viva*, was a veritable roller-coaster ride.

In many ways the two were perfectly matched—imperious, ambitious, driven. "Like Anna, Kathy was another haughty, princesslike figure, and Anna was very pretty, wore gorgeous clothes, and acted and looked like she was not of us, that she was of a much higher order than we were," notes Carol Mithers, then a young *Viva* editor.

But others, like Stephanie Brush, couldn't imagine a bond between them, professionally or personally. "Kathy showed up at work with these halter tops, totally bare in the back," she says. "She was a real trash queen extraordinaire— big hair, the whole deal. What would these two women have to talk about? Kathy was South African, an ex-stripper; Anna was British, wore Yves St. Laurent, and acted like royalty. I can't imagine they had any common ground."

Beverly Wardale watched the dynamic between the two and came to believe that Anna only "tolerated" Kathy and felt she was "in the second division" by working for the Guccione organization.

"Anna thought the whole company was *tainted*," asserts Wardale. "She didn't find anybody who was a kindred spirit. If it had been Condé Nast, and we'd had fashion editors who went to Paris every five minutes, she would have thought it was a wonderful place. But there wasn't anyone there on her real wavelength. There weren't that many people at *Viva* who were interested in fashion, who were that driven about fashion, that artistic. Certainly she didn't think Bob and Kathy were—they were coming from one direction, she from another."

Susan Duff, on the other hand, feels that Kathy "loved" Anna and believes Kathy was interested in Anna's ideas. "When the two of them were together, it didn't even seem like Kathy was the boss." At the same time, though, Duff concedes that Anna "definitely felt superior in kind of a class way—to her surroundings [the magazine], toward Kathy and Bob."

On one occasion, after an editorial meeting, Keeton had praised Duff for some work she had done and Duff had mentioned it to Anna, who never complimented her for her efforts as her writer, which was Anna's style. On hearing Duff going on about Keeton's kudo and how she felt the boss liked her, Anna remarked tersely, " 'Kathy would fire you for sneezing.' In other words," observes Duff, "Anna was saying don't feel good about yourself. But she also may have been expressing her own insecurities and vulnerability regarding Kathy."

Nevertheless, Keeton liked Anna well enough to invite her for a girls' night at the Guccione house, a bizarre evening of drinks, dinner, and girl talk. The house was a thirty-room, seven-story pleasure palace filled with art by Van Gogh and Picasso, and featuring an indoor pool and a ballroom. Once a struggling artist working in London, Brooklyn-born Guccione had started *Penthouse* on a shoestring in 1965, essentially copying the *Playboy* format. His golden philosophy was if there's room for one, there's room for two. A decade, two wives, and two sons later, with a net worth of more than $100 million, he bought the house at 12 East Sixty-seventh Street, the largest privately owned town house in Manhattan. The Guccione place eclipsed Hugh Hefner's pad for sheer elegance and kitsch: A piano that once belonged to Judy Garland, a statue of a female saint, and two lead sphinxes with the head of Marie Antoinette were just part of the bizarre picture.

Guccione was out of town on business the night Anna, dragging Duff along, visited the mansion to spend the evening with Keeton, who presumably had little better to do. Like Anna, Keeton had few close female friends, was lonely at the top, and wanted some company, so when the boss calls, the help comes running. Anna and Duff sat dutifully on either side of Keeton, who perched herself at the head of a dining table that looked like the flight deck of the USS *Forrestal*.

"The mansion was a weird, strange, creepy place. The whole scene was very Gothic," recalls Duff. "Kathy was going on about how wonderful it was when the man's away and you can get your facial and pedicure and just hang out and have girl talk. She had this maid who I think was drunk or something and was falling all over Kathy, slobbering on her neck. I looked over and Anna was just sitting there rolling her eyes."

It was probably the one and only time Anna visited the mansion. She absolutely never made an appearance with some of the other women editors who were asked to fill in the ranks with *Penthouse* Pets, who were supposed to look like normal guests, when Guccione was entertaining advertisers at the house, and it wound up being four women for every man.

Relations between Keeton and Anna often became strained, especially over expenditures. While Guccione poured money into *Viva*, which always lost it—some savvy staffers saw the place as a glorified tax write-off—Keeton kept a sharp eye on costs; she may have been a scantily clad dancer when Guccione first set eyes on her in the Pigalle club, in London's Soho district when she was twenty-six, but she was a scantily clad dancer who read the *Fi-*

nancial Times and played the market. Anna, on the other hand, acted as if Guccione had handed her a blank check at *Viva,* which sometimes turned Keeton into a veritable Shylock over the most trivial expenses.

The longer Anna was there, and she'd been at *Viva* about a year by the close of 1977, the more she and Keeton seemed to go at it, money being just one issue.

"One of the things that went wrong was, Anna had a head-to-head with Kathy," recalls Joe Brooks. "Kathy was of the opinion that anybody who wanted their clothes in *Viva* should pay for the shipping to and from the shoot, which is evidently not the way it goes in the trade."

While it was peanuts, Keeton thought it was an unnecessary expense and felt strongly that the magazine wasn't going to foot the bill. Moreover, she was out to rattle Anna. And it worked. Anna was seething because she was on the magazine's fashion front lines and would have to explain the situation to her friends in the business. At this point, whatever Anna wanted to do, Keeton put her two cents in, and whatever Kathy wanted to do "wrinkled Anna's nose somehow," states Brooks. "It was *not* a match made in heaven."

Beverly Wardale believes that Keeton "initially had been somewhat in awe" of Anna, "but toward the end she and Bob thought Anna was expensive. She only knew about photographers of the caliber of Helmut Newton. She wasn't going to use someone with a box Brownie. That was her trademark. She was costing the company money. Anna never did anything on the cheap. She'd never say, 'I have this up-and-coming *inexpensive* photographer, or this young up-and-coming *inexpensive* model.' If it wasn't someone or something that could be in *Vogue,* it didn't exist for Anna. It always had to be the best, the most expensive, the chicest. That's Anna, and it got to Bob and Kathy."

There also were increasing arguments between Keeton and Anna over the fashions being used in her flashy layouts, with Keeton complaining that the clothing was pure fantasy, and that women readers in Des Moines wouldn't get it. "But Anna didn't care," says Wardale. "She cared for the total look, which was an extension of herself. She didn't care what people who live in trailer parks thought. She was selling Anna Wintour, the package. And the package was being able to pick out a fashion or a trend before it happens. That's what she's all about, and that's why she eventually got to where she is."

Outside the office Anna began complaining about Keeton to friends. To

Vivienne Lasky she made it clear in several telephone calls that she wasn't happy with the way the job was going, that she felt she was being edged out by a "bimbo."

What Anna and most other staffers didn't know was that Guccione had new, costly ventures in mind—gambling casinos in Atlantic City, books, records, television—and another new magazine, a slick futuristic monthly called *Omni*. He also had sunk a reported $17 million of his own money in the X-rated film *Caligula,* based on a script by Gore Vidal and containing a scene with six hundred extras having an orgy. As a result, unnecessary expenses, such as those racked up by Anna, were being slashed, and there were secret discussions at the mansion about killing the money-draining *Viva* altogether. Keeton's seemingly petty cost-cutting dispute with Anna was just the tip of the iceberg. And the beginning of the end.

Always considered a Daddy's girl, Anna followed in the footsteps of her powerful London *Evening Standard* editor father, Charles Wintour, called "Chilly Charlie" because of his icy and demanding manner. Father and daughter pose around the time Anna, thirty-seven, became editor in chief of British *Vogue*, where she caused so much mayhem the press dubbed her "Nuclear Wintour." (*© John Timbers*)

Anna's "American heiress" mother, the former Eleanor Trego Baker, nicknamed Nonie, at Radcliffe College, just before leaving for Cambridge, England, where she was introduced to Charles Wintour by their mutual friend, the future noted historian Arthur M. Schlesinger Jr. The Wintours would have a turbulent marriage ending in divorce. *(Courtesy of Radcliffe College)*

A day after Anna celebrated her fiftieth birthday on November 3, 1999, her father, the most influential man in her life, died at the age of eighty-two. A month later a memorial service was held in London. Anna poses with some members of her family. From left, her children, Charlie and Bee; her sister Nora's children, Klara, Tomas, and Luke; Anna's British journalist brother Patrick; and her sister Nora, married to a Swiss Red Cross worker. *(Associated Newspapers)*

The Carter Presidency, by Richard Reeves
Rating the Top-Selling Yogurts
A Guide to Private-School Admissions

ONE DOLLAR

NOVEMBER 1, 1976

New York

Lottery
Fever

"I've been a
gambler
all my life.
Last week
I bought
$1,000
worth of
lottery
tickets..."

By Jon
Bradshaw

Writer, gambler, drinker, and all-around rogue, Jon Bradshaw was considered the one true love of Anna's life. The two, who met in London when she was in her teens and he was a dozen years older, had a stormy father-daughter relationship. Anna was devastated when he died at forty-eight of a heart attack while playing tennis. (*New York* magazine)

Anna had been involved with a number of men before she met Dr. David Shaffer, a prominent child psychiatrist, whom she wed in their posh Greenwich Village town house on September 7, 1984. Older than Anna, Shaffer was said to be her career guru and Svengali, but their marriage would end after Anna began an affair. *(Robin Platzer/Time Life Pictures/Getty Images)*

Anna on the front row with her teenage daughter, Bee, a contributor to *Teen Vogue*.
(Ron Galella/WireImage.com)

Anna with her son, Charlie, named after Anna's father.
(Arnaldo Magnani/Getty Images)

Anna's marriage exploded after meeting the handsome, wealthy, and married telecommunications mogul and Democratic fund-raiser J. Shelby Bryan, a Texan, with whom she fell in love. The two had a scandalous, well-publicized affair that also destroyed his marriage. Like Anna, Bryan's mother, Gretchen, was a glamorous fashionista. *(Evan Agostini/Getty Images)*

When Anna took over British *Vogue*, she made it a living hell for top editors Liz Tilberis (top) and former model Grace Coddington (bottom). "It was the end of life as we knew it," declared Tilberis, who later became editor of *Harper's Bazaar* and competed directly against Anna's American *Vogue*. After eight months of battling with Anna, Coddington quit British *Vogue* but later joined Anna in a top job at American *Vogue*. *(Andrea Renault/Globe Photos)*

(Djamilla Rosa Cochran/WireImage.com)

Anna's debut as editor of *Vogue*, her lifelong dream come true, began on a sour note when a nationally syndicated gossip columnist wrote a controversial item about her and the magazine's powerful owner and media mogul Si Newhouse. *(Patrick McMullan/Getty Images)*

Alex Liberman (left), *Vogue*'s creative genius, recruited Anna to the world's fashion bible from *New York* magazine. *Vogue*'s then editor in chief, Grace Mirabella (below with Barbara Walters), was furious about Anna's hiring, calling her "cold [and] suspicious of everyone loyal to me, and autocratic in her working style." Mirabella was given her walking papers, and Si Newhouse replaced her with Anna. *(Adam Scull/Globe Photos)*

(Robin Platzer/Time Life Pictures/Getty Images)

Despite angry protests from animal rights activists, Anna wears fur and promotes it in the pages of *Vogue*. She started sporting fur as a teenager in London and refuses to give in to the protesters who once tossed a dead raccoon on her luncheon plate. Draped here in chinchilla, she's much beloved by the fur industry. *(Thos Robinson/Getty Images)*

Fur is worn by beautiful animals & ugly people.

**Anna Wintour:
Keeping Cruelty in *Vogue*.**

PeTA **PETA.org**

PETA, People for the Ethical Treatment of Animals, has been a vocal critic of Anna's wearing fur as a fashion statement. This is one of the organization's rabid protest advertisements. *(Courtesy of PETA)*

At six-foot-seven, towering fashionista extraordinaire André Leon Talley is Anna's longtime colleague and confidant who swoons, "The Red Sea parts when she walks through the room." Here, the glam couple makes a spectacular entrance at a New York event. *(Rose Hartman/Globe Photos)*

Anna viewed Bill and Hillary Clinton as "the new Kennedys and the royal family wrapped into one," and during the White House sex scandal known as Monicagate, she oversaw a makeover of Mrs. Clinton that resulted in her becoming the first first lady ever to strike a pose on the cover of *Vogue*. Anna called the future New York senator "an icon of American women." *(Jeff Vespal/WireImage.com)*

"She has star quality—she *is* a star," designer Oscar de la Renta once raved about Anna. And not many magazine editors can draw this kind of star-quality treatment from the media. Anna preens for shooters at New York's Fashion Week. *(Jemal Countess/WireImage.com)*

Looking as glamorous as any Hollywood movie star, Anna turns out in full glitz in April 2003 for the Gucci-sponsored Metropolitan Museum of Art Costume Institute benefit gala and strikes a dramatic pose for the cameras with her trademark bob and sunglasses. *(Evan Agostini/Getty Images)*

eighteen

Out in the Cold

As Anna's relationship with *Viva* was deteriorating, her personal life was in utter chaos.

By 1978, she and Bradshaw had reached the breaking point. The romance was long over, and the live-in aspect had become antagonistic and sporadic, with Bradshaw mostly crashing on the couches of friends, male and female, in New York, Los Angeles, and London.

Possibly with an eye to replacing Bradshaw, Anna decided to do a *Viva* fashion spread using interesting and sexy men as models, among them Bradshaw and Jean-Paul Goude, an artist who later married disco vamp Grace Jones and helped create the amazonian beauty and former model's androgynous look and persona. Carol Mithers, who had been hired as a twenty-three-year-old editorial assistant but was quickly promoted to associate editor during one of the staff purges, was assigned by Anna to interview the "models" and write blurbs about them.

Mithers, who thought of Anna as "not a nice person—cold, arrogant, and haughty in a magazine with an otherwise nice sisterly feeling, but who did unbelievable, absolutely gorgeous spreads," was taking notes from Bradshaw in the photo studio when he began talking about one particular woman in his life. "I remember him saying, 'My last girlfriend said I was a wonderful affair, but would make a bad husband.' He either told me, or I later figured out, that he was talking about Anna."

In the same time frame as the shoot, there was great excitement—and a bit of schadenfreude—in the *Viva* office when Anna had what was described as a crying fit over the split. She was said to have holed up in her office and, according to the photographer Pat Hill, "was hysterical and crying her eyes out." Mostly, though, everyone in the office was intrigued that the ice maiden could actually shed real tears.

Though she appeared heartbroken, a number of friends of both Anna and Bradshaw say it was she who broke it off.

"Anna ended that relationship, not Bradshaw," maintains Earle Mack, a close friend of both, whose fancy Park Avenue digs Bradshaw commandeered at times before, during, and after the breakup. A genial and charismatic businessman, political adviser, and culture maven who would later serve as chairman of the New York State Council on the Arts, Mack had first met Bradshaw in swinging London and through him became friends with Anna after she landed in New York. "It ended," Mack asserts, "because she was fed up with Bradshaw's wild ways—his drinking, his gambling. She just didn't think that he was responsible enough for her. When you're trying to look seriously at someone for the future you want them to be responsible. Anna was a strong woman. She knew what she was about. She knew what she wanted to do. She was very much in love with Bradshaw, and he was everything wonderful to Anna—but she needed someone with more stability in her life."

Nik Cohn, who opened his Upper West Side apartment to Bradshaw, says, "Obviously, there were problems and rocky times, ups and downs, and storms between Anna and Bradshaw. But Bradshaw's thing with Anna didn't just one day end. They were on and off. She certainly loved him very much, and even when he was going through considerable pain [after the breakup], I never heard Bradshaw say anything negative about her personal life or her professional life. He was more like her cheerleader: 'Anna's up to this, Anna's doing that.' The way I saw it, he thought the world of her, [but] they were two exceptionally complex and deeply contradictory personalities."

Through Bradshaw, Cohn had gotten to know and like Anna, and he saw her, as most men did, in a far different light from those who worked with her, especially other women. Cohn compares her back then to a little doe lost in the woods, while those at *Viva* saw her as Godzilla.

"Anna was very vulnerable and spent a lot of time biting the ends of her hair," he remembers. "There was a Bambi-caught-in-the-headlights quality about her. She was highly emotional and high-strung. Her energies were diffused, and she changed her mind at enormous speed about what she wanted."

At twenty-nine, ambitious and determined to climb to the top of the fashion magazine business, Anna had made the decision to break free of her Bradshaw dependency. He no longer fit into her blueprint for success, despite the fact that she did then, and always would, love him. In the wake of the split, Bradshaw had what Cohn describes as "wide mood swings." But he still found time to hang out at some of his favorite New York haunts—Elaine's and Mortimer's. To raise pocket money, he hustled backgammon games in the back room of Othello, a black disco on Eighth Avenue.

Bradshaw also spent considerable time on the road working on freelance pieces as a way, in part, to drown his sorrow over Anna's defection. On a trip to Hollywood, he reconnected with Carolyn Pfeiffer, an American film publicist whom he had met in London in the early sixties. By the seventies, Pfeiffer had become a relatively successful independent film producer. The two suddenly fell in love, as Pfeiffer tells it, and Bradshaw moved into her Hollywood Hills home, though he continued to see other women, drink, and gamble. On assignment in London in 1978, for instance, he stayed with a friend of Anna's and seduced an American woman journalist pal of hers, without telling her of his involvement with Pfeiffer.

Anna wasted no time after the final split with Bradshaw. One of the next men in her life was said to be Eric Idle, a member of *Monty Python*. When Idle once purportedly broke a date with her, a *Viva* colleague says, Anna was furious. "We all could hear this ridiculous conversation she was having with him on the phone. She kept repeating, 'I think that's *very* naughty of you. . . . It's *terribly* naughty of you. . . . It's *horribly* naughty of you.' She wasn't letting him off easy for canceling out on her. She wasn't taking any excuses."

Anna also raised eyebrows at the *Viva* office around this time by appearing rumpled, if not disheveled, at times, with circles under her eyes, and looking like a lost soul, which ignited watercooler gossip. "She was coming to work wearing the same outfit maybe five days in a row, on several occasions," recalls a coworker, one of the few who liked her. "Here she was, this fashion plate, and she was wearing the same dress every day. People were saying she didn't even have a permanent address at that point, that she didn't have any place to go home to. It was all very, very strange."

With Bradshaw out of the picture, Anna asked *Viva* associate editor Stephanie Brush, who was five years younger and no fashionista—she bought her clothes at Alexander's, a low-budget New York department store—to join her in a *Three's Company*-style roommate arrangement. The other roomie was a younger man, a friend of Anna's, who was not a romantic interest.

Anna was unusually fond of Brush. When she learned that Brush was planning a trip to London to visit a boyfriend, for instance, she offered her a list of people to call, among them the novelist Martin Amis. And on a number of occasions Anna invited Brush for drinks or dinner at a couple of her favorite haunts, such as One Fifth, at One Fifth Avenue, a chic and hip restaurant with a nautical theme that was owned by Anna's friend George Schwartz, a radiologist, who always gave her the best table in the house. According to Paul Sinclaire, Anna dated Schwartz for a time, and he gave her a gift of bracelets. Anna's British ex-pat friend Brian McNally, who went on with his brother Keith to open trendy Manhattan restaurants, worked there at the time. One Fifth was a hip spot. A scene from the film *An Unmarried Woman* was shot there while Anna was at *Viva,* and celebrities like Richard Gere, Nick Nolte, and Bette Midler were customers.

Brush never really understood Anna's interest in her. "She was so cool, and I was such a dork, but I think I amused her on some level," she says.

So she was pleasantly taken aback when Anna asked her out of the blue to share an apartment. It was a triplex in the Turtle Bay section of Manhattan, and each roommate would have one level. Brush was interested, so Anna took her to visit the place, and then they went to lunch at One Fifth to discuss arrangements. But that was the last Brush heard of the offer.

"She never said anything more about it, and for all I know she never ended up getting that place," Brush says. "I never did know what happened. But it's always been in the back of my mind that I just wore the wrong outfit that day—a rodeo skirt with a little ruffle at the bottom and cowboy boots, a little cowgirl theme—and that probably turned her off."

Anna seemed desperate for a new roof over her bob and was willing to settle for something as bizarre as a cockroach-infested walkup loft two flights above iffy East Broadway on the Lower East Side in Chinatown, practically under the Manhattan Bridge—the kind of situation no one could have imagined the high-style priestess living in if she was thinking straight. But the break with Bradshaw, and her increasingly precarious situation at *Viva,* was seemingly taking an emotional toll. The loft, with pitted wood floors painted in dark blue enamel, and a couple of partition walls that did not reach the ceiling, belonged to Richard Neville.

On a few occasions, Anna had attended candlelit bohemian dinner parties there—lots of insider gossip from a diverse group of underground journalists and writers—and the place looked interestingly funky and romantic to her, at least in the semidarkness. Besides Neville, the loft's former occupants had included a reporter for the hip *SoHo News* and an up-and-coming young architect, so the joint had some cachet. But in the glare of the harsh morning light the reality was far different.

The drab space included a tiny bathroom, accessorized with a grungy shower, a toilet, and a mirror nailed to the wall. Across a wallboard partition was the minuscule kitchen—both rooms shared one set of plumbing risers—with a cheap fridge, an inexpensive four-burner stove, and a couple of feet of counterspace, though a small expanse of brick wall was trendily exposed. In the main part of the space, some long-ago tenant had left a Ping-Pong table. The ground floor of the building housed a storeroom for groceries; the floor above the loft was a private club for well-dressed Asian men thought to be in organized crime.

Nevertheless, it was serendipitous when Anna, desperately looking for a place to hang her Yves Saint Laurent, learned that Neville was leaving New York for New Delhi to pursue the story of a serial killer of hippies in Asia and the subcontinent, for which Neville had gotten a book contract. (When the book was published, the photograph of his wife, Julie Clarke, on the jacket showed her in an Anna designer hand-me-down.)

"There were a few Australians around who I could have put in the loft," says Neville, "but Anna decided she wanted to rent it because her domestic circumstances suddenly changed. She needed a place in a hurry."

He adds that never in a million years could he have imagined Anna living in such a place and was dumbfounded when she said she'd take it.

One of the Australians who had also been interested was the radical journalist Phillip Frazer, who caught Anna's screeching phone call not long after she had taken up residence.

"Richard had told me that Anna was an English lady of breeding, or at least had that manner, and she and her boyfriend had broken it off, and she needed a place in hurry and was new to the idea of living alone," recalls Frazer. "He told me she was not the sort of person who was used to this kind of living and asked me to be the phone contact in case she had a problem. I never thought I'd hear from this fashion person named Anna Wintour."

But then came the attack of the cockroaches, thousands of them, like a scene out of a Stephen King urban nightmare.

"Less than a week later she called me in a distressed state, saying there were roaches everywhere and she couldn't stand it and had to leave immediately and could I take over the lease. I explained to her how to put down poison, but she wanted to get out of there and go to somewhere more uptown—literally and figuratively."

The next day, Frazer arrived at the loft and met Anna, whose bags were packed, with a taxi waiting. She exchanged a few pleasantries and was gone.

"I never saw or heard from her again, but I never lost track of who she was," he says.

When he moved into the loft, he discovered something Anna had left behind—an expensive designer bedsheet in a beige and dark blue houndstooth pattern. Frazer had it washed and began sleeping on it and found it to be one of the most comfortable sheets he'd ever had. For some reason the sheet stayed in the Frazer family, and by the fall of 2003, a quarter century later, it had become known as the "Anna Wintour Memorial Sheet" and was then being slept on by Frazer's sixteen-year-old son, Jackson.

Knowing that Anna's career has been based on staying ahead of the curve when it came to fashion, style, and trends, Frazer feels it's ironic that she had that brief moment in what had been a very downscale neighborhood that years later became hot and chic. "She sort of jumped the gun," he observes. And Anna probably never forgot her experience there, either, as evidenced by the February 2004 issue of *Vogue* that had the cover line, "Inside the Red-Hot World of New York Fashion," which dealt in part with the cutting-edge designers and shops and living spaces of what became the hip Lower East Side, where she had fled from an army of roaches.

By the late spring of 1978, the situation at *Viva* had become untenable—a virtual pit of vipers. Unfounded gossip circulated that Bob Guccione was about to shut the doors, which had everyone, especially Anna, in a panic, because *Viva* had become a wonderful billboard for her work.

Moreover, there was a heated confrontation between Guccione and two very talented staffers, executive editor Gini Kopecky and senior editor Valerie Monroe, over a cover photo, which resulted in them being fired and morale plummeting even farther.

"The reason they left," recalls Carol Mithers, "is because there was a Pet that Bob [Guccione] had put in *Penthouse,* and he wanted to put a close-up photo of her very seductive, fuck-me kind of face on *Viva*—a cover that didn't belong on a women's magazine."

Kopecky and Monroe, who had been at *Viva* for only about eight months, were furious. "We were trying to make it a more serious magazine, a more literary magazine," says Monroe, who had hired Mithers. "Kathy had told Gini we could do whatever we wanted with the magazine. I was buying stories from Alice Munro and other wonderful fiction writers, but it wasn't a place where anyone had a strong vision. However, *Viva* was a beautiful book, and Anna was doing beautiful fashion pages. Most people left her alone and she was doing whatever she wanted to do."

Still, Guccione and Keeton ran the show. Beverly Wardale remembers Keeton saying, "It's Bob's magazine, and Bob can do what he likes, and if he wants to have this cover, he'll have this cover!" Guccione and Keeton refused to see Kopecky and Monroe's point of view and vision, and they were axed.

"We were told we had to leave," says Monroe. "We were escorted out of the building."

What became the final days of *Viva* began, probably as a corporate subterfuge, with the hiring in July 1978 of a managing editor, Helen Irwin, to replace Kopecky. It threw everyone on staff, including Anna, off guard and scotched the rumors that Guccione was about to stick *Viva*'s head in the proverbial oven.

A onetime runner-up for Miss Pennsylvania in a local Miss America pageant, the tall, thin, ash blond, and officious Irwin had some previous journalism experience, having worked for *Boston* and *Philadelphia* magazines. She secured the *Viva* job because of her friendship with Jim Goode, the editorial director for *Penthouse* and *Viva,* who recommended her to Keeton and Guccione. They hired her because she had a vision to produce "a magazine for today's intelligent, independent and adventurous woman . . . affluent and well-educated and interested in the world around her," according to a publicity memo.

It didn't take Irwin very long to develop the same view of Anna as most everyone else on staff had—a talented and creative ice queen.

"She wasn't an easy person to get to know," says Irwin. "She was cold—and that's not too strong of a word. She was aloof, ambitious, and had supreme confidence and wanted to do well. She gave off this air of 'I'm good. I know what I'm doing. I can do this.' She had enormous style and talent, and I gave her pretty much free rein and treated her as a separate fiefdom because I was not so secure in my own fashion editing abilities. My relationship with her was professional—and at arm's length."

Irwin's only hire was a new senior editor to fill Monroe's slot but not her duties. Catherine Guinness was a member of the hugely wealthy Guinness brewery family in England and was hired mainly because of her contacts in the edgy New York underground, where she was a close friend of Andy Warhol and had worked at his ultrahip *Interview* magazine. Catherine was hired by Irwin on orders from Jim Goode. Guinness says she had no idea who Anna was until she started at *Viva* but was pleasantly surprised.

While virtually everyone on staff headed the other way when they saw Anna coming, Guinness and Anna, two Brits, hit it off. "She was really nice, jolly, and good company." Of all the women who worked at *Viva,* Guinness fit Anna's profile of someone worth courting. She was trendy, part of the Warhol scene, and from a powerful and influential British family, so Anna showed the beer heiress her charming side. They even had some talks about setting up a magazine together, but it came to nothing.

"Anna had great imagination and was the most generous person in that she gave me all her ideas"—a London issue, a Paris issue, neither of which ever reached fruition—"and inspired me without wanting herself to get the credit," says Guinness. "The people at the magazine, like that dreary managing editor [Irwin], thought the ideas were over the top. This bloody Helen woman had stymied all of her ideas, but the ideas were just *too* wonderful."

Guinness felt that there was "an overriding bridge-and-tunnel mentality" among the people who worked at the magazine. "They were pretty much middlebrow, the sort of people who would *not* be allowed in Studio 54."

Apparently hoping subtly to extend her franchise at *Viva* beyond fashion, Anna suggested the story ideas to Guinness along with the names of friends in London who could do them. The ideas, though, were all nixed by Irwin at the direction of Keeton, who by the late summer of 1978 had it in for Anna.

Despite all of the backbiting and deceit, it was Irwin, strangely enough, who had become Anna's biggest booster, as evidenced by a confidential assessment of the staff, dated August 11, 1978, that she had written at Keeton's request.

In it, Irwin described Anna as "one of the strongest assets *Viva* has. In two years with *Viva*, she has made a name for herself, and for *Viva* in the fashion field. Because of her we are able to get top photographers to work for us at fees we can afford."

At one memorable meeting shortly after Irwin came aboard, Anna told her she'd been offered another job, probably a ploy on Anna's part, and demanded a six-thousand-dollar raise from her annual salary of twenty-five thousand, an amount comparable to walking-around money years later when she got the top job at *Vogue*.

In her memo to Keeton, Irwin stated, "Anna says she has received a job offer of $30,000 from a magazine for which she does not want to work but feels with that kind of outside recognition of her talents she should be offered an increase by *Viva*."

Irwin says Anna never revealed the name of the publication that was supposedly competing for her talents and just took her word for it that such an offer had been made. She recommended her for the salary increase because she did not want to lose her.

Had Anna actually received another offer from a legitimate magazine giving her a raise of 20 percent, she most likely would have jumped at it, but Irwin wasn't cognizant of Anna's negative feelings about working for the Guccione organization.

"I would not want to lose Anna right now," Irwin wrote to Keeton. "Fashion editors, especially good ones, are most difficult to replace. To produce the fashion pages every month is an incredibly complicated task. Coordinating an idea with what is current, particularly with our long lead time, with collecting the fashions, models, photographers and choosing a setting, and finally producing the quality of work which Anna has been doing is simply not easily accomplished. Anna has been producing approximately 18 pages of fashion an issue. We are now asking her to produce 25 to 30 pages an issue. Traditionally, more responsibility suggests greater compensation."

Irwin had been made aware by others at the magazine that beyond her salary Anna had her own personal income, the kind of money that permitted her to fly to London on weekends for fun aboard the Concorde. "I went, 'Oh, my God, she did that?' It was just so extraordinary and memorable," recalls Irwin. "Back then I didn't know *anyone* who flew the Concorde." (At least one friend in London, Annabel Hodin, also recalls Anna's weekend Concorde jaunts, and says she was jet-setting in and out with a good-looking man.)

When Irwin first brought up the issue of a raise with the powers that be, she met resistance, the feeling being that "Anna doesn't need the money." But Irwin argued in Anna's defense, insisting that "Anna's income should be regarded as compensation for her own personal efforts at *Viva*."

In the end, Anna received a raise of four thousand dollars, bringing her salary to twenty-nine thousand, a thousand dollars less than she said she was offered by a competing magazine.

If there was any joy for Anna, it was short-lived. Just two months after her raise took effect, in mid-November 1978, Guccione announced at a staff meeting that *Viva* would cease publication with the January issue. He attributed the decision to "the continued prejudicial treatment on the part of the industry" toward the five-year-old magazine. "I blame it on the prejudices of the bloody distributors," Keeton charged. "They always thought it was a dirty magazine for women, despite our expensive advertising campaign to reposition *Viva* on the newsstands. *Viva* meant so much to Bob and me. It feels like we lost a child."

Guccione promised a relaunch of "an expensive, internationally-oriented fashion magazine with secondary emphasis on beauty, health and general service," which never happened. At the time of its demise, *Newsweek* noted that despite *Viva*'s "striking fashion photographs and a collection of articles ranging from salacious to kindly," the magazine "never did manage to find its market."

Of the sixteen editorial employees, Anna was the most devastated.

"I remember the day we were all called in and Kathy told us the magazine was closing," says Susan Duff. "I saw Anna in the hall after the meeting, and I put my hand on her shoulder as she was getting a drink of water. I knew this was horrible for her, not just another job, and when she turned around she was crying."

Helen Irwin says Anna was especially upset because she had just assigned Helmut Newton to do a fashion shoot and was anticipating working with him again. "She was in tears," notes Irwin. "Anna was the most disappointed for good reason. She was the fashion editor, and those pages were so representative of her and her creative abilities, and she lost her forum. The fact that she was more disappointed than the rest of the staff is understandable. She was really losing her stage, and it was a good one."

Although Guccione promised to try to place *Viva* people in other positions within his organization, there was no slot for Anna. She complained vociferously to friends like Richard Neville that she had actually been "locked out" of the office. He had no reason to doubt her. "She was sobbing," he recalls. "I had never encountered the idea of somebody going to their job and the office being locked, that it could happen so suddenly. That was quite a dramatic moment in Anna's life. She was very upset."

When Guccione killed *Viva*, Anna didn't need to stay around. The December 1978 and January 1979 issues were already locked up.

"Anna's departure was abrupt," says Neville.

She is said to have stormed out of the magazine almost immediately after Guccione's announcement. "She really took it harder than the rest of us," says Irwin, "and she just went her separate way."

Anna told another story some years later when she was named editor in chief of British *Vogue*. She said, "We were told on Thursday evening it was closing on Friday and we were asked to leave the same day."

Penthouse editor Peter Bloch says her recollection of what happened is "bullshit."

About a month later, *Penthouse* staff photographer Pat Hill, who had experienced that irksome ballet shoot with Anna, answered the phone in her office. It was Georgia Gunn calling for Anna. "She asked me if I had, or knew of, any styling work for Anna," recalls Hill years later. "I just couldn't believe that she had the gall to have Georgia make the call for her to me. I was like, 'You've *got* to be kidding.' I was thinking, 'Right, Anna will be the *first* one I will call.' Good-bye."

Over the years, *Viva* alumnae who have run into Anna, or have tried to contact her, like Alma Moore, who hired her when she was out of work, were ignored. "She doesn't like to talk about being at *Viva*," says Moore. "She doesn't want that connection made."

nineteen

The Chanel Affair

In the three years since Anna arrived in New York with dreams of turning the U.S. fashion magazine world upside down with her incredibly focused vision of what style is and should be, she was pink-slipped once and given her walking papers a second time when the magazine she detested folded. At both places, she maddeningly butted heads with her superiors, infuriated her peers, and thoughtlessly maltreated underlings. Now, at the close of 1978, she once again was out of work.

Those who had closely observed her unrelenting ambition and awesome creativity at *Harper's Bazaar* and *Viva* expected—would have bet a week's salary, in fact—this determined, aspiring, and difficult fashionista to land on her feet. Most figured she'd instantly fulfill her dream and that her next stop would be where she thought she should have been all along—*Vogue*.

But a funny thing happened on the way to the pinnacle.

Unbeknownst to most in the ranks of fashion magazines and the media that covers that strange world, let alone some of those close to her, Anna, at twenty-nine, dropped out of the rat race, though one would never have known it from the interviews she's given or the profiles that have been written about her over the years.

Like the infamous and mysterious eighteen-and-a-half-minute gap on Richard Nixon's Oval Office tapes, there's a whopping eighteen-month hole, give or take, in Anna's résumé that few are aware of and that she's never explained. Very private and an expert at spin, Anna essentially tells her story as if she had one fashion magazine job after another with no breaks until she reached the summit.

The truth of the matter is that when she was on her last trembling and pencil-thin legs at *Viva,* as it was folding, Anna hit the brakes on her high-speed career drive.

With no prospects of a proper job on the horizon, with a sketchy work history, let alone no formal higher education or even a high school diploma in her Issye Miyake pocket, Anna decided to chuck it all for a time and become delicious arm candy for the good-looking, bright, and well-to-do French record producer Michel Esteban.

For most of the three years that Anna was with Esteban, a pioneer of the Paris punk music scene, she became a high-living international jet-setter.

Anna had been introduced to the dapper and boyish Parisian in 1978 by their mutual close friend, Michael Zilkha, who was a business partner in New York–based ZE (Zilkha-Esteban) Records, a venture that specialized in new wave, punk, and mutant disco, featuring groups like Kid Creole & the Coconuts, Suicide, Daisy Chain, and a new-wave diva named Cristina—the former Cristina Monet—who became Zilkha's first wife. One of her songs has been described as a touching story of two junkies trimming a cactus with their works and some stolen diamond earrings.

Zilkha, the half-Lebanese son of a wealthy Houston energy producer, had graduated with a master of arts degree from Lincoln College, Oxford, where he was a chum of Anna's brother Patrick. In the midseventies, Zilkha came to New York, where he subsequently produced a film about the downtown art and music scene that featured Debbie Harry, wrote theater reviews for the *Village Voice* along with Cristina Monet, and partnered with Esteban in the record company. Zilkha, whose musical tastes have been described as "coolly exotic and extremely experimental," was one of those responsible for Madonna's first album.

A member of Anna's minuscule posse of close friends, Zilkha, five years her junior, was said to have been attracted to Georgia Gunn. Because he was somewhat shy—and was romantically involved with Monet at the time—

Zilkha required the moral support of his friend Esteban for a luncheon date at the Plaza with Gunn, who arrived with Anna.

When Esteban laid eyes on Anna, he was smitten. "I fell for her immediately, and I had the impression it was reciprocal," he says. "It was love at first sight, as Americans say." Unlike most of the men in Anna's life, Esteban was younger, by a year.

His first meeting with her is so memorable that a quarter century later he clearly pictures the outfit he wore the day he met her—a black-and-white houndstooth jacket from YSL, gray trousers, white shirt, and black shoes. "She told me after we met that she thought I was gay," Esteban says, "because all the elegant men she knew in New York were gay."

The two had a quick courtship.

A couple of days after their first meeting, he invited Anna to dinner at a chic Italian restaurant—she adores Italian food. "When I entered the place there was this amazingly beautiful girl waiting at the bar, and for a fraction of a second I did not recognize her," he says, noting that the vision of her "is still engraved" in his memory. "It was Anna, and she was radiant. I was deliciously trapped—and we spent the following three years together."

Anna had recently begun sharing a chic duplex apartment in a tony East Eightieth Street brownstone with her pal Brian McNally. "She was still at *Viva*, but she was waiting for a better opportunity. Anna wanted more," notes Esteban. "I moved in and helped decorate the apartment. We had a beautiful terrace overlooking a garden. It was love, full stop, and it was not necessary for me to know the reasons. Anna was beautiful, intelligent, and witty. She had class. What else could I want?"

McNally moved out a couple of weeks after her new lover moved in.

From then on, it was a whirlwind of high living for Anna in the chic capitals and fashionable vacation spots of the world.

"We were young and we were living a glamorous life. . . . We traveled a lot between Paris, London, and New York," reveals Esteban. "We had holidays in the south of France, Spain, Jamaica, at Chris Blackwell's [Bradshaw's close friend] house in Nassau. I was living my Jay Gatsby period.

"When Anna left *Viva*, she spent more time in Paris than in New York. We were quite in love, and Anna loved Paris because at the end of the seventies it was really the place to be if you were in the fashion business. I introduced Anna to all the great restaurants of Paris—she loved the wine. Also, Anna's family was in London, where she was a fan of the Ritz Hotel, so it was convenient. We had quite a glamorous life back then.

"Anna loved London, where she had friends, and a sister and brothers. She was closer to her mother at that time because her father was leaving her for a younger woman, and she was a bit angry with her father."

Anna was more than just a bit angry. For a long time she refused even to speak to him, and she despised his new wife.

On August 31, 1979, after a two-year separation, Charles and Nonie Wintour were divorced after thirty-nine years of a mostly tumultuous marriage.

On November 9, 1979, about two months after the divorce decree was finalized, "Chilly Charlie," sixty-two, married Audrey "the flame-haired temptress" Slaughter, fifty, a divorcée, in a civil ceremony in the registrar's office in London's borough of Islington. The newlyweds celebrated with their friends and colleagues in the contemporary space of Hamilton's, an art gallery, in the elegant Belgravia district of London. "It was," recalls Valerie Grove, "a very jolly party." No one recalls seeing Anna or any of her siblings there.

"We often joked with Anna about the flame-haired temptress because it's one of those phrases that rolls off the tongue," recalls Richard Neville, who was in and out of Anna's life during the time of her parents' separation and divorce. "Anna accepted that there was an air of jocularity about it. But she hated Audrey Slaughter. Anna was concerned about how her mother was reacting. But it was something that you felt you could mention because it was *so* out there."

Besides his record company, Michel Esteban owned a shop in the working-class Les Halles section of central Paris called Harry Cover that specialized in imported rock and roll and merchandise like T-shirts—"nothing close to Anna's world," he notes. Since he was busy developing ZE in New York, Esteban needed someone to manage the shop, and Anna recommended Brian McNally's brother, Keith, who was then the maître d' at One Fifth. Esteban invited McNally to Paris with his future wife for a two-week stay, to see if he was interested in taking the job.

"I introduced them to all the great restaurants. We had a great time, and at the end of their trip they decided to go back to New York and open a restaurant of their own.'"

McNally subsequently opened a chic downtown place called Odeon, and then others, and became quite successful. But he has shaded the story of that visit to Paris a bit. Interviewed in 2002 for a film documentary about the New York restaurant scene, he said, "I'd been offered a job in Paris, oddly enough, by the woman who is now the editor of *Vogue,* Anna Wintour. She'd offered me a job working in a boutique in Paris with her then boyfriend . . . and in order to try to seduce me into managing the boutique she took me to all these great bistros and I thought I'd rather be working in this kind of environment." His shop, Esteban notes, was not a boutique.

After three years, Anna and Esteban's relationship ended. "Anna was always with older men and, like a lot of women, I think she was looking for a 'father' figure, and I was not that type," Esteban observes. "I guess three years is a good period. We had the best time."

That "best time" was underscored by the new clothing in Anna's closet in the Upper East Side apartment she rented after the affair with Esteban ended. Recalls Paul Sinclaire, "I opened her closet and it was extraordinary—there was one Saint Laurent suit from ready-to-wear after another that she'd bought in Paris, all perfectly hung with the shoes above them, always very high heels. That was our slogan: 'The higher the heels, the better she feels.' "

During the Esteban period, Anna had had bitchy skirmishes with her friend Michael Zilkha's wife, Cristina. As Cristina Zilkha maintains years later, "I wasn't very kindly disposed toward Anna. She's not a girl's girl—she *hated* me."

One of the reasons for Anna's disfavor, according to Zilkha, is that she once had a romantic interlude with the hard-drinking, backgammon-hustling roué Claude Beer. Zilkha maintains Anna was jealous. Another reason is that Michael Zilkha was "like a little brother" to Anna, and she "considered him her property," so she also was jealous of his involvement with the Harvard-educated Cristina, who was an up-and-coming writer said to have an IQ of 165. As a result, Anna "was vicious to me from the first day we met," Cristina Zilkha asserts. "She did gratuitously spiteful things."

In one instance, Zilkha had taken off a year from Harvard and was visiting

England when she received a call from Anna promising her a summer job at *Viva* that Anna said wouldn't wait. "When I got to New York, she told me she'd given the job to someone else and, in front of her assistant, told me how essentially unemployable I was. Then Anna would tell Michael there were no hard feelings and that she'd still owe me this favor. It was like a mineshaft to fall into again."

Another example she cites of Anna's cattiness was the lunch at the Plaza when Anna first met Esteban. Zilkha believes that Anna purposely arranged the date in the hope that Michael would fall for Georgia Gunn and break off with her. "She was always being incredibly bitchy and hostile. But Michael would always say, 'It's all in your head.'" The two women constantly squabbled. Zilkha would hurl zingers about Anna—"Even her shit's chic." And Zilkha remembers Bradshaw saying, "Anna used to wear tidy shoes," and Anna would say, "Ha! Not *that* tidy."

The feud between the two never cooled over the years. To celebrate the Zilkhas' second wedding anniversary and their tenth year together, Zilkha asked Anna, who by then was creative director at *Vogue,* to get a Chanel suit that he could give to his wife as a present. By that point, Anna was wearing nothing but elegant, *very* discreet Chanel as her Condé Nast work uniform.

"Michael said to me, 'You know, you've never had a Chanel suit, so I told Anna that when she sees [Karl] Lagerfeld to get you something from the autumn collections because she gets fifty percent off,'" recalls Cristina Zilkha. "I said, 'I can't believe you gave *that* woman an opportunity like this. God knows what she'll do!'"

The beautifully gift-wrapped present arrived a few weeks later. Zilkha opened it and exclaimed, "I knew it! I *knew* it!

"It was not a suit, and it was not a jacket," she says, the design imprinted indelibly on her memory. "It was half a suit of a really nasty pale yellow with a puce undertone—a Mr.-Livingstone-I-presume double-breasted safari jacket with thick, *huge* gold metal buttons, each of which had a huge 'CC.' It was the kind of thing they make for the Jewish-Kuwaiti-Japanese *nouveau riche* tourist trade who want the signature. It was vulgarity one couldn't believe and something Anna would not have been caught dead in. I said to Michael, 'Look at this horror! I knew she'd pull something like this.' And Michael says, 'Anna said you'd make trouble. She said you'd be impossible.

She said there weren't any nice suits and this was her and Karl's favorite piece in the whole collection and there was only one size thirty-four.'

"It was just the kind of manipulative, devious thing she would have done, to get me something hideously vulgar, unbelievably unflattering, and fundamentally unwearable, and she realized that Michael wouldn't understand the malice of it. So at that point I took the kitchen scissors and cut this *thing* in half and said to Michael, 'Convey this to Ms. Wintour with my compliments.' "

Zilkha then "dined out on the story gleefully all over town," telling gloating fashionista friends of Anna's like the eccentric Isabella Blow and Condé Nast's Gully Wells. "*Everybody* thought it was an uproariously funny story. And Anna in turn said of me, 'That impossible, dreadful girl.' "

twenty

A Savvy Decision

Judith Daniels had a terrible dilemma. She wanted to fire Anna, but Anna refused to be fired.

It hadn't always been that way between them, and the attempted axing wouldn't happen for some months to come. In fact, the two had started off beautifully when Daniels first retained Anna in the spring of 1980 as a free-lance fashion editor for a slick and sophisticated new magazine called *Savvy*, targeted at the executive working woman.

After her relationship with Michel Esteban ended, Anna had jumped back onto her career track, this time determined not to allow anyone or anything to stand in her way. But there was bad news and good news. The job market was poor. She made the rounds of the better magazines, but there was little or no interest in her, or no openings.

Once again she turned for help to Jon Bradshaw, who was spending most of his time in California now with his future wife, Carolyn Pfeiffer.

He did some snooping among his media friends and learned about *Savvy*, a recent start-up. This new breed of magazine was targeting a seemingly un-tapped and lucrative market: ambitious Reagan-era women armed with MBAs who were entering the worlds of business, finance, and government, and needed straight talk on everything from buying the best spreadsheet soft-ware to choosing the most appropriate wide-shouldered pinstripe pantsuit, then in fashion, to wear to an important meeting.

Better still, Bradshaw had known the entrepreneurial Daniels when she was an editor at *New York* and *The Village Voice,* and Anna had met Daniels socially with Bradshaw at parties around town. Daniels had taken note of her and her brio. "I liked her," Daniels states. "She was smart, well read, knew about art, was good company, and was gorgeous and slender." In the late seventies, Daniels, a sharp operator with a low-key style, had been able to preview *Savvy* in *New York,* which was wonderful publicity, because of her close ties to the magazine's editor, Clay Felker. Then it took her a couple of years to raise the necessary financing and gain backers. Now she'd finally launched her baby. The premier issue of *Savvy* hit the stands in November 1979 but was dated January 1980.

Luckily for Anna, Daniels had just started looking for a fashion editor to succeed the first one, the respected fashion maven and journalist Elsa Klensch, who is said not to have worked out. When Bradshaw telephoned, recalls Daniels, he said, " 'What about Anna?' And I like to think I was smart enough to say, 'Oh, of course, why didn't I think of her myself.' At the time I didn't know what Anna was interested in, or doing, so we talked."

All Daniels knew was that Anna had last worked at *Viva,* and she liked what she had seen her do there. At their first meeting, Daniels offered Anna the job of fashion editor, but the position was part-time, offered neither perks nor benefits, and paid very little money—much less, in fact, than Anna was making when she got her short-lived raise at *Viva.* Anna had no other options at the moment, so she gave Daniels an immediate yes. Once again, money was not an issue, but visibility was. Anna needed another forum in New York to attract a truly glamorous fashion magazine job, her hope still being that someone at *Vogue* would see her work and reel her into the place where she felt she really belonged.

Like her position at *Viva,* Anna was given virtually complete freedom at *Savvy* by Daniels, at least at first, during their honeymoon period.

"She was not supposed to be in the office every single day," says Daniels. "Everything Anna did, she did on her own. She was brought in on a freelance basis. We paid her a shockingly small amount each month—it's embarrassing, about three thousand dollars—out of which she was supposed to pay photographers and herself. I didn't even want to know. It was appalling.

"But she just loved the business so much, and fashion so much, and she was so good at it, that she was willing to do it for practically nothing. [In fact, according to another editor, Anna was taking only a thousand dollars a month for herself out of the monthly fashion stipend.] I had met a lot of women with drive and ambition. What I was just very grateful about was that someone with Anna's drive and ambition was prepared to focus it for me. She was extremely generous.

"I was impressed at how hard she worked, how professional and knowledgeable she was, and how much people would do for her. She had her incredible network, even then, of first-rate photographers. I totally trusted her and her judgment in this case, and she delivered, and did it on time. She had no staff (Anna did bring Georgia Gunn along with her) and no support system, but she just knew the job and did it on her own. I don't know how she got the clothes, where she went, how she wheeled and dealed, and who she had to wheel and deal with. *Savvy* was new. Had no budget. It wasn't like she could drop the name of *New York* magazine."

Anna's first layout appeared in the June 1980 issue. The cover carried a head shot of Alice Daniel, a conservative-looking woman with close-cropped hair, wearing a buttoned-to-the-throat simple blue blouse. The profile was about an "ardent civil libertarian" running the U.S. Justice Department's Civil Division. The cover lines included "HOW TO GET THE TITLE YOU DESERVE," "FALSE GRIT. YOU DON'T HAVE TO BE MACHO TO GET AHEAD," and, in red type, the very ironic "TELLTALE SIGNS OF THE DEAD-END JOB."

Anna had come full circle, from the eroticism of *Viva* to big-time magazine Puritanism, or so it seemed from *Savvy*'s cover stories and art. Inside, on page 65, squeezed between an article about the literary quality of notes women place on refrigerator doors and one about various types of scales, tape measures, and timers readers could buy, was Anna's first contribution—the only relatively sexy feature in the whole eighty-page issue. It was called "Stripes," four pages of uncomplicated photographs of models with striped belts, striped one-piece bathing suits, and striped blouses. Anna shared the byline with Georgia Gunn and the photographer Jean Pagliuso, who was now part of her core group that also included exceptional shooters like Jimmy Moore, whom she had been working with since her hiring and firing at

Harper's Bazaar; Guy Le Baube, who started with her at *Viva;* and Tohru Nakamura.

Once again, to the rest of the *Savvy* female staff, most if not all of whom were staunch feminists, Anna appeared like an alien or, as consulting editor Kathleen Fury describes her, "pixie dust sprinkled in among the group, who were very bright, funny, hardworking, young, talented journalists. She was one of us, but she was *not* one of us. Anna floated in and out, weighed about two ounces—and she was like from another planet. You knew that you wouldn't ever get too close to her."

Fury, who had worked for *Redbook* and *Ladies' Home Journal,* says she always had the odd sensation that Anna was watching her and the others as they worked, as if observing some other life-form, just as they looked at her as being from Venus.

"She seemed interested and amused," Fury observes. "We were not fashion people, and she may have been admiring us for our abilities to use the language and our ability to use style. You could actually see her watching us— very quiet, but observant, and it was almost as if she was standing outside of a circle of people who were having a lot of fun, and she was enjoying, but not taking part in, their fun. There was a sense of remoteness about her that said don't get too close."

Another editor, Patricia O'Toole, who came to *Savvy* with a good amount of business reporting and writing experience, and in the early eighties would freelance for *Vogue,* never forgot her first introduction to Anna. "I said, 'How do you do?' And she didn't say anything. She just stared right through me. I took this to be a bad review of whatever I was wearing. Mine is a wardrobe that does not fit even the most elastic definition of chic. But years later when I read that some people called her 'nuclear Wintour,' I thought, Well, that's perfect—that squared with my experience."

Just as she acted at *Viva,* Anna rarely if ever participated in editorial meetings but would breeze into the downtown Manhattan offices of *Savvy* wearing tight white T-shirts and tight designer jeans, or shorts and stylish flats, and discuss privately with Daniels what she intended to do. When the photos were delivered, Daniels, never Anna, usually wrote the copy, and that was always at the last minute because of Anna's continued difficulty in communicating the details of the story. Anna came up with the general scheme but expected someone else to handle the nuts and bolts.

Seeing how Anna worked, Daniels was forced, with all of her other responsibilities, to assign a writer, Carol Wheeler, to write all of the fashion copy for the features produced by Anna. Wheeler says that Anna's role was minimal. "She brought the clothes in, and at some point I would hear that the story was going to be about clothes to wear in the summer in New York, and then I would think about what to write. Anna didn't even tell me what the concept was. I would first hear from Judy, and then later Anna would show me the clothes. Later, I would see the pictures, which were interesting and glamorous, and write from those. Anna was certainly not terribly communicative, not word oriented, and I never saw her even *try* to write anything."

Wheeler recalls learning two new things from Anna. One was how properly to apply mascara. The other was the importance of the British artist David Hockney and his critically acclaimed Southern California swimming pool paintings. Anna brought up Hockney to Wheeler because she was using pools at borrowed homes as backgrounds in some location shoots.

Like most others at *Savvy,* Wheeler thought of Anna as "an exotic flower in our midst." Her presence titillated the staff, but they were by no means in awe of her. Like Wheeler, most found her to be "rather chilly, very British, and very upper class." Wheeler was especially put off by Anna's treatment of Georgia Gunn, whom she saw as her boss's whipping girl. "That's certainly the sense that I had of her," Wheeler asserts. "Anna simply ordered her around, and Georgia did what she was told. She did the heavy lifting, and I don't mean that metaphorically, because there were all these clothes that had to be moved around." Wheeler acknowledges that if there was a mule and mule driver, Anna was most definitely the latter.

A few years after both Anna and Wheeler had left *Savvy,* they practically tripped over one another while walking on Fifty-seventh Street between Fifth and Madison. "I said, 'Hello, Anna,' but she just looked through me and cut me dead, just pretending she didn't know me. It was incredible." (In the summer of 2003, many years after Anna had become *Vogue*'s editor in chief, Wheeler mentioned the incident to one of Anna's young features editors at the magazine. She wasn't surprised. "That happens to people she's working with right now, *all* the time," she volunteered.)

Of the six or seven full-time staffers, Carol Devine Carson, *Savvy*'s very talented art director, worked more closely with Anna, particularly in the selection and layout of photos. While she respected Anna's fashion judgment, she noticed flaws and eccentricities.

"She was always gushing about the clothes," says Carson, who later became art director at Knopf, the publishing house. "We did one whole series of stuff with polka dots, and to Anna it was all '*staggering* . . . absolutely *staggering* . . . these girls are *staggering*.' There was always a little bit of the old self-promotion in her speech when she'd present her stuff. It was never what we thought but how *she* thought about it—'Isn't it *fabulous* . . . isn't she *staggering* . . . aren't these *incredible* photographs.' Everything was always a bit hyped. A lot of people do that and I understand that, but it was constant with her."

As time went on, Carson came to believe that some if not all of Anna's passion about the fashion pages she produced was more an intense neediness to receive praise. "She'd tell me, 'You *have* to make this photo spread look great. They've got to like it. *They've* got to love it.'" Carson says Anna was referring to Daniels, as well as *Savvy*'s hard-nosed publisher, Alan Bennett, who held equity in the magazine, took an active role in its look and feel, and was disliked by most of the staff, including Daniels.

"They" also likely referred to editors at other magazines who keep a keen eye on the competition for creative new talent to recruit. After all, Anna saw *Savvy* as a way station, and she certainly knew where she was headed. Like most everyone on the staff, Carson found Anna to be extremely ambitious and icy—"not the kind to kid around and chat about hairdos and boyfriends."

Some years later, Carson ran into Anna, who was hosting a book party at the St. Regis Hotel. "I said, 'Hi, it's Carol, we used to work at *Savvy*.' I wasn't even on her screen. She didn't react to me at all. She didn't want to be reminded of working there because *Savvy* was a desperation thing for her."

While Anna put off most of the women staffers at *Savvy*, she bonded easily, both professionally and socially, with the one male on board, Dan Taylor, who was younger by seven years, good-looking, aristocratic, and dapper, a Southerner who was hired as Carol Carson's assistant art director and designer because of creative work he had done for IBM and Coca-Cola while working at an agency in Atlanta.

Anna took Taylor to lunch and dinner at chic restaurants like The Palm and Mr. Chow's, had him house-sit for her, introduced him to her drugged-out, wild-man pal Rowan Johnson—"a nutcase from hell," Taylor notes—the only staffer from *Viva*, as it turns out, with whom she remained close.

"Young and kickin'" is the way Taylor remembers Anna from those days. She used to refer to him as "the Thin Man," because she thought he resembled William Powell, and he wore snazzy pleated pants like the dashing private dick of thirties and forties films.

Because they had so much fun and hung out together, Anna's interest in Taylor sparked some tensions for him and Sara, his future wife. Anna frequently tried to fix up Taylor with gorgeous women even though she knew he was living with Sara, who worked in theater.

"Dan really liked Anna. . . . He had a [friendly] relationship with her, and he's an amazing talent and Anna knew that, and she surrounds herself with talented people," notes Sara Taylor years later. "She introduced him to women who she thought would be more suitable for him, and this happened a lot. She introduced him to a lot of upper crusts—usually stylists and French and rather snotty. The possibilities were always there."

Asked about Anna interfering in his relationship with his future wife, Dan Taylor says, "I'd rather not go there."

From the moment Taylor met Anna, he thought of her as exquisite. In the office, she often leaned against his desk coquettishly in tight shorts and revealing T-shirts. "Oh, God, she was well put together," he says, remembering those days. At the same time, he could see beyond her flirtation and knew she was determined, enterprising, and hustling for another job. While her long-term goal was *Vogue*, her sights were now set on one other high-profile magazine. "She told me she was shooting for *New York*," Taylor recounts. "That was her goal at the time. She wanted to keep stepping up to get to *Vogue*. At *Viva*, she at least had a budget to work with. *Savvy* was just a blip. Everybody knew she was going somewhere."

After Taylor arrived on staff, Anna worked closely with him, and he found her both "inspirational" and "a pain in the ass."

"If she didn't like something—a layout, the photos—it was always 'just awful.' The operative word was 'awful . . . absolutely awful,' that was her key phrase during that time period. She was very demanding. She had a lot of drive, and she went through people like toilet paper.

"I was always fighting with her because she always wanted big spreads in the magazine to advertise herself. She wanted flashy pieces that made her look good. The better you made her look with the design and layout, the happier she was. Otherwise she was very, very *unhappy*. If it didn't excite her, she quickly got bored. It took a lot to entertain her and keep her moving. She wanted you to do the best you could, and she'd reject it until you got there. That's an incredible ability for someone."

Like others who worked with her up to that point, Taylor agrees that Anna's forte was finding creative talent to carry out her vision. "She had that ability to get great photographers working for us. She was able to get all these women to pose for her, and it was all off-the-cuff pretty much because we had no money at *Savvy,* we had nothing as a budget. Anna was the inspiration, the center point. She'd get the people fired up, let them run a little bit, but mostly hold them back until she got what she wanted, got them to try to do something for her within the realm of no budget."

On one such no-budget shoot, though, the reputation of the magazine could have gone down, along with Anna's career, because of the damage inflicted.

Like Anna, Taylor thought that Guy Le Baube, her fun-loving French shooter, was a trip, and they sometimes hung out together. Anna used Le Baube on a number of her stories at *Savvy,* and he always was spiritedly playful and would do "atrocious things with the models, or something obscene" to provoke her, to see her fume and sweat, because he knew how serious and driven and uptight she was about the job.

All of that was underscored by what became a legendary incident known among a tight circle of fashion insiders. It occurred in Southampton, at a very chichi home loaned to Anna for a day's shoot, with an exotic cast that included Le Baube as the photographer and a flamboyant transvestite as Le Baube's assistant and hairdresser. Because the assistant was Muslim, he didn't drink or eat pork, though Le Baube tried to mischievously force them on him in the presence of Anna, who, he says, "enjoyed the cruelty of it."

So they were a tight little group that arrived in the tony Hamptons sunshine for the shoot. But Anna was her usually controlled self, and she extracted a pledge from of both of them that there would be no monkey business this time. They solemnly promised to act professionally.

"We said yes, we'll be good boys," chuckles Le Baube.

Anna should have known better, because even though she and Le Baube's assistant usually got along, and she liked the way he cut her hair, he was known as a troublemaker.

"He liked to terrorize Anna and, in fact, Anna sometimes *liked* to be terrorized. So she hired us as two brutes—a nasty heterosexual French photographer and a really faggy, bitchy Muslim queen who was ferocious, who loved to get into the clothes of the models, to put on the high heels and walk around like a tramp," says Le Baube. "He was my friend, but he disgusted me. Naturally, Anna was humorless because she's very efficient, and efficient people don't have time to waste. Because she was distressed, we decided to torture her as a joke." But it was a joke that got out of control.

Anna had given the assistant and Le Baube strict instructions not to disturb anything in the house, and certainly not to damage or break anything, and if something was moved to put it back in the exact spot. The place was filled with valuable art and antiques, and the shoot was Anna's responsibility, with her and the magazine's name on the line.

Not long after Le Baube began to shoot, the assistant went into his schtick—he started to dance, bounce off the walls, and knock into things. Anna was in a state of shock as she watched him go bananas. Suddenly he fell against an *objet* and broke it, collapsing to the floor, clutching his chest, saying he thought he was having a heart attack, his face contorted in apparent pain. Then he slowly got to his feet, twisted and turned around the room, bumped into things, fell into a chair and knocked it over, scratching and damaging the rug and shattering a vase.

Le Baube asserts, "Anna was paralyzed, *astounded* that this was happening. She was freaking out and left the scene. We were laughing so hard we had pain in the stomach."

The damage was taken care of, and Anna walked away with her reputation and job intact. The layout, with models at poolside, appeared under the headline "A Bigger Splash."

. . .

Anna had secured the house through the good graces of the new love in her life, a handsome, athletic, well-to-do man-about-town named Michael Stone, who also appeared in one of the photos, or at least part of him did. "I wanted just the ass of a man diving into the pool and had Michael diving and almost drowning as a prop in the background," says Le Baube.

In fact, Stone appeared as a freebie model in a couple of Anna's stories at *Savvy*. One, headlined "Off-White Weddings," showed him dapper in bow tie and tux with his arm around the waist of a beauty. The caption read, "Starring Here with Screenwriter Michael Stone, Alexandra debuts in a silk plissé evening dress . . ." Though he modeled, he wasn't square-jawed, blue-eyed, blond handsome. In Anna's circle, he was jokingly nicknamed "Hosni Mubarak" because of his striking resemblance to the president of Egypt. "Michael was Jewish and had a swarthy sexiness to him," says a friend of Anna's. Stone's nickname for Anna was "mouse," because she was tiny compared to him.

Stone was a "playboy" and "socialite" who desperately wanted to make a name as a freelance journalist. Before he met Anna, he had owned an incredible whole-floor apartment in an opulent building on Fifth Avenue, where he threw fabulous parties.

The journalist Anthony Haden-Guest, a friend of Anna's and Stone's, quoted him in a book about Studio 54 that underscored his man-about-town flair. "All these Racquet Club guys, the people who used to go to El Morocco, the guys who ran things socially, suddenly they found themselves standing outside Studio 54 with their dicks in their hands."

Like other men in her life, such as Bradshaw, Stone was thought of as "a paternal type with a hugely generous spirit," notes Bradshaw's pal Joanie McDonell. Stone bought Anna jewelry and clothing. One Christmas gift was said to be a twelve-hundred-dollar shearling jacket he purchased at the chic Madison Avenue boutique Dianne B., where Anna was friends with the owner, Dianne Benson, who supplied her with Japanese and French clothing for her stories beginning when she was at *Viva*.

Stone knew his way around, which Anna always found attractive in men.

He took her to the right restaurants to be seen; he was pals with the maître d' at Le Cirque, for instance. At the same time, he was athletically attractive and played a mean game of tennis, Anna's favorite sport. In a match he was considered aggressive, and a friend remembers him being severely reprimanded for spiking the ball too forcefully in a volleyball game.

Beyond that, for Anna's career needs, he had access to fancy locations and other upscale accoutrements that could be used for *Savvy* shoots. He was for her the perfect Mr. Right of the moment.

Anna introduced him to Judith Daniels and, as Earle Mack says, "Anna launched Michael's writing career." Soon, he was not only modeling but also writing for *Savvy*. Like Anna, he was thrilled to have the magazine's New York visibility.

One of his pieces, called "The Gambler," was an intriguing profile of an obsessive female high roller. "Andrea plays backgammon for very high stakes. She plays against the best, she takes risks. But it's not just for the money. It's the life," stated the headline.

In fact, the disguised "Andrea" was Stone's own mother, a jet-setter of sorts who followed the action on the international backgammon circuit and "lost quite a lot of money," according to Mack. Among the "best" she played against, and part of her circle, was, ironically, Claude Beer, though none of that was mentioned in the well-disguised story. After the piece ran, Stone revealed "Andrea's" identity to Judith Daniels and also confirmed it to *Savvy* executive editor Susan Edmiston, whom he later dated after Anna dumped him. As Edmiston says, "Michael knew something about the milieu of rich women."

When Stone and Anna became involved, he was divorced from a European model with whom he had a daughter. He was living in a loft on Broadway. Anna soon moved out of her Upper East Side apartment and into his place, and they quickly became known as a hot couple about town. As a well-placed observer notes, "Anna always had to have a man in her life, felt the need to live with someone. There always was that neediness."

The loft was early eighties, very *New York* magazine trendy, Anna's kind of place: sparse and clean, elegant and cool, with uncluttered contemporary textural furniture and a genuine zebra rug on the floor. "It looked like a show-

room that nobody lived in," says a frequent guest. The bathroom, once photographed for a *Savvy* piece on bath accessories, had a glass-block wall.
Within were a whirlpool tub and a steam shower. The sleek look of the entire
space was accentuated because everything but furniture was hidden in or behind almost invisible built-in closets and drawers, thus creating the illusion
the loft was cavernous.

The highlight, though, for female guests, was Anna's walk-in closet. In
summer, for instance, all of her clothing was in white and shades of white,
and each garment was hung separated by about an inch of space so nothing
touched. She placed her shoes in racks, all in perfect formation, and the space
could pass a drill sergeant's inspection with flying colors.

The couple's bedroom was the sparsest room of all: a king-size, low-to-
the-floor platform bed with night tables on either side, each holding an alarm
clock and tiny framed photo, one of Anna on one little table, one of Stone on
the other. "I found it funny," a lady friend recalls. "I always wondered
whether it was her picture on his side, or her picture on her side."

From the time she started at *Savvy,* Anna had a fashion feature virtually
every month in the magazine.

Among them was a shoot on location in Paris—Anna picked up the travel
tab herself since she was taking the eight-thousand-dollar round-trip Concorde back and forth for weekend jaunts anyway; a piece from the City of
Lights with her byline on it would make her look important to editors at
other magazines.

One of the longest features, eleven pages, was a dramatic spread featuring
her beautiful friend Tina Chow, co-owner of the trendy Mr. Chow's restaurants in London, Los Angeles, and New York. Courtesy of her onetime London beau, John Pringle, who had been head of tourism in Jamaica, she was
able to wangle an American Airlines round-trip flight and a stay at the luxurious Round Hill resort on the island, where she once again did a shoot with Le
Baube and his transvestite assistant. "It was a disaster," remembers Dan Taylor, who went along. "Guy lost some of his equipment, *Savvy* wouldn't pay,
and Anna was furious."

While Anna pleased editor Judith Daniels's bottom line with her low-budget, dramatic-looking fashion layouts—many pulled off gratis because of her professional and social ties—the two strong-minded, assertive women, along with hands-on publisher Alan Bennett, began to butt heads.

As in her three previous magazine jobs, Anna always seemed to reach a point where she became a problem for management.

This time it had to do with the fact that the fashions she was choosing for her layouts were way too sexy for *Savvy*'s executive working woman readership, and some of the shots Anna selected were too artsy, with, in some instances, the models' heads cut off.

"Judy was saying, 'We not only have to see the clothes, we have to see the models' faces,' but Anna didn't think that was very exciting," notes art director Carol Carson. "Anna always wanted to put a spin on it, she wanted a theme. In one layout she wanted a twilight look. But Judith and Alan Bennett, who was our leader, wanted something a little more pedestrian for what they thought was our readers' demographic."

For a cover, Anna once proposed a glamour shot of a model wearing a magenta hat that obscured part of her face, which Anna thought was an interesting, offbeat look. But Bennett and Daniels nixed it. "Anna was told the issue wouldn't sell on the newsstands because you couldn't see the model's face," says Carson. "There was a whole ideology in place that came from the publisher that said women will look at the cover and *want* to be that woman. I thought we were supposed to be about self-confidence, with readers saying, 'I *don't* want to be her.' "

Moreover, Anna had begun requesting more space in the magazine for her fashion layouts, mainly to get the attention of editors at other magazines in hopes of getting a job offer. For a time Georgia Gunn shared the byline, but her name was eventually dropped, and Anna's name shone alone.

"She drove Judy Daniels and all those people nuts because she was so exacting and demanding," asserts Dan Taylor. "Anna wanted more pages and kept building up the pages so she'd get more visibility and recognition, and Judy kept trying to cut her pages down. Anna wanted bigger pictures and less copy."

Taylor enjoyed sitting back and watching them go at it—"two headstrong women going up against each other," he recalls. "Anna came off like an authority, presented herself as an authority, and disregarded everybody else who tried to get in her way. She followed the old adage that if you pretend you're in control, you are in control. Anna and Judy were totally different kinds of women. One was British society world and the other was New York society world, and that's pretty clashy to begin with."

It all became too much for Judith Daniels, according to her second in command, Susan Edmiston. "Anna was trying to do fairly avant-garde fashion for *Savvy,* and Judy wanted her to do more conservative, professional clothing, like the clothes that Judy wore. But Anna would say, I want to do this, I want to do that, and she would just do what she wanted basically. Judy didn't like it, and she was the editor, for God's sake, and she didn't have the ability to influence [Anna's] product essentially.

"At one point, Judy attempted to fire Anna," Edmiston states. "Judy came to my desk and looked so frustrated and threw up her arms and said, 'but Anna *refuses* to be fired.' Judy wasn't one to go into detail, kept things close to her chest, and I didn't ask. But I always thought that's an extraordinary thing. How does one do that? How does one *refuse* to be fired? I thought it revealed an extraordinary quality in Anna."

Years later, Daniels, who left *Savvy* in 1984 to go to Time Inc. and later became a magazine consultant, diplomatically maintains that she never tried to fire Anna. "I never said that . . . that's not ringing any bells at all. Everybody gets annoyed at somebody at some point. I'm sure there are times when everybody thinks of firing someone. I certainly appreciated her. I certainly never had anybody else lined up [as fashion editor]. I never looked for anybody."

The former *Esquire* and *New York* magazine editor Byron Dobell, a friend of Daniels, says he heard "two diametrically opposed" stories at the time about Anna's deteriorating relationship with Daniels. One came from Jon Bradshaw, who helped Anna get the job at *Savvy* and on whose shoulder Anna always cried. "He told me very indignantly that Judy was dropping Anna because Anna was too high couture for Judy's magazine. He said Judy didn't appreciate how wonderful Anna was," recalls Dobell. "But Judy, on the other hand, speaks with great praise of Anna. My feeling is that Judy never realized Anna was ever going to become this grande dame of the fashion industry."

Whatever happened between the two, Anna, now thirty-one, quietly began seriously looking for another job in early 1981 after having been at *Savvy* for just nine months.

One of her first stops was Andy Warhol's *Interview* magazine, which turned into an embarrassing disaster. For three months, Anna had been working in secret, while still receiving her monthly stipend from *Savvy,* on an idea for a fashion insert that she thought would be perfect for the edgy downtown monthly. In mid-March 1981, Anna confidently and proudly showed her layout to Bob Colacello, Warhol's trusted lieutenant and bosom buddy at the magazine, expecting him to be excited and welcome her with open arms into the underground fold. Her hopes were that she'd be hired on the spot.

Just the opposite happened, and it knocked Anna for a loop, at least the way Warhol told it. Colacello "just looked at it for one second and said it was trash and she started crying," Warhol maintained. "And she's a tough cookie that I could never even imagine her crying, but I guess it was her femininity coming out."

In a way, the rejection was a stroke of luck, because the next magazine she visited seeking work, with the same portfolio in hand, viewed her like a messiah.

Anna would finally get the visibility that would catch the attention of *Vogue.*

twenty-one

New York by Storm

All of the doors were opened for Anna's first four jobs—from *Harpers & Queen* to *Savvy*—by men in her life. The role she would always play as the ultimate man's woman paid off well and would continue to earn her big dividends.

Her position as fashion editor at trendy *New York* magazine, which she won in the spring of 1981, was no exception.

Once again, another guy pal in her circle laid the groundwork for her to get the job that would give her the most credibility and visibility since she entered the fashion magazine world a decade earlier, a position that would catapult her to *Vogue* through her own creativity, ambition, and shrewd manipulation.

A colleague at *New York* magazine maintains that "Anna came to *New York* with one goal, and that was to get the attention of [Condé Nast owner] Si Newhouse, and [*Vogue* editorial director] Alex Liberman. She was auditioning for them. We talked about it. She knew what she was doing. She's very smart and calculating, and she knew how to play everyone, especially Ed [Kosner, the editor at *New York*], in order to get to *Vogue*. The goal was *Vogue*, always *Vogue*, and Anna told me that."

Anna's buddy Anthony Haden-Guest, who contributed a number of stories about the modeling business to *New York*, got the gold ring this time around for helping her get the fashion editor's position at the slick Big Apple weekly.

The way Anna told it to a British journalist writing a 1998 profile of her, she got her in through a "fortunate phone call" from Haden-Guest, who rang her up one day "to ask if I was busy for lunch, and out of that came" the job offer. She insists that "no master plan" on her part was involved.

In that profile, as well as others, she never mentioned her stints at *Viva* and *Savvy* or her jet-setting hiatus with Michel Esteban before *New York* hired her.

It's as if Anna had taken half of her résumé and dropped it into a shredder and then pieced together the parts that best served her image.

She also never revealed to the profile writer, Nigel Farndale of London's *Daily Telegraph*, that she was desperately seeking a new job when Haden-Guest called. Nor did she disclose that she had made Haden-Guest very aware of her intense desire to work at *New York*, where he had access to the top brass and could drop her name.

Anna made her hiring at *New York* sound serendipitous.

In any event, Haden-Guest, whom she'd known since her nightclubbing days in London, had put in good words for her and gotten her an appointment with the magazine's managing editor, Laurie Jones.

As it turned out, much of the same material that Bob Colacello at *Interview* thought was "trash" not long before, Jones found exciting and compelling. Anna and Jones also took an immediate liking to each other, even though in some ways they were different types.

A native of the small Texas town of Kerrville, a onetime cheerleader, superb athlete, former Miss Kerr County, and member of an exclusive WASP college sorority, Jones was stylish and immaculate, and would marry into a blue-blooded family. She was a perfect fit for the sophisticated ambiance of *New York* and a match for someone like Anna who knew, a colleague notes, that "she was dealing with someone with credentials, a pedigree, money, and style." Jones also was hardworking, earnest, and highly respected by the troops at *New York*—star writers such as Pete Hamill, Nicholas Pileggi, Lally Weymouth, and John Simon—and was number two on the masthead under Kosner, a veteran journalist. Their boss at the time was the conservative Australian media mogul Rupert Murdoch, whose News Group owned *New York*.

Jones's "vivid recollection" of their first meeting is that Anna told her she was "between jobs" and "wasn't working for *Savvy*." In fact, Anna was still connected to *Savvy* when she met with Jones, and her last feature, presciently headlined "Dressing for Success," didn't run in that magazine until August 1981, some four months after she was hired at *New York*.

Despite the inconsistencies in the timeline, Jones says Anna knocked her socks off with her presentation. "She had brought in story ideas. . . . It was all Polaroided, sort of a map [with photos] of what she'd do with different ideas. Sometimes people come in with ideas to discuss, but she had Polaroids. She had the whole storyboard worked out, I never encountered anything like that."

After their meeting, the ex-cheerleader went into Kosner's office and raved, "This woman is unbelievable. We'll all be working for her someday." (Jones's prediction was on the mark, at least concerning herself. After Anna became editor in chief of *Vogue,* she grabbed Jones from *New York* and appointed her to the powerful post of managing editor, where she remained Anna's trusted lieutenant.) Jones explained to Kosner that she envisioned Anna as a "one-woman show" (with an assistant) and that she would be responsible for generating fashion and style story ideas, overseeing shoots, and attending the collections.

If Jones was unabashedly impressed with Anna, the married Ed Kosner was enthralled, if not infatuated, from the moment he laid eyes on her, and he gave Jones the green light to hire her at a salary that was said to be in the fifty-thousand-dollar range, the most Anna had ever made.

"Ed had shiksa love, we're talking *major* shiksa love, full breakdown time," says a former high-ranking *New York* editor, laughing at the memory. "Anna would go into his office and bat her eyes and get anything she wanted."

Everyone in the office knew it from day one and whispered and joked about it. As Corky Pollan, an assistant editor at the time who worked on the popular "Best Bets" column, notes, "Ed was quite enamored of Anna. She seems to have quite an effect on men."

Years later, from her high perch at *Vogue,* Jones remembers only the fine work Anna produced. "Anna just did fabulous pieces and portfolios—so innovative—and eventually, obviously, it caught Alex Liberman's eye at *Vogue.*"

But all of that was still to come.

With Michael Stone, Anna celebrated her hiring at the expensive downtown Italian restaurant Da Silvano on Sunday, April 26, 1981, where she ran into Andy Warhol, who "couldn't remember her name at first" and didn't think much of her. "She was just hired by *New York* magazine to be their fashion editor," he said in his published diary, adding bitchily, "She wanted to work for *Interview* but we didn't hire her. Maybe we should have . . . but I don't think she knows how to dress, she's actually a terrible dresser."

When Anna came aboard, *New York* wasn't what it had been back in the late sixties and seventies when it was edited by its founder, Clay Felker, the father of the so-called new journalism, who gave legs to iconic writers like Tom Wolfe and Jimmy Breslin. Back then it was a must-read, one of the first city magazines with the best reporting and writing in the country.

Even by the early eighties, *New York* was still *the* place to be seen and heard in the communications capital of the world, where it covered everything from brownstone living in trendy Brooklyn Heights, to the best Upper East Side private schools, to dramatic city crimes, to Manhattan celebrities and power brokers. Before Anna, the most creative fashion and style editor there was the witty, sharp-eyed John Duka, who left to become a style reporter at *The New York Times* and later worked for Anna's *HG* and *Vogue*. He later developed AIDS and died after a surgical procedure.

New York magazine was Anna's big chance. She knew it, and she made the most of it.

The first day on the job she marked her territory and established her stature by refurnishing her alcove off what was called the bull pen, the main newsroom, where the other editors and writers worked. When Felker, an ex-newspaperman, ran the magazine, he had moved it into a relatively new midtown building but furnished the editorial floor like a city room out of *The Front Page,* with secondhand clunky wooden desks and chairs from a defunct insurance company, which was ironic for a magazine that promoted upscale lifestyle. The ambiance, or lack thereof, didn't suit Anna one bit.

"She looked around at the space we'd allocated for her," recalls Jones, "and she said, 'I won't work at a desk like that.' "

The next day, to the amazement of other staffers, Anna marched into the office and had the old desk removed and replaced with a sleek, contemporary Formica-topped affair on two metal sawhorses as legs that she'd brought from Michael Stone's loft, along with a high-tech chrome-framed chair with a seat and back made of bungee cords. It sent a message to everyone around her:

Her majesty has arrived. "No one had even thought to do that, to have a new desk delivered," notes Jones, still seemingly astonished more than two decades later.

That first day Anna's image as a diva was cemented, just as if she were a star who had placed her prints in Hollywood's Walk of Fame.

And an incident involving her sleek white desk underscored to a number of her fellow staffers that she was a temperamental prima donna.

Anna was given the go-ahead to hire an assistant. In her early twenties, creative, quirky, and artistic, the new hire answered Anna's phones, scheduled her appointments, ran her errands, picked up her lunch, and, in general, did her scut work. At the end of each day, Anna demanded that the girl clear everything off of her prize desk—*everything*—and wipe it down with Windex so the Formica glistened. The next time Anna was in the office, she wanted to be able to sit at a spartan, shiny work surface with absolutely nothing on it, which is the way her desk usually appeared to the astonishment of those whose desks were piled high with old newspapers, magazines, press releases, and cardboard coffee cups like real working journalists.

One of the veteran *New York* staffers was Ruth Gilbert, a tough old bird—she finally retired when she turned eighty—who wrote the column "In and Around Town" about things to do in the city. One of her favorite places to visit was Haiti, and she frequently brought back wooden dolls, supposedly good-luck charms, and gave them to special people. As a present, she left one of those tokens on Anna's desk.

The next morning, Anna came in and "freaked" when she saw the curio, possibly thinking it was a voodoo doll that was left there by one of the many staffers whom she sensed disliked her. At the same time, she was furious that someone had, as one eyewitness recalls, "sullied this pristine surface of her desk by leaving her a little gift." Anna is said to have reprimanded her innocent assistant, who soon quit, for permitting the trespass to occur. She was the first in a long line of young female assistants who "came and went like butterflies in the night." The Anna desk incident became the talk of the office.

Compulsive and obsessive was the way a number of her colleagues viewed her after it happened.

When Gilbert heard about Anna's reaction, she, too, was spitting fire. As a colleague notes of the late and lamented editor, "She was the kind of woman who if somebody said something wrong or she heard something unfair would say, 'Fuck that shit!' " And that's what she said about Anna's hissy fit.

Anna felt a lot of animosity from other staffers because of her behavior and attitude, which caused her some insecurity. At one point early on, she let her hair down a bit and plaintively asked a colleague, Nancy McKeon, "I don't really belong here, do I?"

Trailing behind Anna to the new job was her trusted and loyal stylist-helper, Georgia Gunn. In the years since they started working together, nothing seemed to have changed in what appeared to be their master-slave relationship. By the time Gunn got to *New York,* she still worked like a "fucking fiend" for Anna, who "abused her dreadfully," says the *New York* colleague. "Anna's a classic bully and does it around people with whom she can get away with it. People were just afraid of her. Look how Martha Stewart got away with treating people badly all those years. They have the same mentality, a huge amount of hubris. Anna has an incredible force of will."

Jordan Schaps, *New York*'s cover editor, had a somewhat different view. He feels the two had a "love-hate relationship," that there were good and bad feelings between them, and an indecipherable bond that kept them working together. But the source maintains, "Georgia was a slave and she was treated as such. Anybody who worked directly for Anna was treated abominably. But if Anna had to work one-on-one with you, or she needed something from you, she behaved differently. She played nice."

One confrontation occurred early on with some people in the photo and art departments, with which Anna worked closely. Those departments handled her fashion shots and were responsible for making her layouts look good, but the staff could sabotage her work if they felt they were being treated shabbily, which is how they felt from day one.

"She threw fits, she showed no respect, she acted completely inappropriately," asserts the source, who witnessed Anna's behavior.

Complaints were made to photo editor Karen Mullarkey, a six-foot-tall cowgirl type who possessed major clout and had a great reputation in the photography world; she was a protégée of the noted photographer Oliviero Toscani. She'd also worked at *Life, Rolling Stone,* and *Newsweek.* Unlike others, Mullarkey wasn't afraid to confront Anna, and she did. In front of an eyewitness in the newsroom, Mullarkey pulled Anna aside and, towering over her, read her the riot act.

"You don't have the right to behave that way to these people," she said firmly. "They don't work for you like Georgia does. You can treat her like a dog, but not the people who work for me, because if you do it to people who work for me, I'll assume you did it to me, and I'll get ugly. Don't go there. I fight for keeps."

Anna was stunned and said nothing. Aware that Mullarkey could make life difficult for her, she knew when to back off.

"Anna had checked out Karen thoroughly and realized she was not a good enemy to have," notes the source. "Anna's too smart of a general, and she's a believer in keeping your enemies closer than your friends, so she wasn't about to go up against her. I think she was also intrigued by the fact that Karen wasn't afraid of her."

After almost a dozen years in the business, Anna still wasn't considered a writer, so Quita McMath, an associate editor who had the reputation as a "clever writer," was assigned to pen the fashion layouts in consultation with her. "She would sit down and *try* to tell me what point she was trying to make, or what was important about the clothes," says McMath, whose Texas accent was in striking opposition to Anna's British, which drove both of them crazy. "I once wrote something about hats and she kept wanting to say that they were 'witty,' while I was trying to say it another way, using a pun or an American phrase that she wasn't familiar with. All she could say was, 'But they're so *witty*. Can't you see that, they're *witty* hats.' I always had the feeling that she felt I was beneath her social station because we had no personal connection, and I was a little bit intimidated by her."

Anna got fed up with McMath and, during a week when the writer was on vacation, Nancy McKeon filled in for her. Anna went to Kosner and got the green light to have McKeon assigned as McMath's permanent replacement, and McMath was relieved to go back to her other duties. But McKeon ran into some of the same problems every other writer who worked with Anna encountered. "She could not tell me *why* somebody was interesting or dressed well, or what she or he did was of significance," states McKeon. "She'd say, 'But they have such great *personal* style.' All she kept saying was, 'It's *personal* style.' Oh, my God, if I heard that one more time . . . And I'd think, okay, that's three or four words, how does the rest go?"

McKeon, who later went on to become a powerhouse editor at *The Washington Post,* said she should have felt flattered that Anna had chosen her to do her writing. But instead her reaction was like that of others on staff. "We all felt taken over by Anna. . . . If ruthless means being totally faithful to one's own vision and not bowing to anyone else's, then yes, Anna's ruthless. If you're being told that what you've done is rubbish, one of Anna's favorite words, and it's a matter of your own taste, it's hard not to feel hurt or slighted. And Anna doesn't hesitate to tell you."

A *New York* editor had always wondered what made Anna act the way she did, terrorizing and abusing others and making certain people feel bad. By the time Anna left *New York,* the editor had learned enough about her that she felt she had a good take on what she saw as a fascinating, very private, and enigmatic persona.

"Anna was *very* needy, and her ways of dealing with being needy were to always—*always*—be on the offensive, get them before they get you. She didn't care about having good friends. She only wanted to be in control, to be in charge. That was paramount to her and was more important than people liking her. If she controlled everything, she felt safe. And people who have to be in that much control can be out of control. She had this insecurity, this lack of sense of self. She's very studied—every detail was important, every aspect of her life was programmed. Her goals were very clear, and they weren't about human relationships. The reason she never had any good friends was because she decided friends were not going to be the answer for her."

twenty-two

A Territorial Grab

Anna's imperious British manner quickly grated on some of her American colleagues at *New York*. They began to razz her, one by telling her, "Your father's British, your mother's American. Well, honey, it's like Judaism, you're the religion of your mother, so you're an American." Anna, who could dish it out, usually could take it, too, and kept a stiff upper lip. But on at least one occasion she was, to everyone's surprise, brought to tears by an innocent and lighthearted prank.

The temperature in *New York*'s newsroom was either too hot or too cold, and on one particularly scorching summer afternoon Anna pulled her bob off of her forehead and neck and rubber-banded it into a topknot. One of the office clowns, noticing her new look, did the same to his hair, and soon everyone in the office joined in. Even Ed Kosner came out of his office, doffed his Dunhill jacket, and put his hair up.

Anna, who usually ignored everyone around her, had no idea what was going on. "But when she got up from her desk to take a walk through the office, she suddenly looked around and was stunned to see everybody with their hair up just like hers," recalls Jordan Schaps, one of the few staffers with whom she had bonded. "She realized she was being made sport of, burst into tears, and left the office for the day. I guess her English sensibility didn't like being the butt of that kind of humor. She didn't laugh and get the joke."

There were attempts to bring Anna into the *New York* family fold, such as invitations to staff social gatherings, one of which was an old-fashioned New England–style clambake. When she got the invitation, Anna was stymied. "What is a clambake?" she asked a colleague. It's really fun, she was told—lobster, clams, corn, beer, and everyone has a rollicking good time on the beach.

"Everyone was there in old jeans, shorts, and T-shirts, and Anna shows up draped in a complete Issye Miyake white, pleated three-piece outfit, with the stiletto shoes," recalls a colleague, still laughing about the moment years later. "I said, 'You know, Anna, we're going to be sitting on the sand.' But she didn't have to. The men all jumped to attention and laid down blankets and jackets for her, and while everyone was eating with their hands, Anna was using utensils. She could always run the show, even at a clambake."

One of the keys to Anna's success was the way she managed to snag creative photographers to work for her—most of them men—and have them work hard to make her look good. "The thing she did so well was she never acted happy with their work," notes a former *New York* editor, "so these guys were always jumping through hoops and doing backflips for her. And the way she kept them doing that was to let them know they hadn't quite measured up."

Anna was always on the lookout for creative shooters to add to her stable, so when she got a call from Andrea Blanche, who said she had a story idea, she instantly made an appointment to meet for drinks. Blanche hadn't been aware of Anna until she saw a couple of her layouts in *New York* and thought they had a lot of style. An "idea person," Blanche felt that her concept might fit well with the kind of work Anna was doing. "I found her very receptive to meet with me," she says. "My reputation was established, she knew of me, and that's why she took the call and agreed to get together."

While Blanche was a female shooter, she was special to Anna because she shot for *Vogue* and was one of Alex Liberman's favorites. Anna wouldn't have taken the time for anyone less.

They met at a restaurant for about a half hour while Blanche pitched her "journalistic fashion idea" that she felt would fit in with what *New York* was doing. Anna sat and listened intently, leaning back in her chair, her hands resting on the table, not touching her wine and not taking any notes. Blanche, who's outgoing, noticed that Anna showed no reaction, acted "reserved," and appeared "aloof." When Blanche was finished, Anna gave her reaction. "She told me right then and there she didn't like the idea and that it wasn't something she could use or was good enough for the magazine."

Naturally, Blanche was both "disappointed" and "surprised" because she usually had a good take on what editors liked. "I always try to fit the story to the editor, and I believed this fit with her."

Blanche thanked Anna for her time, and the two parted company.

Not long after, Blanche was leafing through the latest issue of *New York* when she froze. Staring back at her was "exactly" the story idea she had pitched and Anna had rejected, shot by a male photographer.

Blanche was shocked, and the thoughts that raced through her mind about Anna at that moment were, as she recalls years later, "not very good things! I think you're always surprised when you feel somebody has stolen something from you and has given your idea to somebody else. After all, my ideas are, to me, how I make a living, so it's hard to take when you know someone's lifted from you." Blanche says the politics at *Vogue* in those days permitted such things to happen, and one had to adapt to it to stay in the game there. "But Anna was a new person, *New York* a new venue, so I took her at her word. When I saw my story in the magazine, I was very upset and I probably shouted some profanities."

Another prominent photographer with whom Anna had problems was Oliviero Toscani—but this time *she* took the brunt of the abuse. Anna was working on a piece with Jordan Schaps, who was shocked by the scene that played out. Toscani had arrived late from Paris and got to the magazine weary from the trip. But Anna, working on a tight deadline, needed to get started immediately.

"We were waiting for him like acolytes because he was a talented, brilliant man, but instead of him being gracious, he was devastatingly brutal to Anna," says Schaps. "He didn't like the clothes, didn't like the girls, and was just a brute, a sarcastic brute. He strode around like an angry peacock and proceeded to criticize everything Anna had laid out, and he was so brutal that he reduced Anna to tears. I was shocked at his behavior and surprised at her vulnerability."

In fact, Toscani admired Anna's taste and creativity, but unlike other photographers he refused to be intimidated by her. As a colleague of his notes, "If Anna tried to pull any of her crap with him, it wouldn't work. He didn't need her approval. She needed his. That's why he could make her cry and is probably why he did it—just to remind her of that."

Not everything with Anna was always so psychologically complex, especially when she was working with the likes of the fun-loving photographer Guy Le Baube, who caused the star of one of Anna's first big fashion shoots for *New York* to have a panic attack. The story was called "Heat of the Night," and featured a stunning young model from North Carolina named Andie MacDowell, who went on to become an actress and a cosmetics spokeswoman.

The setting was a narrow ledge after dark outside the midtown Manhattan penthouse office of Dianne B. Le Baube, mostly given a free hand by Anna because his work was worth it, had decided he wanted to have MacDowell in the foreground, with the Empire State Building in the background, but on a slant and not level with his camera.

This was in the days before something like that could be cheated in with computer software, so Le Baube decided to jerry-rig a platform with side rails and extend it out the window, some thirty stories above the street, and slant it. Anna had borrowed a classic chair from the Museum of Modern Art that would be placed on the platform, and MacDowell would be shot seated in the chair. It was a dangerous setup.

But the only aspect Anna argued against was Le Baube's proposal to have a floor fan blowing up the pantyless MacDowell's designer dress. He thought it would help keep her cool and also give the dress the effect of a billowing sail, with the Empire State Building resembling a sailboat leaning against the wind. But Anna felt it was dangerously windy enough at the altitude where they were working and that MacDowell "didn't need a breeze between her legs."

The actual shooting went well, and the photos turned out beautifully. But Andie MacDowell's physical and emotional state was a different story at the end of the hour of picture taking.

"Andie has very beautiful eyes but very poor eyesight," says Le Baube. "It wasn't until we were done shooting that she realized she was two feet away from the edge on the thirtieth floor with absolutely no panties on—and she suffers from vertigo. She suddenly got dizzy and scared and started to cry, and began yelling she didn't want to be there. What was funny was that Andie is half blind, and she never realized we put her in such a dangerous situation. When she realized it, she started to scream.

"The beauty of it was that Anna dealt with it very well. I always liked to experiment, and Anna let me do exactly what I wanted," he says. "I could have had Andie MacDowell walking on a thread between two buildings and Anna wouldn't have blinked an eye. She just wanted the photos."

More aggressive, ambitious, and confident than ever, Anna saw an opportunity to widen her power base at *New York* from strictly fashion. She was in charge initially of the special spring and fall fashion issues, but she then moved into furniture design, personality pieces, and all forms of style. "She took over design and the food issues," says a former editor. "She talked Kosner into giving her all of that. He was giving her everything she wanted."

Anna saw that she could make such a territorial grab without stepping on many toes. Having closely studied the terrain and now seeing it in a fresh way, she realized there was a style vacuum at the magazine that only she was able to fill. She got Kosner's ear and imposed direction, suggesting ideas no one else on staff had ever thought of, or produced, because her talent was all so visual. So she bulldozed forward, just like any enterprising, ambitious, and driven man who might have been in the same position, and with the same foresight.

"She branched out and made up for the failure of imagination of the rest of us," says Nancy McKeon, who was writing all of Anna's copy. "At the same time, she took herself seriously in a very frivolous profession because her real project and commodity was herself.

"She wanted to clean up *New York* magazine and bring in a touch of style, so she conceived this rotation—a page of home furnishings one week, a page of fashion the next, a page of girl-around-town celebrity something or other the following week—and this rotation brought a whole new level of photography and style thinking to *New York* that was very positive. But everything she did made *everyone* resentful."

For Anna, it was a perfect time to be working as a fashion editor in New York, a period, as she later described it, "when artists, fashion designers, and interior decorators were in fierce competition with each other for celebrity status." She explained her sense of things to Kosner, who gave her carte blanche to take advantage of the situation—"to break away from the usual catalog formula of fashion journalism." As it turned out, the decorators and artists were "delighted to be photographed next to gorgeous girls, and the approach seemed to go down well."

But some of the pieces Anna proposed seemed to have absolutely no relevancy and left McKeon and other staffers baffled.

One girl-around-town story was about a minor British actress named Clio Goldsmith. Goldsmith had performed nude scenes in several French and Italian B movies in the early eighties that showed on late-night cable. It was during that time that Anna decided to feature her in *New York* for no other discernible reason than she was starring in another lame sex farce called *Le Cadeau* (The Gift) and was going to spend a bit of time in Manhattan.

Whatever the reason, Anna directed McKeon to write some text blocks to go with photos of Goldsmith. The wordsmith was, for once, stymied; she couldn't figure out what to do because Anna gave her no other information or direction. Moreover, McKeon couldn't discern why anything about this obscure actress should be published other than the fact that one Brit apparently was publicizing another, and so she went to Kosner and asked, "What the hell is this? Why are we doing this? What can I do here?"

Kosner's lame response was, "Oh, it's interesting. Do it for Anna." And that was that.

According to McKeon and others, Kosner and his wife, Julie Baumgold, a contributing writer at *New York* at the time, had "social ambitions" and saw Anna as a shining star in their glitzy Manhattan firmament. "Kosner saw Anna turning part of *New York* into a fashion, trend-setting magazine, which I guess he figured would work well for him and Julie on the cocktail circuit," notes a colleague.

At the same time, like so many other men, Kosner was captivated and enchanted by Anna, who knew how to work it and how to read him. "She figured here's this guy who has this sort of vision of himself, who's social, who always mentioned that he bought his suits at Paul Stuart," maintains McKeon. "Anna was very sexy in a total, very all-girl kind of way. It was a Japanese moment, so she would wear these outfits loose and without a bra, and she had a succulent body—very slim, but not the anorexic thing she has since done where she's all head. She would always dab on perfume before she went in to see Ed. So she very much had a feeling about herself that she was a weapon, that she herself was a power."

Another editor recalls how Anna would stride into Kosner's office "in high heels, beautifully dressed, bat those big eyes and say to him, 'I know you'll agree with this . . . ,' and get whatever she wanted."

Besides being mesmerized by her, Kosner was knocked out by Anna's work, such as the time she commissioned a group of well-known artists to paint backdrops with models in the foreground. "It was a perfect piece for us and, at the time, a real first," he said later. "It's become such a standard now, but Anna was definitely the first." Anna had developed many social contacts in the art world, such as glitzy New York gallery owner Mary Boone, who represented artists such as David Salle and Julian Schnabel, who participated in the model backdrop shoot. (Anna may have borrowed the concept from what set designers had done on Cathy McGowan's *Ready, Steady, Go!* dance show when she was a teenager in London.)

As Kosner gave Anna free rein to do whatever she wanted within her expanding domain, a territorial fear gripped some of the women staffers, among them "Best Bets" Corky Pollan, who cowrote blurbs with McKeon about things to buy, see, and do in the city. Pollan feared the worst about Anna and became like a modern-day Paul Revere out to warn the villagers about an imminent British attack. And her fear was warranted. Anna despised "Best Bets." She saw it as a mélange of boring pictures, with uninteresting tips, so she got Kosner's ear and started dummying up well-orchestrated still lifes, such as a layout with everything white. "The woman's ego knew no bounds," McKeon says. Realizing that a revolution was afoot in the newsroom, Pollan kept the enemy under tight surveillance from her "Best Bets" desk, which was in close range of Anna's white Formica command post.

"Corky came to me one day," recalls McKeon, "and said, 'We'd better watch our backs.' I asked her what she meant, and she said, 'Well, if we don't watch out, this woman's going to take over *everything*. She's going to take all our jobs.' And two weeks later Anna's profiles, those one-page fashion, home furnishings, celebrity things, started appearing. But 'Best Bets' remained."

One of those shoots involved a piece shot in a house Anna had rented in the Hamptons. The cover photograph Anna was going for was of a model with an extremely expensive piece of cowhide draped over her in a stylish way. Working on the shoot with her was Jordan Schaps, who had certain qualms about Anna's concept and finally felt compelled to express his view. "So you really think," he asked Anna, "that the *New York* magazine woman is going to go out and spend five thousand dollars on a leather hide to throw around?" Anna stared hard at him for a few seconds and then declared, " 'My dear, I don't care if they go to Woolworth's and buy a lump of fabric. It's not about fashion, it's about style.' And I was very impressed by what she said, and *loved* the attitude."

There were three cardinal sins at *New York* under Kosner that could result in an employee's dismissal: lying on an expense report, leaking internal information about a story, and giving copy or photo approval to a subject. Anna committed the third. Anyone else would have been fired on the spot, but because the violator was Anna, Kosner bent the rules.

After completing a summer fashions shoot with the sultry new actress Rachel Ward, Anna approached another editor who worked on the story and requested the final layout photos, saying she wanted to send them to Ward for her approval—an absolute no-no, which Anna knew.

The editor was in for an even greater surprise while examining the model release form. In writing, Anna had actually given Ward, who wasn't a major star at the time, approval over the photos. Bottom line: If the Australian-born actress didn't like the pictures and refused to approve them, the story might have to be killed. "Maybe Anna didn't expect Ward would hold us to it. Maybe Anna thought she could get away with it," speculates the associate years later.

Even back then, long before celebrities became a staple of every form of magazine from sports to fashion, Anna foresaw that sexy stars like Ward on the cover sold copies, and she was desperate to reel one in, at whatever cost.

The editor explained the dire situation to Kosner, who summoned Anna for a private meeting. "Ed was not pleased," the staffer recalls, and the next morning Anna was aboard a flight to la-la land—on her own dime—with the photos in hand, in hopes of getting the subject's approval. Kosner had apparently given Anna permission to ignore the no-show rule in order to salvage the story.

As it turned out, Ward gave her okay for the inside photos but refused to approve the shot of her in a bathing suit destined for *New York*'s cover. A last-ditch attempt was made from New York to get her cooperation, but then she broke into tears on the phone. "She was crying and saying, 'I look so fat! Please don't use it,'" a staffer says, and Ward was told, "'. . . if that's the way you feel, honey, we won't do it.'"

In the end, the story ran, but with a noncelebrity model on the cover, considerably weakening its impact.

Anna acted as if nothing out of the ordinary had happened, never looked back, and plowed forward determined to reach her goal.

And that goal seemed closer than ever because of a fashionista of the first order, a veteran *Vogue* editor by the name of Polly Mellen. Like Anna, Mellen had a reputation as a perfectionist, was difficult to work for, lived for fashion, and possessed a keen eye and astute taste.

Mellen had first spotted Anna back in the seventies when Anna first started covering the collections as a young editor for *Harpers & Queen*. Mellen was intrigued. "Who is *that* beautiful little girl, how fascinating she is, how she dresses, how she mixes," Mellen recalls thinking. "I noticed her intensity and how she *never* took many notes, and I'm always fascinated with people who don't take notes . . . they want to remember what interests *them* the most."

Over the years, when they ran into each other, they'd chat about everything—from clothes to men, especially men, "because Anna liked men in a very interesting way, and she was a flirt."

In 1982, Anna's second year at *New York*, they bumped into each other at a hotel restaurant and Anna used the opportunity to pitch herself to Mellen.

"I sat next to her, we talked, and at the end I told her, 'I wish you were at *Vogue*,'" Mellen recalls.

"So do I," responded Anna, who surely was walking on air by the time she got back to her desk at *New York*.

Meanwhile, back at *Vogue*, Mellen gushed about Anna to editor in chief Grace Mirabella, a Jersey girl who had worked her way up through the ranks under Diana Vreeland. "I said to Grace, 'Grace, you have to meet this incredible young woman at *New York* magazine. She's *so* with it. Her eye is fantastic. She doesn't just dig fashion, she loves houses, she loves art, she loves *everything.'* And it was really what Grace and I had been talking about for some time, which is fashion is not *just* fashion—it's *lifestyle.* I said to Grace, 'I wish you could meet her.'"

Mirabella agreed to a meeting, which Mellen zealously arranged. Anna, of course, had to do it on the sly so no one at *New York* would find out she was starting to job-hunt.

"Anna arrived, and I met her at the elevator and brought her into Grace's office, and I left so they could talk together," says Mellen.

The meeting didn't last long, possibly ten minutes max, before Mirabella's secretary summoned Mellen to come and pick up her visitor.

"I took Anna to the elevator, and I asked, 'How did it go? I so hope it went well!' And she said briskly, 'I'm not sure, but anyway, thank you, and good-bye.'"

The elevator door closed and she was gone.

By the time Mellen got back to her office there was a message waiting for her from Mirabella to come to the inner sanctum forthwith. Such a summons from the usually easygoing editor in chief was a bad sign. The thought that raced through Mellen's mind was, "Oh, my God, not good. What could have happened?" When Mellen arrived, Grace recapped the brief interview, an event the very dramatic Mellen says she's never forgotten.

"At the end, Grace said to Anna, 'If you came to *Vogue,* what job would you like?' And Anna said, 'Well, actually, the job I would like is *your* job.'" Mirabella instantly terminated the discussion and had Anna ushered out. Mellen listened in stunned silence and then managed to utter a few words: "'Oh, dear. Oh, God!' Grace was very displeased. Anna didn't have a chance with her."

Anna didn't get the gold ring this time, but it wouldn't be long before Mirabella's world would be turned upside down by the arrogant young woman she had quickly dispatched.

twenty-three

Mister Big

A new man had come into Anna's life, one who would have an immense impact on her emotional and professional life.

The first indication that Anna and Michael Stone's relationship was on the rocks was heralded by bouquets of flowers from the other man that began arriving for her at the desk of Laurie Schechter, Anna's second personal assistant in little more than a year. Anna's world was her work, she had few close friends, so it was usually her office colleagues who first got wind of changes in her personal life. Schechter's radar caught the first blip.

With enough things on her plate working for a driven boss, Schechter now had to discreetly juggle two bouquets arriving daily—one from Stone, who had always sent a bouquet a day to Anna, and one from the new man. To Schechter, Anna was a "very powerful presence" with "a sexual power . . . an attraction, an appeal" to men.

Schechter was an intense, hard worker whom Anna hired away from the Dianne B. boutique in October 1982. At twenty-four, she was loyal and well liked by Anna, who would become her mentor and help her in the fashion world, where she later became a top stylist and editor in her own right. The two had first met when Anna came to Dianne B. to shop or pull clothing for fashion shoots when she was at *Savvy*, and Anna saw what a detail-oriented, compulsive worker Schechter was—a virtual Anna clone in terms of dedication and devotion to her job.

A graduate of Wesleyan University, where she had been an art history major, Schechter was intrigued by Anna, too. "She was this kind of mystery," she says, "enveloped in the Wayfarer sunglasses, the Comme des Garçons, or layers of Issye Miyake, the bob in her face." Unlike other personal assistants who would toil for Anna over the years and eventually leave or be fired, Schechter had incredible staying power, a strong personality, and "a passion for fashion." Most important, she was a no-nonsense workaholic with unquestioned devotion to do whatever Anna needed, around the clock if necessary.

"There was no basic training," Schechter notes. "Anna's not someone who takes you in hand. It's more she throws you in the water and you'll either sink or swim. If you swim well, you'll do well, and if you don't, you're not long for the position or the association."

The first day the twelve-thousand-dollar-a-year Schechter showed up for work, Anna seemed surprised to see her and immediately sent her out for coffee. Schechter was convinced that Anna had "forgotten I was starting" and "wasn't quite prepared" to deal with her.

By the time she returned, though, Anna began tossing out orders for things she required for a scheduled weekend shoot. "I need a van . . . call Brian Bantry . . . I need Sam McKnight for hair . . ." The list went on and on. Schechter had no idea what was what and who was who, and Anna wasn't telling her. She could see she'd quickly have to figure it all out for herself— "sink or swim." That was life working for Anna. When Bantry hung up on Schechter, saying McKnight wasn't available, Anna's response, "clipped and British," was, "Well, convince him!"

From the Hamptons a day or so later, Anna called to let Schechter know in no uncertain terms that they'd almost been killed in a rainstorm because the van the assistant had rented for her had bald tires and a terrible driver. "I knew by the tone of her voice she was not pleased," recalls Schechter years later, laughing at the moment. "She said they almost died. I was mortified. I called the rental agency and conveyed to them that I was in a new job and unless they got a new van out there they were about to get me fired because I almost killed my new boss."

In her first two weeks working for Anna, the five-foot-two-inch Schechter lost eight pounds and had started drinking cup after cup of strong coffee to keep herself going because of Anna's many demands; Schechter quickly dubbed her "laser brain." At one point another staffer who sat nearby was concerned and asked, "Are you okay?" Looking back to that time, she says, "I didn't stop moving in those first two weeks. Ten cups of coffee a day didn't help." Schechter realized that things had finally started to go well when Anna came in one morning and gave her a gift of clothing, something Anna had started doing as a teen with Vivienne Lasky. In Schechter's case, it was an Agnès B. white cotton skirt. "When Anna's pleased she'll do a gesture like that. She has a very maternal side to her, which she doesn't show a lot, but it's there for people she cares about."

By the time the competing bouquets of flowers started arriving for Anna from her two men of the moment—"the flowers wars," as Schechter refers to it—she had the PA job under control and Anna's many needs and wants down to a near science. Most important, she was discreet and had Anna's total trust. The word in the newsroom was that Anna had told Schechter "not to get too friendly with the other people." And she didn't. While she doesn't recall Anna ever giving her such a directive, she notes, "I didn't talk to people anyway. I'm not a watercooler person."

An assistant with that kind of prudence was necessary for a woman boss who had started having an affair.

After the flowers from the new man started arriving at the office—they were always from a chic florist, and Anna's favorite was a mixed arrangement with fragrant Easter lilies—Schechter began fielding calls from him, usually in late morning. And then Anna would give a breezy "I'm off to lunch." The curious thing was that when she returned from lunch, she'd declare, "I'm *starving*. I have to have something to eat!" So Schechter would have to run out and get her the lunch that Anna supposedly just had.

"I'd be like, okay, I guess it wasn't a *food* lunch."

And soon the new man, a serious-looking and ponderous-sounding South African–born psychiatrist by the name of David Shaffer, began arriving to collect Anna at the end of the day.

She was thirty-two and he was forty-five.

And then Stone would telephone looking for her, and Schechter would tell him, "She left already."

"She played Michael on a short leash," says another associate of Anna's at *New York*. "She was very good at orchestration and knew how to drive him crazy. Michael was jealous."

Anna began her relationship with Shaffer before ending with Stone, according to friends such as Paul Sinclaire, a close member of Anna's circle at the time. Anna was following the same pattern as when she was stepping out on Jon Bradshaw during her time at *Harper's Bazaar*. However, this time she didn't confide in anyone early on, including her trusted assistant, nor did she ask her to make up excuses about where she was when Stone called asking her whereabouts.

"It was not discussed," says Schechter. "Anna's obviously the woman of the unspoken word, so she didn't have to tell me. And I don't think you needed to be a rocket scientist to know what was going on. Maybe at some point she told me 'I have a new address,' and that was kind of the extent of it."

Acquaintances and colleagues of Anna's in and out of *New York* magazine who knew her and Stone had mixed views of them as a couple as their relationship matured.

"Anna loved having great moments in her life, but she was bored out of her mind with Michael," maintains Sinclaire. "I must have been to dinner at the loft at least twenty times, and she would get up and go to bed."

Earle Mack asserts, "Anna was never particularly happy with Michael and certainly not toward the end. She would have left Michael even if David Shaffer hadn't come into the picture."

New York's Nancy McKeon knew that Anna and Stone had been living together, and she had helped Stone edit some of his pieces when he had started writing for the magazine. She didn't think much of him and couldn't understand what Anna saw in him, other than his money. "At one point Anna said to me that she was in love with somebody else, and I asked was he English or American, and she said, 'Ah, English of course,' like it was the accent that got her, and that was David."

Many in the circle knew that Anna had "dumped" Stone, who is said to have been "devastated," although he later claimed that he and Anna had remained friends. In fact, Anna tended to remain on good terms with most of the many men in her life, and they remained loyal to her. "She was always a good friend to men," observes Annabel Hodin, Anna's pal from her *Harpers*

& Queen days. "Being an intelligent woman, she didn't lose them when the romance was over." Stone indicated to former *Savvy* executive editor Susan Edmiston, whom he started seeing when he tried to sell articles to her after she moved to *Redbook,* that he felt the relationship with Anna ended because her career was more important to her than he was. "He once said something along the lines of 'I wasn't as ambitious or as hardworking as Anna,' and he told me that she worked 'eighteen hours a day,' that she was 'very focused,' and that 'the relationship just never worked.'"

Meanwhile, some in Anna's small circle at *New York* were surprised that she would fall for someone like Shaffer, who was so different from the bad-boy types to whom Anna always was attracted.

"I didn't care for the way Michael treated Anna," says Jordan Schaps, who had also worked with Stone on artwork for stories he did at *New York.* "He was supermacho, and kind of like a Sylvester Stallone Jewish version, out to prove to you what a tough guy he was, and felt he needed to express that with her. Maybe he was jealous of her . . . one of those guys who dealt differently with women than men. I thought he was game playing, the way a guy can do with important, strong, elegant women. I don't know if it was rivalry, but I tend to think she was perceived to be more important than he was, and I'm sure he didn't care for that.

"Anna was more professionally assured of herself than she was personally assured of herself, and I think women like that unfortunately are vulnerable to brutes. At a certain point, for whatever reason, she decided she'd had enough.

"David was totally different, though I never found him attractive and always thought it was interesting she'd get involved with someone so quite different from Michael. David was much more refined, subdued, and extremely intelligent. David just appeared one day as a presence in Anna's life, then started picking her up at the office, and then started appearing with her at functions. I liked David and felt he was complex. But I was just surprised that someone as glamorous and elegant as Anna would be with someone like David, who I found rather drab."

News of Anna's new man leaped across the pond, and an item appeared in the gossip column of London's *Mail On Sunday,* presumably written by Nigel Dempster. The blurb said that she was involved with an "ageing divorcé" and noted, "For some reason Shaffer is known to his friends as 'ET.'

Why, I wonder?" The snarky comment was in reference to the extraterrestrial of movie fame, who some apparently thought the distinguished psychatrist resembled because of his large bald pate and big eyes.

The scion of a well-to-do South African family, Shaffer was born on April 20, 1936, and spent his early childhood in a splendorous Johannesburg home where his father, Isaac, was the chairman of New Union Goldfields, which also had offices in London. "His father made a fortune," a Shaffer friend says. Young Shaffer was then sent off to boarding school at the acclaimed L'École Internationale de Genève, which was founded in 1924 by the eminent sociologist Adolphe Ferrière and a German scholar named Elisabeth Rotten, both of Geneva's Rousseau Institute, to cater to the wealthy children of League of Nations officials, businessmen, and financiers.

After he completed high school, he went to London and got his MB and BS degrees at the University of London, was a member of the Royal College of Physicians, and received his academic diploma in psychological medicine at the University of London. While he was a student, the whole swinging sixties London thing was happening, and Shaffer, who had his own fun-loving streak, savored the excitement of the era. The bright and affluent young bachelor, who enjoyed fine food and wine, traveled through some of the same in-clubs as Anna, ate in the best restaurants, and, like Anna, had his own posh crowd—a hip posse that reportedly included Dudley Moore and Jonathan Miller, then starring in the biting social and political satire *Beyond the Fringe*.

Shaffer also had a taste for beautiful women, the younger the better, it seemed. One who caught the eye of the trendy twenty-four-year-old doctor who had decided to specialize in the problems of teenagers was a sixteen-year-old exotic named Serena who favored bright red lipstick and dressed at Biba and Mary Quant. Like other teenagers who were descending on London from the hinterlands to join the party, she wanted more excitement. She'd left her stepmother's home in seaside Brighton, having tired of meals of pigs' feet and headcheese, and was hanging out on the Brighton Pier with the local mods and rockers. One of several gorgeous sisters, Serena wanted something more sophisticated for herself. She found it with Shaffer, and the two fell in love.

In the late sixties, Shaffer was a clinical and research fellow in pediatric neurology and child development at Yale University Medical School. It was during that time in America that he became friends, by odd coincidence, with Anna's first serious teenage love, the writer Piers Paul Read. "He was very good company in a very sort of quiet way," recalls Read. "He was very fascinated with what was going on, very interested in people." One such person, the one who introduced Shaffer to Read, was a wild-looking Australian surreal artist and druggie by the name of Brett Whiteley. Like Read at Columbia University, Whiteley was studying on a Harkness Foundation Scholarship. Shaffer had become close chums with Whiteley at New York's Chelsea Hotel, once described as a "Tower of Babel of creativity and bad behavior," where the two young men had rooms while pursuing their studies. An alcoholic and a drug addict, Whiteley later died of a heroin overdose.

After completing his fellowship, Shaffer returned to London, where he held positions at Maudsley Hospital and continued his relationship with Serena. When she turned eighteen, he took her to meet his family in Johannesburg. Serena was astounded by their opulent lifestyle: Shaffer's mother had her beautiful dining table set with the great Danish silversmith Georg Jensen's Pyramide silverware that was worth a small fortune—the same forks and knives used by royalty. They married when she was twenty and he was thirty in 1966, around the same time Anna was quitting North London Collegiate at sixteen because of the miniskirt imbroglio.

The Shaffers lived a voguish life on Priory Walk in west London, and Serena—like Anna, who was at *Harpers & Queen* at the time—was deeply involved in the London fashion scene as a designer; it's possible the two had even met. As part of the fashion world, she acted as a liaison in London for the designer Ralph Lauren, and when he visited she would show him around and look for British goods that he could remake and put under his label. In return she got a 5 percent commission on anything he ordered. The Shaffers had an interesting social set that is said to have included fashionistas Michael Roberts and André Leon Talley, who later became protégés of Anna's, and lots of artists and writers, like Piers Read, who thought of Serena as "very sweet, very plucky. We [he and Shaffer] were tired of grown-up women. I was, certainly."

Another "very old friend" of David and Serena Shaffer from the early seventies in London was the American upscale fashion retailer Dianne Benson. "Serena was just a *baby* when she and David were married, and he was sort of like a father figure and introduced her to the world of London," she says. "She was much, *much* younger and *very* funky. She was a designer and used to have a little fashion company called Electric Circus or something, and I knew her because I bought her clothing when I was a hot buyer for Henri Bendel in New York before I opened Dianne B.

"Serena had a collection that she designed and sold out of the downstairs of their house, a funky collection she practically handmade herself—checks and big buttons. David and Serena were very social. They entertained constantly and had big dinners in one of those big dining room–kitchen combinations. I have a very fond spot in my heart for the Shaffers because I met one of the great loves of my life at their kitchen table on Priory Walk."

David and Serena Shaffer had two sons in the late sixties, Joseph Jacob and Samuel. The young Mrs. Shaffer liked to dabble in the kitchen, where she started cooking fancy meals, which would pay off down the road, egged on by the British food writer Elizabeth David, who had a trendy grocery around the corner.

In 1977, just as Anna was starting at *Viva*, the Shaffer family moved to New York and set up temporary housekeeping in David Shaffer's favorite bohemian haunt, the Chelsea Hotel, while they were renovating a town house in Greenwich Village. Shaffer took a position as clinical professor of psychiatry at Columbia University College of Physicians and Surgeons. While staying at the Chelsea, his wife became enthralled with the interesting artists and writers who crashed there.

Once settled in their house, "We entertained everybody—my husband was very taken with it all," Serena once said. Their entertaining was enhanced with some twenty place settings of that elegant Jensen silverware that Shaffer had inherited when his mother died. Serena Shaffer viewed the family heirloom as a "symbol of stability, a symbol of luxury, of civility."

In 1982, five years after the Shaffers moved to New York, their marriage fell apart—so much for stability—and Anna and David Shaffer soon became an item.

"We were bitterly not talking to each other," the former Mrs. Shaffer has said. So angry at her husband was she that she tossed the beloved Shaffer family silverware into a suitcase, carted it off to Shaffer's town house, and left it on the floor, but snitched a few pieces before she left because "there was so much of it, I thought he'd never miss it." She left without locking the door, she has said, and someone broke in and walked off with the valuable booty. Looking back on the incident, she said, "I could have had the whole thing."

There are a number of accounts of what happened to the Shaffers' marriage.

Serena once revealed to a friend that the breakup was all her fault. "She said she fell in love with an artist," the friend, who also happened to be a pal of Anna's, says. "Serena told me the artist dumped her pretty quickly, and Serena said she was contrite, was sorry she did it, and felt she had made a terrible mistake. She said she was young and impetuous and did a stupid thing, lost her head and made a horrible mistake. I felt this was coming from the inside, an honest revelation, not the sort of thing you'd get up and tell everybody, and she said it ruefully. It certainly makes for an interesting story, and it made me think of Serena as this hot bohemian—and maybe that's what she wanted me to think."

Dianne Benson said it was her understanding, too, that Serena left her husband for another man. "It was pretty devastating for David," she says. "From what I could see he was a very devoted husband. Serena and the new man had a house in upstate New York, some idyllic life, and she seemed very complacent for a while before she fired herself up again. That relationship fell apart. And then all of a sudden David turned up with Anna. I think Serena and everybody else was quite shocked. One would not have expected that from David Shaffer, at least I would not have. He was something of an intellectual, but he certainly was not a dashing prince."

Serena remarried, to a man named Curt Bass, from a wealthy New York Jewish family in the knitwear business. The couple lived in the New York suburbs and were considering settling in the Virgin Islands, where they were building an expensive home. But the Basses had their differences, and the marriage became increasingly rocky and ended in divorce. Serena Bass went on to build a successful catering business in New York with a celebrity and fashion industry clientele, including *Vogue*. In partnership with her son, Sam, she also opened a trendy little red-and-black bar and lounge with tin palm trees and Moroccan lamps called Serena in the basement of her old haunt,

the Chelsea Hotel, and became a New York celebrity of sorts, a publicity
hound whose name often appeared in the city's tabloid gossip columns.

Sometime while the Shaffers were splitting up, Anna and David Shaffer
met. Some say they were introduced at a dinner party by Eric Boman, the
artist-turned-photographer whom Anna had known and worked with since
her days at *Harpers & Queen*. Others say Cupid was played by Paul Sinclaire,
who had had what he calls "a very special and very private relationship with
Anna over many, many years"—the two often shopped together and even
traded clothes.

Sinclaire became a trusted adviser to Anna. "We'd speak on the phone
three times a day," he says. There were quirks about Anna, though, that annoyed him, such as at times acting as if she didn't know him. "I'd see her in
the front row of a show and rush over and say hi, and she'd briskly go, 'Hello,
darling,' as if she knew me for two minutes. And then we'd have dinner later
that night and I'd say, 'What was *that* all about?' and she'd brush it off and
say, 'Well, you know I can't see very well.' She was wonderful at kind of
working a mystique."

Sinclaire also knew and was friendly with Shaffer separately. "He was kind
of great and kind of very offbeat," he observes. Sinclaire first met him when
David and Serena Shaffer stayed with Dianne Benson and her husband, Irving, who were renting a home in Quogue, in the Hamptons, from model
agency head Eileen Ford.

Sinclaire, very well connected in the art world, claims credit for bringing
Anna and Shaffer together. "I was at a dinner party for [the artist] Lee Kras-
ner, and David was there and I said, 'David, I'm having a small birthday
party at my apartment. Why don't you come?' David had separated from Serena, and they were in the middle of a not-wonderful divorce. He was *so* depressed. I'd also invited Anna, and she arrived with Michael Stone. Anna and
David met at the party and *he* fell in love, he *truly* fell in love. The next thing
I know he's ringing me up at eleven o'clock at night to bring me a perfectly
dreadful Carlos Falci handbag he'd bought for Anna to see if I thought she'd
like it."

Dianne Benson recalls, too, how Shaffer "used to haunt" her shops on
Madison Avenue and in SoHo, "looking for presents for Anna."

Talk about the new man in Anna's life spread when the two were spotted by a friend walking romantically arm in arm on a Manhattan street.

Shaffer and Anna began a serious relationship that would climax in a long marriage, two children, and a scandalous divorce that would hit the tabloids and send shockwaves through the fashion capitals of the world. All of that, though, was far in the future.

A highly emotional event occurred for Anna around the time she was dropping Stone and hooking up with Shaffer. On December 5, 1982, on his beloved island of Jamaica, the man considered the one true love of Anna's life, Jon Bradshaw, married the movie producer Carolyn Pfeiffer—eleven years older than Anna—with whom he had been living for some five years.

"Even though they hadn't been romantically involved for some time," says a member of Anna's and Bradshaw's circle, "Anna was absolutely devastated. It's clear she still loved him in her heart of hearts, still felt possessive of him, still wanted his advice and guidance, and was absolutely jealous he'd gotten married. Not to play armchair psychiatrist, but I've always felt Anna got involved with her shrink [Shaffer] as part of some sort of subconscious competition with Bradshaw, one-upsmanship, if you will. Bradshaw got married, so I'll find someone worthy to marry myself."

Despite Bradshaw's marriage and the couple's subsequent adoption of a baby girl, Anna never cut the connection.

"Even after they broke up, even after Carolyn and Bradshaw were married, Anna continued calling him, seeking his advice," says a confidante of Pfeiffer's, who retained her name after the marriage. "When Anna would call and Carolyn answered, Anna was icy and just barely civil. Anna never tried to chat her up. She'd just say, 'Is Bradshaw there?' Anna was still *very* needy of Bradshaw, and this was very flattering to him. She used to cry *all* the time with him on the phone—she was *constantly* crying—and Carolyn felt that was how she manipulated Bradshaw, how she pushed his buttons. There was a sort of whole neediness that Anna had.

"She would talk to him about *every* decision in her life and what did he think. Anna wasn't terribly open with a lot of people. she's a very guarded woman, but she was *very* open with him. She played like a little girl with him—it was part of her way. She would seek advice from him about her relationship with Michael Stone and other boyfriends. It was a father-daughter thing. Even after Anna married David she would still call Bradshaw. Carolyn wasn't very happy about it because she knew Bradshaw still totally adored Anna."

Carolyn Pfeiffer was more than unhappy, according to the writer Joanie McDonell, who was part of their circle. "Carolyn *hated* Anna," McDonell asserts. "Carolyn absolutely *forbid* Bradshaw from having anything to do with Anna; she wouldn't even want to hear Anna's name. Carolyn and Bradshaw stayed with me sometimes when they came to New York, and she'd say to Bradshaw, 'Anna's *so* ungrateful, that *bitch*! Do you think she'd ever tell anyone everything you did for her! She would *never* tell anyone!' And Bradshaw would just laugh—I can see him laughing—and say, 'Oh, who cares, *who cares*, Carolyn. What difference does it make?'"

twenty-four

In *Vogue*

By 1983, Anna had become a powerhouse at *New York*. She had been promoted to senior editor and was giving the mostly newsy and service-oriented weekly a reputation as a style arbiter with her splashy and creative layouts that encompassed everything from chic fashion to trendy interior design and glamorous home entertaining.

Anna had hit on the right mix at the right time. The era of the young urban professional, the yuppie, the defining figure of the Reagan eighties, was in full swing. With lots of disposable income and sophisticated taste, real or wannabe, this self-indulgent army of cash-rich, plastic-wielding consumers—many of them double income, no-kids-yet couples—were buying like crazy, seeking out clothing, household goods, and home furnishings, and they wanted advice on what to buy and where to buy it. Anna had her finger on their pulse. As a result, her features lured new advertisers—boutiques, restaurants, furniture stores—which gave her even greater cachet.

Around the same time, another creative, driven, and ambitious woman, the onetime stockbroker and caterer Martha Stewart, had earned the sobriquet "Diva of Domesticity" with the publication of her groundbreaking best seller *Entertaining*, which covered some of the same territory that Anna was now marking, which was simply called lifestyle. Stewart's book—and success—had not gone unnoticed by Anna, who was now thought of as *New York*'s

"Diva of Fashion and Style." Both Anna and Martha were catering to the affluent younger generation and promoting the high life.

Anna's byline and features were finally noticed by the sharp and creative
eye of Alex Liberman at *Vogue,* just as she had hoped. Moreover, Polly
Mellen, long a supporter, had also gotten his ear about Anna after Grace
Mirabella had booted her out of her office.

In the spring of 1983, the great man summoned Anna to a meeting at
Condé Nast's headquarters, then at 350 Madison Avenue, where Anna had
had that embarrassing ten-minute session with Mirabella some months earlier. Mirabella had never mentioned anything to Liberman about the young
woman who arrogantly proclaimed she wanted her job. And Liberman never
told Mirabella that he had an intense interest in Anna—who also told him at
their meeting that she wanted to be *Vogue's* new editor in chief. Liberman,
who had developed qualms about Mirabella's abilities, was quite taken with
Anna and had something big in mind for her.

He was impressed mostly by a piece she had recently done in which she
asked a few trendy Manhattan artists such as Francesco Clemente and David
Salle to interpret the New York collections.

It took her over the top.

Liberman and his boss, Si Newhouse, were Anglophiles and had a thing
for young, bright, ambitious—and pretty—Brits. In the same time frame that
Liberman began to focus on Anna at *New York,* he and Newhouse had just
brought a savvy blond, blue-eyed, buxom sharpie named Tina Brown over
from London, where as editor of the venerable *Tatler* she had tripled circulation. They made her first a consultant to the circulation-challenged *Vanity
Fair* and soon after appointed her its editor in chief. She turned the magazine
around with a gossipy and glitzy mix of well-written and -reported stories
about the high and low life of society, with major emphasis on celebrities.

The elegant, sophisticated, and artistic Liberman adored the glamour of
Hollywood and often tacked up on his office walls, to the shock and consternation of his chic subordinates, the garish front pages of the celebrity-driven
supermarket tabloids, telling his editors they should be doing something similar only more upscale. One Condé Nast editor in chief, Linda Wells of *Allure,* once said, "There is a tension that you get from the juxtaposition of the
high and the low that [Liberman] was fascinated with. A lot of delicious

naughtiness can be had using tabloid devices." Tina Brown knew the score and made *Vanity Fair* into what some thought was a slicker literate version of the *National Enquirer.*

A few weeks after Anna's first meeting with Liberman, a second session was arranged, this time with more secrecy. Because Liberman was concerned that Mirabella might spot her, the meeting was held at the country house and sculpture studio that Liberman and his wife, Tatiana, owned in Warren, Connecticut, a short distance from Anna's aunt Jean Read's place.

For advice and counsel, and for his take on the talks, Anna brought along her beau, David Shaffer, who had fast become her "in-house shrink, personal adviser, guru, and Svengali regarding her career and her life in general," as one close observer notes. Another says, "David took care of her. She always needed taking care of. With David, she was looking for security. It was a turbulent time. She had a goal—*Vogue*—and David was responsible, secure, and bright. He could guide her." Paul Sinclaire put it this way: "David was very supportive helping her to achieve keeping it together and getting what she wanted. David was *so* ambitious for her."

The meeting was on a weekday, and Shaffer picked up Anna at *New York* for the ninety-minute drive to Litchfield County. En route they stopped at a motel so Anna could change out of her office outfit into something a bit more alluring, a miniskirt of micro proportions. Later, Liberman would say of Anna, "I was absolutely enchanted with her," though Mrs. Liberman, a sexy woman in her day, was put off by the tiny skirt and the fact that Anna had chosen to bring zinnias as an offering rather than roses or a plant. As usual, Anna had seduced the man and put off the woman.

In any case, Liberman laid an offer on the table—but not the editorship of *Vogue* as Anna had hoped. It was a new position with undefined duties. Essentially, he wanted to get her in place and move her up or around when the need suited him, and mainly get her away from the competition. Nevertheless, Anna was thrilled. All of her hard work, her enormous creativity, her toughness on the way up, her manipulations and machinations had finally paid off. Getting into *Vogue* had always been her goal, and it was about to become a reality.

Back at *New York,* Anna let a few people know that *Vogue* had called with a job offer she knew she couldn't refuse. And so she began pitting her editor,

Ed Kosner, against Alex Liberman and vice versa, hoping to get the best deal possible.

"It was never a question of *if* she'd stay at *New York;* it was always how long it would take for her to get Alex and Si's attention," says a *New York* insider in whom Anna had confided. "Anna told me she heard from Liberman and she asked me, 'How do I play it?' I said, 'Look, sweetie, *Vogue* is where you belong. That's always been your goal.' I said, 'You need to let Ed [Kosner] know in a gentle way, so he will rebound and do everything he can to keep you, which of course will make Liberman want you even more.' Anna played it beautifully. She'd go in and have a private meeting with Ed, and then she'd come out and look at me and smile, and she'd say, 'Now I'm going to have lunch with Liberman.' Then she'd go to Liberman and say that Ed had told her she could have more pages in the magazine and get more money."

At one point, Kosner, who had enlisted his wife, Julie Baumgold, to get involved in the effort to keep Anna from going to *Vogue*, actually thought he had her. Anna did feel an allegiance to the magazine that gave her such great visibility, permitting her to become a big fish in a relatively small pond.

Nancy McKeon says, "It was a little messy. Anna was talking to Ed, she was talking to [managing editor] Laurie Jones, and she seemed not sure what she wanted to do because Grace Mirabella was still at *Vogue*. At one point she decided to stay at *New York*. But then Liberman called again, and she decided to leave. It was a matter of a couple of weeks."

Word of Anna's negotiations got out, and talk flew around the *New York* newsroom that she had sealed the deal by spending a seductive weekend with the Libermans; that Liberman, in his seventies, was chasing her around the swimming pool, and that Anna was coquettishly trying to avoid his advances, all of which was most likely unfounded but made for great watercooler chatter among those who were envious of her success.

One of the biggest sticking points in Anna's discussions with Liberman wasn't over money but rather over title. They didn't want to give her one at first, but Anna (and Shaffer) insisted, according to a *Vogue* insider. They finally settled on a new title that had never been used. It was rather nebulous but had panache and a powerful ring to it. Anna was, in the end, satisfied that the masthead would list her as *Vogue's* creative director. And while salary wasn't a big issue, Anna managed almost to double what she was making at *New York,* with a starting salary of $125,000 annually and many perks, including a clothing allowance, all expenses, and a car and driver, among others, which was typical of the lures Condé Nast used to recruit major talent.

After Anna sealed the deal with Liberman, she immediately telephoned her father in London from her desk at *New York* to proudly announce the news. A staffer who overheard the conversation claims there was a long pause as Anna listened intently to the most influential man in her life. The busybody took the long silence on Anna's end to mean that Charles Wintour was questioning his faith in his daughter's abilities to perform at *Vogue,* because Anna's response, almost childlike, was, "Well, Daddy, *they* think I can do the job."

Anna's first order of business after she was hired, but just before she started at *Vogue* in mid-October 1983—a couple of weeks before her thirty-fourth birthday—was to buy herself an expensive new wardrobe, consisting mainly of chic and sexy business suits that would fit in with the Condé Nast corporate culture.

That dress-for-success advice came from her friend Paul Sinclaire, whose fashion judgment she trusted implicitly. He told her, "*Ahna,* only Chanel will do." Sinclaire accompanied Anna to a chic shop in Millburn, New Jersey, of all places, where she bought "a bunch" of Chanel suits with tight, short skirts.

Soon after Sinclaire started working with Anna at *Vogue,* the magazine's newly appointed features editor, Amy Gross, with whom Anna would work closely, pulled Sinclaire aside and said, "You know, Paul, she's *not* a Russian princess. What's with the '*Ahna*'?"

For the first time since she got into the fashion magazine game, Anna demanded and was given an office, a two-room suite, actually, by her new mentor, Alex Liberman.

It was a sun-filled affair with a view of Manhattan's towers of commerce. She had her name and title placed on the door. And as she did at *New York,* Anna brought in her own desk and furnishings, which were surrounded by glamorous accoutrements supplied by Condé Nast. She also brought along her loyal and hardworking assistant, Laurie Schechter, who had her own little outer office and became the new creative director's gatekeeper.

One wall of Anna's domain was covered with a single-patterned repeating image that had no borders, and each pattern blurred into the next in some curious psychological-like fashion, inspiring some to wonder whether Dr. David Shaffer himself had decorated the office.

Grace Mirabella was beside herself. As she put it, "Anna created an office within the office . . . and *against* me . . . to undermine my thinking and my authority."

She was furious about Anna's hiring. She was incredulous that Anna would be given the new executive title of creative director, which she saw as a position that Liberman had handed to Anna on a silver platter because he was so infatuated with her. Mirabella knew the score, she'd heard it from Anna's own lips, so she knew she was in for a battle. As Polly Mellen, one of Mirabella's key lieutenants, put it years later, "Anna loves men and had a special appeal to men. It's not an appeal that every man would dig, but for the ones that dug it, her appeal was special. She's an incredible flirt and it hit certain men hard. That's what happened to Alex Liberman and to Si Newhouse—they were smitten, *totally*. Not only did she have the brains, but she had the come-hither. She knows how to do it."

Mirabella saw Anna as the enemy or, as she venomously put it later, "a vision of skinniness in black sunglasses and Chanel suits . . . cold [and] suspicious of everyone loyal to me, and autocratic in her working style."

Mirabella had come to the realization that Liberman, whom she always thought was *her* mentor and supporter, had become a turncoat and fallen "so in love" with Anna that he gave her "the power" to do whatever she wanted at *Vogue.*

Notes Laurie Schechter, "It was obviously a painful experience for Grace. . . . Anna was obviously a threat, and Grace was right in thinking so."

Now that Anna had been hired at the world's fashion bible with a high-sounding title, she was, for the first time, on the news media's radar. In her previous jobs in the United States and in England, she was essentially small-time, not worthy of big-time coverage, except for the nasty bits that appeared in the British gossip columns and in *Private Eye,* therefore, the extremely private Anna had been able to keep her personal life well hidden.

But coming to *Vogue* put her in the big leagues and would change all of that. From 1983 on, her every move, her every promotion, her every appearance at an event, the women she lunched with and the men she was seen with, became fodder for the news and gossip machine. Anna's movements and decisions were dissected and speculated upon by the press, both fashion and general. Anna's past was virtually unknown to the media and the public, but her present and future lives would be placed under a journalistic microscope as if she were a newly discovered life-form.

One of the first articles appeared in the trade magazine *Adweek* under the glowing headline "The Up-and-Comers: Wintour Displays Knack for the New."

Mirabella and her loyalists read the puff piece and shuddered. Anna, with amazing chutzpah, boasted that she was "working on every aspect of the magazine, from the choice of photographers to the overall design." Taking a direct shot at Mirabella, Anna claimed, "There hasn't been someone who can stand back a bit and say, 'What can we do with this fashion sitting to make it different? Maybe there's a new photographer we should try. Maybe we can mix painting and illustration to add dimension to the pages.' . . . One of my concerns at *Vogue* is to bring in other aspects, to mix fashion with anything that's cultural. That's the direction I think things are going."

Interestingly, in discussing her early years, Anna mentioned nothing about her schooling, or lack thereof, but made claims such as having "studied the classics with an emphasis on English literature" and possessing "a fondness for Jane Austen." The article stated erroneously that Anna moved to the United States and "spent several years working for Carrie Donovan at *Harper's Bazaar,*" when in fact she worked there less than a year and was fired. There was absolutely no mention of her tenure at the cursed *Viva,* let alone *Savvy,* or of her Paris fling.

She turned on the charm and the author of the article gave her four stars, declaring that Anna "has been expanding the traditional boundaries of fashion coverage," that her "influence has begun filtering through the pages" of *Vogue,* and that her articles "made for provocative reading." While the *Adweek* piece states that "colleagues praise her knack for discovering new talents and producing new talents and producing inspired fashion and interior design features," none was quoted, an indication of the fear that now permeated *Vogue.* Anna defenders were worried about repercussions from Mirabella, and Mirabella advocates were afraid of what would happen to them if Anna took power. The only person who was quoted by name didn't even work at *Vogue*: Her old boss and acolyte, Ed Kosner from *New York* magazine, called her "a real star."

What Anna hadn't told the reporter from *Adweek,* and what no one leaked to the press because of fear of reprisal, was that she had started arrogantly showing up at meetings of the editorial board, "shaking her head, obviously disagreeing" with everything Mirabella said or did.

Mirabella soon discovered that Anna, on the sly, was redoing layouts without the editor in chief's permission, was contracting for new photos that Mirabella and her fashion editors weren't aware of, and was beginning to oversee fashion sittings that weren't in her domain.

Anna was carving up the magazine as if it were her own and reporting only to Liberman. Looking back on that time, Mirabella stated that Anna was so optimistic that she'd be named to the top job that she considered her more "a momentary inconvenience than a person she might have to answer to or contend with."

All hell was breaking loose at America's most elegant and ladylike fashion magazine, and Anna, anxious to take over, was the wily provocateur.

twenty-five

Golden Handcuffs

While Grace Mirabella and her capos were blindsided by Anna's blatant efforts to sabotage the old regime, the new creative director also worked in more subtle ways to infuriate her editor in chief.

One instance of her cattiness once again involved Andrea Blanche, the photographer whose story idea she had stolen and used in her early days at *New York* magazine. Long associated with *Vogue*, Blanche had learned that Anna had been hired before many others knew. "I remember getting this pain in my stomach when I heard. At that moment I had a premonition that things were not going to be easy for me at *Vogue*. What happened when she stole my idea had always stayed with me."

But Anna's shabby treatment of Blanche at *New York* was then, and this was now, and Anna realized she had to play nice because she knew that Blanche was special to Alex Liberman.

As with Anna, Liberman had first seen Blanche's photos in *New York* magazine long before Anna had come to work there.

"I had these pages that were very successful, and Liberman called me to his office and said, 'Why do I see these in *New York* and I don't see them in *Vogue*?' And that's the same reason he hired Anna—because her work was getting so much attention. Plus, she's very beguiling and attractive, so I could see where he could fall for her. He was a big flirt, Liberman.

"I worked very closely with Alex and he had sort of taken me under his wing, and he wanted Anna and me to get along, to *try* to get along, and he kind of put us together, so she had to deal with me," says Blanche. "Anna was on a turf that I had been working on since 1979, and I had to protect myself, but I wanted to create a situation where we could work together."

The two went to lunch. Blanche was naturally wary and this time didn't toss out any story ideas but knew she would have to pitch Anna and sell herself to her once again. And she was quite aware that the only reason Anna was acting as if nothing bad had ever happened between them was that she knew Liberman adored Blanche.

But it still came as a shock to Blanche when she received a call out of the blue from Anna inviting her to a social event at a new Manhattan discotheque called Palladium. "I almost dropped my pants!" she remembers. "It was right out of left field."

As Blanche would soon realize, Anna may have had subtle ulterior motives for asking Blanche to join her and David Shaffer and her cousin Oliver James, who was visiting from England, for an evening of what was supposed to be fun.

Their party eventually grew to include a business entrepreneur and acquaintance of Anna's named Sam Waksal, who would gain notoriety and go to prison years later in the ImClone trading case that also indirectly caused Martha Stewart's downfall. At the time of the Palladium event, though, Blanche and the high-riding Waksal were "kind of in and out of a relationship." And Waksal had started seeing Anna's friend and *Vogue* contributing writer Joan Juliet Buck, who also showed up that night. So it wasn't very pleasant for Blanche and caused her to wonder, "What's going on here? Why was I invited? Is this a bad dream?"

The next morning the apparent reason for the curious machinations of the previous night appeared to come into the photographer's focus.

Blanche arrived at a scheduled meeting at *Vogue* to discuss an assignment with Liberman and Mirabella. Anna also showed up, at Liberman's side, where she always seemed to position herself as if they were epoxied together.

But before they got a chance to discuss the proposed shoot, Anna enthusiastically jumped in and raved to Mirabella about the absolutely marvelous time she had had the night before with Andrea Blanche, whom she made to seem like her new best friend.

"This, of course, made Grace *crazy*," notes Blanche, who began to speculate that Anna had invited her to the disco party for the sole purpose of being able to boast to Mirabella about it, make it seem as if Blanche was in Anna's corner and "totally piss off Grace and put me in a really awkward position. I felt I was brought into something very messy, with mind games going on. I thought it was very Byzantine *and* Machiavellian."

Soon Blanche found herself getting less rather than more work from *Vogue*. In one instance, Anna had Blanche shoot a portrait of her but afterward said she didn't like it. "Anna's relationship with me was frosty," she observes. "I don't think she ever really liked the fact that I was Liberman's 'baby,' so to speak, and that she had to deal with me. I was not *her* find, so she just never really embraced the situation or me."

Down the road, when Anna was named editor in chief of British *Vogue* at Liberman's behest and returned to London for a time, Blanche would find herself in an even more distasteful situation.

The fear of Anna that gripped *Vogue*—the palpable dread of what she would or wouldn't do to the venerable magazine, and who would or wouldn't be demoted, axed, or sent off to the North Pole to cover deep-freeze couture— was so widespread it also devolved onto her assistant, Laurie Schechter.

At her job interview with a Condé Nast human resources woman, she was sternly informed, "Even though you're working for Anna Wintour, you're *not* going to have any power."

Schechter was dumbfounded. "To me what she was saying was, 'We are all so scared here of [Anna's] coming.' It revealed the fears at Condé Nast even about someone who was going to work for Anna as an assistant. But obviously Anna's demeanor was forbidding and foreboding. Everybody was quaking in their boots. It's that sink-or-swim attitude at Condé Nast—if they drown, we'll just get new ones." But Schechter had learned one big lesson from Anna that helped her move forward: In order to get ahead she had to "charm it and work it, do whatever you needed to do, and not be afraid."

Though she had the total support of Liberman, Anna was lost in her early days as creative director, mainly because everyone was afraid and didn't want to get too close. She got little cooperation from the old guard. Just as Anna was showing her claws and pushing herself into every area of the magazine, Grace Mirabella was defending her long-held domain with equal ferocity.

"It was a tough transition for Anna," observes Schechter. "She had no friends at *Vogue* per se. Anna can live without friends, but she didn't have *any*. She didn't have any supporters there, quite honestly."

Besides Liberman and Si Newhouse, her greatest cheerleader was David Shaffer, who continued to send her a daily bouquet of flowers to show his love and keep up her morale. Anna had a virtual hotline to him, was on the phone with him constantly seeking advice and guidance.

"He was supportive as a partner, and his professional knowledge and experience was important to her," says Schechter. "How much better could it be to have your shrink at home. They had a very strong relationship. They communicated a lot. I'm sure if . . . she was at a point of being broken to some extent, then he would be a great help." But Schechter doesn't feel Anna was "broken," but rather faced "culture shock of sorts in the sense that she tried to contribute and do things she may have been mandated to do corporately."

Next to Liberman, Schechter worked more closely with Anna than anyone else did during her creative director period, and she saw the toll the job was taking on her. "She had a hard time at first because prior to that she was a fairly big fish in a good-size pond. Now she was a big fish in a pond of barracudas, and that can take you off your center, and it did to some extent. It wasn't like people were nasty to her, but people just didn't necessarily go out of their way. They did their job and protected their territory."

Schechter, who watched Anna closely, states she suffered "a bit" emotionally during that time. "And that's where David came in. Thank God he was a psychiatrist!" To help Anna, he even chatted up difficult staffers, making them wary of him.

Anna did a supreme job of hiding her fragile emotions from the staff, but every so often a few got a glimpse of what she was going through and were taken aback, because the general consensus was that she was "one tough bitch" and nothing or no one bothered her or got in her way.

"Tell me, I can take it" was her macho response when she bluntly asked colleagues whether or not they liked one of her ideas.

But then there were those other moments.

Polly Mellen had an office next to Anna's, which was several doors down from Mirabella's, and was passing by when she heard a sound that stopped her in her tracks. "I went in and Anna was facing the window, and I realized she was sobbing, her shoulders were heaving, and she was trembling, and when she realized I was there she tried to get control for reasons of pride because she was a very strong young woman." Mellen asked Anna what was wrong, and she said she had had a disagreement because an idea that she had proposed had been accepted by Mirabella and then killed by Mirabella. "This happened more than once, and Anna was totally frustrated," maintains Mellen. "I realized she wanted to be involved in *every* part of the book, but she was being held back. She told me, 'I can't take it . . . I can't go on.' I said, 'Don't say that, please.'"

Despite those scenarios, Anna claimed a couple of years later, when she took over British *Vogue,* that if there was resentment toward her, "I didn't feel it," though she acknowledged "it was very hard in the beginning."

Schechter also saw examples of Anna's anxiety and stress. One afternoon she walked into her office and was surprised to find Anna teary-eyed and extremely upset. When Schechter asked what was wrong, Anna sobbed that she'd broken a tooth, which seemed an odd reason for the emotions she was showing. "I don't know if it was true," Schechter says years later. "I didn't say, 'Open your mouth and let me see.'"

Stressed by the job, Anna, who was as organized as a Palm Pilot, began misplacing or losing important personal items, such as her Ray-Ban Wayfarer sunglasses. She'd go to lunch or to a meeting, and when she returned to her office she discovered they were missing, which drove her up the wall. She'd inadvertently left them in a cab or a restaurant and had to constantly order new ones that were customized for her by an optometrist in SoHo. Because her face is small and Wayfarers are oversize, she'd pay extra to have them constructed to fit her face.

Stories have circulated over the years as to why she always wore sunglasses, inside and out, day or night: for image, was one; to hide behind, was another; a third was that her eyes were sensitive to the bright lights at fashion shows; still a fourth was to hide bags under her eyes.

However, the main reason for the shades was the fact that Anna had very poor eyesight and a dread of losing her sight altogether. The trendy-looking glasses, therefore, weren't just for show and image but were fitted with strong prescription lenses to help her see.

Out of vanity, she chose to wear the stylish Wayfarers, which gave her a glamorous air of mystery, over regular prescription eyeglasses. The glasses are often mentioned by critics of Anna's, such as one writer who noted tongue-in-cheek that there was "reason to believe" Anna was "Satan" and that the sunglasses "are very likely hiding glowing red eyeballs."

A colleague discovered otherwise. She had wandered into Anna's office during her creative director stint and saw a pair of the trademark specs sitting on her desk. Since Anna was away, the staffer couldn't resist trying them on, curious about how she'd look in them.

"I almost fell over because they were such a strong prescription. I got dizzy," she says. "It seemed like she was blind as a bat, and I thought to myself, 'God, how many times have I stood across a room from her and she probably couldn't see me if she wasn't wearing her glasses. I was probably a blur.' She has received so much attention and criticism over the years for wearing sunglasses, but if critics knew that she couldn't see without them then they might have been more sympathetic."

Anna's fear of losing her eyesight had some basis in fact. As her father aged, his eyesight became increasingly worse, and in his last years he'd gone almost completely blind. Friends and his second wife had to read to him, and he purchased from the United States a powerful magnifying frame that was attached to his television set on which books were projected in exceptionally large type, and he'd sit practically with his nose against the screen to read.

"It really was terribly piteous to see this editor who had existed his entire life so keenly on reading newspapers and magazines and books go nearly blind," says his longtime *Evening Standard* colleague Alex Walker. "I was told that there was a congenital illness in the Wintour side of the family that had resulted in this particular kind of blindness. This was an ailment that apparently was hereditary. If Anna, who constantly wore sunglasses, was aware of this, and no doubt she was, the use of those exceptionally dark glasses might not be affectation so much as protection."

After a number of emotional scenes involving Anna, most, if not all, out of public view, Liberman, a genius at Condé Nast corporate politics, took his protégée aside and told her that some battles were worth fighting and others were not winnable—and to forget about the latter.

"Initially, it was hard for Anna," says Schechter, who "adored her" and "felt blessed" to work with her. "Even though she had the title, a great salary, the car service, and the other perks Condé Nast offers, in some ways it was as if she was wearing golden handcuffs because she did not have the same freedom she had before. She had to battle to get people to do work for her, to like her, to want her to be there.

"Anna's not one to reveal herself. It wasn't like suddenly she got a whole lot thinner or had huge horrible bags under her eyes. I know it affected her, but as a professional she would never reveal that. She wouldn't come into the office and slam her door and throw a temper tantrum, or curse someone out behind their back. She didn't work that way. She keeps a very steely exterior, but she's a woman, and human inside. I felt for her because I recognized it was difficult for her, but I never, ever thought, 'Oh, poor Anna,' because I knew she was strong. And I knew how important David was to her as a sounding board, a support system, a sympathetic ear. He was another editor, so to speak."

During this stressful period, Schechter noticed some eccentricities in Anna's behavior that struck her as odd—such as how she'd stand alone in her office and go through her purse picking out pennies and tossing them in the wastebasket, one by one. "I never asked. I just figured pennies were too small for her to consider keeping. She was someone who never had to count her pennies." The other odd thing was Anna's lunch. When she didn't go out for lunch, she had Schechter pick up soup for her at a little place in the West Thirties. While there's nothing strange about soup for lunch, Anna ate it in a curious manner. She'd put a big gob of butter on top, let it melt, and then eat only the butter and little of the soup. "I just saw the soup as a vehicle for the butter, a way to eat butter without seeming so obvious."

Meantime, Mirabella was freaking as Anna continued her assault, taking one hill after another in hopes of reaching the summit and toppling the leader. When Anna couldn't do an end run around Mirabella's veteran fashion editors, such as Polly Mellen and Jade Hobson (Hobson had been at *Vogue* since 1971, and Mellen since 1966), she'd "harass and criticize them," the editor in chief claimed. She asserted that Anna demanded Polaroids of shoots over which she had no say, showed up at sittings that weren't her responsibility, and in some cases, ordered that they be done over.

"I was not a big fan of Anna's," says Hobson, shuddering at the memory of the early days of Anna's tyrannical reign as creative director. "Anna didn't seem to want to work with *any* of the existing staff. She wanted to bring in freelance people, and that didn't sit so well with a number of us."

Anna's desire, as it had been in her previous jobs, was working with her own team of freelance photographers and overseeing the shoots herself. Single-handed power and control and the originality that emanated from it had always been her game, and that's what had caught Liberman's attention in the first place. However, *Vogue* was an entirely different kettle of fish. At *Viva*, at *Savvy*, at *New York*, the fashion coverage was a small part of the over-all editorial content, so Anna, hidden in a corner with an assistant, was able to run things her way, be creative, and make herself and the fashion pages stand out. But *Vogue* had been doing that spectacularly with an army of people, all working together as a team, for decades.

Under Mirabella, the job of overseeing and directing major fashion shoots was the longtime domain of the two talented editors, Hobson and Mellen. "We had absolute autonomy, and she started coming to the shoots, kind of excluding the editor, talking to the photographer, and she just made it *very* uncomfortable and it was rather disruptive," declares Hobson.

A shoot is a creative process—something Anna well knew. It involves a close working relationship with the editor, the photographer, the stylist, and other principals, and the shoot often doesn't take shape until midway through the process, and often the original idea is scrapped or the direction changed because someone conceived a better idea. But Anna's constant intervention virtually destroyed that very important process.

"Her interference made it much more routine and not as creative," asserts Hobson.

Hobson, Mellen, and others felt that Anna was watching over their shoulder, "and *not* in a friendly way, and *not* in a supportive way," says Hobson. "She was rather exclusionary of the editor. It wasn't taken to very happily by the two of us."

Winter collections. Paris, spring 1984. Showdown time, big-time.

Hobson and Mellen were overseeing a shoot in a studio when Anna appeared unexpectedly. "All of a sudden," Hobson remembers vividly, "it was a cast of thousands, it seemed, watching and directing, and she destroyed the whole process."

The two editors were beside themselves, according to Mirabella. Furious, they returned to New York and declared "Never again!" in an emergency summit meeting with Liberman and Mirabella. Hobson remembers telling her bosses, "You've got to stop this. We can't deal with it. It's the magazine that's losing out." Mirabella said that the angry editors had actually threatened to strike if Anna didn't get out of their hair. " 'We can't stand her,' they said, and they began, as much as they could, to shut her out of their work."

Years later, however, Mellen says she *always* thought Anna was the right person for the job and that fashion wasn't Mirabella's forte. "I saw Anna as someone who couldn't be avoided, someone you could not turn your back on because that would be a mistake. But I had to be very careful because I was also very close to Grace."

To put a stop to the constant catfights, Liberman was forced to handcuff his protégée. With no other choice, and to avoid a mutiny, he essentially banned Anna from the fashion coverage—a "tough blow to her," observes Schechter, because fashion was what *Vogue* was all about and why Anna always dreamed of being there. "Grace basically went to Liberman and Newhouse and said, 'If she must be here, fine, but I don't want her involved in the fashion.' "

Liberman, who had been devoting his efforts to strengthening the magazine's features section—books, entertaining, living, and style—now assigned Anna to work in that area with features editor Amy Gross, who had been recruited from *Mademoiselle*. Anna's job, as described in a blatantly vague staff announcement, was to "enrich the looks of the pages and bring to the pages other aspects of women's interests."

After that she reluctantly left editors like Hobson and Mellen alone.

Anna wasn't happy with her new assignment, but she brought in some new and talented photographers to work on features and was able to have some influence in that area.

As Schechter points out, "Features was off Anna's work agenda. However, she obviously had a good relationship with Mr. Liberman. I'm sure he fell in love with her, because she can be *very* charming, and I can't define that charm because I'm not a man, and he recognized her talent. I felt instinctually that features was certainly not going to be her resting place. I knew only too well that she was a focused, goal-oriented person and whatever she was looking to accomplish, she would accomplish it."

twenty-six

Marriage Made in Heaven

Anna and David Shaffer had a relatively quick courtship, and in short order he proposed, but she declined to give him an immediate answer. She held on to the expensive ring he gave her but didn't wear it. It wasn't until some months later, in early 1984, that he got the yes he was waiting for, but in the oddest way imaginable.

Shaffer had accompanied Anna to the collections in Paris, the same trip that sparked the showdown with Jade Hobson and Polly Mellen. During their stay she met her father for drinks at the bar at the grand Ritz Hotel. Anna communicated very little with Charles Wintour at that point for a couple of reasons. Besides being totally immersed in her career in New York, she was still seething over his marriage to Audrey Slaughter and his shabby treatment of her mother.

As father and daughter shared a rare intimate moment over drinks, Wintour noticed a "very nice" diamond on the fourth finger of Anna's left hand. When he asked her what was what, she revealed it was her engagement ring, and Shaffer was the lucky guy.

Although he knew that Anna and Shaffer were deeply involved, and he thought of the shrink as "an absolute saint" because of how he looked after her professional and emotional interests, Wintour had no idea their relationship had reached the point of marriage. He was thrilled.

As Wintour admired Anna's ring, Shaffer suddenly arrived at the bar, and his future father-in-law offered him hearty congratulations. Shaffer "looked slightly stunned," and had no idea what was going on. Then Anna slowly raised her hand, and Shaffer saw that she'd finally placed the sparkler on, which caught him as much by surprise as it had her father.

As it turned out, Anna had told Shaffer when he first proposed that she'd put on the ring only when *she* was finally ready to marry him and not before. She chose that relatively unromantic moment at the Ritz bar with her father by her side to signal to Shaffer that she was now saying yes.

Later, Charles Wintour said, "David always tells Anna that was the evening *I* proposed to *him*."

The curious way Anna handled it all said something about the complexity of her relationship with the man who would become her husband, and which partner was ultimately in control in their relationship. As those who know her have stated, Anna's "the *ultimate* control freak" in both her professional and private worlds. It also said something about her relationship with her father and how important his approval was to her at all times, despite her feelings about his remarriage. How many women let their father know they've accepted a proposal of marriage before letting the husband-to-be in on it? But her father's acceptance of her future husband was of supreme importance to Anna. While many in her circle thought Shaffer was an odd choice, he was probably the first man in Anna's life whom Charles Wintour genuinely approved of—and Anna always was a daddy's girl who sought his approval.

Back in New York, Anna dove back into the *Vogue* wars, and she and Shaffer, still not having set a wedding date, began overseeing the renovation of a four-story mid-nineteenth-century brownstone in Greenwich Village. The house, with its warren of small rooms, had been neglected for years and was a shambles, but Anna envisioned it becoming her dream house.

She retained a friend, the high-tech New York architect and designer Alan Buchsbaum, to creatively preserve the original details of the house but also make it modernistic and different.

Anna had met Buchsbaum while she was at *New York* magazine. She had chosen him along with some other well-known interior designers to do some rooms for a dramatic and idiosyncratic layout. Buchsbaum was an architect-designer to the stars who had done work for Christie Brinkley, Bette Midler, Diane Keaton, and Ellen Barkin, among others. But he and Anna had a special relationship, and they often socialized, had dinner together, gossiped, and talked style. He was one of many gay men in her circle, mainly because of the fashion world in which she was immersed. Like Anna, Buchsbaum was reserved, but he lit up whenever he saw her. Sadly, he was one of the first American victims of AIDS in her life, at fifty-one, in 1987. After his death, the disease became one of Anna's causes through a New York fund-raising fashion event called Seventh on Sale.

According to Davis Sprinkle, who had been Buchsbaum's business colleague, Anna ran the whole house renovation show. "She really had some very particular ideas about the feeling of the interior," Sprinkle notes years later. "David was certainly less involved with the entire project. He definitely let her call the shots. She controlled most of the process. If she didn't like something, she would certainly let me know." Had she been difficult to work with? "With time," he says, "we forget the bad stuff."

With a fetish for neatness and stark minimalism, Anna wanted lots of open space, so walls were torn down, and at least one room, the dining room, had a pair of columns rather than a door marking the entrance. "Working at a magazine is an endless feast for the eyes; you spend your days looking at things," she once said in discussing the renovation. "Therefore, I prefer a more calm environment at home."

Along with his work on the house, Buchsbaum designed a high-tech and elegant power desk for Anna, which later was marketed by the French firm Ecart International as the "Wintour Table." Its wooden frame and legs, set on the diagonal, were made of ebonized mahogany, and its top was a lacquered sheet of cold steel. Anna prized the desk more than anything she owned and had it shipped twice across the Atlantic—when she took over British *Vogue* and when she returned to become editor in chief of *House & Garden* and then American *Vogue*.

Like her bob and sunglasses, the desk became an element of the Wintour signature, and she was still running things from behind it in 2004 in her second decade in charge of *Vogue*. She has described it as "very clean," "a bit quirky," and having "a sense of humor." The desk has no drawers because she said she likes to have "everything out in the open," and she loves its narrowness, because "I don't want people to feel far away when they're talking to me. . . . It's not so corporate." (Because Anna's desk was a table, anyone could see through the bottom. "It was funny," recalls Laurie Schechter, "because Anna sat behind her desk like a man, with her legs apart . . .")

With the renovation at the house ongoing, Anna and Shaffer rented a loft with Hudson River views in what was then the far West Village, near the West Side Highway. The apartment, which permitted Anna to see the *QE2* arrive and depart, was in a forbidding building that had once been a penitentiary. The owner of the loft was a British woman named Charlotte Noel, who had been part of Anna's small circle when she first arrived in New York a decade earlier. Noel was escaping the area and moving uptown, and Anna and Shaffer decided to lease her place because it was close to their town house renovation and friends in the area.

"It was an ordinary loft with very little furniture and not very comfy, and the area was very grim, pretty ugly, quite bleak when they rented from me," she says. "Dead bodies were being fished out of the river, the Mafia controlled all the garbage trucks, and there were all those gay S&M clubs. It was really rough." But Anna and Shaffer didn't mind, thought it was a cool milieu, and took the place after a brief negotiation over the rent.

"Anna was really very brusque, very businesslike, and David was rather sort of pathetic, asking things like, 'Could I go and get the sofas covered?' " recalls Noel. "What I'm saying is, Anna did nothing, and so he was left to do a lot of what you would think of as sort of womanly tasks. It was an odd relationship, and I always thought it was an odd coupling. They didn't seem to match physically or mentally."

Still others had an opposing view—that the editor and the psychiatrist were in love and were good for each other. Shaffer had intellect, was a solid father figure, and Anna was cool and sexy and younger, someone who was good for the shrink's ego and gave him panache. "Anna wanted children. She wanted stability," a friend notes.

On Friday September 7, 1984, in their town house on MacDougal Street, Anna and Shaffer, then chief of the child psychiatry department of the Columbia Presbyterian Medical Center and the New York State Psychiatric Institute, were married in a ceremony conducted by New York Civil Court Judge Elliott Wilk. In two months, Anna would turn thirty-five. Shaffer was forty-eight. The brief notice in the next day's *New York Times,* probably the first time Anna had ever received a mention in the paper, noted that she would retain her last name. Of her previous work history, only *Harpers & Queen* and *New York* magazine were mentioned, presumably based on information she had submitted.

Other than the engraved invitations that had gone out, there was nothing fancy about what one guest describes as "a very beautiful, very simple, very quiet intimate family wedding—very civil, not splashy."

After the ceremony, all of the guests, about twenty, including Anna's divorced parents, her father's new wife, Anna's siblings, and work friends of Anna's, such as Ed Kosner, Jean Pagliuso and her husband, Laurie Schechter, and Georgia Gunn, adjourned to the living-room area, where a long table was set up for a celebratory supper.

At the table, Charles Wintour stood and offered a toast to his favorite child and her groom. He told the gathering that Anna was finally fulfilling a dream, to be an editor at *Vogue.* Years later Anna recalled that day: "My father is enormously kind in a subtle kind of way. At my wedding, when he made his speech, he mentioned each of David's two children at length to show them they were an important part of the family." (The two teenage boys from Shaffer's first marriage would live with the newlyweds.)

"It was a lovely wedding," says Schechter. "They had written their own vows. To me it seemed like a good match."

Others, like Anna's colleague and friend Paul Sinclaire, felt differently and were surprised that they had tied the knot. "I would have bet that the wedding would not have happened, and if it did their marriage would have lasted a year and a half, let alone having two kids," he says, looking back years later, after the affair that ended the marriage. "I think she married David because he was so smart. A beauty he never was."

Some seven months after the nuptials, around April 1985, Anna became pregnant.

That same month, in London, an event occurred that also would have great implications for her future. After twenty-one years at the helm of British *Vogue,* fashion doyenne Beatrix Miller announced her departure, saying she was leaving to write books. Like Anna, Miller was a tough cookie and a taskmaster. To a potential employee, she would proclaim gruffly, "You have exactly two minutes. Tell me about yourself." She once called some four dozen staffers into her office and told them, "I want you all to know that, as far as I'm concerned, the July issue is a write-off. There is a mistake on page 136." But she was beloved. Now the staff pondered their future as rumors began to float across the pond that a nuclear blast in the skinny form of Anna Wintour was coming their way. But top management at Condé Nast—Si Newhouse and Alex Liberman—remained mum as to who Miller's replacement would be.

Meanwhile, the pregnant Anna was busy pushing her way around the front of the book at *Vogue* and becoming stepmother to Shaffer's sons.

Mutual friends of Shaffer's ex-wife and of Anna and David Shaffer observe that the psychiatrist "must have applied his own brand of psychology to the kids" because they turned out so well. "The boys were always extraordinary and precocious in the best way, and always seemed close to their parents," says Dianne Benson.

Shaffer's sons occupied the ground floor of the couple's beautiful town house, starkly furnished with simple but elegant English and American antique pieces—a Federal sofa, a Queen Anne tallboy, Empire chairs, lots of books, bare wood floors, area rugs. Anna lived the life *Vogue* represented, and that was a gold bullion asset, which had made her even more of an attraction to Alex Liberman and ultimately to Si Newhouse.

The top floor of the house had been gutted from four small rooms into the couple's large master bedroom suite, minimally furnished with a bed covered with a simple white down comforter, two Victorian slipper chairs, a Queen Anne bureau, an English oak chest, and Anna's collection of small pieces made of ivory. The bathroom was large—British-style, the kind Anna was used to—and had a fireplace, an old porcelain tub, a marble sink, a large wood-framed mirror from England, and a nineteenth-century wicker chair.

Anna had decided that every room had to be airy, open, uncluttered; she didn't want a Victorian mélange, which she believed "can look ridiculous when it's re-created in New York apartments. . . . When it's genuine nobody does it better than the English," she boasted in *The New York Times* Sunday *Magazine*, which in 1986 deemed the elegant house and its powerful *Vogue* creative director now worthy of her first big spread.

Regarding Americans and their level of taste, Anna said they were too brand-name and designer driven, which was a curious statement from an ed-

itor at a magazine that promoted and derived its power and revenue from designer and brand names. Nevertheless, she thought the Yanks (wealthy ones,
presumably) were overly obsessed "with owning Biedermeier this or Josef
Hoffman that," and that "designer homes" bored her to death. She noted
that some of her neighbors didn't "get" the redo of her house. When invited
to tour her domicile, she said they "looked around quite perplexed and said, 'I
guess this is what you call a loft house.' "

Back at the office, Anna had given Laurie Schechter more responsibility—of
coordinating photographers, locations, and such for the nonfashion front of
the book, which Anna now loathingly had to handle at Liberman's directive
alongside Amy Gross. With the Schechter promotion, Anna announced that
she would hire a secretary/editorial assistant to take over the day-to-day routine work. Schechter was relieved—for about a minute.

The new girl was the Hon. Isabella Delves Broughton Blow—Issy (pronounced Izzy) to her friends. She was a busty, voluptuous, beet-red-lipped,
microminiskirted eccentric Brit with a braying laugh who was sort of well
connected back in Mother England. Her grandfather was the wealthy businessman Jock Delves Broughton, the central character in the nonfiction
book and movie *White Mischief*. During World War II, in Kenya, the jealous
Broughton had fatally shot a playboy named Lloyd Erroll, who was fooling
around with his beautiful and much younger wife, Lady Diana Broughton
(played by Greta Scacchi in the 1988 film). Lady Diana was Issy's grandmother.

So into the *Vogue* wars came this fascinating new character as Anna's aide
de camp.

Blow saw an immediate bond with Anna. "She loved fashion with a passion like me. If you look at her, she surrounds herself with obsessive people
like André Leon Talley, all absolutely obsessed with fashion."

Blow says that most of her work for Anna consisted of simple errands like
taking her shoes to the shoemaker to be reheeled—"really dull stuff." She
said she was "very frightened" by Anna's "organization and steely determination. When someone rang up, Anna put the message in a folder. *Everything*
would be filed, *every* conversation would be filed, *every* single piece of paper."

To avoid being criticized by Anna for being sloppy, Blow began washing her own desk at the end of the day with Perrier.

She also saw during her nine-month stint how much Anna leaned on her husband for moral support. "David used to guide her," she says. "I don't think she could have done the job without him. David was a great strategist. He was so rational and precise. Because he was a psychiatrist, he thought more clearly. She spoke to him on the phone all the time. As a psychiatrist he would know how to deal with people."

The bottom line, though, was that she found Anna to be "an inspiration. I idolized her."

Anna liked Blow, Schechter says, "because she was a character. Issy was like a wacky, eccentric British bird. She would come to work in the miniest of skirts and fishnet hose that had rips, probably not because she meant it to be that way but because she tripped and ripped them, and her lipstick was always off the side of her mouth."

Blow's style began to impact the well-oiled functioning of the creative director's office and a war within a war started. Schechter found herself working twice as hard to make sure Blow, who spent a lot of time talking on the phone to friends, was functioning. And other more serious issues arose, such as the time Blow "lost a photographer's portfolio" and "he was threatening to sue for a hundred thousand dollars," asserts Schechter. When Schechter first started working for Anna at *Vogue*, she lost about ten pounds because she'd run up and down thirteen flights of stairs to complete errands rather than waste time waiting for elevators. Now, with Blow on board, "I was near a nervous breakdown. Everyone adored her because she was Dizzy Issy—'Isn't she funny? Look at her torn stockings.' But she was vitriolic toward me."

After a time, she could take no more and complained to Anna. "I finally had to go to her because she was going to lose me—not so much because I was going to quit, but because I was going to fall over."

As luck would have it, Blow had bonded with Anna's protégé, André Leon Talley, who "adored" her and viewed her as an eccentric muse, and asked her to come to work as his assistant. "After three months," says Schechter, "she and André weren't talking," and she left.

After she returned to England, Blow tried unsuccessfully to freelance stories for *Vogue* but quickly learned that "Anna's a great one for rejecting pieces. She's famous for it, if it's not right. She's a perfectionist."

By 2004, Blow had become famous in her own right in England. As a fashion stylist, she had worked for British *Vogue* and now was fashion director of the London Sunday *Times* and *Tatler,* where she kept a rack of her own clothing, aside from the forty-thousand-dollar custom-built closet she had at home. Over the years she has been credited with discovering such designers as Alexander McQueen and Philip Treacy.

"When I go to the shows, Anna always asks me to the American *Vogue* parties. She always says she was proud of me when I worked for her. They call her the ice maiden, but I don't think she is an ice maiden at all. I think she's like the Concorde, flying through the clouds."

twenty-seven

Baby Makes Three

Anna didn't boast to friends and *Vogue* colleagues—the few with whom she communicated—that she was going to have a baby, and most couldn't even tell she was pregnant, since she stayed thin and perfect-looking.

When one colleague finally found out she was with child, she asked Anna how she kept it so together. Anna's response? "Willpower."

Instead of wearing boring, unchic maternity clothes, she simply opened the back of her short, tight Chanel skirt a bit to make room for her tummy, and always wore the suit jacket when she was in the office, which helped to conceal her delicate condition. No comfortable shoes for her, either; she still clicked around in her stilettos. She was as energetic as ever. As her number one lady-in-waiting, Laurie Schechter, marveled, "It wasn't like she was rushing out to go throw up. She sailed through it."

One of the few who were in on her secret early on was her own father. The wife of a British journalist who had been mentored by Charles Wintour in the early days at the *Evening Standard* recalls running into him one day at the BBC, and he was beaming. "She asked him how he was doing and he was just beside himself with excitement. He said, 'My daughter Anna's going to have a baby, and if it's a boy she's going to call him Charlie after me.' It was very thrilling for him."

When Anna finally began to reveal to select female colleagues that she was "up the duff," as they say in England, a number of them were taken aback, mainly because they couldn't imagine her taking any time from her career to raise a child, let alone envision the formidable ice queen holding a baby to her breast and being nurturing, warm, and loving. Anna Wintour, driven editor, yes; Anna Wintour, mother, no. To some, it seemed like an oxymoron.

"I thought it was kind of disconcerting to see her as a mother," says the photographer Andrea Blanche. "I just never saw her that way. You know, warmth, those qualities that I attribute to motherhood. I just never envisioned Anna like that." The photographer Jean Pagliuso happened to be on the elevator with Anna after a meeting at *Vogue* and "she just sort of dropped it as an aside," Pagliuso recalls. "At that time she didn't want anybody to know she was pregnant. She seemed happy, more than I would think for Anna."

Along with a grandchild, "Chilly Charlie" Wintour was going to have his favorite offspring, a chip off the old block, back home in Britain, too.

Rumors had begun circulating in the British press in the summer of 1985 that Anna was the leading contender for Beatrix Miller's job as editor in chief of British *Vogue* and that Anna had spent a week in London being wooed but had turned down the offer. She told Nigel Dempster at the *Daily Mail* she wasn't taking the job because her husband had taken on a research project on teen suicide, his specialty, and couldn't leave New York, and she wasn't going without him. "I'd love to work in London and have a British baby, but he can't leave," she stated with a straight face.

Some weeks later, on September 18, 1985, Condé Nast managing director Bernard Leser confirmed the rumors. After top secret plotting and planning, and putting off the press, it had been decided that Anna would, in fact, become the new editor of British *Vogue*.

Unbenownst to most, Anna had been in on some of the clandestine talks and wasn't exactly thrilled with the outcome. She had lobbied strenuously, and believed she deserved, to replace Grace Mirabella now rather than later. But Newhouse and Liberman convinced her that the time would come. She even played the motherhood card and complained that she'd wind up with a transatlantic marriage. But none of it held water with the suits. She had no choice but to play corporate ball.

In making the public announcement, though, Leser did a quick two-step when asked why the appointment had taken so long. "American *Vogue* did not relish the idea of losing her," he said, which was fine for press and public consumption.

But for those in the know who worked with her at American *Vogue,* the sooner Anna left, the better. There was no sense of loss, only glee. Her promotion was a dream come true and the end of a nightmare. Her many detractors, especially Mirabella, would finally be rid of her.

A brief mention about Anna's new job appeared in *Women's Wear Daily,* but the British press was breathless with anticipation over the change in command. *The Times* declared that Miller was "a hard act to follow" and speculated (oh, so wrongly) that Anna "can be expected to stay a decade and display the glamour and eccentricity that have marked out *Vogue* editors since 1916."

That group included one who went on to run a fashion house and then spent the rest of her life in bed, another who always wore purple, and one who was a Communist.

The eccentricity of *Vogue's* lineage would end with Anna's reign. It now would be all business.

The *Guardian,* where Anna's brother Patrick became a political correspondent, was on the mark, reporting, "In New York, they see her as wintry . . . Wintour is defined by her iron will, the cool single-mindedness, the success . . . the appearance of things."

The London *Times,* quoting an unnamed Wintour colleague, described her as "elegance personified . . . Everything about her is the finest, simplest and most exquisite of its kind." Calling Liberman the "grand panjandrum of the international *Vogues,*" the *Times* said he gave Anna "a little extra polish" when he appointed her creative director and "instructed her to 'use her elbows.' A minister without portfolio, she sized up the situation and rather quickly became the jewel in the Condé Nast crown."

Five months pregnant, Anna acted as if she was thrilled, but *the* job—the flagship *Vogue* in New York—was still out of her reach. Schechter says Anna saw London as an opportunity to be an editor in chief of another *Vogue,* but she didn't show great enthusiasm. "But you don't *ever* see Anna get excited. She was never someone to jump up and down and be excited in some vocal way."

If Anna wasn't overjoyed with the appointment, Mirabella and her court were ecstatically dancing in the halls. Literally. "I was home sick the day they made the announcement," recalls Jade Hobson. "My colleague Liz Tretter called me to tell me, and I could literally hear hoots and hollers on the floor. It was pandemonium. A lot of people, including myself, were very pleased she was going."

For Mirabella, the decision to ship Anna to London came as a relief. The editor in chief had had it with the creative director's aggressive and insensitive attempts to push her out. Mirabella had been pummeled with rumors that she would be axed at any moment and replaced by Anna. The gossip had run rampant, from the lowliest clerk in the mailroom on up, since the day Anna arrived two years earlier. Outside of *Vogue,* the fashionistas who lunch speculated on nothing else—Grace was out, Anna was in, any day now. The rumors ricocheted from the elegant avenues of Madison, Park, and Fifth to the fashionable Avenue Montaigne in Paris and chic Via della Spiga in Milan. The fashion and general press had a field day speculating, too, chasing anonymous and sometimes well-placed insider tips that an announcement would be made any day that Anna would get *the* job.

But Mirabella taught herself to ignore the speculation, or otherwise she'd drive herself crazy.

Liberman, who loved to instigate, manipulate, and provoke, knew how Mirabella felt, and while he told his pride and joy, Anna, one thing, he told Mirabella another—comforting her and imploring her not to worry.

"Alex laughed off suggestions that anyone might be after my job," she said. "And, very solicitously, he led me to believe that keeping Anna Wintour around was in my best interest." He convinced her that if *Vogue* didn't hold on to Anna, the competition, like *Harper's Bazaar,* would snap her up.

Mirabella came to believe her nemesis was being groomed to be sent back whence she came to run that other *Vogue* and that would be the end of that. Later, she realized that by agreeing with Liberman Anna had "dug my grave with my blessing."

But that was still several chess moves ahead.

For now, Mirabella had to sit back and watch Liberman's adoration of his protégée.

"He loved her look, her glamour," the incensed editor in chief noted later. "He loved the intrigue of her clicking around in her high heels, trusted by and trusting no one except him. He thought her work, which combined the glitz of the eighties with elements of street art and design, was brilliantly 'modern.' He'd often show up at my office and, with all the pride of a cat presenting a dead mouse to its owner, show me samples of art that Anna Wintour had brought in. 'Isn't this wonderful,' he'd say breathlessly. 'Look at what Anna has done.'"

And, indeed, Anna had made a visible contribution to the magazine's look, despite Mirabella's feelings. Before she was bumped out of the fashion coverage, Anna did a slick story on England's new designers that was styled by a discovery of hers, a young designer by the name of Vera Wang. Working with the features editor, Anna saw ways to better illustrate front-of-the-book stories to make then "hipper, younger," notes Schechter, who coordinated many of those stories. One such piece was about the gentrification of and the growing art and music scene in New York's East Village. But, as Schechter points out, "it wasn't like Anna was saying, 'I think we should do a feature on this or that.'" Anna essentially was finding ways to improve the visual level of those stories. She read domestic and foreign fashion magazines constantly, looking for new ideas.

When the announcement was made that Anna was off to jolly old England to run *Vogue* and modernize "its dowdy, exclusive, and outdated-looking pages," as Mirabella described it, she patted herself on the back, thinking she had been correct all along about Anna's future, that it would be in London, not New York, and she'd finally be out of her well-coiffed hair.

Because Anna was pregnant, it was decided that she'd have the baby in New York and afterward cross the pond to take on her latest challenge. Anna was due in January 1986 and scheduled to be in her new office in London that April.

The only difficulty she faced in her final trimester was early contractions, which occurred around Thanksgiving. She was taken to the hospital for a day or two, watched over, and given some drugs. "I remember David joking and saying that the whole reason why she went into early contractions was because the baby wanted to come out and have a good meal," says Schechter.

In December, friends in the business, those in her circle and hangers-on, started throwing rounds of lunches and dinners for her as time drew near—not for the the birth of the baby but rather for her coming ascension to the throne of British *Vogue*. On Fifty-seventh Street, at Mr. Chow's, her pals Michael and Tina Chow feted her and fawned over her. It was one bash after another. As one observer noted, "It was a performance of staggering discipline."

Right on schedule in January, Anna, at thirty-seven, became a mother for the first time, delivering a healthy boy. As promised, she named him Charles in honor of her father.

There was talk that Anna had induced Charlie's birth so that she could attend the couture collections, which she vehemently denied through her publicist when *The Times* of London repeated it—a whopping sixteen years later. Anna claimed she took off two months. The story came to prominence from fashion editor Liz Tilberis, who was one of Anna's detractors when she arrived at British *Vogue*.

Within what seemed like days, whatever her claim, Anna was back in her office making final preparations for her transfer to London. She asked her trusted lieutenants to join her: Schechter, once again to be her assistant, and Paul Sinclaire, to be a fashion editor. She got neither.

Sinclaire, who had angered Anna by not coming to her wedding because he was out of town, agreed to take the job, but he later backed out and earned Anna's wrath. "She had asked me to come to English *Vogue*—she didn't offer me some *enormous* position—but I had accepted the job, and she was depending on me. I had already moved a lot and I just thought it's too big of a drag, I didn't feel like moving to London. I called her up and she was *enraged*. David even called me to say, 'You *better* come.' Anna was *really, really, really, really* angry. She was still mad at me for not coming to the wedding, but my not going to English *Vogue* put her over the top. Anna saw it as two betrayals."

Schechter, too, had qualms about going to London. While she saw Anna's invitation as "an amazing opportunity," she still wanted to explore other possibilities. Anna gave her exactly one month to do so. "I'm sure she hoped that I wouldn't find options here and that I would come with her, but I just wanted to see the lay of the land."

As it turned out, the promised land was *Rolling Stone*, where the twenty-seven-year-old Schechter became the magazine's first full-time fashion editor. Anna was seriously disappointed. Later she said she "intellectually understood" Schechter's decision, "but emotionally it was very hard to take."

Anna now desperately needed to find an assistant in London she could trust, someone as loyal, sharp, and hardworking as the one she had with her since *New York* magazine. Anna asked for recommendations. Schechter recalled having some luck with an ambitious young woman who worked for

Condé Nast in London named Gabe Doppelt who had done some research for her. She proposed her name—a recommendation she would come to regret. Anna and Schechter would work together again, but her star would fall and Doppelt's would rise.

By mid-March 1986, Anna, two-month-old Charles, and a full-time nanny were ensconced in a lovely Victorian town house rented for her by Condé Nast in picturesque and grand Edwardes Square—with its lovely private garden in the center—in chic Kensington. Her temporary home, befitting a *Vogue* editor, was within walking distance of the old Wintour family home in Phillimore Gardens, where Anna's interest in fashion first burgeoned some two decades earlier.

Anna complained that the logistics of the move and the transatlantic marriage were "terrible" and claimed at the time she woke up at night in "a cold sweat . . . parts of me think, 'I'm crazy. I should stay home, look after my baby, have a nice quiet life.' But I didn't think I wanted to have a kid in New York. I've worked so hard for fifteen years [in New York]. . . . British *Vogue* was always the magazine I wanted to edit. Will it work? Ask me in six months." Meanwhile, her husband stayed in New York, and both commuted via the Concorde to see each other. Anna's personal frustration was, in part, taken out on her new colleagues.

The Wintour of British *Vogue*'s discontent was about to begin.

twenty-eight

Anna's Guillotine

The January 1986 issue of British and American *Vogue* had the same model on the cover. In the UK edition, her hair was a bit tousled and the freckles on her face stood out. In the edition produced in New York, she had a more glitzy, glamorous look—a Madison Avenue Madonna, a Barney's Brat.

Anna, who had arrived in London with a corporate mandate essentially to Americanize British *Vogue*, compared the two issues and concluded that there weren't very many women she knew in New York who walked down the street dressed like the models in the out-of-touch *Vogue* she was taking over. Beatrix Miller used to call her seventy-year-old magazine *Brogue* to distinguish it from American *Vogue*, but Anna would trash that concept soon enough. There would be *no* difference between the two, if she had her way. The fantasy, fancy, and eccentricity that had been *Brogue*'s signature was about to be pummeled to the ground and, some would later believe, robbed of its singular personality.

A couple of weeks before she started the overhaul and the bloodletting—and blood would flow as she swung her ax—she gave some hints of what was to come to one of the many London fashion scribes lining up at her majesty's doorstep for interviews. "I enjoy my work, and I work very hard," Anna declared. "In New York I used to get in at eight and the office was full. When I first started work in London [at *Harpers & Queen*] we used to droop in around ten." And then she emphasized (or threatened), "I do think New York brought out my competitive streak."

Just like the fear that permeated Madison Avenue *Vogue* for the two years before Anna made her exit, a feeling of dread hovered over the offices of Vogue House on Hanover Square upon her arrival.

Before formally making her entrance, Anna began holding high-level private meetings in her home with the editors who were Beatrix Miller's top lieutenants: fashion director Grace Coddington, the most senior, and Liz Tilberis, second in command, both of whom would have major battles with Anna. Both knew her from her days in London, were aware of her reputation in New York, and shared mutual friends—and so they didn't trust her for a second. Moreover, their backgrounds were so very different from Anna's.

While working as a waitress in the late fifties, Coddington had started to model, often for *Vogue,* just as the fashion boom of the swinging sixties was kicking off. She was the epitome of the era's look—tall, skinny, and leggy— and could look haughty or decadent. One of her last photo shoots was conducted by Helmut Newton, who posed her in a tiny black bikini at night, in a swimming pool, wearing red nail polish and sunglasses.

By 1968, her modeling days were numbered and she was hired by *Vogue* as a fashion editor, where she could be icy, dismissive, and terrifying if she had it in for someone. She was a fashionista big-time, who would go from flaming red hair to dyed punk color at a blink of a perfect eyelash. At the time she joined *Vogue,* she was married to Anna's friend, the restaurateur Michael Chow, and cruised around London in a flashy beige convertible Rolls-Royce, an amazing change in lifestyle for a poor girl who grew up eating ham sandwiches for dinner every night.

Liz Tilberis, who long ago had closely bonded with Coddington, was two years older than Anna, the daughter of an arch-conservative ophthalmologist. Her mother came from a wealthy Scottish family that made a fortune in the fabric-dyeing industry. Tilberis was sent to a fancy boarding school, after graduation took a secretarial course, and then went to one of Britain's finest art schools, where she studied fashion design—around the same time Anna was dropping out of North London Collegiate. Over the years her family's money disappeared, and by the time Tilberis joined *Vogue* in the sixties as a lowly intern, she had to earn her keep; there was no private income such as that enjoyed by Anna and by many of the *Voguettes* with proper backgrounds who worked there in those days—a virtual finishing school populated with socially connected young women who gossiped about who among them was seeing Prince Charles or one of the Beatles.

Tilberis had covered the lingerie market with Anna in the early seventies, when Anna was a junior at *Harpers & Queen* and Tilberis was just getting her feet wet at *Vogue*.

While glamorous, these were not high-paying jobs. A story that has made the rounds over the years, apocryphal but on the mark, is of a pretty society girl editorial assistant who complained. "I have to get a real job. Daddy can't afford to send me to *Vogue* anymore."

Coddington wasn't very interested in the editor in chief's job when Miller stepped down because of the politics and other obligations involved—she cared only about fashion. The more competitive Tilberis, on the other hand, made her interest known, though she felt she didn't have much of a chance because of her lack of experience in production and features. She was married to an artist and had two adopted sons. Neither Coddington nor Tilberis knew that Anna was already the chosen heir to the throne.

Miller was disappointed when she heard that Anna got the crown. "Beatrix is not a great admirer of Anna," says onetime *Vogue* staffer Drusilla Beyfus Shulman, a friend of Miller's and of the Wintour family. "She didn't like Anna's values. She felt Anna was all about shopping, sex, slickness. Beatrix always tried to imbue *Vogue* with a kind of higher quality of culture and intellect. That was her aim at *Vogue*."

When Anna arrived in London, one of the first things on her to-do list was to call Tilberis, offer a perfunctory hello, and demand to know where she could put her fur coats in storage. "No one I knew in London wore furs," Tilberis stated later, "and *I* certainly couldn't afford them." Anna also began using Tilberis's hair salon, swanky MichaelJohn in Mayfair, where celebrity clients have ranged over the years from Tony Blair to Nigella Lawson. Anna used the same cutter, too—an eccentric named Charlie Chan who liked to chatter about his New Age interests while cutting her hair. Anna is said to have told him to put a sock in it.

Anna's ascension was a gold mine for *Private Eye,* which published many gossip items about her. It noted that her arrival at *Vogue* was "the occasion for tears and near hysteria" among the magazine's fashion writers, who "have long been able to indulge their favourite designers as well as photographers. . . . La Wintour has said she wants 'total control' of the content." *Private Eye* was getting constant leaks from *Vogue* insiders. One report had it that Anna had called *Vogue*'s longtime managing editor, Georgina Boosey, asking if "she knew of a gym that opened at 6 A.M. A little shaken, Boosey said no. 'Well where do you all go?' demanded La Wintour incredulously. There has been a sudden rush, I understand, to purchase items of designer sportswear among the tremulous staff."

Private Eye also broke the story that Anna had negotiated a whopping $160,000 salary for herself, the rent on her house, a car with a full-time chauffeur, and a nanny—"thus lightening the burden of motherhood for her. To maintain social contacts in the states," the report continued, "the workaholic harpy will be provided with 2 return airfares each month, via Concorde, of course."

"She was *incredibly* focused and organized when she got to London," notes Shulman, a veteran *Vogue* features editor who would be fired by Anna soon after she took over the magazine. "She just had the baby and immediately went to work straight off the obstetric table.

"Wonderful David Shaffer started to commute by Concorde in order to see her. Charles [Wintour] always referred to him as a saint, and he was. Never be saintly to a wife that's so ambitious. But David admired her. She was just all so terrific within that narrow compass of fashion. One might ask, is it worth feeling like that about a fashion magazine? And who cares, since it's just selling advertising, really." (Some time after Anna's reign ended at British *Vogue,* Shulman's daughter, Alexandra, became its editor in chief. Beatrix Miller is her quasi godmother.)

In her meetings with Tilberis and Coddington, Anna was "civilized," "polite," "reassuring." But Tilberis saw her as having an American outlook on fashion and foresaw herself and others at the magazine "heading for a direct culture clash."

The British press, such as the *Daily Telegraph,* noted that Anna was about to do a "major shakeup on one of Britain's greatest and grandest institutions." She told the paper, "I want *Vogue* to be pacy, sharp and sexy. I'm not interested in the super-rich or infinitely leisured (which, of course, she was, as time would tell). I want our readers to be energetic, executive women, with money of their own and a wide range of interests." Interestingly, that was the same concept Anna had adapted to and carried out a few years back when she was at *Savvy*. In fact, there was nothing new in the philosophy she was now espousing—but it was new to London.

Anna's meetings and blunt memos said it all. She was going to turn British *Vogue* upside down and inside out, and shake out the cobwebs. As Tilberis noted sourly, she was planning to make the magazine "faster and busier, directly addressing the concept of the modern working woman, and it scared the hell out of us. She hated anything . . . too archly British."

On Anna's first day on the job, Tilberis had handed to her some black-and-white photos of a model whose head was swathed in bandages—the kind of offbeat layouts she liked to do and that had long been a staple of the magazine. To Anna, Tilberis proudly exclaimed, "This is very new!" Anna, looking as if she'd been handed a bag of soggy fish and chips, replied, "Oh, my God, I'm back in England."

It would only get worse.

The more traditional stories, the fashion shoots at country castles, were scratched, replaced by models toting briefcases at Lloyd's of London.

"She wanted smiling, happy, athletic, professional pictures," declared Tilberis. "She wanted saneness and sameness. It was the end of life as we knew it."

Anna ordered the complete renovation of Beatrix Miller's office, which was expedited over one weekend. One wall was knocked down to make a new entrance, all walls were painted linen white, Anna's Buchsbaum desk and a Biedermeier sofa were delivered, bookshelves for bound volumes of the magazine with a large NO SMOKING sign on one shelf were installed, and the carpets were torn up and the floors finished to a gleam. Now she was ready to get down to the business of chopping heads.

Anna's debut issue, with a circulation of around 170,000 (big for Britain, minuscule for the United States) appeared on the newsstands in August 1986. The size of the type was larger, the graphics had a sleeker look, and sections like travel and "Men in Vogue" were moved from the back to the body of the magazine. Anna had plans for additional arts coverage, more health and fit-ness stories, celebrity profiles, and even a horoscope—all in all, as American as a women's magazine can get.

Excised from the masthead were two fashion editors, the living editor, the restaurant critic, the associate editor for features, the nutrition editor, and some others. Anna added another high-ranking fashion editor, her friend Michael Roberts, to work with Coddington, who was one name above his on the masthead; she remained fashion editor but he was given the fancier title of fashion director. Tilberis got a raise and was promoted from fashion editor to executive fashion editor. (The raise was unexpected, and when Tilberis said to Anna, "I don't know what to say," her boss's response was a chilly "You could say thank you.")

Anna kept Georgina Boosey as managing editor. She'd been at *Vogue* since the midfifties and knew everything there was to know about production, printing, and budgets—important information Anna needed. Anna brought in a new arts editor, a beauty editor, a senior fashion editor, and two lower-level fashion editors. Her friend Emma Soames, granddaughter of Winston Churchill, was brought back to *Vogue* as features editor, and four fashion assistants were added to the staff list, all with perfect *Vogue* first names— Phillipa, Arabella, Annabelle, and Venetia. Gabe Doppelt was listed as Anna's assistant, the job Laurie Schechter had passed on.

Among the first to be fired, curiously, were close Wintour family friends and longtime colleagues of her father, among them Alex Walker, the august film critic of the *Evening Standard* who played with Anna as a child and for more than sixteen years wrote a monthly show business column for *Vogue*. Another was Milton Shulman, the *Evening Standard*'s drama critic who began his newspaper career with Charles Wintour and had a similar deal with *Vogue* to write a cinema column.

Milton Shulman was the first to get the pink slip. After it happened, he called Walker and said, " 'You're next.' And I said, 'No, don't be silly.' And then, of course, when I did get sacked, Milton rang up and said, 'I told you so.' "

Almost two decades after he was pink-slipped, Walker was still upset and saddened by Anna's rude and frigid handling of him. "I'm a well-brought-up child, and I would have thought it would have been perfectly easy for someone in Anna's position to call me up, particularly because she knew me personally, and say, 'Alex, I'm making a lot of changes. I want it to be a different magazine from Beatrix's. I know you've been here a very long time and I hope you don't mind if I thank you very much, and say well done, and hope you'll be able to contribute occasionally.'

"There was none of that. The work that I'd written in advance simply didn't appear in the magazine. I was paid for three months, and that was the end of it—never a letter, nothing, absolutely nothing. I thought it was an absence of politeness, not an absence of gratitude, because there was no reason why she should be grateful. For her, it was easier to exert power through the negative aspect of dropping someone rather than dropping a line and saying, 'I'm sorry.' Charles would never have handled it in such a backhanded way. He would have said, 'I don't think things are working out. Have you anywhere else you'd like to go?'

"I'd had a good time with Beatrix, and I contributed regularly once a month for sixteen and a half years, so my career wasn't being nipped in the bud. I just felt saddened that there was a lack of social grace in how she handled it." (In 2002, a journalist who wrote a profile of Anna for the London *Times* asked her if she found it difficult firing a loyal family friend like Walker. "Well, I'm sure it was," she responded briskly. "I'm afraid I don't remember.")

A few years after Anna was named editor in chief of American *Vogue*, Walker was in New York "full of himself," as he notes, because he'd just been named critic of the year in the British annual press awards. He was walking along Madison Avenue and suddenly realized he was in front of the Condé Nast building and decided to go in and say hello to Anna, wish her well—he held no grudge against her.

The receptionist at the lobby desk called upstairs and Anna's assistant answered. When he explained who he was, he was told she was very busy. After he said he just wanted to say hello, Anna got on the line, asked two quick questions—how he was and what he was doing in New York. As he started to explain, she cut him off, saying, "I hope you enjoy yourself. Give my regards to the people back home. Good-bye." Click.

Once again, Walker notes, "I felt crushed, not in vanity but simply by the fact that it would have been nice for her to say, 'Oh, do come up. How nice to see you again.' But—nothing. Anna always had her order of priorities. People like myself simply didn't feature in them."

Drusilla Beyfus Shulman knew it was only a matter of time before she faced Anna's guillotine. She'd known Anna as a child and a teen, was a long-time friend and colleague of Charles Wintour's, and liked and respected Nonie Wintour. But she viewed Anna as "a threat to all editors" at the magazine. "When Anna was appointed, her first statement was that she wanted to move the magazine up a generation or two. I worked for British *Vogue* for seven years, was close to Beatrix Miller, and knew Grace Mirabella. I belonged to the old guard, so I realized it was only a question of time."

The firings and the general all-around shakeup at the venerable fashion monthly were watched closely by a gleeful and gloating British press. Anna's firm and frosty Americanized management style and high-profile visibility became fodder for the pundits of Fleet Street. She was dubbed "nuclear Wintour" by press and staff, and one scribe described what was going on at *Vogue* as "the Wintour of Our Discontent." Even her retired father's old paper, *The Evening Standard,* now under new management, noted Anna's "habit of crashing through editorships as though they were brick walls, leaving behind a ragged hole and a whiff of Chanel."

One of those covering fashion for *The New York Times* at the time was Michael Gross, who wrote a column called "Notes on Fashion." He was able to schedule an interview with Anna while he was covering the collections, and it was then that he learned that she despised the adjectives the British press had been using to describe her. That became clearly evident the moment he walked into her office and the first words out of her mouth were, "You will *not* refer to me as 'nuclear Wintour.'" She wasn't kidding. If he wanted the interview, he had to pledge he would not use those words. Anna didn't want Si Newhouse and Alex Liberman reading the *Times* and seeing what they thought of her in London, if they didn't already know, or care.

Gross agreed to Anna's condition. After the interview, he went back to his office and, having now spent some time with her and finding her "chilly and a little bit forbidding," he described her in his story as "tightly coiled." But the two words were edited out. When he complained, he was told by an editor, "You can't describe Anna Wintour as an asp,' and I said, 'It's accurate. She's tightly coiled. That's what she is.'"

Anna was constantly reporting back to Liberman in New York. She was determined to keep him on her side, knowing he might be hearing some negative talk about the way she was handling things. She was concerned that the distance between London and New York might *not* make the heart grow fonder, so she kept him in the loop, at least for now.

"Anna was very possessive of Alex, of their relationship," a colleague of both observes. "With Liberman you were always aware of his position and that he had the power of life and death over your career. He was a snake, a hypocrite, and you had to be to survive in that environment. That's how *he* survived all those years. Anna had to be very political to really thrive and survive in that climate. Alex was the head of it, so everybody followed his lead. Alex established the corporate culture at *Vogue,* at Condé Nast. His thing was to divide and conquer. He also was the ultimate father figure. You *wanted* to please him."

With all of that in mind, Anna sent him dummies of her layouts for his approval and phoned him often asking if he liked a particular cover. And she sometimes requested his help. "When she had problems with the front of the book," he once stated, "she came to New York and we redesigned it for her."

In London, Anna cracked down on photographers, demanding that they turn in *everything* they shot, giving them less creative freedom. When she was a fashion editor in the trenches in New York, she accepted their choice of the best of the best shots. Now, however, as boss woman, she wanted every single roll of film, every print, every Polaroid to be turned over to the fashion editor overseeing the shoot. Anna would have final approval. Where the photographer once was the key, if not lead, creative member of the team, the fashion editors at British *Vogue* now were given greater importance and power under Anna—that is, as long as they carried out her vision.

The New York fashion photographer Andrea Blanche, who had her innings with Anna in the past, was traveling through Europe when she got word that Anna had a couple of assignments for her. She was both delighted and apprehensive, having been burned by her before. Looking back, Blanche believes Anna's decision to use her again "was definitely political because she knew Liberman liked me. I'm a good photographer, so why not have me work for her."

Blanche had shot for British *Vogue* when Bea Miller was editor, so she thought she knew the terrain. But that was then. Anna now wanted the photos to be "very up, joyful"—models smiling, jumping, and running.

Blanche, on the other hand, was more artsy, and her photos tended to be moody and sexual. While Anna gave Blanche no special instructions and didn't say make it upbeat, the photographer was aware that Anna had done a one-eighty from the old days. "The things she was doing when she worked at *New York* magazine were much more aesthetic, but when she started working for British *Vogue* she was doing things that were more lively, more commercial."

The assignments were simple enough for Blanche—one was shooting casual clothes in the studio, the other photographing a model in different cocktail dresses in various locations around London. Blanche shot thousands of frames for the latter, not atypical, and one of the pictures was of the model getting into a London taxi with her arms enthusiastically in the air, a big toothy smile on her perky face, a very natural moment, looking very buoyant. Working with a young *Vogue* fashion editor, Blanche went through her shots and decided to send all but the "natural moment" frame to Anna. When the editor protested, Blanche told her to forget it, she didn't like the photo. After all, it was her eye, the photographer's eye, that made such decisions. Or so she thought.

"We had three garbage bags filled with thirty-five-millimeter slides, and I sent only three or four shots from each situation to Anna, which is what I sent to *Vogue* all the time," Blanche says.

A few days later Anna called and demanded to see *everything* Blanche had shot.

"I said, 'No, I'm not going to do that. That's all I send to American *Vogue* and that's all I'm sending to you.' And then Anna said, 'I want to see that shot of the girl with her hands in the air. I want to see *that* shot!'"

While Anna could be furious on the inside, she rarely, if ever, showed anger on the outside, so controlled was she. But this time, sitting in her hotel room, Blanche felt Anna's fury burning through the phone line.

"She got hysterical that she wasn't going to get the film," she says. "She became unglued. She wasn't as calm and collected as I knew her to be. The pitch of her voice kept rising. I thought it was a bit amusing to hear her sound that way. I said, 'No, I threw the picture away, I edited it out,' or whatever, because I didn't like it, didn't think it was up to my standards.

"Whenever a question arose with Liberman, ninety-nine percent of the time he would give me my way. So I wasn't used to somebody being that demanding. In all the time I knew Alex, maybe he once questioned how much film I sent him, and then when I talked to him about it, it was fine. I don't remember ever having to send more film. It was just something that wasn't done, and my judgment was never questioned.

"Anna wanted the power and the creative control. She got that if she saw all the film. Then it's not my decision, the photographer's decision, but her decision. It makes the photographer more dispassionate."

Blanche heard nothing more about it. Because of the dispute over that one photo, she never worked for *Vogue* again. She says that when she later went into therapy, Anna, Liberman, and the insanity at *Vogue* constantly came up in sessions with her shrink.

Several months after Anna's fit over the photo, the photographer was leafing through British *Vogue* when she came upon her cocktail dress layout. And there, right in the center, was the disputed picture Anna had demanded and that Blanche had refused to turn over.

"I was really surprised when I saw that picture, and I laughed, and I really felt sorry for that poor fashion editor," says Blanche. "I can hear Anna saying, 'Well, you've got to go back and *find* that shot.' And so there it was in the magazine. That editor had to go through every single slide—three garbage bags full, several thousand slides—to find that one shot. That's a lot of work.

"But that incident shows how driven Anna is. And I have to say, I tip my hat to her. Who could be angry when somebody is so determined and perseveres like that. I thought that was quite something."

twenty-nine

Lover, Friend, Mother

By 1986, Anna's former lover and longtime soul mate Jon Bradshaw, who had helped her so much over the years, was in the midst of a personal and professional midlife crisis, while she was skyrocketing to the top.

At forty-eight, he was especially despondent about the state of his career. His first serious book, a biography called *Dreams That Money Can Buy*, about the wild and tragic life of 1930s torch singer and playgirl Libby Holman, had been panned by critics.

Bradshaw had worked obsessively for five years on the book, enlisting talented author friends like A. Scott Berg to help in the rewriting, and had had big dreams of it becoming a bestseller and being made into a movie. He also had been involved in cowriting a screenplay about the "Lost Generation" in Paris, called *The Moderns*, and was working on a novel about a James Bond-*ish* character much like himself, called *Rafferty*, which he hoped would become a series.

But nothing seemed to be panning out. While he envisioned himself making it big in Hollywood, where his wife was a successful independent producer, and lolling tanned by the pool at the Beverly Hills Hotel flirting and drinking, he had little motivation and had to be constantly pushed and prodded by his friends.

Along with his career lows, he'd let himself go physically. After years of eating rich foods, smoking two or three packs of cigarettes a day, drinking heavily, and partaking in recreational drugs, he'd become overweight and was beginning to lose the roguish luster that had initially attracted Anna and other women and men to him.

Worse still, around the time of Anna's thirty-seventh birthday in November 1986, as she was enthusiastically whipping British *Vogue* into shape, Bradshaw, increasingly dispirited, was whipping himself about how life and success were passing him by.

Maudlin over drinks with friends, he began talking about his own death and the funeral he wanted for himself.

One of his confidants during this depressing period was Scott Berg, who would go on to win a Pulitzer Prize for his biography of Charles Lindbergh. The two had met at a Hollywood party in the late seventies—Bradshaw had conned a waiter into giving him a bottle of Johnny Walker Red, not just a drink, and the two split it. They had bonded around the time Bradshaw got married and Berg's acclaimed biography of Max Perkins was published.

Like so many others in Bradshaw's life, Berg became "obsessed" with Bradshaw. "It was love at first sight," he emphasizes years later. "I just adored him. I thought he was an old-fashioned rogue, and he first, last, and always reminded me of a kind of toothless bulldog. He snarled and complained, but in fact he was really kind of a softy. Anna was absolutely still calling him, crying on his shoulder. I don't know that Bradshaw ever lost a friend or a lover. People never let go of him. Anna's name would come up every now and then. He'd reminisce about when he was with her, and he often talked about how beautiful and attractive she was."

To their mutual Hollywood friends, Bradshaw and Berg became thought of as an odd couple, even though Bradshaw was married with an adopted daughter.

"I can't tell you to how many dinners people would invite Bradshaw, and I would just sort of show up," recounts Berg, who in 2003 had only one framed photo on his desk. It was of Bradshaw. "After a while, people learned to just set a place for me. I used to say I was his Margaret Dumont [a character actress in thirties and forties wacky films, including Marx Brothers comedies] and he was my Groucho. He would just sort of be outrageously Bradshaw, and I was the matronly old lady that he would offend."

Women who knew Bradshaw over the years swore he wasn't gay or bisexual, though there were suggestions of a leaning in that direction in his manner and style. Marilyn Warnick, an American journalist who worked in London and adored Bradshaw, observes, "He was a man who loved women, who liked the way they looked, the way they smelled. He liked their problems, liked talking about their emotional situations. That was certainly the case with me when I was crying on his shoulder about this bastard I was dating at the time. Bradshaw was like a girlfriend, except he was virile and enormous fun. It's true, though, that men liked him enormously."

Sometime in October 1986, Berg was having dinner with Bradshaw at Adriano's, a trendy restaurant at the top of Beverly Glen in Los Angeles. Bradshaw was drinking heavily, talking about how he hoped to see his adopted daughter, Shannon, grow up, and that led to his talk of dying and a list he bizarrely dictated to Berg of his fantasy memorial service.

In the predawn hours back at home, Berg wrote down the itinerary for Bradshaw's future funeral service: who should speak, what they should speak about, and in what order they should speak. That's the kind of obsessive detail Bradshaw had laid out for him.

"He wanted Nigel Dempster, his friend in London, to speak. I said, 'Is he your *best* friend?' And he said, 'Oh, Scott, you're like some little schoolgirl—"Who's your best friend?" Nigel's my mate!' "

Among other old pals he wanted present was the sixties British actress Fiona Lewis; the queen's cousin, Patrick Lichfield; Jimmy Bradshaw, his brother, whom most didn't even know existed; and his journalist pal A. J. Langguth. He didn't mention Anna, though, probably for his future widow's sake. He also wanted *three* memorial services: one at Morton's in Los Angeles, a second at Elaine's in Manhattan, and a third in London, not necessarily in that order.

Berg thought it was all so absurd that Bradshaw was being so mawkish that night. At the same time, he was aware that his friend "was almost a textbook case for how to get heart disease. He ate nothing but red meat. Butter was on everything [Anna had a similar propensity]. His favorite dessert was bananas Foster, which is just bananas, booze, and a lot of butter. It's just like *drinking* butter. He was always under some professional pressure, the crunch of being a freelance writer. And once every month he would play a killer game of tennis, just going from zero to one hundred."

About a month after that distressing dinner, just a couple of days before Thanksgiving, Berg got home and a call was waiting for him on his machine from another close friend of Bradshaw's, Jean Vallely, who for years wrote for *Esquire* and had once been married to one of *Washington Post* owner Katharine Graham's sons. She and Bradshaw had bonded and would spend weekends together with his little girl—Bradshaw's wife often was away on business—and Vallely's children; they were like two single moms.

Vallely's message urgently instructed Berg to get to the UCLA Medical Center: Bradshaw had had a heart attack. He was in intensive care and had not regained consciousness. Berg was dumbstruck. He immediately thought of that dinner and how it now appeared to him that Bradshaw had foreseen his own demise. As it turned out, Bradshaw had collapsed on a tennis court while playing with two pals, Dick Clement and Ian LeFrenais, both Brits, who were a successful screenwriting team in Hollywood.

"Dick put him in the car to drive him home, and by the time they pulled into the driveway he was unconscious, we called nine-one-one," remembers Bradshaw's widow, Carolyn Pfeiffer. "He never regained consciousness."

Berg and other close friends, including Barbara Leary, the wife of psychedelic drug guru Timothy Leary, rushed to the ICU to see their larger-than-life hero on life support at such a young age. "We're in intensive care and Barbara Leary looks around to see if any nurses are there and she lights up a cigarette," recalls Vallely. "Barbara, whom Bradshaw adored, said, 'Bradshaw wouldn't have gone this long without a cigarette for any of us."

On November 25, three days after he was stricken, Bradshaw died. It was decided that the plug be pulled because it didn't appear he would ever regain consciousness.

The next day in the *Daily Mail,* Nigel Dempster noted his passing and pointed out that "for years Bradshaw lived with Anna Wintour, now editor of *Vogue* in London, but they split up in 1977 and he moved to California. . . ."

Scott Berg had never seen a corpse before, "but somehow I just felt I had to see Bradshaw one last time, and I went to the morgue at UCLA." He was accompanied by Vallely and Barbara Leary. "The three of us walk into where they keep the dead bodies," recalls Vallely, "and it's freezing cold, and there he is, and Barbara says, 'Oh, my God, I just saw him yesterday, and now he looks awful, just awful!' And Scott turns to her and says, 'That's because he's dead. Yesterday he wasn't dead.'"

Says Berg, "I said good-bye to the Pied Piper, and he was a Pied Piper to many people who loved him."

After his death, a story circulated that Bradshaw's kidney had been donated to a powerful Hollywood studio head, and in exchange someone close to Bradshaw got a three-picture deal from the studio.

The obituary in the London *Times,* written by a close female journalist friend of Bradshaw's, stated that his full name was Jon Wayne Bradshaw. The middle name was an inside joke about how macho he had acted.

After his death there was talk that his Libby Holman book would be made into a movie starring Debra Winger and that his novel *Rafferty* would be turned into a film, but nothing ever came of any of that. However, his cowritten screenplay *The Moderns* was produced, got decent reviews, and starred Keith Carradine and Linda Fiorentino.

As produced by Bradshaw, the three memorial services came off as planned, including the singing of an old Princeton school song at the service at Morton's. Bradshaw had once accompanied Berg to an event where it was sung, and he became enamored of it. For Bradshaw, it was all image, even in death, since he had never gone to Princeton, or even graduated from college. But by having the song sung at his memorial service, people might think he was an Ivy Leaguer.

"He sort of wished he had gone to Princeton," says Berg. "When he asked me at our last dinner together that the song be sung, I said, 'Bradshaw, I have a moral problem with that since you didn't go to Princeton.' And he said, 'Well, change the lyric to 'In Praise of Old Bradshaw.' And by God when I had the program printed up, I had the lyrics printed out. 'In praise of old Bradshaw, my boys—hoorah, hoorah, hoorah.' And everybody got up and sang it. People were just standing there sobbing. It was hilarious."

In January, two months after his death, Bradshaw's widow and their daughter took his ashes to the home they owned in his beloved Jamaica. He was given a formal funeral and his ashes were buried there.

In London, Anna, hidden behind her sunglasses, attended one of the three memorial services, also held in January, at trendy Church of England St.

Paul's, in Knightsbridge, where debs got married and aristocrats were memorialized. "It was very formal, with a choir, trumpets, famous people—Bradshaw would have absolutely loved it," observes his widow. Other mourners included Anna's predecessor at *Vogue*, Beatrix Miller, who knew and liked Bradshaw and gave him some of his earliest magazine assignments in London. The London *Times*, which wrote about the service, listed all of the mourners. David Shaffer was not among them, and Anna was listed as "Miss Anna Wintour." She sat with her mother. Many spoke about Bradshaw, including Anna's father, who read the lesson; Patrick Lichfield, who gave the main address; and *Queen* founder Jocelyn Stevens, who read from Dylan Thomas.

Anna didn't speak, but someone saw her wipe her eyes under her Ray-Bans.

"She was devastated—*devastated*—that Bradshaw was not in her life anymore," says a colleague. "After the service, she went home and cried her eyes out."

One of the most important men in her life was gone. Now one of her closest female friendships was about to end.

It had been almost a decade since Anna and her best pal growing up, Vivienne Lasky, had seen each other. The last time had been that hellish weekend in Connecticut.

Over the intervening years, though, Lasky had kept up close ties with Anna's brother Jim and with Nonie. It was while Anna was ruling British *Vogue* that the two onetime bosom buddies got together one last time.

Lasky, her husband, and their children, two-year-old Nicholas and three-year-old Amanda, had come to London twice in eighteen months to visit her father, who had suffered a heart attack. Lasky's stepmother had designed to the nines a beautiful grandchildren's apartment, two floors of a lovely house near Harrods, and she also provided a nanny when they visited. It was during their second stay that Nonie Wintour told Lasky that Anna "would love to see you and the children."

Anna was quickly catching up to Lasky on the domestic front. Because of the odd way Anna had acted when Lasky got married, she had come to believe that Anna was jealous of her domesticity. Now Anna had a husband and was only one child away from being even with Lasky in the motherhood sweepstakes.

In December 1986, around the time of Lasky's visit, Anna became pregnant again during one of her weekend Concorde jaunts to New York to visit her husband.

Lasky naturally had qualms about seeing Anna after how badly their last visit turned out. But Nonie assured her that there was no ill will and that Anna really and truly wanted to have a reunion. A few days before the scheduled visit, Lasky's husband broke his foot and couldn't accompany her, but her two children and their nanny, Rosie, did. Knowing how upset Lasky had become the last time she saw Anna, Lasky's husband instructed the nanny to "watch out for my wife."

Lasky, her small brood, and Rosie, the newly proclaimed bodyguard, arrived around three for tea at the Wintours' house and were greeted by David Shaffer, who came to London to be with his family as often as his work in New York permitted. It was the first time Lasky had met him. "I was like, *this* is who she picked? He had no charisma, just seemed old and tired. He wasn't a handsome fellow and was balding. My thought was, 'If this is one of the great child psychiatrists of the world, we're all in trouble.' Warm and fuzzy he wasn't."

Neither was Anna, who barely greeted Lasky and accepted her gift for baby Charles—pants with a corduroy British riding jacket—by responding, " 'Oh, how *very* Ralph Lauren.' She gave me a look like it was acceptable as a gift." Anna noted how adorable Lasky's children were. And that was that.

As Anna's and Lasky's nannies disappeared to the kitchen to get cookies for the children, Anna turned to another woman in the room, whom Lasky hadn't noticed at first, and proceeded to chat with her, ignoring Lasky completely and never introducing her.

"Her husband never once went over to whisper in Anna's ear, 'You're ignoring your friend, darling.' My husband was very protective, very proper, the kind of person who would have gone over and said, 'What's going on here?' "

Lasky sat on a couch, as if she didn't exist, about to burst into tears. Anna and the other woman—lots of makeup, red streaks in her hair, most likely someone from *Vogue*—sat facing away from her "like I was chopped liver. I thought, 'Well, I put myself in this situation,' but Nonie had said, 'Anna really wants to see you.' If my husband had been there, he would have said, 'We're leaving now.'"

As she looked around the house, Lasky was surprised at how badly furnished it was. "It came furnished and it was hideous," she remembers. "I wondered how Anna could bear this ugly furniture because she cared so much about that kind of thing and was such a snob about it."

The fact that Anna *hadn't* redone the place to her very precise tastes was a strong clue that she knew her stay at British *Vogue* was temporary and that she'd soon take over Grace Mirabella's office in New York.

Thankfully for the upset and embarrassed Lasky, Anna's mother and brother arrived earlier than expected.

"Nonie said, 'Anna, why haven't you served anything yet? I thought this was a tea party. Vivienne's come all the way from America. Where are the things you ordered? Where's the tea?'"

Anna rolled her eyes and instructed Shaffer to get the housekeeper to bring up the tea and food from the kitchen.

Watching husband and wife interact for the first time, Lasky didn't see a match made in heaven. "I didn't see the rapport. I saw no chemistry whatsoever," she recalls. "What I'd seen with Bradshaw and her, here I saw *nothing*."

Mainly, Lasky couldn't believe that this visit with Anna was a repeat of the last horrific one. "It was god-awful, a really awkward, bad afternoon," she says. "I asked her husband to call for a taxi for my nanny to take the children home. My nanny said, 'If I hadn't seen it, I wouldn't have believed how rude and unfeeling she was, and this was your best friend.' We left Anna with her friend in the living room to get away from that situation, and I said to Jim and Nonie, 'Do we have to stay any longer? Once I get my children off to their destination, let's go,' and they said, 'That's a good idea, we'll have more time together,' and they whisked me away. We had a lovely evening together. What happened was not discussed. Not one word was said about Anna's rude behavior. My mother might have apologized for my poor behavior. Nonie said nothing."

And that was that. Lasky had had it with Anna. After a close bond that was cemented more than two decades earlier, they never spoke to or saw one another again.

In 2003, Lasky, her voice choking with emotion after having looked back on all those years as Anna's friend, had no answer as to why she treated her the way she did. Yet, she notes, "Anna's still part of my life, like an unfinished sentence."

On her visit to London, Lasky was surprised to see how drastically Nonie Wintour's circumstances had changed since the divorce. She had moved into a simple, tiny town house in a rather drab area far from the vibrant center of London where all of her friends were, many with whom she had lost touch or simply severed contact. "She seemed sadder," notes Lasky.

After the divorce from Charles, Nonie had seemingly disappeared from the scene altogether, and some thought she might have returned to the United States to live with her sister, Jean. In fact, she had decided to live alone in the working-class suburb of Balham and to drown herself in her social work. Blue-collar Balham, a part of which was known for street prostitution through the seventies and eighties, also was a target for comics like Peter Sellers who poked fun at the place in a popular British sketch called, "Balham, Gateway to the South."

The one *Evening Standard* staffer who always was a favorite of Nonie's from the early days was Alex Walker, who was shocked by Nonie's new lifestyle. "Balham's not the part of London where I *ever* would have imagined Nonie living," he says. "It's not where Nonie would find her kind of intellectual, with-it, stimulating company."

Walker had visited Nonie once there but found it all too depressing. "It was a small place she lived in, and everything was a bit cramped, perfectly comfortable but not Nonie's style," he recalls. "There was a wariness about mentioning Charles. One didn't do it. It was as if Charles didn't exist.

"It struck me that she was filling her time with social work. There were all kinds of files in her place, case histories and so on that she brought home from her office. Nonie was probably doing very good work with unfortunate children, and I would guess many of them were in the Balham area. She had resigned herself to that life.

"Nonie had made her choice, and her choice did not lie with the friends she had known when she was married to Charles. It lay in the work that she had accustomed herself to doing and felt compelled to do.

"Both Nonie and Charles believed in suffering in silence," Walker observes. "Nonie was a Boston Brahmin character who believed life was hard. And Charles was an English county man who thought that any expression of emotion was a bit vulgar."

After that one dismaying visit to Balham, Walker invited her to dinner at a fine restaurant in London to cheer her up, to talk about books and films, their favorite mutual passions. But then he lost track of her. She'd moved and no one knew where or how to contact her.

After years of her husband's womanizing along with their other problems, she had come to despise marriage. Anna, though, had a different, more positive view of the state of matrimony, at least one that she had begun expressing to colleagues in London during her editorship at British *Vogue*—a time when she and her husband talked daily by phone but were lucky if they saw each other and spent time together with the baby once or twice a month.

"Anna was going on and on like she was on a soapbox about marriage and how she felt it identifies you," recalls one of her colleagues. "She said she thought marriage was a very important thing. She said, 'Marriage says who you are.' She said people should be committed enough to *say* who they are. Of course, she never used her married name. I got the feeling she felt it was more bold to be married than not married. But I thought it sounded more like a shrink talking than her talking. I thought it was David talking through her.

"I asked her about her marriage. I said, 'He's so much older than you, don't you think about that?' And she said, 'Oh, he has the most energy of anybody I know. I talk to him many times a day and I miss him.'

"And then she said, 'Right now, I think he's wonderful.' She left it kind of like it might not be forever."

thirty

Beginning of the End

Liz Tilberis and Grace Coddington felt that their days were numbered, that Anna was out to get them.

Ratcheting up the pressure, Anna constantly demanded reshoots. Coddington's first had to be done three times until Anna finally signed off. When Coddington was on location, Anna commanded that she shoot a Polaroid of the setup (before the actual shooting started) and have a courier rush it back to the office. Anna would then scrutinize it and telephone Coddington, declaring, "Like it" or "Don't like it." If she didn't, which was often, Coddington would have to start all over, wasting time and costing the company money.

"It was pure harassment and bullying on Anna's part," an editor maintains.

Used to the rules of the old regime, Coddington tended to be late—to work in the morning, back from lunch in the afternoon—which infuriated Anna, who once tracked her down to a restaurant and demanded that the former model who had controlled what went onto *Vogue*'s fashion pages for two decades return to the office posthaste, as if she were a lowly intern.

Tilberis was equally harassed. On the morning of her father-in-law's funeral, she received a hand-slapping call from Anna, lecturing her that she was over her budget and ordering her not to take her assistant on a scheduled trip to New York. Tilberis was "horrified" and felt she was being "reprimanded like a willful child."

Anna had a negative attitude about everything Coddington and Tilberis thought or did in regard to fashion. At the "horribly tense" editorial meetings to decide what would go into the magazine, the imperious and dictatorial editor in chief positioned herself on a hard-back chair, and if she didn't like an idea she'd loudly tap her pencil on the desk, sending a chill through everyone present.

As one staffer who quit in disgust says, "She's the first female bully I ever met. She treated everyone, except for her own little coterie, like trash. You could tell she got off on it. A real little bully of a woman, and for what? Power for her was what it was all about. Power's Anna's aphrodisiac. I mean, *Vogue*'s just a fashion magazine, a catalog to sell clothes, for God's sake. And people had to be tormented so she could get a pat on the bum from Liberman and Newhouse, and get Grace Mirabella's job."

Anna and the veteran editors were on opposite sides and on a disastrous collision course. "She was horrified at the sort of work I was doing, the iconoclastic images that differentiated British fashion coverage from anything in American magazines," Tilberis has stated. "I began to wonder how long I'd last and whether it was worth the angst."

Anna trusted only a few, such as André Leon Talley, whose presence came as a shock to her subordinates because of his flamboyant manner and dress: patent leather pumps, striped stretch pants, red snakeskin backpacks, faux-fur muffs all superimposed on this gentle black giant who, in another world, could have been playing for the New York Knicks with his six-foot-seven frame. But here he was at British *Vogue*, advising her—the two of them and a few others against all the rest.

Most all the old guard's layouts, concepts, and story ideas Anna declared she hated. Staffers wanted highbrow features, Anna demanded middle-of-the-road. "There is still a place for those wonderful, creative mood pictures for which British *Vogue* is famous," Anna told a fashion reporter for the *Sunday Telegraph*, "but I also would like to see a balanced, modern approach to fashion—less drifting-through-the-woods and more realism."

Anna especially detested a photo Tilberis had David Bailey shoot of future supermodel Christy Turlington wearing an almost open man's shirt. She spiked it.

"Peremptory," "rather tactless," "unconcerned with 'the little people,'" "quickly bored," "didn't let anything so mundane as courtesy get in her way," is the way Tilberis saw her. She viewed Anna's appointment as the start of a "reign of mediocrity."

A major confrontation involving Anna, Tilberis, and Coddington took place at the collections in New York. The three were unhappily ensconced in a suite at the Algonquin Hotel trying to decide which clothes should be photographed when a firefight erupted over a Ralph Lauren double-layered coat.

Coddington loved it and demanded that it be shot. "It's fabulous," she said. Anna hated it. "It's ridiculous," she said. "It's the look," Tilberis said. The battle went on, Coddington fighting for "the look" and Anna always thinking ahead to what the reader's (and Liberman's) reaction would be. It got so bad that Tilberis suddenly felt panicky, began gasping for air, and excused herself and ran out of the room. Later she claimed the stress and anxiety of the situation had caused an attack of asthma, from which she would suffer for years.

"She was quite a whirlwind," observes former fashion editor Sophie Hicks, who fled *Vogue* about six months after Anna's reign of terror began. "When Anna took over, people were quite shocked because she was very dynamic and fast and took the job at great speed, and that was quite unusual. She was a *blast*—not a breath—of fresh air, worked much longer hours than any previous professional with a capital 'P.' Things were professional before Anna but much more relaxed. She hit the ground running and wanted to redo the magazine in her own image, worked extremely hard at it and expected others to work extremely hard—and they did mind that."

Hicks saw an immediate change in the look and feel of the magazine under Anna's watch. The issues were "more coherent . . . there were isolated things of more interest. It became less quirky, less individualistic. Some of the fashion before was better than after Anna came. But over all, if one adds it all together, the worst of *Vogue* was better, but the best was *not* better."

Anna was bothered by certain British attitudes, one of them that English women, as she saw them, "are embarrassed to spend money on themselves, which is a shame." Through *Vogue* Anna hoped to change all that. "If you earn the money," she intoned, "it is yours and if you have a certain self-respect, it is terrific to go out and spend it on yourself." Geraldine Ranson,

who wrote the piece for the *Sunday Telegraph,* pointed out that Anna earned
an enormous salary, so "it may take her a while to come to grips with the reality of most of her readers' domestic finances."

Coddington felt as if the roof had caved in on her. In control for so many
years at the magazine, she now was being treated horribly. To make matters
worse, she was one of those who early on had supported Anna for the job.

"Anna turned out to be beastly to her," states Winston Stona, a Jamaican
businessman who was a friend of Coddington's and had been a close pal of
Jon Bradshaw's. "Anna was terribly unkind to the point that I remember going to England and seeing Grace, and I said to her, 'Listen, leave the bloody
place.' She was devastated at how Anna treated her."

Coddington heeded his advice. Eight months after Anna took power, Coddington quit. She'd had it. "You don't need a fashion director, because you're
it," she said when she gave notice to become design director for Calvin Klein
in New York.

Although Tilberis despised Anna, she lobbied with her for Coddington's position. Anna put the job on hold and told Tilberis that if she wanted to keep her
current position—let alone get a promotion—she had better shape up, do what
she wanted her to do, stop complaining, and support her decisions and demands.

Tilberis, power hungry in her own right, played ball, and a month after
Coddington quit, she got her job.

"I never became a convert to Anna's themes," Tilberis claimed later, "but I
decided right then to be a dutiful number two. . . . I carried out Anna's bidding directly."

Things got slightly better between them, but skirmishes continued to rage
at the magazine.

Anna was the attacker at *Vogue* but played the victim of the British press.
She had come to hate the media. She considered herself a journalist, she was
the daughter of a noted one, and she had been involved romantically in the
past with many—yet in private and later in public she attacked Fleet Street.
"The British press are worst," she declared in 2002 while discussing its treatment of her when she was at British *Vogue.*

Everything about her became a target for criticism. Her father's old paper,
the *Evening Standard,* sent a reporter to interview her, and the story noted
that Anna had offered the scribe a "Valium . . . to calm my nerves," that

Anna's smile "seems brief and insincere," that after a decade in New York Anna was "not quite British," and that her only enthusiasm was for articles on "career women, business suits and working out. . . . 'There is a new kind of woman out there. She's interested in business and money. She doesn't have time to shop any more. She wants to know what and why and where and how,' Anna declared. 'So I feel the fashion pages, as well as looking wonderful, should give information.' "

The *Evening Standard* piece asked, "Is there anything nice to be said about Anna? Well, friends say she is a pushover—a mug for men, able to take a joke . . ."

The British press weren't the only media doing unkind reporting about her. *The New York Times* noted that Anna "is a thorn in the side of London's trendy set, who say the magazine has become too bland." Anna's response? "Any reaction is better than none." She added, "A new editor is going to change a magazine. People resist change. British fashion was a little insular. One had to open it up."

Around the same time the press was going after her, someone had designed a button meant to criticize Anna's drastic makeover of the magazine. Thom O'Dwyer, the style editor of London's *Fashion Weekly*, was spotted wearing one at a fashionable London restaurant. It read: "Vogue. Vague. Vomit."

Anna had bigger problems, though. Her second in command, Tilberis, had become the subject of a spirited headhunt between Ralph Lauren and Calvin Klein, who both wanted her to come to New York and take big jobs with them in the wake of Coddington's defection. Lauren had been the first to call, but when Tilberis swore Coddington to secrecy and told her of the $250,000 offer from Lauren, Coddington went directly to her boss, and the next thing Tilberis knew Klein was also courting her.

When Tilberis went to Anna's office to offer her resignation in June 1987, Anna was shocked that she was leaving and then proceeded to denigrate Seventh Avenue and people like Lauren and Klein, who were its royalty. But Tilberis had already accepted Lauren's offer, the press had announced she was following Coddington to America, and friends were planning going-away parties. Her family, she told Anna, was packed and ready to go, their house sold.

Anna called Newhouse and Liberman.

A couple of days later Tilberis (and soon the fashion world) got the shock of her life. In a secret meeting, Anna disclosed in confidence that she was actually the one leaving British *Vogue* and she offered Tilberis her job, which she accepted right then and there.

Rumors about Anna's possible departure from *Vogue* and her future in the United States had been swirling since earlier in 1987, around the same time reports appeared in the press that she was pregnant again.

One story in *The New York Times* about the speculation caused problems in the Condé Nast executive suite on Madison Avenue. Fashion reporter Michael Gross had concluded a column by quoting Liberman as saying, "It is possible that Anna Wintour will come to the U.S., within a certain period of time." Gross ended by noting, "That should keep the rumors roiling."

When he arrived at his desk the next morning, a series of urgent phone messages awaited him from Liberman. The reporter called instantly, and the first words out of Liberman's mouth were, "Dear friend, it seems that *we* have gotten *me* in some trouble. What are *we* going to do to get *me* out of it?" According to Gross, Liberman gave the strong impression that he had been chastised for his comment—probably by Newhouse—and he was now demanding a correction.

"Obviously he had been read the riot act that morning," says Gross, "and it took me forty-five minutes to talk him out of the correction, which I did by explaining to him that by the end of the day his parakeet will be shitting on the story, and if there's a correction, all you're going to do is keep this alive. It's much better to let it pass."

Anna's second child was due to arrive on July 30, and she intended to work right up until July 29. "It's not an illness," she firmly explained to the *Daily Mail*. Anna had a scan done and knew it was a girl.

The talk about Anna leaving *Vogue* started just after Si Newhouse, who was aware of her growing discontent, had flown to London for a breakfast meeting with her. He wanted to placate her, buck her up, tell her that her time was coming, and offer her a new job back in New York.

Anna thought this was the big moment for which she'd been waiting, that Newhouse was going to hand her the editorship of American *Vogue*.

In mid-August, the gossip that something big was going to happen to Anna was confirmed.

She was returning to New York—not to *Vogue* to unseat Grace Mirabella but rather as the new editor in chief of Condé Nast's revered shelter magazine, *House & Garden*. That magazine's longtime editor in chief, Lou Gropp, learned he had been canned three days after Anna's appointment had been announced. "Lou was very brutishly fired," says a former high-ranking editor at *House & Garden*. "He was on vacation in California, and he phoned the office every day, and one day he phoned from a public phone in a parking lot and Si told him he was history."

Anna was, as she stated later, "totally stunned" by Newhouse's offer, and not happily stunned, because she could practically taste American *Vogue*.

"I went right back to the office and called Alex, and he said, 'Absolutely, you have to come.' It was apparently Alex who pushed for me to go to *House & Garden*."

To *The New York Times*, though, she put up a cheery front, saying nothing of substance and talking only on the condition that she not be asked about her plans for her new magazine—mainly because she had none. "I've missed New York terribly," she said. "I'm enormously looking forward to coming back." Speaking of her tenure in London, she said only that "Some people did not like what I did."

By the time of Anna's new appointment, British *Vogue* had gone through the most traumatic time in its seven decades: More than two-thirds of the staff had been replaced, she banned lunchtime drinking, she made sure her top editors were there at eight in the morning by sending cars to pick them up, most arriving rather bleary. It wasn't quite the Blitz, but to those who worked in the trenches at *Vogue* it felt like it. While the look and feel had changed during Anna's brief, controversial watch, circulation and advertising had stayed about the same.

As Drusilla Beyfus Shulman notes, "Everyone was delighted when she got the editorship of *House & Garden* because every editor at British *Vogue* could breathe safely."

Anna rationalized, defended, and denied some of the changes she made during her tenure in London. She said she felt that everyone at *Vogue* "thought I was some sort of American control freak," charged that the press had portrayed her as "a wicked woman of steel," and claimed, "I only remember letting only two or three people go. But, no doubt fearing my awful reputation, a number left of their own accords."

She said she was attacked because she decided to "infuse the magazine with a bit of American worldliness, even toughness." She asserted that the "cozy but mildly eccentric atmosphere" at the magazine struck her "as out of date" and "out of step," and "not responsive to intelligent women's changing lives."

In early August 1987, as scheduled, Anna had a baby girl whom the Shaffers named Kate but who would be nicknamed Bee, mainly because when she first started talking, the toddler had a difficult time saying her actual name, uttering something like "bah-bee." So Bee it became. Fleet Street reported that Anna, after giving birth, was back in the office three days later. But Anna's brother James told Vivienne Lasky that there was some concern about the baby's health, enough that Nonie flew over from England to be at her side. But the emergency soon passed.

Some six weeks later, on September 9, Anna started the overhaul of her new magazine. Already speculation was rampant that she would be at *House & Garden* temporarily, a short respite before pulling out the rug from under Grace Mirabella.

The first day Anna was out of her hair, Liz Tilberis, the new editor in chief of British *Vogue,* resurrected that photo Anna had killed of Christy Turlington and made it her debut cover. She and her family celebrated Anna's long-awaited departure with a real English-style dinner of takeout fish and chips washed down with expensive champagne.

thirty-one

The Parking Lot

No one would ever think of referring to elegant *House & Garden* as a parking lot. But in fact that's how it was described ironically and in private by high-ranking editors at the magazine and top executives at Condé Nast. They called it that because Anna had been placed there temporarily until the time was ripe to give her Grace Mirabella's job at *Vogue*.

"Anna was just being parked for a short time at *House & Garden*," a tuned-in magazine executive says. "She threatened Si that she was going to go to another magazine, so he gave her *House & Garden* and parked her there while he worked out his Machiavellian scheme to get rid of Grace. None of what he did made any sense because he could have just gotten rid of Mirabella and stuck Anna at *Vogue*, and *House & Garden* could have remained a lovely magazine. Anna came in and destroyed it."

Laurie Schechter, whom Anna hired away from *Rolling Stone* to work with her at *House & Garden* as a decorating editor, says, "She told me that she couldn't stand being in England and told them [Newhouse and Liberman] that she didn't care what they had to do, but that they had to bring her back. And so they gave her *House & Garden*."

At *Vogue*, Anna's cheerleader, the fashion editor Polly Mellen, watched the move and suspected what was going on. "Anna did an oblique, and I thought, wait, what's going on here? I had a very strong feeling, a hopeful feeling she was on her way to *Vogue*."

Just when Mirabella thought she was finally safe from that skinny shark draped in Chanel, she started hearing the *Jaws* theme song ringing in her ears again. With Anna back in New York to run *House & Garden,* Mirabella's job was in even greater jeopardy than when Anna was at *Vogue* as creative director—for a couple of reasons.

Not only had Mirabella's relationship with Alex Liberman deteriorated after Anna decamped to British *Vogue,* but now Anna had returned to the Condé Nast headquarters a conquering hero who had seemingly turned the magazine around in less than two years. At least that was the perception that she and her guardian angel Liberman promulgated.

Mirabella was furious, especially because Anna had instituted at British *Vogue* "everything she'd seemed to disdain about *my Vogue*" during her time as creative director. Mirabella was well aware that Anna was a shrewd operator and a savvy corporate politician and had completely won over Liberman and Si Newhouse with her brief reign in London.

As Mirabella acknowledged later, British *Vogue* "established Anna as a player on the editor-in-chief circuit."

Seeing the handwriting on the wall, Mirabella began telling confidants that she was thinking of leaving *Vogue,* but she wanted to do it on her own terms. At the same time, she still refused to admit to herself that she was swimming in dangerous waters and that Anna was circling in for the kill.

Meanwhile, Anna scoffed at suggestions that she had her eye on Mirabella's job, declaring to *The New York Times*—nudge, nudge, wink, wink—that *Vogue* under the current editor was "fantastic" and that Mirabella was "doing a wonderful job."

But Condé Nast veterans knew or suspected otherwise.

Just as fear gripped American *Vogue* and British *Vogue* when staffers knew she was coming, the same mood now existed at *House & Garden.* "Everyone was scared to death because she was known to be a *terrible* woman," a veteran of more than a dozen years at the magazine recalls vividly.

Anna began pulling together her own creative team, which included André Leon Talley, who had been working as a style reporter at Condé Nast's *Vanity Fair.* Talley would be, as Anna said at the time, "covering the waterfront in his own special way."

Laurie Schechter's new position was to oversee a newly minted style column that would encompass interior decorating, living, and fashion.

When Schechter arrived, Gabe Doppelt, the young woman she had recommended to Anna to be her assistant in London, was now listed as an editor, six names underneath Anna's, while Schechter's was eight names below Doppelt's, an indication of things to come.

Doppelt was quickly earning a reputation as difficult and bossy like Anna, having been her right hand since London. "Gabe was wretched," notes a female former *House & Garden* editor who had been waiting to have a meeting with Anna but was getting put off by Doppelt, who kept saying, "Anna's getting ready for you . . . don't worry, everything's fine." After being fired by Anna, the editor went into Doppelt's office and declared, " 'You were very sweet when you were lying to me.' When I left I certainly wished both of them ill."

Anna had also brought in a Park Avenue and international mix she called "consulting editors" and put them on the masthead. This posh and glitzy group included diamond-studded socialite Brooke Astor; Anna's restaurateur pal Michael Chow; her friend Oscar de la Renta; Dodie Kazanjian, who was about to cowrite an authorized (and some would say hagiographic) biography of Alex Liberman; and John Bowes-Lyon, who was related to the queen of England. Most were there mainly for their contacts and insights into the world of the rich and famous.

Gone were editors like Denise Otis, who was a top lieutenant to fired editor in chief Lou Gropp. "I'd been there a long time, but I didn't stay very long after Anna took over," says Otis. "The new management got bored with us, or annoyed with us, because we didn't seem to move fast enough. But you can't move beyond your readers. Anna's approach was a fashion approach, and at that time Condé Nast was still a fashion company. They were used to the fashion pacing."

Anna personally and viciously went after those leftovers from the old regime who had not already read the writing on the wall and resigned. Many needed jobs and stayed on as long as they could.

From behind her steely cold Buchsbaum desk and surrounded by tubs of pink peonies, Anna held personal meetings in her office with most staffers.

"Although she looked young, she looked like a person who was never a lit-tle girl and never played with dolls—unless she put pins in them," recalls one female senior editor who was axed on the spot by Anna. "In that British ac-cent of hers, she said, 'Well, *you* won't fit in.' I said, 'How do you know? I have this idea, and that idea,' and I showed her a long list. We ended up stand-ing up and yelling at each other, and I told her I hoped she fell on her face."

About a half hour later the two ran into each other at the elevator. Anna looked through her and refused to acknowledge her presence.

In her first days at the magazine, Anna met with everybody "except people that she hated, those who were the age of her mother," a senior staffer asserts.

Those who fit in that category felt age discrimination radiating from the bobbed, slender, and fashionable new editor in chief. "Young, young, young," says one creative and talented older editor who soon left. "She didn't want older people. She was mean to older staffers. My son is a lawyer, and as soon as I realized what she was up to I called him and said, 'I think I'm going to need a lawyer.' You don't wait until the shit hits the fan. As soon as you see the fan, you hire a lawyer."

The editor felt an age discrimination suit might be in order. Her son put her in touch with an attorney who specialized in such cases, and he advised her to make detailed notes about things Anna said, particularly if she ever used the word "youthful." Luckily, for Anna's sake, the editor never heard her utter it, though it's certainly a part of Anna's lexicon.

Other editors ran out to get new, hipper-looking wardrobes in the hopes of placating Anna and making her think they had a youthful image and attitude—and save their jobs, even if their hair was turning a bit gray. "Everybody had to shorten their skirts," recalls one editor.

A few who didn't pass muster, but whom Condé Nast wanted to keep around because Liberman liked them, were sent to the fourteenth floor, known in the parlance of Condé Nast as "the elephant's graveyard," where they would serve out their time and retire, some with full pay and medical benefits.

Veteran staffers who weren't fired were kept around because Anna didn't know the shelter business like she knew the fashion business, and she needed experienced editors and writers who had covered that scene for years for

House & Garden to take her to the showrooms and introduce her to the industry. They were treated shabbily before finally getting the boot.

Anna's planned retooling was not the first time since the beginning of the eighties that Si Newhouse had shifted strategy at the magazine to try to make it into a winner.

In 1983, while Anna was still doing her dog and pony show at *New York*, Newhouse, chairman of Condé Nast Publications Inc., had reduced *House & Garden*'s circulation to make it an elite rather than a mass-market monthly. His hope was to put it in league with *Architectural Digest*. But *House & Garden* bombed, and a dark horse called *Metropolitan Home* raced into the lead of the shelter magazine pack. Soon more would come along, such as *Elle Home*. Eventually, Newhouse ended the competition with *Architectural Digest* by simply buying it.

Now Newhouse put his money on Anna to make *House & Garden* a success, if there was enough time before he canned Grace Mirabella and gave Anna her job. Anna was Newhouse's favorite British editrix after Tina Brown at *Vanity Fair*.

The word was out that under Anna, the doddering eighty-six-year-old *House & Garden* was in for an extreme makeover. That included more than just larger pages, a new square format, lots of fashion coverage, and features on celebrities and socialites and nobility. Something far more drastic was in the works.

After almost nine decades, its name was changed—a corporate decision made by Newhouse, with Anna's support. Her name first appeared on the masthead in the January 1988 issue, and the name on the March cover of the magazine became *HG* in three-inch-high letters. Nowhere in the magazine was there a mention that there had been a transition of editors or that the name had changed. Thinking it was a new magazine, many subscribers put it aside and continued to wait for their beloved *House & Garden* to arrive in the mailbox.

The first issue with Anna's imprimatur got mixed reviews. Charles Truehart, who covered the magazine world for *The Washington Post*, observed that the new *HG* looked more like it had been "shot up with amphetamines" rather than redesigned.

"There is no question of subtle transitions under Anna Wintour . . . The new *HG* is as different from the old as a remake can comfortably be. This one is born to be scanned: Its pages give the eye kiss after kiss of sumptuous color and snazzy scenes, little bites of information and dazzle, the glow of modern luxe."

One major criticism of the first and early issues was that the graphics were distracting, especially to designers who saw their work cropped. One architect, after leafing through the first issue, said the layouts looked as if they'd gone through a Cuisinart.

Anna had also introduced *Vanity Fair*–style celebrity tabloid fare. That first issue included looks at the home life of Bette Midler, David Hockney (both of whom also appeared in *Vanity Fair* around the same time), Dennis Hopper, and some of the new Rothschilds. A column called "View" in *Vogue* was similar to one called "Talleysheet" in *HG*. It all tended to make readers of both think they were seeing double, and it infuriated Tina Brown, who felt that Anna was intruding on her celebrity territory.

Anna assigned pieces to her pal Christopher Hitchens, who wrote about the George Bush White House as a place to live and advertising executive Jerry Della Femina's "graphic" Manhattan penthouse.

A mixture of fashion, wealth, and elitism was in.

One photo underscoring the new look was of a guitar-playing Princess Gloria von Thurn und Taxis draped in S&M leathers while posed on Marie Antoinette's bed in one of her palaces in Bavaria. One *HG* cover displayed a playwright's rumpled bed with his pet pugs and books; there was a photo of Michael Chow standing on his head with an Eileen Grey pedestal nearby; and then there was the model lying spread-eagle on a needlepoint rug on a beach. Anna planned one issue around a Gauguin exhibit in Washington, D.C., which sparked anger from *HG* contributor John Richardson, a noted art historian. He was furious that she would use such art to hawk commercial design.

As she did at British *Vogue,* Anna turned *HG* inside out and upside down, fired and hired, raided other magazines for writers, including Tina Brown's *Vanity Fair,* with whom she was enmeshed in an ongoing rivalry.

Most shocking of all, she arrogantly tossed into the trash upward of two million dollars in story inventory (text and photos), so she could start from scratch and do things her way.

"In her dark glasses, she went through every piece of inventory," recalls a senior editor. "Every editor had to come into the room, which had light boxes to view the Kodachromes around three sides of the room. Everyone came in with their inventory. The photographers had been paid, the writers and editors had been paid who had stayed in fancy hotels during those shoots; it was a very lush life. But Anna got rid of everything—*everything*—except for maybe seven or eight stories."

Put off by the celebrity and fashion coverage, longtime readers canceled subscriptions—a special toll-free hotline was hurriedly established to deal with the onslaught of fuming subscribers. Designer advertisers who were hooked on the magazine's reputation for spectacular layouts of elegant interiors—not cushy, nouveau riche celeb party pads—began to bail out, although the business side claimed that advertising had held its own. While some fashion advertisers gravitated to the magazine, most traditional *House & Garden* advertisers couldn't make heads or tails out of what Anna was doing, and the same went for those in architecture and publishing.

Another problem for Anna was that former editor Lou Gropp was well liked in the home magazine industry and every month wrote a cozy "from the editor" column reminiscing about houses he had lived in. Under Anna, the once warm and fuzzy feeling of the magazine was replaced by a stark stainless-steel and granite coldness, representative of its editor.

"Anna was a bad fit," observes Denise Otis. "The mood about her wasn't very good. You got the feeling there were 'in' people and 'out' people, and that hadn't been true of the magazine before."

While Anna had dealt with interior design stories at *New York* magazine, running an entire magazine based not on fashion but on fanciful shelter quickly took its toll. When Anna began showing fashion along with interiors, the magazine earned the sobriquet *House & Garment*. When she introduced celebrities—including trendy artists, hip architects, and old- and new-money Brits and Euros—wags began calling her magazine *Vanity Chair* and *Hot Gossip*.

Where there were once "pristine, people-free rooms," *The New York Times* noted, "there was now a zippy mix of fashionably dressed models in quirky environments . . . 'society' lady decorators in their designer duds" and a playwright petting his dogs in an unmade bed.

Despite the criticism, Anna felt as if she had revolutionized the home magazine genre. "Up until she changed things, the layouts were of very staid rooms that were perfectly attired and looked like nobody had touched them," Laurie Schechter observes. "They were dust free, forever. Anna so dramatically changed the book. But it was very jolting to subscribers who were the older garden people, and to people in the interior design world. I don't think they [Condé Nast] were prepared for that world to be *so* set in its ways. For those people who were so addicted to the old format, the new one was more irreverent and mixed things up more. You rarely see a total repositioning of a magazine. Ideally, you don't want to alienate your readership but increase or broaden it."

One of Newhouse's goals in putting Anna in the editor's chair was to play catch-up with *Architectural Digest,* but that would never happen during her watch. *HG* lagged far behind by some sixty thousand issues a month, though its circulation grew slightly. "Our instinct told us we needed to make *House & Garden* into more of a living magazine than a typical shelter magazine," said Bernard Leser, Condé Nast Publication's president. Liberman and others wanted to beat *Architectual Digest* at its own game by being distinctly different. That they got. But business reportedly went south; the publisher of *Architectural Digest* boasted that as many as twenty of *HG*'s advertisers had jumped ship and come aboard his publication because of the changes Anna and her team had wrought.

Anna's blueprint for *HG* was to show, as she put it, "the connection between fashion and style and design and decorating." But she denied at the height of the controversy over her remake that she had turned it into a fashion magazine, although by early summer 1988 four of its first five covers showed women in designer dresses. Inside, stories of the fashion genre abounded, such as one that had models in classic little black dresses standing on classic little black chairs. Despite her denials, Ralph Lauren's fashions appeared on the cover, with Yves Saint Laurent's inside; celebrity hairdressers Kenneth, Christaan, and Didier Malige were featured cutting topiary.

While so many were displeased with Anna's product, Newhouse acted overjoyed. In fact, he acknowledged that he pampered it as if it were their baby. "I saw it before it was published," he said. "I saw it when it was laid down with the photostats."

Liberman also came to her defense. He said he saw every layout because "Anna wanted my approval. I personally questioned the introduction of fashion, but she was so innovative and daring about it, and Si loved what she was doing. We were both stimulated and excited by the idea of a total magazine of style."

By early June 1988, rumors once again were rampant that Anna was set to replace Mirabella, all of which were denied by Condé Nast brass. After all, Mirabella had made *Vogue* a great success, and Anna was just getting down to business at *HG*.

She told *The Times* of London, wearing what was described as the briefest white tweed skirt Karl Lagerfeld could devise, that the rumors "are ridiculous. We've only just started, it would be crazy to leave now."

The reporter noted that Anna "even dissembles with style."

But the question remained, Why make a change?

thirty-two

July Fourth Massacre

On August 20, 1985, an American version of a trendy French fashion magazine called *Elle* appeared on American newsstands. Overnight, it became a publishing success story.

For Si Newhouse, it was the end of the world as he knew it. Well, almost. *Vogue,* he believed, faced its greatest threat and stiffest competition ever.

From that moment on, the message on high to Grace Mirabella was to make *Vogue* more like *Elle,* which had shrewdly picked up on the MTV generation's short attention span, offering its quickly growing younger readership montages of flashy fashion layouts, crisper and spunkier headlines, shorter stories without jumps, and lots of exuberant hot models wearing youthful, sexy fashions.

Sister of the legendary thirty-year-old Parisian fashion magazine, American *Elle* was not designed to tell someone how to put style in her life, which *Vogue* subtly did—Mirabella's philosophy was "give them what they never knew they needed." *Elle* was aimed at fashionistas and wannabes who already had a thread of style, in everything from the clothes they wore to the food they ate to how they decorated their living spaces.

Newhouse must have been especially concerned when he read the May 5, 1986, issue of *Forbes* and noted that in just eight months *Elle* had "elbowed its way into the magazine racks alongside *Vogue.*" The director of print media for one of the world's largest advertising agencies declared *Elle* "a fabulous success story." And *Elle*'s publisher stated that the magazine's readership was younger than *Vogue*'s and less didactic than other women's magazines. Circulation, the business magazine noted, was way up and, better yet, ad rates were less expensive than *Vogue*'s.

A quiet panic had set in at the upper echelons. On a cover shoot, Alex Liberman was said to have called the studio every twenty minutes demanding to know, "Does it look like an *Elle* cover? Does it look like an *Elle* cover?" At one point he actually called back and ordered that the model's hair be cut shorter "just like an *Elle* cover."

Mirabella was told in "charming and not-so-charming terms" to give *Vogue* the feel of *Elle*. She couldn't and she wouldn't, which of course did not go over well with the big guy upstairs, who passed the word that she was out of touch with young people and with women in general.

That message was usually funneled to Mirabella by Liberman, through whom she communicated with Newhouse, an odd setup and not a great career enhancer. Not talking directly with the head of the whole company because she disliked him intensely and never took him seriously was Mirabella's curious style—and against Liberman's advice.

Many times he had told her to get to know him. But she refused. Later, she pondered the possibility that some key two-way information regarding her views about *Elle* and other issues never made it to the intended party. "Alex," she pointed out, "controlled the flow of information as it suited his purposes."

But her biggest career faux pas was not following *Elle*'s lead, which is what Newhouse wanted. She firmly believed that *Vogue* was still the magazine some 1.2 million women a month turned to for their fashion fix, and that *Elle* "offered very little. . . ."

Bad decision, as she would later acknowledge.

Through the month of May 1988, top secret meetings took place in the executive suite at Condé Nast with Si Newhouse, Alex Liberman, and Bernard Lesser. Planning was under way for Mirabella's dismissal and Anna's ascension, the job she could taste practically since the first time she shopped at Biba in the midsixties. According to Liberman later, it was Newhouse who wanted Mirabella out and Anna in. "I didn't push for Anna Wintour," he maintained. "She was a demand of Si's."

Whoever made the decision—and most find Liberman's assertion hard to swallow, since he was Anna's biggest booster—she was elated. Her time had finally come.

"There were endless meetings with Si and Alex at which we talked mostly about dates and timing, because Alex was so undecided" about the timing, she stated later. "Sometimes it was going to be September, and sometimes the following January. The whole thing was unfair to Grace, who had not been told, and unfair to me, because I had to come back from the meetings and try to do a magazine that I knew I wasn't going to be at for very long, and lie to all the people. It was awful, really awful."

Anna and Mirabella had two things in common: their passion for fashion and the fact that both had taken doctors for husbands. Mirabella's, Dr. William Cahan, was a cancer surgeon affiliated with the prestigious Memorial Sloan-Kettering hospital in New York.

On June 28, 1988, upscale New Yorkers who didn't have to punch a clock were already escaping the city for the long Fourth of July weekend, heading for beach houses on Long Island or country places in Connecticut, both especially popular with the fashion, style, and design crowd.

Mirabella was still at her office, but Cahan was at home relaxing after a stressful day in the operating room when the telephone rang. A family friend was urgently calling to tell him to turn on Channel 4. A promo said that the syndicated gossip columnist Liz Smith, who had a segment on "Live at Five," was about to dish some major gossip about Grace.

He switched on the TV just in time to hear Smith in her annoyingly creaky Texas voice tell viewers that his wife, at age fifty-eight, the editor in chief of *Vogue* for seventeen years, was about to be axed, and that Anna, who had a tempestuous history in the fashion magazine business and wasn't liked by many, would be her successor four months before her thirty-ninth birthday.

"The hot publishing story is that this will probably happen on September first," Smith stated. "Don't ask me why Condé Nast would want to replace Grace Mirabella. *Vogue* is one of the healthiest, heftiest magazines in the Condé Nast chain. You know, if it ain't broke, don't fix it, but they're going to anyway."

One of Smith's greatest assets as a highly paid gossip is her ability to have it both ways—to stick in the knife while still appearing sympathetic to the victim. Someone at the top at Condé Nast had dropped a dime and she ran with it, even though Mirabella considered her a friend.

With the holiday weekend near and rumors about her demise flying, Mirabella should have expected something like this. Newhouse had a tendency to fire top editors before or during a holiday or vacation. He had notches on his belt to prove it. The most recent victim had been *House & Garden*'s Lou Gropp. Now Anna was going to replace another Condé Nast veteran, just ten months after she took over *HG*. "What was a constant in all of Si Newhouse's seemingly erratic behavior," Mirabella would later observe, "was a kind of extreme insensitivity to the feelings of his editors."

There was still another clue that something bad might befall Mirabella's career. In early June, instead of attending an important furniture trade show in Chicago where the editor of *HG* was expected, Anna was in Paris front row center at a fashion show, which didn't escape the keen eyes of both the furniture and the fashion people, and the drums started beating.

The Tuesday when the story broke Anna had left the office early in the afternoon, which was curious to her *HG* team because she had been spending long hours there molding the magazine in her image. But on that particular day, as if she knew that a dirty bomb was about to explode, she had oddly disappeared. Many later wondered whether she knew the leak was coming and didn't want to be around to answer to anyone. The other question was whether she herself had leaked the story, either directly or indirectly. No one would put it past her, but no one ever knew for sure.

Refusing to believe what he was hearing, Mirabella's husband immediately telephoned his wife, who had been told nothing about being replaced—she was innocently going about the business of locking up the next issue. Now they both were in shock.

In response to his question "What's going on?," all she could mumble was "I have no idea . . . I have no idea."

"It had all the makings of a soap opera," *Newsday* reported a few days later. "The formidable yet fallible editor of the world's most vaunted fashion magazine is ousted. The hauntingly beautiful upstart ascends to the helm . . . with reports of plots and coups and tales of behind-the-scenes sniping."

Mirabella headed upstairs to the office of her mentor to find out if there was any truth to the broadcast gossip.

"Grace, I'm afraid it's true," Liberman told her,

When she demanded an explanation, he claimed the axing wasn't his idea and advised her to talk to Newhouse. "I had nothing to do with it," he maintained.

She told him, "You're going to regret this," because of how it was handled.

Later, Liberman raised more questions than he answered when he described the succession as "a series of misunderstandings and mix-ups" and asserted that "the way it came out was unfortunate."

Anna was jubilant that late afternoon. Her dream had finally come true. She'd been crowned editor in chief of *Vogue,* the world's fashion bible and the jewel of the Condé Nast publishing empire. She had become the fifth editor of the nearly nine-decades-old magazine. But she was in hiding, no one knew where. She'd known for more than a month she had the job but had covered up and lied to everyone she knew, except for her husband.

Mirabella, meanwhile, was numb and in the spotlight.

She couldn't believe that Newhouse had replaced her with an editor who many felt made a "fiasco" out of *House & Garden,* where ad pages were down and subscribers had disappeared. Newhouse, on the other hand, put forth that Anna had turned *HG* into a magazine of "wit, excitement and controversy." And he was seemingly unbothered by the mess she'd left in her wake at British *Vogue,* so adoring he was of her.

To Mirabella, her dismissal and replacement by Anna was unconscionable and insane.

But Anna was the ultimate company girl, and Mirabella wasn't. She'd thumbed her nose at Newhouse for too many years, and now she'd gotten her due, as he saw it. And so had Anna.

As one keen but cynical Condé Nast observer notes years later, "Anna was so far up Si's you know what, she could see his fillings."

A few hours after her brief meeting with Liberman, Mirabella reached Newhouse by telephone at home. Yes, he confirmed, he'd sacked her, and he told her to meet with him in his office the next morning to make arrangements for her departure and a financial settlement.

Early Wednesday, June 29, she found him at his desk in his stocking feet. It was just nine A.M., but he'd been working since five, so he was relaxing.

"Well, it's been a long time," he said as he dropped the curtain on her career.

He asked her to stay on until mid-July to oversee the completion of the October issue and then sent her off to meet the corporate secretary to work out a severance package. Mirabella thought the offer was low and telephoned her friend the attorney and literary agent Mort Janklow. He came up with an alternative plan that his friend Newhouse accepted immediately.

That afternoon, this real-life melodrama continued to play out when Mirabella called a meeting of her staff to formally announce that she was leaving. "Unfortunately, management has seen fit to have me go earlier," she said. Then she added, "Anna Wintour will be the new editor of *Vogue*."

Some, who hadn't heard about the TV report, were shocked. Others, who watched the Liz Smith spectacle, had tears in their eyes.

Co–fashion creative director Polly Mellen performed her and-now-Mr.-DeMille-I'm-ready-for-my-close-up routine. As Mirabella later described the scene, "Grabbing her breast, she threw herself against the cabinet that held our TV and VCR and shouted, 'My God, Grace! My God! How could this happen?'"

Only moments before, though, Mellen, long a champion of Anna, had told a colleague that she supported Mirabella's firing, which Mirabella was aware of when Mellen gave her Oscar-worthy performance.

Later, Mirabella said, "I thought of Diana Vreeland's line: 'The stage lost its greatest actress when Polly Mellen joined *Vogue*.'"

Another editor bitchily pointed out to Mirabella, "Well, you don't need the money" and mentioned something about the magazine needing "new blood."

The other fashion creative director, Jade Hobson, immediately let it be known she was resigning. Hobson destested Anna and never forgot how Anna had treated her and others during her tenure as creative director.

Another veteran editor, astonished by what had transpired, stood by Mirabella's desk and observed sadly, "This is a tough place. Very tough. I had no idea."

While everyone knew she had been fired, Newhouse issued a memo to the staff that afternoon announcing that Mirabella had retired. Later, Mirabella would claim that she intended to leave the magazine of her own accord later that year or the next, which might have been her rationale to lessen the blow.

The next day *The New York Times,* in announcing the dramatic change in editors at the world's most powerful fashion magazine, noted that the appointment of Anna "comes as *Vogue* is thought to be losing ground to *Elle*" and quoted a top national media director as saying, "The scuttlebutt in the fashion industry is that *Elle* could be the new standard for the fashion industry, and that's got to be disconcerting to *Vogue.*"

Newhouse later told the *Times* that he long felt it was time to "reposition *Vogue* for the 90's." This despite the fact that under Mirabella, circulation had tripled.

Anna's takeover, therefore, raised an important question: Why would Condé Nast, as Liz Smith had asked, fix something that wasn't broke?

While *Elle* was certainly making a name for itself, *Vogue* was still far ahead of its competitors in advertising revenue. In 1987, *Vogue* had $79.5 million in ad revenue, while *Elle* had $39 million and *Harper's Bazaar* stood at $32.5 million. However, Elle's paid circulation had catapulted to 851,000 by 1987, while *Vogue's* had stayed around 1.2 million. *Vogue's* newsstand sales had slipped and advertising pages were flat.

While speculation about Anna replacing Mirabella had been floating around ever since Anna first came to *Vogue* as creative director, her succession still shocked the fashion world, particularly in the shabby way it unfolded and how Mirabella learned about it.

"For Ms. Mirabella," *The New York Times* noted later, "it was an undignified ending to a highly successful career." And Mirabella told the *Times* that the manner of her removal was "very unstylish, for such a stylish place." She also stated that she never spoke to Anna about the rumors, noting Anna was "not anybody I have long conversations with."

The firing didn't have as much impact on Mirabella, though, as it did on *Vogue* editor of yore Margaret Case. Case was so upset by the shabby way her own dismissal was handled, the eighty-year-old fashionista, ill with cancer, depressed, and alone, committed suicide by jumping out of her fourteenth-floor apartment window.

In Mirabella's case, she'd bounce back in the fashion magazine ball game big-time soon enough.

Meanwhile, *HG* advertisers were left flabbergasted by Anna's abandonment. "To have the person responsible for those changes get up and leave after a few months is quite a surprise," declared the director of advertising for a major furniture company. "You just don't take a magazine the caliber of *House & Garden,* change it around, and walk away."

At *HG,* Nancy Novogrod, a former book-publishing executive editor who had joined the magazine a few months earlier, succeeded Anna. Novogrod said she planned to "inch" the magazine "back to interior design," the same place it was when Anna took it over. *HG* lasted a brief time before Newhouse closed it down but later reopened it.

Shortly after that memorable July Fourth weekend massacre, Anna was having lunch at the plush Four Seasons Grill Room. At another table was Grace Mirabella, who had just locked up the October issue and was ready to bid a final adieu to the magazine that had been her home for years.

The two editors never exchanged a glance.

Vogue was now Anna's baby.

As one wag observed at the time, "Condé Nast editors may all breathe a sigh of relief because Anna had landed the only job where she may safely be expected to stay."

thirty-three

Anna and the Boss

Anna began her reign as editor in chief of *Vogue* even before Grace Mirabella had signed off on the final piece of text and the last photo for her curtain-closing October issue.

By late July, in her virtually empty *HG* office on the fifth floor of the Condé Nast building, she had started pulling her team together and making her power felt by interviewing shaken *Vogue* staffers every half hour or so. Members of the old regime would do what they had to do for Mirabella and then report directly to Anna, who often put them on the hot seat by asking them what they did, why they thought they should continue doing what they did for *her,* and who *they* felt should or shouldn't stay. The do-you-still-beat-your-wife tactic sent a chill through the place.

With Anna about to take over, paranoia and fear ran rampant among those employees who saw their worlds crashing down under the new boss woman.

Mirabella remembered those last days as being "a strange and ugly time" with people walking around "whispering and looking over their shoulders to see who was listening." She was especially peeved when she saw Si Newhouse actually walking the corridors of *Vogue,* where he was rarely seen, carrying baskets of jewelry and other things in and out of Anna's office to preview for her first issue. It was, she felt, "like a slap in the face" to see him so involved.

Monday, August 1, 1988, Anna's first full day as the head of *Vogue,* started horrendously. Liz Smith had another scoop that was profoundly disturbing. The item alleged a romantic link between Anna and Newhouse, a rumor that had begun back when Anna was recruited by Alex Liberman and Newhouse from *New York* magazine, and one Anna was well aware of.

Nevertheless, the spanking-new editor in chief went ballistic. Not only did it cause problems for Anna and Newhouse, but the bitchy item would put what was described as a severe strain on Anna's relationship with her husband, who is said to have gotten deeply involved behind the scenes in the imbroglio.

A catty item of this sort appearing on her debut at *Vogue* was almost guaranteed and shouldn't have come as any great surprise. It had been open season on Anna ever since she had taken over British *Vogue* because so many people in the fashion magazine business and the rag trade had it in for her—either jealous of her success, or a victim of her imperiousness, or both.

But Smith felt the rumor had enough legs to warrant running with it.

Was it payback?

Despite the fact that Smith had run the item about Mirabella's firing, she was known to be close friends with her. Mirabella later stated that Smith "was furious" with Condé Nast for giving someone the green light to "leak" the story before telling Mirabella.

Besides suggesting an intimate relationship, the item essentially repeated that old antifeminist saw that any successful woman who makes it to the top probably slept her way there. And while Anna was far from being a feminist, the assertion made her see red.

Rather than simply ignore the gossip, or laugh it off as the bitchiness of the fashion business, Anna was loaded for bear.

Within a week after the item ran, she called a mandatory morning meeting of her editorial staff and anyone else in the organization interested in hearing what she had to say.

"She was outraged—*outraged*—about the Liz Smith item and was not going to let it go by unanswered," says a female former Condé Nast executive who had worked closely with Anna. "She was very upset that people thought this was still a world in which women couldn't get ahead without sleeping with the boss.

"I thought David was completely behind the speech," the former executive says. "There were certain things Anna said that I didn't think she was capable of. I didn't think that she could be the architect of such a speech. It was strong. It took the issue on where I wouldn't think she would have taken it on. She sounded angry, but appropriately so.

"It was a difficult thing to do in light of the fact she'd just taken on this huge job, and the person she's accused of sleeping with owns this huge company. Anna was very prepared and I could tell, knowing her, that this was something she had genuinely discussed with somebody very close to her, that this somebody was also very upset and had thought it through and addressed it. And that would have been David.

"Anna did it in a very dignified way, saying people still think this is the way women got ahead. Anna rarely ever held these kinds of meetings. It was one of very few such performances, and it was not a very English thing to do."

Anna stood on stilettos throughout her remarks, which lasted less than twenty minutes in a meeting room on the twelfth floor where advertising and promotion was located. After finishing, she took no questions and told her people to go back to work and move forward.

If anyone applauded, no one can recall.

"It wasn't like everyone was shocked," says the former executive. "While unusual, it was probably a smart thing for Anna to do. Her comments didn't sound like Bill Clinton's 'I didn't sleep with that woman, Ms. Lewinsky.'"

Afterward, staffers gathered in small groups to talk about the shocking events. "I, for one, thought she was telling the truth, and I always thought it was handy for people at *Vogue* to believe that she had a thing with Si because they didn't want to see Anna validated," says the former executive.

Newhouse eventually and genially commented to Smith that he was flattered by all the gossip but declared that he was "very much in love with my wife and my wife's dog," and stated firmly that there was no truth to what Smith had printed.

Around the same time as the Liz Smith item ran, *Newsday* did a major story about Anna's takeover at *Vogue* and quoted an unnamed "fashion veteran," who also asserted, "Si is in love with her. He loves the way she looks, he loves the way she flirts. . . ."

Despite Anna's sincere and forceful denial, talk of a cozy relationship between Anna and Newhouse continued.

"There were longtime and long-standing rumors that Anna and Si were romantically involved, and it was never anything but smoke," says fashion writer Michael Gross. He said it was never the kind of gossipy story *The Times* would have ever chased and pointed out that "people in the fashion world are vicious, envious bitches—male and female.

"Anna's rise caused a lot of envy and bitchiness. All you had to do was see Si Newhouse and Anna Wintour in a room together to realize that Si was *very* pleased to have Anna around him. Now, can you extrapolate sex from that? If you're a fashion editor sitting in your three hundredth fashion show subsisting on cigarettes, coffee, and champagne in the nineteenth row looking down on Anna Wintour in the front row, sure, one could come up with that. But there was never enough there that I even chased it. Anna was already with David. She was breeding. Mothers don't usually go off and have affairs." (Down the road he'd be proved wrong about the latter, though the man in question wasn't Si Newhouse.)

Laurie Schechter, who had come over to *Vogue* as style editor with Anna, also remembers her as being "highly disturbed and upset" about the Liz Smith item. "I don't think Anna's speech was a case of thou doth protest too much," she maintains. "But she definitely has a way with men. They become enamored of her. She's a striking woman and she has that mysterious allure, and her charms get turned on for men. But I didn't think, personally, that the rumor was true. How pathetic that people couldn't acknowledge she was at *Vogue* because she deserved to be there and not because she slept with Si Newhouse. Men can be carried a long way on the enamored quality of a woman like Anna. It doesn't have to be physical."

For Anna, her appointment seemed almost inauspicious. If there was a celebration of her coronation, no one was aware of it. So much venom was being spewed, so much anger and angst abounded. The Liz Smith story was like pouring gasoline on glowing embers.

Some fourteen years later, having been involved in a real, well-documented, and highly publicized extramarital affair that destroyed her marriage, Anna was still oddly vexed about that old and yellowed gossip item.

As a recipient of a 2002 Matrix Award for magazines, sponsored by New York Women in Communications, she brought up the gossip that most everyone had forgotten—the latest scandal, involving her and wealthy Texan Shelby Bryan, being much more current and scrumptious.

While the mood at the award luncheon was described as upbeat and gracious, Anna took a "defensive tone" in her acceptance speech. She recalled for the audience, including Walter Cronkite, who was on the dais, that on her first day as editor in chief of *Vogue*, "a nationally syndicated gossip writer said that an alleged affair with my boss had got me my job." Anna emphasized that she believed "none of this would have happened if I had been a man." A surprise and ironic speaker at the affair after Anna accepted her award and vented was an iconic figure who over the years had been embroiled in extramarital affairs—William Jefferson Clinton.

Besides Laurie Schechter, Anna brought with her to *Vogue* a team that included André Leon Talley; Gabe Doppelt, who had bonded closely with Anna; Charles Gandee; Derek Ungless, *Vogue*'s new art director, who along with Anna was responsible for some of the controversial changes at *HG*; and a couple of other creative talents.

Among those who left were Jade Hobson, who went to Revlon for a time (but the other fashion creative director, Polly Mellen, stayed on); managing editor Lorraine Davis left but stayed within the Condé Nast organization; features editor Amy Gross accepted a position at *HG*; associate editor Kathleen Madden also resigned but stayed at Condé Nast; the two-person living department was killed off, and Anna's once close friend and colleague Paul Sinclaire, who had been a fashion editor at *Vogue* where he also was a close associate of Mirabella's, went to *HG*. In all, some thirty staffers either were pink-slipped or turned in their resignation within a month or two of Anna's ascension.

With Anna gone from *HG*, new editor Nancy Novogrod added the old name *House & Garden* in small letters under the big *HG* initials, in hopes of winning back subscribers who had jumped the garden fence when Anna was in residence. The magazine didn't have long to live, though, in its latest incarnation. In 1993, Si Newhouse killed off the more than nine-decades-old monthly because its comeback wasn't fast enough. That same year he bought its rival, *Architectural Digest.* Anna's shoddy renovation of *HG* apparently couldn't be repaired.

The biggest surprise addition to Anna's team was one of the giants of British *Vogue* who had fled from Anna's flogging—Grace Coddington. She had been working for Calvin Klein in New York for about eighteen months when Anna came into power. Coddington missed the fashion magazine world and she felt, after working in New York, that she had a better understanding of the American woman and her fashion needs. She telephoned Anna and said, "I'd like to come back," and Anna responded, "I'm starting on Monday. Why don't you start with me?" Anna gave her the title of fashion director and put her high on the masthead. There was talk within the industry that Coddington took a substantial salary cut and ate lots of crow to come work for Anna again.

"Anna's very mercurial," notes Schechter regarding Anna's decision to hire Coddington. "She's a lot like fashion—short skirts this season, long skirts next. She can be a bit like that with people, too. Even when she was pursuing André [Leon Talley, when he was a freelancer], she used to say to me, 'Oh, I think his work is so over the top, don't you?' That's the way she is. It didn't surprise me that Grace went back. Working for a fashion designer like Calvin Klein is a very singular point of view and doesn't allow the depth or range that working at a fashion magazine does, working with a lot of different designers' clothes and points of view rather than just one."

Anna, who despised the Brit mentality that ran *Vogue* in London, now did a complete one-eighty and acknowledged that when she took over American *Vogue,* "I took the British approach with me because it seemed what was needed was some sort of combination of the two."

Anna's immediate goal for *Vogue* was to "put a happier face on things," says Schechter—models smiling and looking exuberant. "Even Anna's first cover was a big departure because it wasn't just a beautiful face, it was a smiling, beautiful face."

That cover, dated November 1988, was far different from anything Grace Mirabella or Diana Vreeland or any of the others before Anna had ever dreamed or had nightmares about. It showed a pouty-lipped nineteen-year-old Israeli model named Michaela Bercu with mussed hair wearing tight, faded fifty-dollar jeans—*jeans,* of all things, on the cover of glamorous *Vogue,* the old-line fashionistas gasped—and sporting a ten-thousand-dollar Christian Lacroix T-shirt designed with a bejeweled pattern in the shape of a cross.

"I wanted the covers to show gorgeous real girls looking the way they looked out on the street rather than the plastic kind of retouched look that had been the *Vogue* face for such a long time," declared Anna. "I wanted to bring in new photographers and just liven the whole thing up a bit."

Critics were astonished at what the new arbiter of American fashion had done with her first issue. As *The New York Times* pointed out, "It may well be the first time blue jeans have appeared on a *Vogue* cover—without a belt and with the model's tummy showing, no less."

"Weird" was the way a Neiman Marcus executive described the cover.

Anna's view of mixing jeans with couture was to convey to the readers that a woman can "make an outfit her own by how she puts it together." She called the issue "transitional" and pointed out that "*Vogue* girls have a kind of 'don't touch me' look. I think we have a freer attitude toward fashion. When we looked at the couture this time, we tried to look at it in a more accessible way."

Besides the startling cover, the models inside had a more informal look.

It was what Si and Alex had been demanding of Mirabella but never got. It was *Elle. Vogue* called the look "haute but not haughty." As Schechter notes, "The *Vogue* under Anna didn't look or feel like the *Vogue* under Grace. Anna obviously had a different approach. Even the content that Grace railed against for whatever reason when Anna was creative director—all of it was very palatable commercially. Anna's smart. She's not going to do something that's going to put her outside the corporate popularity."

Much later, Mirabella felt certain she would never have been fired if she had only followed Newhouse's wishes and made *Vogue* look just a little bit more like *Elle.*

Anna had followed Newhouse's mandate to the letter, nudging *Vogue* ever closer to the look and feel of *Elle.* One of her first acts after unseating Mirabella was to lure to *Vogue* a glamorous, high-ranking *Elle* editor who had the *Elle* spirit of being fun, mixing things up. She was an important addition to the staff in those early days.

thirty-four

Madonna, Di, and Tina

Anna's first full year at the top of *Vogue* was not a pleasant time for the fashion industry. A deep recession had taken hold.

The U.S. dollar had fallen like a rock, by as much as 50 percent against the British pound. Everyone from the rag trade to couture was feeling the pinch. As a result, Anna and other power brokers in the U.S. fashion scene went so far as to ignore Fashion Week in London in spring 1989. Everyone was in the doldrums.

Anna, meanwhile, devoted as much as twelve hours a day to performing cosmetic surgery on what she and Newhouse perceived as the wrinkly face of *Vogue*—tightening it here, nipping it there, tucking it everywhere—always working toward making it look younger, getting it closer to that kicky *Elle* look that had intrigued Newhouse so much that he canned Grace Mirabella because she didn't get it.

What Anna didn't do was a complete makeover as she had done at *HG*. She'd learned her lesson about proceeding with extreme surgery without a real plan or a true feel for the marketplace.

Those first year of *Vogue* covers under Anna ranged from a young model in a tank top sporting a Byblos hat costing less than a hundred dollars to a formal photograph taken by the famous Irving Penn. It was all part of her loosening-up process, without going off the chart.

That included putting hot young celebrities on the cover—and none was hotter, sexier, or more erotic at the time than a singer and entertainer formerly known as Madonna Louise Ciccone.

André Leon Talley went forth to Los Angeles to check her out for Anna, met with her, was psyched, and thus the May 1989 issue of *Vogue* had the Material Girl on its cover, with a ten-page spread of her house inside, *HG*-like.

"We put Madonna on the cover," Anna intoned, "because we want to show the range where fashion comes from."

In fact, Anna actually put Madonna on the cover for "S&S—sales and Si," asserts a well-placed *Vogue* source. "Madonna in those days would have sold a roll of toilet paper if she was on the packaging. Anna was all about celebrity, putting a supercelebrity on the cover sold big-time, and Si was walking on air. She was doing what Grace didn't do, and what Si wanted."

The New York Times, though, noted that Madonna was "hardly the elegant, carefully coiffed woman of whom *Vogue* was enamored" in the past.

But Anna's youth orientation didn't show an upward spike in newsstand sales, which represented some 65 percent of *Vogue*'s circulation. That number remained much the same as when Mirabella was running the show. However, advertising pages increased somewhat, by about forty-seven pages compared to Mirabella's final year.

As *The Times* observed, "The jury is still out on how effective Ms. Wintour is doing."

Meanwhile, *Elle* was right on *Vogue*'s tail, having replaced *Harper's Bazaar* in both circulation and advertising. Some in the industry had begun looking at Anna's baby as a "me-too" magazine, meaning Anna was copying the *Elle* look and feel, which to a great extent she was.

Aware of the criticism, she declared that *Vogue* had the responsibility to "report which way fashion is going." She added, "It is an attitude, not an age. The magazine is younger looking because that is more contemporary, but age is not the issue. We have to tread a narrow path . . . be on the cutting edge" or "lose the buzz."

Anna had Newhouse's full backing. His plan was to raise by 10 percent the circulation that the magazine guarantees its advertisers, what's known in the industry as the rate base. A step like that was seen as a calculated risk and hadn't happened since the late 1970s.

Anna was now moving on all fronts—from fashion to features—and seeking less and less input from the one man who had guided her to the pinnacle, Alex Liberman. She essentially demanded that her mentor keep his nose out of what she was doing. "Anna told Si she didn't want Alex meddling, that she wanted *total* control over what went into each issue," a *Vogue* insider maintains. "When the word got around that Anna was dissing Alex, she claimed it was all nasty gossip, 'rubbish.'"

But Alex felt out of the loop he had controlled forever. The man who had helped get her to *Vogue* in the first place came to the realization that he was no longer of any use to her. "He had done for Anna what she required, and now she felt it was time to break the cord," notes the insider. "Alex complained and Si finally had to put Anna on notice to keep Alex involved."

Later, Anna acknowledged that she "probably forgot how much [Liberman] had been involved before," which is difficult to imagine since she was at his side from the moment she first came to *Vogue* as creative director and relied on him to consult on and approve her pages when she was at British *Vogue*.

"I guess," said Anna later, "I was trying too hard to prove that I was not going to be like Grace Mirabella."

She said that when she took over from Mirabella she had meetings with Liberman, who appeared concerned about his future role. He kept asking her, "'What will it be like?' and 'How will we get along?' I was probably too pushy, and all the people who had been with me at *HG* were used to reporting to me. But Alex and I talked . . . and gradually things got worked out."

Under orders from Newhouse, Anna brought Liberman back in the ball game—somewhat—by running layouts by him and by showing him potential covers but doing what she wanted to do anyway. She placated him and he felt relieved that he wasn't being discarded.

He saw Anna as bold and audacious in how she handled the magazine and its personnel. While he thought Diana Vreeland when she took over *Vogue* was "daring" in an "artificial" way, that she was all "flamboyance," Anna, he determined, if he hadn't long ago, was "closer to pure femininity" and felt "her great genius is feminine seduction. Maybe this is what it takes to make *Vogue* exciting . . . I may have made *Vogue* handsome . . . but I don't think I made its fashion pages exciting."

Besides *Elle*, a new magazine had joined the fashion follies.

It was called *Mirabella*.

Anna simmered. She thought Mirabella was out of her hair forever. Now she was back.

About a week after Anna was named editor, Mirabella received a telephone call from Ed Kosner, Anna's former editor at *New York* magazine, who told her that his boss, the media baron Rupert Murdoch, wanted to have lunch with her. Mirabella wondered why a publisher known mostly for his gossipy tabloids (but also 50 percent of *Elle*) wanted to meet, but she went along for the ride. No one turns down an audience with Murdoch.

At the fancy French restaurant La Côte Basque, he talked to her in detail about women's magazines, asking lots of questions, especially about what was lacking in them and which audience of women was being ignored. They parted company with Murdoch saying the magic words, "Let me go over the figures," which meant the man had a plan.

Mirabella heard nothing more. Murdoch was busy that summer buying *TV Guide,* the *Daily Racing Form,* and *Seventeen.* Then, when she thought he was off to other things, he called and they had another lunch. It went well. A few days later, she sat with one of his colleagues in a private room at another restaurant and was told she was going to be given a new magazine. She was floored when she heard it would be called *Mirabella.* Murdoch's philosophy was "a magazine has to have a name," and Mirabella's was as good as any.

As Anna was working to get her first spring 1989 issue locked up, Mirabella was preparing for her first issue, which she proudly described to the media as "an upscale fashion book for women who know who they are. It's for women who are more than fashion groups. It's not about bubble gum and hula hoops."

A top executive of Murdoch Magazines, though, was more specific about the target audience: "It's aimed at the reader *Vogue* abandoned ten years ago. She's interested in substance, not glitter."

Once *Mirabella* began readying its launch, *Vogue* would fight tooth and nail to keep anyone from even thinking of defecting. Those who did, or were known to be negotiating with the enemy, were threatened with blacklisting from *Vogue.* That went for models, photographers, writers, and editors. It became nasty. Some key players were forced to sign contracts giving *Vogue* exclusivity, causing them to lose their other markets.

That was an outside feud, one of many Anna would have with editors of competing fashion magazines.

Within the Condé Nast organization, Anna's main competitor was seen as "that other Brit"—*Vanity Fair* and later *New Yorker* editor in chief Tina Brown. The media loved to play up a good catfight, and magazine industry wags were constantly weaving bitchy scenarios about the two.

Anna versus Tina made for hot copy. They had become symbols of the glittery Condé Nast universe: glamorous icons presented like movie stars playing at being editors. They both ran glitzy journals in tight skirts and high heels, lived glamorous public lives, were celebrities in the gossip columns. Everything about their high-flying worlds became grist. They were *the* dons of Condé Nast's British Mafia.

The feud between Anna and Brown wasn't totally imagined.

Rancor between the two dated back to their younger days in London. Brown's father, George Hambley Brown, a British B-movie producer, despised Charles Wintour because the *Evening Standard* had panned some of his films. "Charles thought Brown was a hack filmmaker," says Alex Walker. "I didn't think much of him, either, and my reviews reflected both of our thinking."

The resentment carried over to their daughters once they were together in the same arena.

Embarrassed by her lack of a formal education, Anna was envious of Brown's, who had been a proper and serious student, and graduated from Oxford's St. Anne's College. Unlike Anna, Brown had no problem with writing and, as was said later, took to magazine editing "like a deb to a canapé." But while Brown was blond, tiny, buxom, and five years younger, she was no seductive glamour puss like Anna, and that caused her to be jealous.

"Here were two women who could not have been more different," observes a female former Condé Nast executive who worked closely with both of them. "Tina is *so* smart, *so* good at what she does, and Anna is beautiful and icy and knows how to play the game.

"Their relationship with Si had many elements of a classic family structure—a classic *dysfunctional* family structure—with Si as the father figure and Anna and Tina vying to be the favored daughter. Si appreciated them each. Tina's perception was that Anna was the prettier sister, more girly-girl, more popular. But Tina was brilliantly finding this magazine niche that had never existed and was getting all that media attention, and that made Anna jealous. Both used their charms on Si."

What the two did have in common was unvarnished ambition, undistilled drive, Olympian competitiveness, and an incredible need for success—all worthy traits in the bitchy magazine world.

They also had a friend in common, the London gossip columnist Nigel Dempster.

In November 1989, Anna and Brown put aside their differences for a few hours and cohosted a party for Dempster in New York to honor the publication of a book he had written about the tragic life of billionaire playgirl Christina Onassis. The event took place in a trendy downtown café owned by Anna's pal Brian McNally.

The guest list consisted of some two hundred so-called classic-A talents and literary masters of the universe, a nice way of describing the usual suspects who show up to get free books, free food, free drinks, and a free bold-face mention in Liz Smith's mostly hagiographic column. At one point during the party, both Anna and Brown showed their wicked side, laughing hysterically when Dempster, probably soused, accused one of the guests of murdering Onassis a year earlier.

When Anna was editing *HG* and had started including celebrity coverage, Brown was livid. She couldn't believe that Newhouse would permit her to trespass on her glitzy domain since *Vanity Fair* was all about the idolization of celebrities.

"Can you *believe* Si did that!" Brown once complained to a friend. "He's humiliating my father. He knows Anna's father and my father are mortal enemies! He knows!"

A knowledgeable observer, however, says, "I always thought Tina used the feud between the fathers as an excuse. Tina just saw Anna as being far more beautiful and had far greater ease, and that Si found her sexier. They were like teenagers vying for his eye."

Anna's pal, André Leon Talley, who once worked for Brown at *Vanity Fair,* is said to have thought of her as "tacky-tacky-tacky, dowdy-dowdy-dowdy" and accused her of wearing "borrowed designer dresses." Talley reportedly presented his views to Brown in a snarky note when he left *Vanity Fair* at one point to work for Anna.

Their resentment toward each other grew more intense in the 1990s.

In June 1992, Brown was named editor of America's most esteemed but money-losing weekly, *The New Yorker*. The move caused quite a stir in the literary and media worlds, but for Anna, Newhouse's decision to place Brown there came as welcome news. Rumors had been circulating that Brown was being considered by Newhouse as Liberman's replacement as editorial director of all Condé Nast magazines. Anna lobbied strenuously against it, telling friends privately that she'd quit before having to report to Brown. It would have been a battle royale.

By June 1997, Brown had turned *The New Yorker* around, Anna was nearing her eighth successful year running *Vogue* and, while there would never be a peace treaty between the two, things appeared copacetic. In fact, Anna had arranged for a very private lunch with one of the world's most famous women, Diana, Princess of Wales, at the Four Seasons in New York, and had graciously invited Brown to join them.

Since *The New Yorker* for the most part wasn't into celebrity and fashion reportage, Anna's fear of competition from Brown had faded somewhat. But Anna's invitation to Brown was Machiavellian, mainly because of a nasty piece Brown had written for *Vanity Fair* in the mid-1980s before she became its editor, a piece of journalism that Di would never have forgotten.

That story, which received international attention, painted the prince and princess as a highly dysfunctional couple. Called "The Mouse That Roared," Brown described an emotionally unstable Di who spent hours isolated, listening to her Sony Walkman, dancing alone, and studying her press clippings. And she described Charles as "pussy-whipped from here to eternity."

By the time of the lunch, though, Diana seemed to hold no grievance against Brown and opened up to the two editors, confiding her negative thoughts about Prince Charles as the future king of England. It was strictly a social lunch and everything discussed was off the record, supposedly.

Cut to September 1997 and the horrible car crash that took Diana's life in Paris. Brown rushed out a special *New Yorker* commemorative issue and there, as part of the package, was a blow-by-blow account of that lunch with Di, which became a journalistic cause célèbre. While *New Yorker* newsstand sales rocketed, critics like Jonathan Yardley at *The Washington Post* lambasted Brown for breaking Di's confidentiality, calling the piece "an exercise in self-display, so odious as to shame everyone in journalism."

Odious, shmodious, Anna was livid and complained vociferously to Newhouse and others in the media who she hoped would go after Brown for breaking the confidence. Mainly, she was upset because she'd been scooped by her archrival.

"Tina never so much as inquired whether Anna was okay with her using the entire off-the-record conversation," says a *Vanity Fair* editor and writer who had a ringside seat at the imbroglio. "There was no courtesy call by Tina to Anna, which there usually is from one editor to another in the same organization under such circumstances. All's fair in journalism, but Anna was fit to be tied. She was the one who had arranged the lunch and she was embarrassed—mainly because it was Tina and not her who had run with the story."

But the brouhaha over the Di story paled in comparison to the controversy still to come over how Brown would use the pages of her next magazine, *Talk,* to go after Anna and her lover after the scandal about their extramarital affair became tabloid news.

As one highly placed Condé Nast executive observes, "When it involves Anna, it's a bitch-eat-bitch world."

thirty-five

The Assistant

Anna had brought Laurie Schechter a long way since she first hired her as her personal gofer at *New York* magazine. With Anna as her mentor, Schechter had earned the kind of respect and hash marks that got her the first fashion editor's job at *Rolling Stone* and was brought back by Anna as a ranking editor at *HG* and now at *Vogue*.

Schechter's name had become known in the fashion business and the media, and she was viewed as a contender. When Anna was running British *Vogue,* she had even recommended Schechter to Carrie Donovan at *The New York Times* for a prime spot on the Sunday *Magazine* style section staff and had made that generous gesture despite the fact that Schechter had disappointed her by not following her to London.

Anna clearly saw in Schechter the same kind of ambition and drive that had taken her to the top of the fashion magazine field. She liked and respected her spunk and hard work, or at least that was the feeling Schechter had, and there was never a reason to feel otherwise.

Anna even felt maternal toward Schechter. That was amply and graciously demonstrated when Schechter eloped and Anna, overwhelmed with launching *her Vogue,* actually took time from her hectic pace to plan and toss an elaborate dinner for her.

It was quite an affair, held in Anna's town house with celebrity florist Robert Isabell handling the flower arrangements and celebrity caterer Glorious Foods preparing the supper. While Anna offered Schechter the option to choose from the menu, she strongly suggested lamb, so that's what Schechter chose. Do as the boss does.

Most of the organization for the party was handled by Anna's new favorite lady-in-waiting, Gabe Doppelt, who had taken the job of Anna's assistant in London when Schechter declined to make the move. And Condé Nast picked up the tab. After all, this was a bash Anna was tossing, Schechter was a respected employee, and a lot of big names in the fashion world were invited— Marc Jacobs, Simon Doonan, among others. Anna's philosophy was always to combine pleasure with business. And her world was the job.

"She was charming about throwing the party for me and I thought it was all very wonderful to have a close relationship with her," says Schechter.

By 1990, though, Schechter was getting antsy for a couple of reasons. She hadn't moved up the ladder under Anna as she thought she would, and she could see that Gabe Doppelt had gotten closer to Anna in *Vogue*'s inner circle. Schechter had kept her eye out for other opportunities, and one suddenly came along. *Interview* magazine, which had once rejected Anna for a job, had approached Schechter with "an appealing offer" to oversee fashions and style.

She went to Anna and told her, and was shocked by her reply.

"She said, 'I'm *not* supposed to tell you, but there's something they've been talking about for you at Condé Nast, and in light of this situation, it's something you should know about. Go back to your office and I'll call you.'"

Within the hour, Anna called and told Schechter, "Go see Si Newhouse."

Schechter couldn't believe what she was hearing. Newhouse was telling her that she was being seriously considered for the top job at *Mademoiselle*. "He said it wasn't a move they were going to make right away, but that they were considering it," says Schechter, who saw the possibility "as my dream job. I was thrilled." The only hitch was that the editor, Amy Gross Cooper, was married to *GQ* editor Art Cooper, and they had a complex clause in their Condé Nast contracts that if one was fired, both would have to receive severance. "It was a sticky deal, and they were still kind of muddling through the idea," says Schechter. "Art Cooper made a fuss, but in the meantime, Mr. Newhouse told Anna that he wanted her to train me for the job."

The training, for the most part, involved following Anna in and out of meetings and watching her operate, though Anna wasn't big on editorial meetings and was usually in and out in minutes as opposed to the hours Grace Mirabella was said to have labored over decisions. Anna got bored quickly and left it to her subordinates, for the most part, to handle the details.

Anna also strongly urged Schechter to put together a detailed plan for what she'd do with *Mademoiselle*—once described by the snarky *New York Observer* as the "Jan Brady of Condé Nast"—when and if she took it over. "If *I* were you," Schechter recalls Anna saying, "*I* would write one." Schechter got on it immediately. She gave a copy to Anna and one to Newhouse, but the reaction in the executive suite was not positive. "They [Newhouse, Liberman et al.] weren't ready for a rehaul," Schechter says.

After a few months, having watched the *Interview* job grow wings and fly away—a great career opportunity lost by heeding Anna's advice—Schechter was told that the editorship of *Mademoiselle* was on hold indefinitely. By shrewdly holding out the carrot of a major editor in chief's job, Anna, Newhouse, and Liberman had kept the talented Schechter from going to the competition.

And now they had another so-called opportunity for her. They said she was needed to help launch a new beauty magazine called *Allure*. The prototype, she says, was a disaster and "they had to throw it in the garbage. They needed me to come from *Vogue* to get it off the ground, format the whole thing and put it in order."

The problem was that *Allure* had an editor in chief, thirty-two-year-old Linda Wells, who did not take kindly to what she viewed as Schechter's interference, coming over with the title of creative director—the same one Anna had when she first wreaked havoc at *Vogue* under Grace Mirabella. At the same time, Schechter thought Wells was a lightweight who didn't have her kind of magazine experience. Wells did have journalistic cachet, though; she'd been the food and beauty editor at *The New York Times Magazine* for five years. Schechter, though, felt that Wells got the job through family connections.

"But I was encouraged to go to *Allure* by Alex Liberman, and I had a message that Mr. Newhouse strongly urged me to take the position. I was sort of between a rock and a hard place because I had to go to *Allure* whether I wanted to or not. It would have been career suicide to tell them to go jump in the lake."

The petite Jewish Schechter and the taller, blond, and WASPy Wells—

both of whom had worked at *Vogue* at the same time as assistants—were like oil and water, like Wintour and Mirabella. The two didn't mix.

Anna could have stepped in to help Schechter—she certainly wielded enough influence with Newhouse and Liberman. But to Schechter's surprise and dismay, Anna quietly removed herself from participation in the matter. Years later, Schechter looks back on that time and observes, "Maybe she didn't want to go up against them. Anna is the kind of person who will give you the rope. If you're going to hang yourself, then that's what you're going to do. She's not going to necessarily help you either way. If Anna really didn't want me to go, she could have taken a stand, but she didn't because Si and Alex wanted me there. Politically, Anna wouldn't have taken a stand against them."

Was the very Machiavellian editor in chief out to "get" Schechter in some way? "Maybe." Schechter says plaintively.

She notes that Anna "knew about my capabilities, and if you're a potential threat to her, competition to her, she's not going to help you do a better job at competing with her. Anna's smart. I was a *Vogue* editor at *Allure* and that's obviously a problem, that having a *Vogue* editor at another publication is going to be viewed by her as a possible threat. When I was fashion editor at *Rolling Stone,* I wasn't a threat to what she was doing, as I was when I was at *Allure.* Not to say that Anna didn't want me to do well, but I knew that to some extent I would appear as a threat to her."

While *Allure* was mainly a beauty magazine, it did get involved with fashion, an arena that competed head-on with *Vogue,* and Schechter believes that concerned Anna because she would have started getting good word of mouth because of "my influence, my story ideas."

Although Anna knew of the problems that existed between Schechter and Wells, she didn't intercede or try to help Schechter. In fact, Schechter believes that Anna was "more helpful" to Wells.

While all this was going on, Newhouse had decided for a number of reasons, ranging from the economic climate to the resources required to get *Allure* launched, that this wasn't the best time to change editors at *Mademoiselle* after all, so that possibility became a dead issue for Schechter.

She began to feel that she was in the middle of a horrific nightmare that wouldn't end. "It was kind of a no-win situation at *Allure,*" she states.

As creative director, she was supposed to work on all aspects of *Allure.*

"With Linda, what happened was she wouldn't let me do anything, basically." It was the same situation Anna had faced as creative director under Mirabella.

Schechter stayed at *Allure* for about six months during the late fall and winter of 1990, then resigned in spring 1991.

About eighteen months after Schechter left Condé Nast, her rival, thirty-two-year-old Gabe Doppelt, with Anna's full support, was named editor in chief of the 1.5-million-circulation *Mademoiselle,* the job Schechter originally had been promised. "It was my finding and recommending Gabe to Anna," she says, "that started Anna's relationship with her, and they became close friends."

Schechter wasn't at all surprised that Doppelt got the job that she had coveted. "Gaby's clever, knows how to play her cards right, has contacts, knows a lot of people, she's very British, and she's very private—and in that way she's very much like Anna. Anna was a great supporter of hers and has done great things for her."

Doppelt replaced forty-five-year-old Amy Gross Cooper, editor since 1980. Her "promotion" to editor at large for all Condé Nast publications was reported to have been a "complete sham . . . the standard move when a veteran employee isn't wanted at a certain position anymore."

A native South African whose family moved to London when she was in her midteens, the brash and aggressive Doppelt was the invention of the two most powerful women in the business: Anna and Tina Brown. Doppelt had been a loyal assistant to both, starting by answering phones at eighteen for Brown when she was the editor in chief of Britain's *Tatler,* then moving on to Anna, beginning at British *Vogue,* from where Doppelt rose to editorships under her at *HG* and American *Vogue.*

On taking on her powerful new job at *Mademoiselle,* Doppelt declared, "We live and breathe frocks, but we also want to make the magazine face issues in a modern, amusing manner."

In less than a year, she failed miserably.

Her first issue appeared on newsstands in March 1993. It included a recipe for peanut butter pie and Cool Whip from the *Junior League Cookbook* and an advice column on spotting and removing one's own nasal detritus. The covers were even more over the edge—druggy-looking, grungy girls, with cover lines that read "Cool Clothes from Kmart."

Six months later, on September 29, 1993, she was out, though the Condé Nast press release, with Si Newhouse's name on it, diplomatically stated that she had resigned. "I had one vision of the magazine," she said. "They had another." Newhouse said that there were "conceptual differences that we have been unable to resolve."

If Anna feared possible competition from Schechter, whose ideas were mainstream and commercial, she had little to fear from Doppelt, whose ideas were off-the-wall—and that's most likely why she backed Doppelt for the *Mademoiselle* job.

A day after Doppelt cleaned out her desk, Elizabeth Crow, a forty-seven-year-old magazine and publishing veteran, was named as the new editor. Just as Newhouse wanted *Vogue* to be more like *Elle*, he mandated that Crow give *Mademoiselle* "an *Allure* feel." It went through a few more iterations but was finally laid to rest by Si Newhouse on October 1, 2001. At the time of its demise, it was being edited by another Brit, Mandi Norwood.

Looking back more than a decade later, now running her own successful fashion-styling business, Schechter says, "I don't know if Anna betrayed me. But a couple of my story ideas that I had in my proposal for *Mademoiselle* turned up in *Vogue*. Anna's a good editor, and a good editor is good at appropriating. She's a very competitive person, and I don't think she could be where she is today without being . . . very aware of what her competition is doing and who her possible competition might be."

thirty-six

Fashion Battlefield

In the summer of 1991, a monster rumor began sweeping the fashion world. The hot buzz was that Liz Tilberis, who loathed Anna, and whom Anna detested, was on the short list to take over American *Harper's Bazaar*.

This would mean all-out war between the two, the fashion magazine equivalent of Operation Desert Storm, which had been launched at the beginning of the year in the Persian Gulf. If the rumor came to pass, Anna and Tilberis would be the opposing generals on the fashion battlefield.

Bazaar—the first magazine to hire Anna when she arrived in New York and the first one to fire her—had fallen far behind *Vogue* and *Elle* in popularity over the years. The editor who was said to have canned Anna, Anthony Mazzola, was still in charge. The talk was that the wife of the head of the Hearst magazine empire was pushing for his replacement and that Tilberis seemed the best candidate.

Hearst wanted to get *Bazaar* back in the game and take on *Vogue*. There had always been an intense rivalry with Condé Nast, with each using every opportunity to steal talented personnel. Now Hearst felt that with Tilberis in charge of *Bazaar*, it might have a shot at playing catch-up with *Vogue*. Tilberis would be *Bazaar's* Anna Wintour.

The chatter about Hearst's plans for Tilberis and *Bazaar* had gotten so intense—bouncing back and forth across the Atlantic—that Si Newhouse's cousin, Jonathan Newhouse, who ran Condé Nast's European operations, demanded a meeting with her. Over poached eggs and coffee at Claridge's, he noted generously that she was due for a raise. He warned her she'd hate living in New York and added an ultimatum: If she took the job, she would "never work for Condé Nast again."

But Tilberis had a number of trusted cheerleaders telling her to go for it when it was offered. Among them, surprisingly, was Anna's own fashion director and top lieutenant at *Vogue* and Tilberis's closest friend, Grace Coddington.

"Get your ass over here," Tilberis was told by Coddington, who didn't seem to have problems with the two of them being "friendly competitors."

But Anna certainly would.

Coddington even helped Tilberis come up with alibis in case she was spotted in New York holding top secret meetings with Hearst brass: say she was on an anniversary trip or shopping. Coddington and Tilberis even had discussions about possibly joining forces again, becoming a team like they were in London when Anna came over and forced Coddington out. But they decided against it because Coddington had always been Tilberis's superior and probably would have trouble working under her. Moreover, Coddington was now happy working with Anna. "We [Tilberis and Coddington] trusted our ancient friendship enough to figure out a comfortable compromise between our usual wont to dish and a more sensible policy of don't ask, don't tell," Tilberis said.

Top fashion photographers, like Patrick Demarchelier, who could make *any* woman look stunning, told Tilberis that *Bazaar* was a great opportunity for her, and he would work for her if she was able to hire the controversial French art director Fabien Baron, who had been at Italian *Vogue*.

Tilberis was building a highly respected staff, and she hadn't even gotten the offer yet.

But she was taking the advice of her friends and colleagues seriously. Since Anna left four years earlier, things had gotten worse at British *Vogue*. There had been management shifts at Condé Nast in London that did not sit well with Tilberis. And just like the stiff competition Anna's *Vogue* was getting from *Elle*, Tilberis's *Vogue* was fighting what appeared to be a losing battle for the hearts and minds of its readers with what she saw as the "slightly pornographic" five-year-old British upstart *Marie Claire*. It now outsold *Vogue* by more than 10 percent with its mix of sexy articles and models.

During the Paris collections in October 1991, the forty-four-year-old Tilberis met for the first time with the president of Hearst magazines, D. Claeys Bahrenburg, and the two hit it off. After subsequent meetings, she wrote a detailed series of demands: full editorial control, the best photographers, big editorial and promotional budgets. She also wanted to fire existing people and hire her own staff because she knew from watching Anna take over British *Vogue* "how difficult it was to inherit a recalcitrant, embittered staff."

In short, if she were to take the job, Tilberis wanted carte blanche.

She then had a sit-down in New York with Si Newhouse. The meeting did not go well. She voiced some of her unhappiness with the way things were going in London, and he hardly responded. Later, Tilberis noted, "If I hadn't had another job offer in the background, I would have left his office feeling thoroughly dejected." Had she got a better response from him, she might have stayed.

Tilberis wasted no more time and cut a deal with Hearst. Tony Mazzola had already resigned but agreed to stay on to edit a 125th anniversary issue of the magazine.

On January 6, 1992, she was named editor in chief of *Harper's Bazaar,* putting Brits at the helm of the most venerable fashion magazines in the United States.

Anna's only immediate public response was not one of congratulations. To *The New York Times* she said merely, "The more British editors, the better."

Spy magazine, New York's equivalent of *Private Eye* in London, was prompted to publish a humorous piece called "The New British Invasion: How American Publishing Has Been Taken over by People with Charming Accents and Bad Teeth." An illustration by Al Hirschfeld showed a Beatles-style group called "The Brits," with Anna and the *New Yorker's* Tina Brown on guitars and Liz Tilberis on drums. They were just several of dozens of British writers and editors—women and men—who had come to the United States, many working for Condé Nast.

In a similar piece in *The New York Times,* Edwin Diamond, media critic for *New York* magazine, surveyed the phenomenon of fashion editors from the UK invading America. He concluded, "I don't think there is any confirmed data that says that British women have better taste or sharper editing instincts than American women."

Image, accent, and snob appeal were thought by observers to be the Brits main selling point to U.S. magazine publishers.

Anna didn't offer a private salute to Tilberis, either. "I didn't get any flowers of congratulations from her," Tilberis said later. "No matter what either of us said [pleadingly and privately to reporters] to play down our personal rivalry, the press on both sides of the Atlantic were intent on setting up a catfight. Anna versus Liz, *Vogue* versus *Bazaar*, Condé Nast versus Hearst—it was far too juicy to resist."

But it was true—the catfight, the rivalry, and the media circus.

In London, readers awoke to the headline, "Liz and Anna wage savage Frock War," in the *Daily Express*. The story declared that Tilberis's appointment "has set handbags flailing in the outwardly elegant, intrinsically vicious world of high fashion." It went on to report that Anna "is certainly not laying out the welcome carpet. The Frock War between the Boadiceas of fashion is savage and fingernails are blood red."

There was truth to what Fleet Street was reporting.

In Paris, at the couture previews, Anna sat stone-faced at a table just a few feet away from Tilberis and never said a word to her, refused even to acknowledge her presence. Ponytailed Karl Lagerfeld, a designer for Chanel, fluttered between the two of them in hopes of warming the chill, but to no avail.

Threatened with being banned from its pages, *Vogue* photographers and models were put on notice not to work for *Bazaar*. The other side made the same declarations. A *Vogue* editor at the time says, "Every time a photographer got an offer from them we upped the ante. If they beat us and got a photographer we wanted, it cost them huge money."

Tilberis tried to convince photographers that they would have more freedom working for her than for Anna. "Anna Wintour's style, as I knew from working with her," Tilberis said, "is prescriptive. She tells people what she wants and they have to come back with it. If it's not what she has in mind, she kills it. I kept repeating that *Bazaar* was going to be far more democratic."

The battle for the photographer Peter Lindbergh, who shot Anna's first

American *Vogue* cover, underscored the kind of hardball both sides were playing. When Tilberis got word that Lindbergh was ready to sign a contract with *Bazaar*, she booked the next flight to Paris to meet with him. But when she arrived at Kennedy Airport, she ran head-on into Si Newhouse, also Paris-bound and determined to have Lindbergh sign a *Vogue* contract for more money. Tilberis won; the creative freedom she promised did the trick. She also got Demarchelier to shoot exclusively for her. All of this Anna brushed off. Her philosophy, and that of Condé Nast, was that there are always others out there.

Tilberis's salary along with perks was more than one million dollars. Anna was the highest-paid magazine editor in the world, earning close to two million, with built-in bonuses in her contract for circulation gains that could bring in seven more figures. She had a bottomless clothing budget and an enormous editorial budget, was surrounded by the most beautiful people in the world, had flower-filled suites when she traveled to the world's most glamorous fashion capitals, had a Lincoln Town Car at her disposal, could catch a flight on the Concorde whenever, and was wafer thin (while Tilberis wore a size fourteen, about which the British press had a field day). Indeed, Anna had the kind of glamorous, glitzy Olivia Goldsmith–character life any woman worth her Manolos would covet.

Still, she was envious of what Tilberis was getting from Hearst.

In New York, a key *Vogue* editor under Anna at the time says, "She was fuming. She had no respect for Liz's work, thought she was still way behind the times, and couldn't believe she'd worked such an incredible deal for herself. Anna put out the word: Destroy *Harper's Bazaar* at any cost. She wanted to see Liz Tilberis embarrassed out of her job. Anna's all about beating the competition, keeping herself on top, pleasing Si Newhouse. I felt like we were on a war footing. We *were* on a war footing."

Attempting to put a happy face on their very real and unpleasant feud, Anna described her relationship with Tilberis as "friendly" and said they even intended to have lunch "real soon." The media "is just trying to make something out of nothing," she maintained. "We had a conversation just the other day—about face-lifts."

In fact, Anna wasn't about to give a break to Tilberis or, for that matter, anyone who wanted to glorify her in any way.

Such was the case with the veteran British journalist Georgina Howell, who had interviewed Anna and her father for a candid London newspaper profile years earlier. Howell had won the *Vogue* Talent Contest at sixteen and later had served as fashion editor of the *Observer*, had worked for the *Sunday Times*, and had written a number of books, including *Vogue Women* and *In Vogue: Sultans of Style and Season*. Howell had also been Tina Brown's deputy editor at the *Tatler*.

By the early nineties, with the feud between Anna and Brown bubbling, there was a bidding war for Howell's services. Brown wanted her for *Vanity Fair*, and Anna for *Vogue*. "I had to decide between the two," Howell says, "but Anna just offered me *so* much money that I had to accept it." Howell also had an arrangement to write pieces that would appear only in Great Britain for the London *Telegraph* magazine, which at the time was edited by Anna's friend Emma Soames.

One of Howell's first assignments for Soames was to go to New York and write a profile of the newly appointed Tilberis, who was, Howell says, "the toast of the town. Everyone thought she was wonderful." The article was only for British circulation for the *Telegraph* and would not appear in the United States.

"And so, as I always did when I went over to New York," says Howell, "I dodged into Anna's office and said hello, and she asked, 'What are you doing here?' "

When Howell said she was interviewing Tilberis for a *Telegraph* profile, Anna went ballistic. "She said, 'Do you not consider that a conflict of interest?' I said, 'Well, no, because it's for England, not America, and it's part of my London contract.' And Anna yelled, 'WELL, I DO!' and that was the end of it. . . . My contract with American *Vogue* ran to its end and wasn't renewed. I thought Anna and I had an excellent relationship. But Anna and Liz Tilberis were rivals in the marketplace."

Looking back years later, Howell says she was "sorry to lose the money and sorry to have offended Anna, but as I reflected, and I've gone on reflecting over the years, I think perhaps Anna could have been *bigger* about it. But she does tend to demand total loyalty in a way that I reserve for private relations, not for business. I didn't see it in my mind as being disloyal to Anna. It never occurred to me that it would be a problem for her.

"Liz [Tilberis] was a good friend of mine. She was a good friend of Emma

Soames, who was a great friend with Anna, and they were in constant touch, and I did think that Emma wouldn't have asked me to do it if she'd seen any problem with Anna. Now I've concluded I *never* really had a personal relationship with Anna. I was surprised it turned out that way."

The big question facing the magazine industry, still in a recession and with advertising revenue nose-diving and newsstand sales pale, was whether *Vogue, Elle, Harper's Baazar,* and the newly minted *Mirabella* could be supported in such lean times. In 1991, for instance, ad pages had declined as much as 26 percent for *Bazaar* and almost 15 percent for *Vogue* compared with a year earlier. But Anna's *Vogue* still received all of the kudos. One head of a major media buying and planning service described *Vogue* as "the gold standard of fashion for intelligent modern women. *Elle* doesn't have the substance of *Vogue* and is more for the superficial external woman. I like *Mirabella,* which skews a tiny bit older. It's a good threesome, and it's possible to look at *Harper's Bazaar* and say, 'Who needs it?' "

And that's precisely why Tilberis was brought in to do battle.

"With Liz there, it will be stronger," Anna conceded. "I think she will do a good job, but I am not going to edit this magazine any differently because she is over there. We know we can have an impact if we have strong features and a point of view. Do women still want fashion? Of course they want fashion. They'll always want fashion."

Even with the new competition, the horrible recession, and staying on top of her game, Anna was deeply involved in putting together the hundredth anniversary celebration of *Vogue* in April 1992. To honor the occasion, a huge black-tie bash was held in the vaulted lobby of the New York Public Library, along with a century retrospective of *Vogue* photographs chosen by Anna and Alex Liberman.

The anniversary party—Anna oversaw the guest list—was like the Academy Awards and the Emmys and every contemporary Paris, Milan, London, and New York fashion show all wrapped in one big glittery ball. Movie stars, socialites, supermodels, titans of industry, media moguls, the world's top designers—Lacroix, Lagerfeld, Gaultier, Versace, Blass, Beene, Karan, Klein, Lauren, de la Renta, Jacobs, and Mizrahi—were there, plus all of the A-list fashion photographers. The designers and the photographers were fantasy makers, and fantasy was what the fashion industry was all about, and *Vogue* transmitted the message to the masses. All the beautiful fashionistas ate, drank, and danced to Tito Puente and C&C Music factory.

Anna was in her element, the queen of the ball, dressed in an elegant long cream Geoffrey Beene beaded dress. "We wanted to turn the music up really loud so that all the old people would leave, including me," she joked. Only because her longtime friend, *The New York Times*'s street fashion photographer Bill Cunningham, who had been shooting Anna since the early seventies, asked her to, she posed with one of her guests, Liz Tilberis, who was wearing a Chanel dinner suit. Both also wore boilerplate smiles and played nice, offering no hint of the animosity that existed between them. But, of course, everyone present knew otherwise.

Still, despite the contempt in the air, it was one of New York's memorable parties.

As Anna's friend the designer Anna Sui declared of the fabulous evening, "Anyone you can think of is here."

Meanwhile, a mile uptown, the average Joes of New York and tourists from the Midwest peered into the windows of Bloomingdale's flagship store on Lexington Avenue trying to figure out what was what. The show windows were lined with Anna clones—many, many mannequins with bobs, sporting sunglasses, and perched on gold chairs with pencil-thin legs crossed as if they were in the front row at a fashion show. The dummies wore either Isaac Mizrahi slip dresses or Chanel jackets with skintight white jeans, which had become Anna's latest look when not dressing for success.

With all of the pressures of the job, the battles and feuds and personality conflicts, Anna needed to get away from the *Vogue* hot seat. In the midnineties she kicked off her Manolo slingbacks in favor of chic little flats, shed her Chanel for fashionable black slacks and tight Ts, and took what became known as "the vacation from hell."

The location was the CM Ranch, situated in a bucolic, secluded valley in Dubois, Wyoming. The spread had been a longtime summer vacation spot for the American side of her family. Though charming, it was a funky, rustic old dude ranch that featured events like square dancing and horseshoe tossing, and was one of the last places in the world that one would expect to find the queen of glam chilling. Anna's thing was urban luxury.

Her party included the flamboyant Donatella Versace and her two children, Allegra, the ten-year-old heiress to the Versace fortune, and her brother, Daniel; Donatella's husband, former model Paul Beck, described in the press as "his hunkyness," who was head of menswear operations for Versace; Donatella's handsome bodyguard, Albert Orlangi, called "a gorgeous stud" by ranch help; Anna's husband, David Shaffer, and their two children, Bee and Charlie; Anna's stepson, Sam Shaffer; Manhattan restaurateur Brian McNally, who spent the week with a cell phone epoxied to his ear, shouting "buy this, sell that," and his chic wife, Anne McNally, a fashion editor at *Vanity Fair;* Gabe Doppelt; a nanny or two; and a couple of other children.

In the weeks preceding Anna and her posse's arrival—all bills sent to Condé Nast, of course—there were daily calls from her harried assistant at *Vogue* to ranch bosses Lisa Petersen and Barbara Shoemaker. Petersen says she tried to make Anna's assistant understand that the old CM was not a fancy spa but a classic dude ranch with 1920s log cabins heated by woodstoves, with showers but no baths, with Indian rugs on wood plank floors, and down-home front porches. There were several fancier houses, but all but one had been booked far in advance. Anna graciously—and shrewdly—gave the vacant one to Versace, a major *Vogue* advertiser. "Her assistant said, 'Anna wants the *real* experience,'" recalls Petersen. "I said, 'Well, I hope this is going to work.' I was definitely a little suspicious."

Shoemaker says the assistant called every day. "Anna wanted this, Anna wanted that. I told her to tell Anna to lighten up a little, and the assistant said, 'Ain't it the truth.' I can't think of a worse job in the entire world than what that poor girl had. I'll bet when deadlines come and things get tense, it's like handling explosives. Me? I'd kill her about the first week and that'd take care of that."

Petersen and Shoemaker were correct to have qualms. On arrival—by helicopter—Anna, wearing her sunglasses, which she never removed in public, even at night, during the weeklong stay, demanded an in-house hairdresser and an in-house masseuse to cater to her and her friends' sybaritic needs, which the ranch couldn't supply. So Anna immediately chartered a plane to shuttle back and forth daily to the tony little town of Jackson for shopping, shampoos, comb-outs, and body rubs. She also had a chauffeur at her disposal to take her and her friends by limo to the stables, which were within walking distance, when one of them got a hankering to ride.

Anna was one of the most difficult and demanding guests the ranch had ever seen. "We didn't forget that one real easy," notes Shoemaker.

By coincidence, one of the young people working as a cabin girl and waitress was a young American relative of Anna's, Delia Gilkyson, the teenage daughter of Anna's cousin Eliza, whom she hadn't seen or spoken to since that family reunion back in the sixties.

"It was one of my daughter's first jobs," says Eliza Gilkyson, "and Anna *knew* that a relative was working there, but Anna never even spoke to her, gave her the cold shoulder. Anna knows about us, the Gilkysons, and couldn't care less. She's a snob!"

Word of Anna's snub soon spread to other Gilkysons, including Patti Gilkyson Agnew, who felt Anna hadn't changed much since her chilly visit in New York as a teenager years earlier with Agnew's sister, Neal Thorpe. "I heard Anna was very cold to Eliza's daughter," says Agnew. "She didn't pay much attention to Delia."

The first evening, the glitzy Wintour party showed up at the ranch's homey family-style dinner. Anna clearly wasn't a happy camper. Summoning Petersen with a patrician wave of her hand, she said, "*You* understand. *You're* from New York. *This is not* acceptable! We *need* the other two houses."

Petersen told her she was sorry, but the houses were already occupied.

"Well, move *them out!*" Anna snapped.

Petersen was startled, said she would do no such thing, and advised Anna "to sit back and observe and start to enjoy the place, or we can pack you up . . . that's your choice. That kind of snuffed her a little bit. I think she was *stunned* to find herself where she was. I guess she didn't read the brochure her assistant gave her."

From that point on, Anna avoided the ranch as if it were an outlet mall. Almost daily, she had her driver whisk her to the one-horse airport in Dubois, ten minutes away, where she boarded her chartered plane for the half-hour hop to Jackson, where she spent the day.

When she was at the ranch, she acted like a spoiled child who couldn't get her way and was having a 24/7 hissy fit.

"She didn't speak to anyone," recalls Shoemaker. "She was totally antisocial, totally disagreeable, didn't blend in with the other guests at all—*intentionally*. She went riding once, maybe twice, no more, and always rode way behind everybody. She just wouldn't socialize or do anything that was friendly."

Versace, accompanied by her bodyguard, strolled up and down in front of the dining room and office where the other guests could see her, wearing low-slung, skintight, black spandex shorts that, according to bug-eyed eyewitnesses, "just barely covered the essentials," and was always puffing a cigarette. At home, she moisturizes her toes with $150-a-bottle Crème de la Mer and rarely goes out without being draped in jewelry worth a small fortune. So the CM was big-time culture shock as much for her as it was for Anna.

"Everybody staying at the ranch was very aware of Wintour's iciness," maintains Shoemaker. "They laughed about it all week. Anybody sitting in the dining room at night wearing sunglasses is something of a novelty," says Petersen.

thirty-seven

The Party's Over

From ejecting veteran staffers to igniting in-house competition for stories to establishing dress codes and odd rules of behavior, Anna turned *Vogue* into her vision of what a great fashion magazine should be.

Some longtime staffers fled in terror or disgust at the changes or their treatment—like Grace Coddington had done in London before she came back into the fold. Others left because their departments were abandoned, or they were axed, or they retired.

"Anna had a very interesting way of establishing herself," recalls Elizabeth Tretter, who was a seventeen-year veteran of *Vogue,* a honcho in the fabric department, which Anna dismantled to streamline the operation. "She took a look at the staff as it was and scheduled lunches with the ones she wanted to keep, and if you didn't have lunch with her, you knew what was up."

Luckily, Tretter got an invitation, and Anna took her to Tretter's favorite restaurant, the Oyster Bar at Grand Central Station. They had a pleasant chat, but soon Tretter was gone.

"Age," she says, "could have been a factor." She was a decade older than Anna, and "Anna's mandate was young, spirited, enthusiastic. Hip-hop editors like Gabe Doppelt came in. I was not hip-hop."

Tretter's department was closed, and she was assigned to the tedious job of shooting pattern pages, something everyone abhorred.

Tretter had mentioned to a younger friend all of Anna's talk about w
ing everything youthful, and the friend thought "that is actionable" and s
gested that an age-discrimination suit might be in order, a repeat of what I
happened at *HG*. "But that's as far as it went," she says. "So was I pushed ou
Possibly, by the trend of things, the way it was going."

Over the years at *Vogue*, Tretter had made many contacts in the fabri
business, so when things started to look very bleak she had opportunities ou
of *Vogue*. "I said to my husband, 'I think the party is over.' I went to speak
with Anna and I said I thought I had to go someplace else. She didn't say,
'No, you can't leave.'"

Another older, longtime editor, who left six months into Anna's reign but
stayed within Condé Nast, also thought age figured in Anna's personnel decisions. "There was that whole thing about young, young, young," she asserts.
"Anna was kind of peeling out everyone who was older. Anna was just
adamant that everyone be young. And the thing is, she inherited Polly
Mellen, who one wouldn't call young. But Polly transcended the age issue because she was such a character and tried so hard."

Mellen, who had been at *Vogue* almost three decades, had been Anna's biggest
cheerleader during Grace Mirabella's reign and was the one who set up that ill-
fated meeting in which Anna told Mirabella she wanted her job. Anna was aware
of Mellen's support, and Mellen was the first one she told that Grace Coddington was coming on board. "I got a phone call from Anna saying, 'I want you
to be the first to know,' She told me Grace was going to be creative director,
and she said, 'Do you like her? Do you get along?' And I told her, 'I *love* her.'"

Coddington and Mellen were supposed to work closely. But after a time,
less and less of Mellen's sittings and ideas were getting into the magazine, and
finally none were.

"It was sad, in a way," recalls a colleague. "Polly was sitting there with her
thumb up her you-know-what. Nothing of her work was getting into the
book. Anna and Grace were sending her a message."

Mellen says she was aware that Anna's mission was to have everyone
"young and beautiful," but Mellen believed that "performance was still number one." She also reached the cold realization that "two strong editors," like
her and Coddington, working together "does *not* work."

Mellen held out as long as she could, hoping things would get better, but she finally saw the writing on the wall: "I began to feel like I'm not really doing shoots, maybe I'm not really young enough for Anna. The time comes when you can sense it, and I'm pretty good at that. I had to do some real soul-searching and say, 'Come on, you've had a wonderful life. You're the spoiled brat of the fashion world.'"

Anna had decided she'd given Mellen enough rope and it was now time delicately to drop the trapdoor.

Si Newhouse handled the job for her. He called Mellen to his office and asked her what her dream job was. "I said, if you can believe it at my extreme age, I'd like my own magazine."

He didn't have that to offer, but he told Mellen that Linda Wells at *Allure* needed a creative director, post–Laurie Schechter.

Unlike many of the others who fell by the wayside, Mellen made the move and carved a niche for herself there. And she gives all the credit to Anna, who, she says, had "guts, passion, daring, caring, a point of view, and, number one, total focus. She's the biggest influence in fashion in the world in the twentieth century. I put her right up there with Coco Chanel. People will argue with me, but I'm a fan."

Under Anna, *everything* changed.

When Mirabella ran the show there were endless lengthy meetings. Recalls one editor, who was close to Mirabella and disliked Anna, "I remember sitting in a Grace run-through and it was like, 'Oh, my God, tell us what you want for heaven's sake. It's not brain surgery.' And then with Anna you were going, 'Hmmmm . . . this is too damn easy,' because the meetings were over in a flash. It was one extreme to another. With Anna there was no waiting, she was always prompt. In the past you sometimes hung around forever."

Michael Roberts, a longtime British friend of Anna's who became *The New Yorker*'s fashion editor in the midnineties under Tina Brown, had observed Anna closely over the years and came to the conclusion that she "simply likes to keep things brusque, abbreviated, and to the point."

Anna's imperious manner manifested itself even in the elevators and hallways of *Vogue*.

Toby Young, a British journalist who became a contributing editor to *Vanity Fair* in the midnineties, claimed there was an "unwritten rule" that Anna didn't permit anyone to ride on the elevators with her and that staffers "were expected to let her go first and take the next one."

He recalled how a jokester who worked as a researcher at *Vanity Fair* had talked about hiding behind a pillar in the lobby, waiting with a bunch of friends for Anna to appear, and when she got on the elevator would "pile in with her." His stunt would be carried out after having consumed lots of beans and beer the night before.

There was even a rule imposed about how Anna was to be addressed and when and where one might speak to her.

The teenage daughter of a *Vogue* department head had gotten a job as a summer intern and was warned by her mother never ever to speak to "Ms. Wintour." One day the girl was walking down the corridor when she saw Anna heading her way. Frightened of a confrontation with the boss woman, according to Young's account, she walked quickly and looked straight ahead, hoping they would pass safely like two ships in the night. But just as they got virtually face-to-face, one of Anna's high heels broke and she fell to the floor, sprawling at the girl's feet. Remembering what her mother had told her, she "gingerly stepped over Anna's prostrate form" and hurried to her mother's office, where the child was told she'd done "the right thing."

As Young saw Anna, "Here, at last, was Patsy from *Absolutely Fabulous* in the flesh."

Under Mirabella, everything was a team effort, decisions were made by committee, long and drawn out. People who came up with an idea were assigned that idea. All that changed drastically under Anna.

"Everyone was sort of an Indian, out doing their own stories, with a smallish story pot to pick from," says one editor who quit in less than a year, refusing to contend with Anna's demands and warp-speed drive.

"There would be a list of designers, and each one of the editors would want, of course, the same thing," she recounts. "So you would be crying, 'Me, me, me! Please, please, please.' It was funny and pathetic. We were like children. People were fighting. You'd bring in an accessory to use and hide it in a closet from everyone else. . . . You had to start wearing body armor because everyone was fighting for their piece of the turf. Anna really allowed powerful personalities in there to do their thing. It was like the end of the dinosaur era."

Anna brought in new writers. Some lasted, some didn't. One in the latter category was the magazine writer and novelist Julie Baumgold, Ed Kosner's wife, who had played an unsuccessful role in trying to keep Anna at *New York* when she was being wooed by Alex Liberman.

Anna viewed Baumgold as someone who could handle the kinds of celebrity stories she was now jamming into the magazine—some worthy, some puzzling, like the makeover layouts featuring tabloid faces such as Lisa Marie Presley and Ivana Trump.

In the late nineties, Baumgold's first assignment was a profile of Brad Pitt. "I never met Brad Pitt, and I wrote a quick piece on Brad Pitt because they had some wonderful Brad Pitt pictures—and nobody changed a word," says Baumgold. "It was sort of male beauty and I mentioned that Marilyn Monroe and Elvis had their noses fixed and that Brad Pitt had a little scar on his cheek."

That kind of piece was Anna's speed. She was thrilled and invited Baumgold to lunch.

"She asked me to become a contributing editor, and remembering that experience [writing about Brad Pitt], I said yes."

That was the last good experience Baumgold had working for Anna at *Vogue*.

She says her dealings with the editor in chief after that "were never direct. It always came filtered through other people, which was a mistake. It was always, 'This is what Anna wants . . .' And that wasn't the best way to have things filtered. It wasn't direct and then I never quite got it because it changed all the time."

On a piece Baumgold did on femmes fatales, she was told "Anna wants you to include Kate Beckinsale, Anna wants this, Anna wants that . . ."

Eventually, after several more pieces, it all became too much for Baumgold to deal with. "I worked for Anna for six months and couldn't stand it and quit," she says, laughing at the memory. "I can say that was the last time I enjoyed working in journalism. I left. That was it for me. This was a weak point in my magazine career."

While Baumgold made the cut with Anna but couldn't take dealing with her indirect demands, others felt that the corporate culture and journalistic direction of the magazine wasn't a perfect fit and fled.

Such was the case with highly respected fashion reporter Robin Givhan, who wrote for the lively *Style* section of *The Washington Post*.

Anna, who knew Givhan and had been interviewed by her for fashion stories over the years, approached her to become an associate editor, a job that had just opened up. Givhan was very flattered and thought, If I'm ever going to write full-time on fashion for a magazine, it's not going to get better than *Vogue*.

Givhan had always been impressed with Anna, especially by her "incredible decisiveness." She notes, "I would interview her, and there's never any hesitancy, always a really clear opinion, thought out, always supported. I'd talk to her about putting someone like Hillary [Clinton] or Oprah on the cover. . . . She always had a vision about why those covers mattered . . . saw how those decisions would have a ripple effect within popular culture. She can talk about that in a way that moves beyond just talking about clothes."

Anna pursued Givhan, who agreed to join the team. "Anna's very good at getting what she wants," Givhan notes. "She can be very charming."

But within a matter of a few months, Givhan began to have doubts about the job and began questioning whether Anna was the boss she wanted to work for and *Vogue* the place.

One reason had to do with the magazine's objectivity, or lack thereof. Givhan quickly discovered that the focus of any article she wrote or considered had "to be changed to accommodate the *Vogue* point of view." A newspaper like *The Post*, as Givhan well knew, chose people to be interviewed based on diversity, whereas at *Vogue* the rule of thumb was much narrower.

"You're looking for women who have a sophisticated point of view—not a suburban soccer mom but maybe a suburban charity worker. You're always thinking about what these women look like. They're going to be photographed so they need to project a *Vogue* sensibility."

In many ways, Givhan felt, writing for *Vogue* "was preaching to the choir, people interested in fashion, not women with an estranged relationship with fashion."

One story that intrigued Givhan and that she proposed to Anna never saw the light of day. It was about a designer who had a terrible reputation in the fashion industry, was disliked and self-destructive but continued to excel and draw public praise. "I thought it would make an interesting piece and give an insight to the goings-on behind the scenes."

But Anna didn't buy it.

"The point of *Vogue* is not to tear down the industry, but to celebrate it," emphasizes Givhan. "My story wasn't celebratory. *Vogue* takes the creativity of fashion seriously. It takes its readers' love of clothes seriously. A woman who just adores shoes is very easily mocked, but the magazine doesn't do that. They say, 'You know what? *You* love shoes, *we* love shoes, and there's nothing *wrong* with loving shoes.'"

After four months, it had all become too much for Givhan. But when she mentioned to a friend that she was thinking of packing it in, she was advised, "Honey, buck up. There are people out there who would mow down a crowd for your job."

After six months, Givhan turned in her resignation, left on what she felt was good terms with Anna, and returned to her fashion beat at *The Post*.

Anna had developed close ties with *The Washington Post*. She was friends with Katharine Graham, the owner, as was Anna's father. And Anna had become pals with Nina Hyde, the longtime fashion editor, who died from breast cancer, a cause Anna felt strongly about. So she tended sometimes to focus, when she was hiring editors and writers, on *Post* people. Another was Stephanie Mansfield, who earned a reputation for her bitchy stories and profiles of politicians and celebrities in the *Post's Style* section and was brought on as a contract writer by Anna. Their relationship didn't last long, either.

One of her assignments was a profile of the designer Donna Karan that was considered tough on her by *Vogue* standards—not negative, but realistic, dealing with her personal relationships, among other things.

"Maybe Anna had not read the story before it went in," says Nancy McKeon, who had worked with Anna at *New York* magazine and was a *Washington Post* colleague of Mansfield. "Anna took Stephanie out to lunch, and she was trying to kind of tell Stephanie, you know, we have to be careful with these people. And Stephanie's remark to me was, 'I don't know what those girls think they're doing up there, but it sure isn't journalism.'"

Then there were those who were so desperate to work for *Vogue* and were so fearful of Anna that they found themselves fibbing to her in order to be accepted for a job.

One such example of fabrication-for-Anna's-sake involves the blond, leggy, men-on-the-brain writer Candace Bushnell, who described the editor in chief as "one of the most frightening women in the world. I don't care what anybody says."

Anna had offered Bushnell a job and the two went to lunch to seal the deal, when the white lie slipped out.

"She's eating a steak that's like, bloody, like it was just killed in the street and brought in. I'm trying to eat a lamb chop. I'm, like, shaking," recalled Bushnell. "She's like, 'Well, Candace, you are exactly our demographic. You live in an urban area and you're thirty-two.' I was, like, 'Okay, I'm thirty-two.'

"I was actually thirty-six. But I was so frightened [of her] that I didn't want to say that I was thirty-six because I was convinced I would get fired before I even started to write this column. So then I started dating the publisher. So then I couldn't tell him [her true age] because I'd already lied to Anna and he and Anna talk all the time so it would've come out."

Bushnell, who as a columnist for the *New York Observer* created what became HBO's blockbuster *Sex and the City,* called her Anna experience "one of these horrendous situations you never ever think you'll get in." (A friend of hers tipped gossip columns and her real age eventually surfaced.)

Anna also killed stories if the subject wasn't attractive, thin, and beautiful. "She's monstrous-looking, have you seen her?" an editor recalls Anna saying of one well-known star.

Similarly, Anna is said to have killed an essay by a hugely successful author after she saw his photo that was to run with the piece and ruled he wasn't good-looking enough to grace her pages. The editor of the piece is said to have argued to no avail with Anna that it was all about the writer's words, not his looks.

Anna could be arrogant to major figures in the fashion world, such as the red-carpet diva Cindy Crawford.

Crawford, scheduled for the important September cover, was forced to attend three separate shooting sessions because Anna wasn't satisfied with her look. In the end, Anna killed the Crawford cover. When the model's people complained, they were told, "Cindy Crawford's just another model. I'm Anna Wintour!"

Under Anna, more celebrities and fewer known models made the cover. In 1998, for instance, Anna put on *Vogue*'s cover the likes of Liz Hurley, Sandra Bullock, Claire Danes, the Spice Girls, Renée Zellweger (whose fashion look Anna would control into the year 2004), Oprah Winfrey (Anna demanded she lose major poundage before appearing on the cover, and the queen of daytime TV obliged), and Hillary Clinton. As *The Guardian* in London pointed out, "Supermodel Carolyn Murphy, the August cover girl, actually seemed out of place in their company."

Anna would continue the trend, and by the time of the new millennium most *Vogue* covers were graced by celebrities.

As a new managing editor, Anna had hired Laurie Jones, one of her great supporters at *New York* magazine, who had been at the weekly for two decades.

It was Jones who had been so knocked out by Anna's portfolio that she brought her to the attention of Ed Kosner, the editor, who hired her on the spot and gave her the visibility that caught Alex Liberman's eye at *Vogue*. And it was Jones who, hoping to convince Anna to stay, told her, " 'You can't leave *New York;* you're the only one doing fashion. If you go to *Vogue* you will be lost.' I knew it would be impossible to replace her."

Now Jones was working for Anna and was still Anna's trusted lieutenant in 2004, a dozen years later.

Jones started at *Vogue* the day after the 1992 presidential election and re-members how enthused Anna was to see Bill and Hillary Clinton replace George Bush. "Anna'd been out at various parties," Jones recalls, "and she was very excited he'd won."

Anna was smitten with Clinton's charisma and sexiness, and could per-ceive the bad boy in him that was always so attractive to her in men. Having gone through the Gennifer Flowers scandal and survived to get elected, Bill and Hillary were celebrities, along with being shrewd politicians, Anna felt. "Anna told me the Clintons were the new Kennedys and the royal family wrapped into one," a *Vogue* editor at the time observes.

As the Monica Lewinsky sex scandal unfolded, the first lady was troubled about her look. She was never a fashionista. As a Beltway wonk, she favored navy blue pantsuits and low heels to hide her heavy legs, her hair was a disaster, and she had those fearsome eyebrows. The president's spouse realized that she required a mega-makeover. She started meeting with celebrity hairstylist Cristophe, and she conferred with haute-couture king Oscar de la Renta, who placed her in Anna's able hands. The two struck up a friendship.

Under Anna's tutelage—and Anna had an agenda going in—Hillary's wardrobe became more fashionable, even glamorous. She began wearing neutral-colored suits with long jackets that hid her wide hips, her hair became blonder and straighter, and she began wearing softer matte makeup. Anna scoffed at the look of some of the other female players in the Clinton drama, such as Lewinsky and Linda Tripp. "If you're going to make accusations about the president," she intoned, "you had better have a good hairdresser."

Anna's savvy bonding with the first lady and future New York senator resulted in a huge scoop for *Vogue*.

During the politically charged Ken Starr versus Bill Clinton year of 1998, Anna put a glamorous new Hillary Clinton on the cover of the December issue, the first time a first lady had ever struck a pose there. There she was, the stand-by-your-man wife of the embattled president looking poised and self-assured in a velvet dress, and beautifully coiffed.

Hillary Clinton's sitting ignited worldwide press so immense that the publicity department at *Vogue* sent the thick set of tear sheets out in a binder book. The issue sold more than a million copies on newsstands alone.

"The press hit way before the issue was out," Anna told *The New York Times*. "People have seen it as a vindication for [Hillary Clinton], that being on the cover of *Vogue* is beyond power and politics. It proves in a way that she is a woman of stature and an icon of American women."

Anna was extremely proud of her friendship with one of the most fascinating first ladies of the land since Jackie. So proud, in fact, that, after one of her visits to the Clinton White House she returned to New York with a stack of souvenir White House stationery. During a subsequent visit to London she gave some of the letterheads and envelopes to her brother Patrick, a political reporter at *The Guardian,* in London, who found her idolization of the first family rather amusing. "Patrick makes fun of Anna," says cousin Patti Gilkyson Agnew. "He wrote me a letter on the White House stationery and said, 'This is from Anna, and Anna's love of Hillary Clinton.' He said Anna brought the stationery over and left it, 'so don't think I'm writing you from the White House.'"

At *Allure,* Linda Wells jumped into the Clinton competition with an issue featuring a makeover given another of the commander in chief's women, the Minnie Mouse–like, big-haired Paula Jones. Tina Brown, not to be outdone, put "that woman, Ms. Lewinsky" on the cover of *Vanity Fair,* and a year later, Brown had Hillary Clinton discussing her hubby's infidelities in the premier issue of her new magazine, *Talk.*

But it was Anna who first saw star quality in the Clintons and scooped her Condé Nast competition.

Laurie Jones paints Anna as a superwoman of sorts. "She's very stoic, very strong," she declares. "She's fearless. Everything is done very quickly. There are a lot of meetings, but nothing goes for any length of time. Anna handles it all very efficiently. She approves all the story ideas. She does the run-through where all the clothes are brought in on the rack. When the pictures come in, she picks the pictures."

Anna's schedule was rigorous. Up at six A.M., she usually played a mean game of tennis before having her hair and face done professionally. In the office around eight A.M., she had rounds of meetings and made dozens of quick editorial decisions before going out for a high-protein lunch of a lamb chop or a hamburger, with hopes she didn't run into the animal rights activists who have constantly gone after her, once even throwing a dead raccoon in her plate, which Anna nonchalantly pushed aside and continued seemingly unfazed with her chopped steak. She usually left her office around six, and her evenings were as filled as her days. There were charity events that she had to attend—Anna has graciously given her time as a power in the fashion world to AIDS awareness and breast cancer. There were parties where she had to make an appearance.

At glittery events, she went from ice queen to glamour queen at the sight of the cameras aimed at her, preening and posing and smiling. There are literally thousands of photos of her doing it up for the lenses and modeling every kind of expensive outfit imaginable, many of them freebies from friendly designers.

Every night during an issue closing cycle she had to go through and approve stories and photos in the "book"—a sacred, thick, bound volume that is delivered to her home by an assistant. The layouts are in the order of their appearance in the magazine. The book, considered Anna's bible, is returned to the art department the next morning.

"Anna has gone over every layout, every page, and after she's reviewed it, the pages are filled with her Post-it notes," says Jones. "There could be a collage of different photographs, and something the size of a postage stamp, and Anna may say she doesn't like that dress, that whoever's wearing it wore it to such and such party on such and such date. Her attention to detail is phenomenal to me."

Jones emphasizes that Anna takes home manuscripts every night and "reads *everything* that comes into the magazine."

Well, almost everything.

In 1997, after a decade of research, author Patricia Bosworth's biography of her father, Bartley Crum, was published. Bosworth had written about her father's colorful career as a high-powered lawyer, his work as an adviser to Harry Truman, his crusade against the Hollywood blacklist, and his suicide in 1959 at age fifty-nine.

Acclaimed for her biographies of the dark lives of Montgomery Clift and Diane Arbus, *Anything Your Little Heart Desires* also was well received and got a full-page review by Mary Cantwell in the book section of *Vogue*'s April 1997 issue.

"*Vogue* reviewed my book wonderfully, which, of course, was enormously helpful," says Bosworth.

Bosworth's book wasn't a best seller, but the author did win a Survivor of the Year Award from the American Foundation for Suicide Prevention, a group in which David Shaffer was involved because of his expertise in the area of teen suicides.

The organization's annual awards dinner was held at a New York hotel several months after the review appeared. "Judy Collins sang to me, and it was all very emotional," says Bosworth, who was seated at a table with Anna and her husband, and couldn't help but notice that they had "no interaction" and "didn't talk to one another."

"Because *Vogue* had given me a huge spread, I leaned over and I naturally thanked Anna. But she had no idea what I was talking about. To my surprise, she told me she hadn't read my book and didn't even know the review was in her magazine," says Bosworth. "I just assumed she had read it, but she didn't know anything about it, and I was surprised since she's the editor in chief. I was struck by that, and I'm not an egomaniac."

A couple of months after the event, Bosworth ran into Richard David Storey, the features editor at *Vogue* who had overseen the review of her book, and told him what had transpired.

"I just said, 'I can't believe this. My God, she didn't read it.' It was then I found out that wasn't an isolated incident. He told me, 'Oh, no, it's par for the course. She never reads, or very rarely reads the copy for the books and movies—the arts coverage.' I found that absolutely staggering."

Along with all of her editorial duties, Anna gave Laurie Jones the responsibility of interviewing potential assistants.

Few were ever as hardworking, dutiful, and ambitious as Laurie Schechter or Gabe Doppelt, so Anna went through a number of them. But some were well liked by Anna. "She takes good care of her assistants," emphasizes Jones with pride. "Anna's very devoted to them. One moved on to be the assistant to the sittings editor."

But one especially turned out to be big trouble for Anna.

She was a tall, cute, preppy blonde just out of college who wanted to be a writer—a perfect *Vogue* specimen, or so she seemed. Her name was Lauren Weisberger.

"I was the one who hired Lauren Weisberger," acknowledges Jones.

It was a gutsy admission for Jones to make, because Weisberger's name, if whispered and overheard by Anna in the hallowed halls of *Vogue,* could lead to a career beheading.

Weisberger spent less than a year as Anna's assistant. After she left, she wrote a roman à clef called *The Devil Wears Prada* about life as an assistant to the barely fictional Miranda Priestly, described as the most revered—and hated—woman in fashion, the editor in chief of a fashion magazine called *Runway.*

Even though Weisberger repeatedly denied it, everyone in that rarefied world of fashion knew that Miranda and Anna were one in the same, only the names were changed to protect the guilty, and the author from possible legal action.

The book, part of a genre called chick lit, written and read by young women, became a bestseller in 2003 and followed in the wake of *The Nanny Diaries,* a fictionalized tell-all written by two former short-time nannies who worked for rich East Side Manhattan mothers. Both were the precursor to a 2004 best seller about beautiful Manhattan man-hunters called *The Bergdorf Blondes,* penned by a former *Vogue* writer and British pal of Anna's. The books appealed to the same demographic of twenty- and thirty-somethings who watched *Melrose Place, Friends,* and *Sex and the City,* and fantasized about having glamorous lives and studly lovers.

Publishers Weekly, the publishing industry trade magazine, gave *The Devil Wears Prada* a rave review: "As the 'lowest-paid-but-most-highly-perked assistant in the free world,' [Andrea Sachs, the protagonist] soon learns her Nine West loafers won't cut it—*everyone* wears Jimmy Choos or Manolos—and that the four years she spent memorizing poems and examining prose will not help her in her new role of 'finding, fetching, or faxing,' whatever the diabolical Miranda wants, immediately. . . . Weisberger has penned a comic novel that manages to rise to the upper echelons of the chick-lit genre."

In London, *The Daily Telegraph* dubbed the genre "Boss Betrayal" and noted that Miranda Priestly "is a stick-thin, British, steak-eating, tennis-playing, fur-and-Prada-wearing editrix with two children, who resembles Wintour in every observable way except that she invariably sports a white Hermès scarf while Wintour is know for her sunglasses."

The article pointed out that, in the interest of avoiding a lawsuit, no doubt, Weisberger "gives the real Anna Wintour a walk-on part."

Many of the reviews and articles about the bitchy novel actually turned sympathetic toward Anna. Some journalists felt the book was unfair. As *The Telegraph* article pointed out, and it seemed to represent the views of many others on both sides of the Atlantic, "Wintour is tough in her position, you have to be. You also have to be dedicated, hard-working, passionate about fashion, and self-disciplined."

The story quoted the newspaper's own fashion editor, Hilary Alexander, as saying, "I'm sure she [Anna] is probably quite tough to work for, but she has to be. She probably does make life impossible for her assistants sometimes because she has an iron will. It's the nature of this business. Fashion is full of workaholics for whom it is their whole lives because they love it."

With all the publicity, Anna had to say something, so she told *The New York Times,* "I am looking forward to reading the book." Hamish Bowles, her European editor at large, said the book should be laughed off as "very inventive fiction."

Privately, Anna fumed. "She was spitting fire," maintains a *Vogue* editor. "Anna felt she had been used and abused by Weisberger."

What the book did do, besides giving Weisberger her fifteen minutes, was to place Anna squarely in the mainstream celebrity pantheon. Besides the gilded venues of New York, London, Paris, and Milan, Anna was now known and talked about over Big Macs and fries under the Golden Arches by young fashionistas in Wal-Mart denim in Davenport and Dubuque.

Laurie Jones, who claims she never read the book, says Weisberger "wasn't here very long. When Richard Storey left"—the editor who revealed to Patricia Bosworth that Anna didn't read everything in her magazine—"she went with him. She wanted to be in features and there aren't many positions that open up there, so she asked to go with Richard as his assistant. While she was here she seemed to be a perfectly happy, lovely woman."

When Jones had to fill the position vacated by a more recent assistant of Anna's who was promoted, she had to do a lot of interviewing. "All those people had read the book," she says. "One of them asked me, would she have to walk Anna's dog. I said, no. I guess that's in the book.

"Anna doesn't share a lot of details about her personal life," acknowledges Jones. "She is slightly enigmatic, doesn't pour out her heart to people. There *are* questions, things people wonder about her—'nuclear Wintour' and all that. We go our separate ways, but we've always been able to talk about things."

thirty-eight

An Affair to Remember

It was a banner year for Anna, 1998. *Vogue* revenues were booming. In the previous twelve months it had posted its richest period since 1892, when *Vogue* was founded, and forecasts were even more optimistic. Along with being the world's diva of fashion, Anna also possessed the Midas touch. Her praises were being sung by the royalty of the magazine and fashion kingdoms.

Sir Si-*ness*, Si Newhouse, called Anna "the greatest *Vogue* editor of them all."

King of designers Oscar de la Renta raved, "She has the star quality—she *is* a star. There has never been a *Vogue* as important as *Vogue* is now."

Arie Kopelman, head of Chanel—designer of Anna's *Vogue* uniform—declared, "She has become a persona."

Her longtime colleague and court jester, André Leon Talley, noted, "The Red Sea parts when she walks through the room."

The designer Marc Jacobs was ecstatic. "If I design a grey thermal cashmere sweater, and Anna's wearing it, and it's also on Stella Tennant on the cover of American *Vogue,* the effect on sales is phenomenal. There's definitely a flock who follow what Anna does . . . she's a celebrity icon." Jacobs wasn't exaggerating. Anna did wear his gray thermal sweater, Tennant was on the cover sporting it, and it sold like Manolos at a fire sale.

The designer John Galiano described Anna as "my fairy godmother. Anna's influence cannot be underestimated."

Despite headline-making protests by animal-rights groups like PETA, the fur industry had come to worship Anna. The Fur Information Council of America, the fur trade group, observed, "Anna has had a huge impact on the amount of fur being used in fashion. The point about Anna is she influences the influencers."

Along with fur, Anna also was far ahead of the competition when it came to athletic wear for nonathletic activities. Bloomingdale's fashion director Kal Ruttenstein, always a big fan of Anna's, said his chain "rushed to the market to look for these kinds of clothes" after *Vogue* presented them to readers. And he declared, "Where Anna leads, it seems, the rest of the world follows."

"Simply put," observed James Truman, the British editorial director of Condé Nast who had succeeded an aging Alex Liberman, "Anna is running the industry, far beyond her influence as a tastemaker. All designers check in with Anna about what she thinks is modern, what she thinks is hip. She gives them the broad trend ideas about what the public is ready for."

October 1998 had the greatest significance for Anna. It was a landmark for her, her tenth anniversary as editor in chief. For a decade she had run the most powerful fashion magazine in the world, turned it around, and made it soar with a more contemporary mix of celebrity profiles, trendy features on food and style, and fashions more accessible to mainstream women.

None of her competitors was ever able to knock her out of the box. Not Liz Tilberis at *Harper's Bazaar,* who, dying of ovarian cancer, published a memoir in 1998, the year before her death, that was highly critical of Anna. Not Grace Mirabella, whose *Mirabella,* called by the media "the magazine born with a silver spoon in its mouth" because of Rupert Murdoch's backing, couldn't really compete and officially ceased publication with its May 1995 issue. It got a brief reprieve when another publisher, Hachette, picked it up with plans to publish six times a year, but it didn't survive. Not *Elle,* which continued to pursue *Vogue* vigorously but never could jump into the lead. And there was no horse race with other fashion monthlies that popped in and out.

Vogue was Anna, and Anna was *Vogue*—an unbeatable combination.

"She's far more than just another well-paid hack," pronounced *The Guardian* in London in a piece celebrating her decade at the helm. "She's the most influential person in fashion today. . . . Wintour is either the fashion world's fairy godmother, championing new talent and keeping the industry hip and modern; or she's its answer to *The Godfather,* single-handedly controlling a $160 billion global industry."

In a major story in *The Washington Post* headlined "Anna's World: In Industry of Glamour, Editor of Vogue Turns a Lot of Heads," it was noted that Anna "has been both deified and demonized" over the past decade of her reign. But the article pointed out that however people felt about her, "just about all agree she has taken *Vogue* to a whole new blockbuster level as the bible of fashion—and that she has become an icon in the process."

Not bad at all for an obsessive fashionista who had reached the pinnacle of the fashion magazine world without even a high school diploma, with no journalistic writing or communications skills in the pre-*Vogue* years of her career, and with a wild side.

Anna's philosophy at *Vogue* was to determine and define fashion—and to help fashionistas choose what was and wasn't fashionable. She believed that because there was so much clothing in the marketplace, most women required guidance and direction. Thus, *Vogue* under her started and shaped fashion trends by focusing on the work of favored designers, many of them Anna's discoveries and pals.

Through the years, a good deal of the magazine's content has been a reflection of her personal taste, though she has asserted that her editors were sometimes "much better at spotting trends" than she was. "I know they wouldn't be working for me if they didn't feel the magazine did justice to their eye as well as mine," she once said.

Nevertheless, it was she who ran the industry, she who designers touched base with about what she thought was "in" and "hip." Like a guru, she sent down the message from on high about what she thought the public wanted.

Early on Anna was *the* poster girl for Chanel, was a strong supporter of Yves Saint Laurent, Christian Dior, Azzedine Alaia, Bill Blass, Geoffrey Beene, Helmut Lang, Narciso Rodriguez, and Gianni Versace; of the Japanese such as Issey Miyake and Kenzo whose sensibilities were mixed with European elegance. She wore them, and promoted them. Anna was one of the earliest champions of Vera Wang and her beautiful bridal dresses. The furs of Adolfo, Ben Kahn, Marco Gianoti, and Dennis Basso—much to the consternation of animal-rights advocates—have been favorites of hers, and have been *Vogue* advertisers.

Marc Jacobs, whom she has championed, said his design work is often influenced by what Anna tells him in broad strokes. "She'd never say, 'Oh, don't do this or that,'" he has said. "I don't fax her designs—I usually tell her what I'm thinking about." But designers do send her their ideas for her approval. "I'll call them before the couture or the collections and say, 'What are you thinking?' and sometimes they'll send me sketches."

As Condé Nast's editorial director James Truman has noted, "Anna is not a newspaper editor, spending weekends with Tony Blair. *Vogue* has always been half in and half out of the industry, and Anna fully comprehends both aspects of it. Anna is a strategist. It is through her relationship with designers that *Vogue* has become the bible of fashion. It pays dividends in ads and how esteemed the magazine is. I can't say which comes first."

And that's why she's *the* fashion world's most powerful figure, one who can make or save a designer's career. One whom she saved was another favorite, John Galiano. When his business was struggling financially, *Vogue,* unlike other fashion magazines, continued to prominently feature his designs. Anna had also come to his rescue by footing his costs for a trip to New York and a salon show, and helping him to find an investor. He called what she did for him "an act of loyalty unheard of in the industry."

In the new millennium, Anna would champion the careers of young designers like Tom Ford, Stella McCartney, and Zac Posen. An Iranian-born designer, Behnaz Sarafpour, had started working for Anne Klein and Isaac Mizrahi, but then Anna issued an edict that Sarafpour was about to be the next fashion star, and the world of fashionistas took notice of her independent sexy line.

Twenty-something Lazaro Hernandez, an aspiring designer, ran into Anna at the airport in Miami, gave her a note telling how much he idolized her and fashion. A few weeks later, Michael Kors—another acolyte of Anna's—sent him a note saying, "Anna Wintour says you should work here." Several years later Hernandez and his design partner, Jack McCollough, won the Perry Ellis Award for new talent. They are the two behind the label Proenza Schouler.

Anna also became a huge supporter of the work of young Swedish designer Lars Nilsson, whose background was in French haute couture and the tailoring of men's clothing. He became the head designer of Bill Blass. Anna helped his rep by wearing one of his shirts to the VH1/*Vogue* fashion awards.

There's always reversible sides to every story, to wit: Anna has had her battles and feuds with designers, such as Geoffrey Beene, Alexander McQueen, and Georgio Armani.

"Wintour is a woman of simmering discontent, a boss lady in four-wheel drive who ignores or abandons those who do not fuel her tank. As an editor, she has turned class into mass, taste into waste. Is she not a trend herself?"

So declared Beene in the midnineties after Anna stopped covering him, and he refrained from inviting her to his shows.

When McQueen failed to make a showing at one of Anna's favored events—the Metropolitan Museum's Costume Institute gala—she was said to have gone ballistic, threatening to boycott his future shows. They reportedly had a rapprochement.

In the early nineties, in the middle of New York Fashion Week, Armani decided to throw a party at the Museum of Modern Art. It was not the best of times to expect a joyous turnout because Anna and the rest of the fashion crowd had just returned exhausted from the shows in London, Paris, and Milan, and it was raining that night.

Furious, Anna did make a showing at the party and also a fashion statement underscoring her anger. She wore a bright yellow sequined scuba jacket designed by Karl Lagerfeld for his Chanel collection.

"It was a blatant signature piece of a collection that was the diametric opposite of Armani's look," recalls fashion writer Michael Gross, who was there that night. "Anna was a walking fuck-you. She absolutely wore it to send him a message. It was her way of saying, you know what, buddy, making me come out tonight to see a Milanese designer in the middle of New York Fashion Week is simply not right, so I'm going to wear this glaringly insulting outfit.

"It's bad enough to wear another designer, but to wear the bright yellow runway piece to the command performance gala of the designer who epitomized imperiousness said to me that I had underestimated this woman.

"Fashion is a power game, and Anna has come to epitomize fashion as a power game. She clearly had this will to power and that was the first night that I saw that there was more to her than the imperious fashion editor hiding behind glasses with her legs twisted around like a corkscrew and her arms crossed in front of her, always seemingly cagey and hiding. I always thought it was a cover for some vast insecurity, but that night I admired the shit out of this woman."

Despite her enormous success and power professionally, Anna's personal life was in a dreadful state by the late nineties. Her seemingly happy marriage to her guru, David Shaffer, was on shaky grounds. Just as 1998 was an extraordinarily wonderful and joyous year for Anna, 1999 would turn out to be one of the ugliest periods in her otherwise glam life—a year filled with carnal scandal, tear-jerking heartbreak, and stranger-than-fiction irony.

Though Anna and Shaffer tried to keep their private life very private, there were signs of growing discord and discontent.

The two were seen together at public events less and less and, when they were, the psychiatrist looked glum while the editrix-wife switched on her brilliant, albeit enigmatic, smile for the photographers. The couple barely communicated. During a vacation in tony St. Barth's in their fourteenth year of marriage, Anna and Shaffer sat together on the beach but never spoke a word and were described by an observer as sad and bored looking.

A high-profile journalist who covered the fashion world recalls how Anna and Shaffer had angry dinners together in an Italian restaurant near their Greenwich Village home. "They would fight so bitterly at the table that often one or the other of them would get up and walk out, and the other would sit there alone finishing their meal. They were the kind of public rows that one would think that a stylish, image-conscious person like Anna would not engage in. Other times she'd eat alone if they weren't talking. She would walk into certain restaurants in her neighborhood and demand a certain table. If it wasn't ready she would blow her top. There was tremendous anger there."

This source says he "never understood" the marriage. "David is certainly no Adonis and he's such a mild-mannered guy, though he was her Svengali. It was amusing that he married Anna and that he specialized in disturbed teenagers—somehow that always rang true to me."

Despite all of Shaffer's love and support over the years, Anna is said to have gotten bored with the marriage, just as she got bored with the length of skirts, or photographers who had served their purpose, or assistants who didn't act slavish, or designers who no longer turned on her fashion juices.

"She was numb, tired of their routine—playing Scrabble was one of their pastimes—and she wanted more excitement in her life," says one close observer of the marriage. "David was so different from all those men she'd been involved with in the past. Not to sound mean or cynical, but I think David, who is really brilliant and very charming, had served Anna's purposes. He gave her two lovely children, was a great father, was her guiding light through the most important years of her career. But I think after all of her success Anna felt omnipotent, felt she could handle it all on her own. She needed a new beginning—and then Shelby came along."

At a glitzy New York City Ballet gala at Lincoln Center in late 1997, Anna met a new man, and her life was about to be turned upside down. She was chatting at the table of the diamond-encrusted socialite and philanthropist Ann Bass when she was introduced to tall, sexy, rugged, extremely bright and wealthy entrepreneur John Shelby Bryan. Bryan, three years older than Anna, was the top man at the five-hundred-million-dollar ICG Communications, headquartered in Denver. He also was a major fund-raiser for the Democratic Party and threw political events at the posh East Seventy-first Street town house that he shared with his second wife of some seventeen years, Katherine Bryan, a psychologist and marriage counselor, and their two children. As a money-raising star in the Democratic Party, he was an "FOB," friend of Bill. When President Clinton learned of Bryan's affair with Anna, he called Katherine Bryan, with whom he once flirted, from Air Force One to offer his condolences.

"Shelby was the Marlboro Man to David's Pillsbury Doughboy," maintains a well-placed observer to Anna's blossoming relationship. "Anna, who is one of the world's great flirts, and Shelby, who is a skirt chaser extraordinaire, fell for each other the moment they locked eyes at that gala. She was like a schoolgirl, acting sexy with him. And he was smitten. It took a while for them to *really* get serious—they were both married, for God's sake!—but their meeting that night sealed the fate of both of their marriages."

Until she met Bryan, Anna had been viewed as a caring and loving wife, which was quite a feat, especially during the period when she was alone in London running British *Vogue* and later spending long hours changing *HG* and American *Vogue* into her image.

Friends say that, despite her ambition and drive and the demands of her career, Anna had always tried to be compassionate and sensitive to her hus-

band's needs, as he was to hers. "There was a point about midway through
their marriage when David was going through major suffering from ulcers,"
says a pal who knew Anna from her days with Jon Bradshaw. "Anna was just
so concerned, and I don't think my wife would be as sensitive and caring to
me as Anna was to David. I was there at their house in the Village one day
and David had the ulcers and there were tears in Anna's eyes. She was worried
about getting the right doctors for him, and the fact that he couldn't eat this
and couldn't eat that. And she was hugging him and holding his arm and crying. I was truly moved because in all my years of marriage, I've never seen
that from *my* wife."

Anna and Shaffer were also concerned and loving parents, and would do
anything in the world for their children, Charlie and Bee. They were active as
much as they could be in their very fancy private schools. They attended parents' nights and orientations regarding the course curriculums for the year,
and Shaffer at one point volunteered to be a safety patrol crossing guard at his
son's school.

But they rarely mingled with the other parents. "Anna always sat by herself
at all school functions," says a parent. "When she and David came together
before they broke up, they sat next to each other and apart from everybody
else. They were cold and aloof and felt they were above everyone else."

However, they made at least one halfhearted attempt to be friendly when
they invited a group of parents for cocktails and hors d'oeuvres. They'd even
hired transportation and bought tickets to treat them all to a Neil Simon play.
It was a gracious gesture and an apparent attempt by Anna to be more of a
down-to-earth mother. But it turned into a strange scene because the Shaffers
at the last minute never joined the others at the theater. Recalls one parent,
"We had been rushed in and out of the house, and after they didn't come
with us to the theater, everyone was like, 'What's with them?' That sort of
sealed their fate with the parents in the class from then on."

Not long after Anna met Bryan, he began sending her flowers and little
gifts. Once things started heating up, Anna would close the door to her office
at *Vogue* to chat with him on the phone, and she soon began taking long
lunches, seeing him secretly. Anna knew the game well; she'd played it when
she was with Jon Bradshaw.

Unlike the Euro types Anna had been involved with over the years, Bryan was all-American, his roots buried deep in the oil-rich Texas soil. The man for whom the city of Austin was named, Stephen F. Austin, was his great-great-great-great-uncle, and the town of Bryan, Texas, was named after another ancestor. The man for whom Shelby Bryan was named, Evan Shelby Smith, his maternal grandfather, owned enormous tracts of land in Brazoria County. Bryan's father, James Perry "J.P." Bryan, was a lawyer, his employer for many years was Dow Chemical, and he was a regent at the University of Texas. Bryan's older brother, named after their father and also called J.P., was hugely wealthy, the money flowing in from a Houston oil and gas company he founded called Torch Energy Advisors.

Bryan was something of a jock. At high school in Lamar, Texas, he was a football player. "He also was a pompous ass at fourteen," recalls a co-ed who became a prominent Houstonian. "Shelby was cocky, self-assured, and *very* good-looking. He was involved with the most beautiful cheerleader, he was big man on campus, handsome, and muscular—the same as he looks now [2004], but minus thirty or forty pounds. He was *very* popular and everyone adored him, for the same reason why people like him today. He's a guy's guy, a man's man. Just very macho."

She could have been talking about Bradshaw.

At the University of Texas, where he studied history and art, Bryan played some football and at one point was a Golden Gloves boxer. He went on to get a degree in law. A pal, Fred Baron, now a powerful Dallas attorney, called him "the Great Gatsby—you could tell he was going to be successful." In the early seventies, when Anna was just starting out in the fashion magazine world in London, Bryan worked for Ralph Nader in Washington, D.C., then went to the Harvard Business School, and for a time was at Morgan Stanley. From there he eventually got in on the ground floor of the cellular phone business and made a bundle.

Along with being a macho jock, with a good business head on his broad shoulders, Bryan was "a mama's boy," says another Houstonian—and that might have something to do with why he fell for Anna, and she for him.

For the two, mama and Anna, were remarkably alike.

Bryan's mother, beautiful Gretchen Smith Bryan Chandler Josey, who died of cancer in the early 1990s, was a fashionista par excellence who draped herself in Chanel or mixed and matched it with Yves Saint Laurent. She was a culture maven, involved in the Houston opera and in charity work, and was driven and ambitious.

"Gretchen was very Dina Merrill–*ish*," says a friend. "Thin, not tall, she had the look of society, *very* country club, with a little edge. She had the pretty blond frosted hair, not the cookie-cutter haircut. She had an artistic flair—her clothing, her whole look was different from other Houston women. She was a style setter. If Shelby was looking for a woman like his mother, he couldn't have chosen anyone more like her than Anna Wintour, in terms of style, glamour, and fashion."

Shelby Bryan's mother also was said to have figured in the demise of the marriage of wealthy "old money, old guard" Houston oilman Jack Josey. "Gretchen didn't come from old money, but she married into Jack's family and Jack's reputation and Jack's social standing," says a friend, "and *then* the closets became *full* of designer names and couture."

Josey had followed in the tradition of the legendary married Houston oilmen who kept one or more women on the side, and it was rumored that Shelby Bryan's mother, before Josey married her, might have been one of them. As a friend said of Josey, who died in 2003, "He loved to party. He liked the women. Shelby followed in his footsteps."

There was one legendary Houston oilman who is said to have built an apartment complex in which he housed all of his ex-mistresses, took good care of them, which kept them from talking. As one knowledgeable Houstonian noted, "Jack Josey's father had mistresses, too, and he also had a very understanding wife. Every time she caught him, she got diamonds. That's how these rich Houston men grew up. It was a way of life."

The wealthy Josey was Shelby Bryan's mother's third husband. Her second, after she arrived in Houston with Shelby and his brother after her divorce from their father, was to a much younger local TV news personality. That marriage lasted only a year or two, but they remained friends.

During that time she was the proprietress of a chic little antiques shop.

As the friend points out, "Gretchen married well but divorced better. Jack Josey was a great catch with a money-is-meant-to-be-spent-and-have-fun philosophy."

By the time his always glamorous and chic mother married the millionaire oilman, Shelby Bryan was grown and earning his own fortune.

The Joseys had one of the grandest houses in all of Houston. Though she had decorators, she was very involved in supervising style, design, and theme—just like Anna. The house was filled with antiques that she chose and a world-class art collection that she and her husband pulled together. Art and the love and knowledge of it was another interest Shelby's mother and Anna had in common.

"Gretchen was one of the most beautiful and fashionable women Houston had ever known," notes her friend Diane Lokey Farb, a powerful Houston real estate agent. "You couldn't take your eyes off her. Gretchen was always in Chanel. Beyond that she was a very driven, very strong woman. Whatever Gretchen wanted to achieve, she would just go forth and achieve."

Anna appeared to be a virtual clone of her new lover's mother.

Shelby Bryan tended to pursue interesting, chic women. Anna wasn't his first.

At twenty-two, just out of law school, Bryan married Lucia Ann Rawson, a pretty Houston society woman two years older than him whom he had started seeing in college. Like Bryan's mother, his mother-in-law, Natasha Rawson, said to have been a Russian ballerina in her day, was a fashionista.

"I always confused Natasha with Gretchen," notes a Houston socialite friend. "Natasha was divine, glamorous, a natural and great beauty. Lucia looked nothing like her mother. Lucia's a nice, cute, lovely, and charming gal—quiet and low-key. But her mother looked just like Shelby's mother—*breathtaking*, with fine bone structure and clear transluscent porcelain skin. I would see her and I would think, 'Why are you in Houston? You belong in Paris.'"

Shelby and Lucia Ann Bryan had two children, Ashley, who was born in Boston in 1973, and Alexis, born in New York, in 1976.

Four years after the second child, the marriage fell apart, and the couple separated on November 1, 1980. Bryan filed for divorce on the grounds that his marriage "had become insupportable because of discord or conflict of personalities."

The divorce was final on August 6, 1981, a few weeks before what would have been the Bryans' thirteenth wedding anniversary, and she got a nice settlement that continues to the end of 2024. From their house in exclusive River Oaks, Bryan was permitted to take a punching bag. But he also kept property the couple owned in the tony Wainscott area of East Hampton, a condominium in Houston, some fifty-six acres of land in Brazoria County, Texas, along with the Porsche, the Jaguar, and the Pontiac, and stock in a number of companies.

He wasted no time in remarrying, tying the knot for the second time some seven months after the divorce. On March 12, 1982, he married his girl-friend, Katherine Gurley, a brunette Kansas beauty with a young son—but not before she signed a prenuptial agreement. Some six months after the Bryans' wedding, their first son, John Austin Bryan, was born. A second son, James Alexander, was born in 1985.

Anna and Bryan tried to keep their affair a secret, but they were reportedly spotted early one morning leaving an elegant Manhattan apartment building, Anna draped in a chinchilla coat meant for evening wear. The sighting reached the media, and in 1999 the scandal broke. At home, David Shaffer learned of the affair when he found a message Bryan had left for Anna on their answering machine.

The psychiatrist called Katherine Bryan, the psychologist. "Your husband and my wife," he is said to have told her, "are fucking each other."

The gossip press was all over the story like Chanel on Anna. The outrageous Internet fashion industry Web site Chic Happens, overseen by Ben Widdicombe and Horacio Silva, two thirty-something Australians working in New York, was the first to break the story based on an anonymous e-mail. Chic Happens was designed for fashionistas and people within the industry who wanted to drop a dime on their colleagues and bosses. Where else could one find items such as "Which aging glossy editrix dyes her pubic hair to cover the grey?" Because Anna was at the summit, she was a particular target of Chic Happens, and the Web site ran bitchy items about her. But the story about Anna's adulterous affair was the biggest. Widdicome, who later became a gossip columnist at the New York *Daily News,* and Silva, an editor at *The New York Times,* never revealed their Deep Throat but noted that most fashion magazines "treat their staff like dirt . . . if you screw someone they get on the phone. They want revenge." The pair believed that Anna had subsequently attempted to censor their appearances on cable TV; they were told by station executives they could not mention her name, or any of Condé Nast's magazines, on camera.

"Page Six," the must-read gossip column in Rupert Murdoch's tabloid *New York Post,* was running neck and neck with Chic Happens, and ran a blind item in February 1999 asking, "Which fashion oracle—who appears to have an ideal home with a loving husband and kids—has been having a year-long affair with a telecommunications titan who also appears to have a wonderful marriage?"

By mid-June, the "Intelligencer" gossip column of *New York* magazine, Anna's alma mater, reported under the headline "Wintour of Discontent?" that after a "series of teasing half-blind items in the tabs" Anna's "love life is fast becoming a public drama." The item didn't mention her lover by name but described him as a "millionaire Democratic fund-raiser" and said that they'd been involved "for more than seven months, in a none-too-secret dalliance that has raised eyebrows all over town."

Asked for comment, David Shaffer stated, "I have no plans to get divorced, and I hope Anna has no plans to get divorced."

In London, Anna's father's former newspaper, *The Evening Standard,* quoted an anonymous "close family friend" as saying, "I think for the first time in her life, she is madly in love with someone and she finds the whole experience totally overwhelming."

When *Texas Monthly* did a small profile on Bryan in the wake of the breaking scandal, he confirmed that he and his wife had separated. But regarding Anna he stated, "There's an old-fashioned view that your personal life should be kept private, and that's my view."

In her syndicated column in *Newsday,* Liz Smith called Bryan "the romantic fly in the sticky ointment of Anna Wintour's marriage. . . . And let me add this, I have heard only the most unsettling things about Mr. Bryan, all about how 'fascinating, naughty, thrilling, exciting, and bad-boyish' he is said to be. Conversation about this tycoon makes him a cross between a movie star and Lord Byron. And I am told by everyone observing that the delectable Wintour is over the moon in love with him, more excited and happier than she has ever been in her formidable and controlled life. It isn't just his money, either, although, of course, money is always in vogue."

While Anna refused to talk to the press about the scandal, her and Shaffer's high-powered New York lawyer and spokesman, Ed Hayes, put up a smoke screen. "I promise you that I'm not doing a divorce. They're together, they love their children, and they're going to stay together," he said.

Every September, the world's fashion press descends on New York for the annual rag trade bacchanal called Fashion Week, when the beautiful models strut their stuff, when fortunes and reputations of designers and manufacturers are won or lost, depending usually on how Anna reacts to what she sees and what *Vogue* subsequently features in its glossy pages.

But all the attention for the 1999 Fashion Week was on Anna herself, seated, as usual, front row center. Her marital scandal was on everyone's glossy lips.

As the fashion reporter of London's *Daily Telegraph,* pointed out, "the fashionistas loved it. After all, this is an industry that thrives on celebrity gossip at the best of times, and when the target is one of its own—indeed the widely feared queen of them all—you can virtually hear the shears being sharpened."

That week, the September 20 issue of *New York* magazine, with every fashion person in the world in town, chose to make Anna its cover girl. The story was headlined "The Summer of Her Discontent," and it went into gossipy detail about Anna's extramarital relationship. The article called Bryan "a flashy extrovert . . . with a notoriously roving eye."

On the outside, Anna was very British stiff upper lip, but on the inside, according to a close source, "She was embarrassed and devastated. For someone like Anna, who is so private and secretive, to have her dirty laundry strutted down the runway for the world to see, to have the biggest skeleton in her closet on display, it was the worst. She railed against the press, against her competitors at other magazines who were gloating. Anna's never been much for introspection, but she suddenly was doing a whole lot of soul-searching. She felt guilty. She felt sick. She didn't know which way to turn."

And, indeed, there was great schadenfreude in the bitchy, wicked world of fashion.

Despite her disgust at all the horrendous gossip, the media-savvy, tight-lipped, ultraprivate Anna actually cooperated somewhat with *New York* magazine as it was preparing its story and gathering photos. Surely she must have realized that the weekly was rubbing its hands together and was going to do a number on her. But she agreed to be interviewed, to a point. The article quoted her as saying just forty-two words regarding the scandal. Over lunch at her favorite table at the Four Seasons with the writer she said, "There are certain things that no one wants to read about in the tabloid press." She added, "You know that your friends and your family have one vision, and if the outside world has another, then that's just something that you don't focus on." She also acknowledged that there was nothing in any of the reports that she wanted to correct.

However, Anna's involvement with the photographs that ran with the article was an entirely different story. While she agreed to the brief interview, she refused at first to pose for an exclusive photo and instead sent over to cover editor Jordan Schaps, her longtime friend at the magazine, a box containing pictures she was authorizing the magazine to use.

"One was in black and white taken by [*Vogue* fashion photographer] Mario Testino," says Schaps, "and it had Anna with bangs down to her eyebrows, big sunglasses, and a fur coat pulled up so you barely saw her. It could have been Audrey Hepburn or Greta Garbo. She looked to be concealed, hiding, and very removed."

Schaps went to the editor overseeing the story, told him he didn't like the photo, and asked to be told when the interviewing was finished. He said he had a plan. When he got word that the editorial side had finished, he called Anna.

"I told her, 'Look, we all know the story is not going to be a puff piece; it's going to be tough. Why should you not look terrific, look courageous, look open on the cover? If the readers see a great cover they'll think it's a great story, no matter what. We'll go into a studio and not come out until we're all satisfied.'" It was the weekend. Anna said she was taking her children to see a tennis match, but she'd think about it.

A few days later she called Schaps and agreed to pose, but not with the photographer he had suggested, whom she did not know. She wanted the famed fashion and celebrity shooter Herb Ritz. Schaps agreed, and the shoot was scheduled for the next day at Chelsea Piers, a commercial and entertainment complex on the Hudson River.

Anna arrived in a tank top over a short skirt, and with her was André Leon Talley, who was there as her stylist, "fussing and mussing and making sure everything was fine," Schaps says.

In the end, *New York* got an exclusive cover photo of Anna. It showed her unsmiling, looking determined, her bob streaked with blond, wearing a tight white wife-beater, her skinny but toned arms defiantly crossed. It was a hot shot, but she wasn't thrilled with the story.

"I heard it had a very devastating effect on her," Schaps says.

At *Vogue,* managing editor Laurie Jones contends that "Anna allowed them to profile her," which was not actually the case. The magazine was going to do the story whether or not she cooperated, but Anna's hope was that by offering some cooperation they might go easy on her.

Jones says she was "not surprised" that Anna agreed to participate to the extent that she did, and notes that she herself was offended by the article. "I told Anna I wanted to write a letter to the editor, which I did to complain, but she never would have asked me. She never feels she's being picked on unfairly and never complains. She would never say anything, and there have been things in print which are totally inaccurate and unfair, but she wouldn't complain. She just thinks these are things she has to deal with, and she deals with them by herself. She is a very strong woman."

As for Anna's affair, Jones says, "I was very surprised . . . it was something nobody really expected, but she seems very happy."

thirty-nine

A New Life

November 1999, the cusp of the new millennium, was the cruelest month for Anna.

Even in the best of times—and those were the worst—she wasn't looking forward to it.

For November marked a major milestone in her life: the big five-o.

Turning fifty, a difficult rite of passage for most, was even tougher for Anna, whose whole being and philosophy, both for herself and for *Vogue,* was based on looking young—model young, movie star beautiful young, mini-skirt and Manolos sexy young.

But now she faced fifty embroiled in a horrid, very public extramarital affair and a hellish divorce. Moreover, she was concerned whether her relationship had legs, because in recent months her lover had been on and off her radar.

"Shelby was cooling his heels," says an insider. "Katherine had caught Shelby before. He had apologized and said he'd never do it again if she took him back. Now he got caught again, this time with Anna, and he was profusely apologizing. At that point I don't think he wanted to divorce his wife for Anna."

Another knowledgeable source observes, "Shelby was not the epitome of the monogamous guy, and Katherine knew that. He had a reputation as a ladies' man. Katherine knew very early on that Shelby had hooked up with Anna, but I don't think Katherine ever thought it would come to much."

For a time there was speculation that Anna and Bryan had ended it, and that Anna was trying for a reconciliation with an angry David Shaffer.

A woman writer friend of Jon Bradshaw's, who also knew Anna, was shocked when she first saw Bryan and noticed his resemblance to Bradshaw and how similar they acted around women. "I met Shelby one night at my literary agent's house and he was already with Anna, and flirted with me. I couldn't believe it!"

On Wednesday, November 3, Anna celebrated her fiftieth birthday.

The very next day, she got an urgent call from her brother Patrick in London. Anna's father, *the* most important influence in her life, whose icy manner and editorial style she inherited and emulated, had died in his home in Tisbury, Wiltshire. At his side was his second wife, Audrey. Wintour was eighty-two years old, and the cause of death was cerebroarteriosclerosis, or a hardening of the arteries in his brain.

Along with all the turbulence in her life, Anna was now struck with great sadness over her father's passing.

"She was devastated, in a state of shock," says a longtime family friend. "First of all, there was all of the horrible chatter over her affair, and then came her father's death. It was too, *too* much, even for Anna, and she's like the Rock of Gibralter. Charles really was the most influential man in Anna's life. He was her teacher, her guide, her adviser. She was like him in many ways—tough, stern, icy, creative. It's a cliché, but she really was Daddy's girl."

Now both of her parents were gone. Nonie had died three years earlier, on January 5, 1996, eight days before her seventy-ninth birthday. The passing of the divorced, lonely, and retired social worker came as she was being treated for pneumonia and a preleukemia blood cell disorder at London's prestigious Royal Brompton and National Heart Hospital. Friends from when she was married, such as the film critic Alex Walker, weren't even informed of her death. According to an American cousin, Anna telephoned to tell her of her mother's death, one of their few contacts. In London, a small memorial service was held. Prior to Nonie Wintour's hospitalization, she had been living in a flat in Chelsea where Patrick Wintour and his wife, Madeleine Bunting Wintour, also a *Guardian* journalist, lived, and they watched over her. The couple later divorced.

On word of her father's death, Anna dropped everything and flew to London to deal with funeral arrangements (he was cremated) and a memorial service.

The *Guardian* said in its obituary, "If the test of a good editor is the ability to stamp a new sense of style and purpose on a newspaper, then Charles Wintour . . . was one of the greatest editors of the second half of the century. He was one of the acknowledged masters of his trade . . . a courtly man with a sharp pen and a sharper private tongue. . . . Those who worked for him did not always love him, but he commanded universal respect for his shrewdness and speedy decisiveness. He was, with military precision, the general in every battle."

When Anna's sadness diminished, anger erupted when she discovered a shocking clause in her father's will.

The document was dated August 23, 1993, when Anna and David Shaffer, always considered a "saint" by Charles Wintour, were still together. The clause stated: "I DO NOT leave a share of my residuary estate to my daughter Anna Wintour Shaffer as she is well provided for but I wish her to know that I am very proud of her great success and achievement and I am equally pleased that she has combined her career so happily with her family life."

Anna's happy family life was now a thing of the past.

And to Anna's chagrin, her father's estate, valued at upward of one million dollars in stocks, shares, and personal and real property, was left to his widow, whom Anna much resented; the widow's two children from a previous marriage; and Anna's three siblings.

Anna wasn't as much upset about not being an heir as she was that her stepmother and her father's stepchildren were beneficiaries.

With a memorial service for her father scheduled for December, Anna returned to New York, where she was met with yet another emotional blow.

On November 20, Alex Liberman, who first spotted Anna's talents and was the dominant creative and political force in guiding her career through Condé Nast to the summit at *Vogue,* died at his retirement home in Miami. He was eighty-seven. For Anna, who owed her career to Liberman, his death, just two weeks after her father's, came as a jolting shock.

In Anna's rarefied world, November appeared to be a cursed month. Thirteen years earlier, almost to the day of Liberman's death, Jon Bradshaw had

suddenly died. And it would have been the fifty-ninth birthday of her brother Gerald, whose death in that car-bike accident in 1951 left the Wintours in emotional shambles.

On December 6, about a week before her father's memorial service, Anna made an appearance at one of her treasured events, the Costume Institute Gala that she cochaired at New York's Metropolitan Museum of Art. It was a very special occasion that year because the institute was opening a new exhibit of rock and roll fashions. The place was packed with boldface names— Henry and Nancy Kissinger, Ahmet and Mica Ertegun, Prince Pavlos and Princess Marie-Chantal of Greece, Jerry Seinfeld, Jennifer Love Hewitt, Elizabeth Hurley, Debbie Harry, Kate Moss, Elle Macpherson, Donatella Versace, and Calvin Klein.

But there in the center ring was the spectacle of Anna, with all of the scandal buzz focused on her, crying in public with mascara running down her cheeks, her tear-filled swollen eyes covered by her sunglasses. Some thought she was upset because Shelby Bryan had to leave the party early on the night that was planned to be their most public appearance since they decided to divorce their spouses. One of the celebrities present, Whitney Houston, who had her own marital problems with her husband, Bobby Brown, was quoted as saying that Anna was so furious she would "fuck that boyfriend up!"

In fact, it was the death of her father and Alex Liberman, along with the roller-coaster ride of her affair, that had caused Anna to fall apart that glittery evening.

"Anna felt as if a dark cloud had descended over her and would not clear away," says a friend who saw her in London when she returned for her father's memorial service.

Hundreds of VIPs, celebrities, and journalists turned out for the celebration of Wintour's life, held in the Vilar Floral Hall of London's Royal Opera House on December 13. David Shaffer was not listed among them, but Shelby Bryan was.

Anna spoke lovingly about her father and also talked compassionately for the first time in anyone's memory about how his second wife had made the last two decades of his life pleasant. There seemed to have been sort of a rapprochement, at least publicly. Anna's speech was believed to have been written by her brother Patrick.

The journalist Paul Callan, who had started out in newspapers working for Charles Wintour, "was suddenly struck by how closely she reminded me of her father in voice and manner. When I closed my eyes, I thought it was Charles speaking."

After the service, Anna posed with family members for a photograph. She was the only one smiling for the camera, as if she were on the red carpet at an awards dinner. Susan Summers, who had worked for Charles Wintour at the *Evening Standard*, went up to Anna, who was wrapped in mink, to offer her condolences and say a few nice words about her father. "I reached out, and she recoiled—actually recoiled! I don't know if she was expecting me to throw paint on her mink or what, but it was an actual physical recoil. She's sort of like the queen. You're not supposed to talk to her."

In the new millennium, Anna and her husband were divorced in New York, the papers sealed by the court. But, as a friend of the couple asserts, "Anna was very generous with David." Anna's brother Jim, however, told Vivienne Lasky, "Anna got to keep two houses."

In New York, Katherine Bryan filed for divorce in Manhattan Supreme Court on March 10, 2000, charging "adultery" and "cruel and unusual treatment." Five days later, Bryan sued her in Houston, three days after what would have been their eighteenth wedding anniversary. He felt it would be more financially beneficial for him to get the divorce in the Lone Star State, although he owned three homes in New York, because that's where their prenuptial agreement was written and signed and was covered by the Texas community property law. Moreover, Texas had no-fault divorce, which meant details of his affair with Anna wouldn't be made public. His Houston lawyer, Don Fullenweider, said his client was more a Texan than a New Yorker. "He's a fifth-generation Texan," the lawyer declared. He pointed out that besides New York, Bryan had property "everywhere," operated an oil company in Houston and belonged to that city's fancy River Oaks Country Club, and had a ranch in Brewster County. His wife's lawyer, Bernard Clair, claimed that New York was the proper venue. The lawyers, clocking big-money hours, fought on.

As part of his divorce petition, Bryan asked the court to enforce the prenup. Under it, Katherine Bryan had agreed to seek no more than half of the community property and not to seek any interest or share of his separate property. The prenup also called for a couple of options. One was for him to pay her nine hundred thousand dollars. The other was to be an amount equal to 10 percent of his after-tax net worth in excess of ten million, payable in four equal yearly installments. A clause called for similar amounts for alimony, and fifty thousand dollars a year in child support until their children reached the age of eighteen.

At the time Bryan met Anna, he was said to be worth thirty million dollars. But in August 2000 he resigned from his lucrative position as chairman and chief executive officer of ICG Communications, operator of a nationwide voice and data network. Between the spring of 2000 and the day of his resignation, the company stock, of which Bryan owned 2.3 million shares, had dived from $39 a share, to $6.47, a loss, at least on paper, of $75 million. The New York *Daily News* observed, "It looks like some kind of karma just caught up with" Bryan. "Given the new circumstances, it will be interesting to see how long Bryan remains in vogue with Wintour."

That summer, despite the financial mess, Anna reportedly vacationed with Bryan in the south of France, with her two children and his two sons.

Then, in November of 2000, high-flying ICG Communications filed for Chapter 11 bankruptcy protection. Press reports said that the company was riddled with debt.

Nevertherless, Bryan was still well off, and he and Katherine Bryan reached a settlement and were divorced. Their town house, where Bill Clinton was once entertained at a Democratic fund-raiser, reportedly sold for eleven million dollars, and the former Mrs. Bryan moved to Park Avenue.

Just as Audrey Slaughter had made Charles Wintour a happier and less icy man when she hooked up with him, Anna appeared more relaxed and less frosty with Bryan then she had with David Shaffer. She lightened and highlighted her signature bob and in public wore her sunglasses less. And there was talk that she even looked younger—a nip and tuck here and there wasn't out of the question. At a New Yorkers for Children Fall Gala, Anna boogied with Bryan to the Village People's disco gay anthem "YMCA," and the boyish Bryan grabbed Gwyneth Paltrow and Oscar de la Renta, and he and Anna danced with them.

Anna's divorce appeared to have little emotional impact on her children.

As a family observer notes, "Bee and Charlie live in a world of friends whose parents have affairs, whose names wind up in the gossip columns, who get divorced. They just felt it was a way of life."

Anna has always had a close bond with her daughter—the child attended her first fashion show in her terrible twos with her mother—and some were later convinced that Bee Shaffer, as one fashion wag observes, "is Anna squared without the shades and the bob."

By age ten the two didn't see eye-to-eye regarding fashion. "She doesn't listen to anything I say," complained Anna. "She likes overalls and sweatpants, and she doesn't like dresses. As long as she's happy, that's fine, but occasionally, I would love her to wear a dress."

The child often confronted Anna when she was dressing to go out for the evening, critiquing that what she was wearing was "too revealing." Declared Anna, "She'd like me to go out like a monk."

All that changed when the youngster entered her teen years and became what one fashion journalist described as a "beautiful young fashion plate in her own right." At an event on the arm of Olivier Theyskens, who designed for Rochas, she wore a "flattering, dreamy, frothy, pale strapless full skirted tulle gown."

In the spring of 2003, when at Anna's prodding Condé Nast saw fit to jump into the pop tart arena with a fashion and style magazine aimed at young girls called *Teen Vogue,* sixteen-year-old Bee Shaffer was named a contributing editor—nepotism, like wearing fur, had never been a problem for Anna. Anna felt that girls who could barely see over the edge of a catwalk were budding fashionistas. "They see media coverage . . . They are so much aware of what is going on in fashion than girls used to be. And that's the magazine's reason for being."

Anna's daughter became involved in the first issue, said the magazine's editor, Amy Astley, a protégée of Anna's. "I really love what Bee has to say. She's obviously the ideal *Teen Vogue* reader. She and her friends are a ready-made focus group. They're smart and really sophisticated and clearly know a lot about fashion, but they're still normal girls."

Every so often, Anna and her sleek, shiny-haired, and buxom daughter, who has been described as the *Vogue* editrix's "mini-me," sit together on the front row at the shows and occasionally attend cocktail parties together.

A Wintour family friend, the publicist Paul Wilmot, said Anna's daughter, considered poised, elegant, and regal, has "the DNA and, by osmosis, she's got the exposure and experience. . . . Don't be surprised if she winds up a young editor somewhere."

Or America's next hot model.

By mid-2004, there was talk that several agencies had interest in representing Bee, but she had her sights on going to college, something her mother hadn't done.

With her divorce out of the way, Anna was on top of the world. As always, *Vogue* was number one and Anna was in total control. And she now had Bryan all to herself.

And then she got word that her longtime nemesis, Tina Brown, now running gossipy *Talk* magazine, was about to strike, having assigned a "grudge" profile of Bryan. Brown had left enemies behind when she jumped ship at Condé Nast to start *Talk*. Anna was at the top of the list.

"Tina has a very visceral hatred for Anna," discloses a close observer of the two women. "It was not predicated on anything logical, or anything that Anna did to her, but was predicated once again on the innate rivalry that would arise between these two very driven and tough British editors."

Brown focused on Bryan in particular, the insider asserts, because Brown's husband, the editor Harry Evans, allegedly had affairs. "Tina was very bitter about that and was asking friends why nobody was concentrating on other editors who had bad marriages. There had always been stuff about Harry, blind items in the tabloids about him, so Tina was very bitter—not only about the negative press, but about her husband's womanizing. So suddenly there's Anna messing around with Shelby, and Tina couldn't wait to do a story in *Talk*. From what I gather it was a grudge piece."

Another element in Brown's decision to go after Anna by publishing a piece about Bryan was the fact that an unauthorized biography about her marriage was in the works by *Vanity Fair* (Condé Nast) writer Judith Bachrach. Brown expected that the book about her life with Evans would be a hatchet job.

"Even though Bryan made for a legitimate news story, Anna was beside herself when she got wind of the *Talk* piece and made a slew of telephone calls to Brown pleading with her not to run the story," says a publishing insider. "Brown told her not to worry, but that she planned to continue pursuing the story. Anna contacted every power player she knew in media to try to get the piece killed. From what I hear, she pleaded with Graydon Carter [the editor of *Vanity Fair*] and went to Si [Newhouse] to see if he could help."

The *Guardian* in London, where Patrick Wintour was a reporter, jumped on the war between the two British magazine queens and noted that Brown "has heartlessly ignored Anna's pleas" not to run a piece about "Anna's arm-candy. . . . The enmity between them runs deep."

The unflattering piece was headlined "The Talented Mr. Bryan," and went on from there.

There was a full-page photo of the onetime Golden Gloves boxer, hands on the hips of his pinstriped two-button business suit, looking ready to take on all comers.

The photo on the contents page showed a sunglassed Anna with a slinky off-the-shoulder dress next to a tuxedoed Bryan. The very first line of the story, which was supposed to be about Bryan's business practices, began, "Last June, having just returned from a vacation in the south of France with his girlfriend, *Vogue* editor in chief Anna Wintour..."

The article touched on the affair and also quoted a number of women who made claims about Bryan's "louche behavior."

In her book, Bachrach notes wryly that "Tina was good enough to send Wintour a copy of the published article, with a 'With Compliments' card attached."

Indeed, Brown had done what appeared to the media to be another number on Anna, and she was surely out for revenge.

Neither Bryan nor Anna took any legal action against Brown's magazine for the article, but Bryan successfully pursued a libel claim against the London *Daily Telegraph*, which had picked up material from the *Talk* piece under a headline "English Queens of New York in Clash over Wintour's Boyfriend." Five months after its piece ran, the *Telegraph* apologized to Bryan and admitted that certain facts in the story were erroneous. The newspaper apologized to him in a published story and agreed to make a generous donation to a charity of Bryan's choice and to pay his legal fees.

The fashion Web site Chic Happens, which broke the story of the affair, pointed out that "Britain's more lenient libel laws" made a judgment in Bryan's favor "more likely" and noted that "a victory in the UK—the home turf of both Wintour and Brown—would be that much sweeter." The writers added, "If you're reading this, Shelby, 'WE DON'T HAVE ANY MONEY.'"

With Bryan on her arm, Anna began to have another love affair—with the glitterati of Houston, her lover's hometown, where the glamorous twosome began making stopovers and where Anna was treated like visiting royalty. Anna and Bryan also sparked whispers and gossip with their openly amorous ways. At a party for his brother at the exclusive Bayou Club, which includes high-powered members such as George W. Bush, Bryan and Anna acted like a pair of going-steady adolescents at a spin-the-bottle party.

"In front of the world, Shelby and Anna spent a good part of this party making out, tongues down each other's throats, seated on a bench in a little foyer to the party room," asserts a well-placed observer of the Houston social scene.

Anna became friends with a number of the city's wealthiest and most powerful fashionistas, women who read *Vogue* as closely as they do a prenuptial agreement, fashion horses who spend at least tens of thousand of dollars a year to fill their closets with designer duds.

One with whom Anna eventually bonded was Becca Cason Thrash, a gorgeous fifty-something wife of one of the city's gazillionaires who had to expand her closet by more than a thousand square feet to fit all of her elegant Chanel, Lacroix, Helmut Lang, Stella McCartney, Gianfranco Ferre, Sergio Rossi, Marc Bouwer, Jean Paul Gaultier, and La Perla. Name it, she had it. In Houston—and in New York and Paris—this daughter of a Harlington, Texas, TV sportscaster who married right was a boldface name, written about in the *Houston Chronicle*, *Women's Wear Daily*, *Town and Country*, Tina Brown's *Talk* before it became defunct, and *Harper's Bazaar*, in which the fashion diva was profiled as one of "Couture's Big Spenders." The magazine had followed Thrash and two others through fittings in Paris.

Thrash had once been dubbed "the high priestess of posh" and had earned the sobriquet "TriBecca," because she usually changed her sexy, gorgeous outfits three times at the extravagant parties she threw in her twenty-thousand-square-foot mansion: indoor pool, two-thousand-square-foot kitchen, glass-floored second level. The place was once described as looking like a "cutting-edge art museum."

"Anna just *loves* Texas, she *loves* it," declares the exuberant Thrash, who had invited Anna to be the guest of honor at a party at her home for the Houston Stages Repertory Theater, an evening that included an abbreviated performance of *Full Gallop,* a one-woman show about the life of *Vogue's* onetime vaunted editor Diana Vreeland.

"We on the theater board were thinking about various ways to really make the evening interesting and we came up with the idea of inviting Anna," Thrash says. She notes, though, "There's no comparison between Anna and Diana Vreeland other than the fact that they both held the same job. Anna absolutely does not compare herself to Mrs. Vreeland."

The arrangements for Anna's royal visit were made by another Houston fashion powerhouse, Susan Criner, who was a close friend of Bryan and of his mother. "Susan and Gretchen were so close," notes Thrash, "that when Gretchen died, a lot of her Chanel couture and a great number of her Chanel suits went to her. Susan owns and wears them to this day."

Until the glittery night of the big party, Thrash says she felt "intimidated" by Anna. "I'm not easily intimidated, but there are no words to use to describe to what lengths Anna herself, her persona, intimidated me. When I would see her at couture at the fashion collection, I'd be intimidated. She'd come in with those signature sunglasses on and take the best seat on the front row, and I'd think, 'God she's a *very* imposing, *intimidating* character.' You *know* who she is. The world *knows* who she is. Everyone *knows* that's Anna Wintour, *the* most *influential* woman in fashion, *globally*."

It all was too much for Thrash to comprehend, so Anna became a scary figure to her.

Everyone who was anyone in Texas and the fashion world seemed represented at Thrash's party—politicians, celebrities, designers. Thrash had custom lighting installed to give the walls a red tint, and models were hired to move among the guests in dresses by the designers who were there: Mark

Badgley, James Mischka, Diane von Furstenberg, among others. One woman was overheard complaining about her "jewelry elbow," apparently all the bracelets and rocks she was sporting were too heavy.

Anna, wearing a silvery Chanel suit, minus the sunglasses, arrived fashionably late, holding hands with Bryan. All eyes were on her. The local press had reported little if anything about their extramarital relationship. Gossip like that just doesn't see print in Houston. Lawyers threaten suit *before* items run. But everyone in Thrash's wide circle knew all the dirt about Anna and dished about it incessantly. One of the guests noted that without her glasses Anna's eyes blinked rapidly and that she did a double take looking at the bountiful new breasts of a Texas rose in a low-cut Ralph Lauren gown who introduced herself, practically bowing to the editrix from New York.

That night, the once intimidated Thrash bonded with her imperiousness when they shared the table of honor.

"It was just the eight of us"—Anna and Bryan, the Thrashes, the Criners, and Bryan's brother and sister-in-law—"and we spent three or four hours at the same table and interacted, and I just thought Anna was great, and I was no longer intimidated," emphasizes Thrash. "Anna was delightful, and she is completely one-hundred-percent misunderstood. It's just that she's a slow warm-up, really. I do think she is *very* British, *very* reserved, and for a Texan that can be misunderstood.

"At my parties, I never seat people next to each other who are sleeping together, so I put Anna between my husband and J.P. [Shelby's brother], so my husband was her dinner partner, and he *adored* her, thought she was fabulous and *very* sexy—not in a blatant way, but in a subtle way."

At a certain point during the evening, Thrash's besotted mate got up to talk to another party guest, and Bryan, "who is so very effervescent and fun, dashed over and sat in his chair as fast as he could, and Anna and Shelby leaned over and kissed," recalls Thrash fondly. "They're like a young couple in love. And when all the speeches and presentations were done, Anna and Bryan were the first ones on the dance floor. My girlfriend was dancing next to them and she told me, 'God, they were kissing, and he was *all* over her.' It was just like at a prom."

The following Monday, once again all business, Anna, who never had a real prom, was at her huge desk in her enormous corner office with a wall of glass that gave her a spectacular view of Times Square from the new Condé Nast tower.

She was on top of the world, professionally and personally, ready to start work on another lushly beautiful, catalog-thick, very lucrative, style-setting, sexy-celebrity-on-the-cover issue of *Vogue*.

And as always, she was prepared to do battle with her competition and, as usual, come out the victor.

By the middle of the first decade of the new millennium, her relationship with Bryan was still golden. The two were seen together at fashion shows, cocktail parties, and cultural events in New York, holding hands. But when the photographers moved in to take pictures, Bryan usually evaporated into the background, leaving Anna in the spotlight. Their affair was no longer considered hot news and had long been out of the gossip columns.

But in May 2004, their life together once again became tabloid fodder. The *New York Post*'s Page Six ran a headline that blared: "Anna, Lover in 'Illegal' Sublet." The story alleged that Bryan was illegally subletting an enormous $5,800-a-month penthouse loft from the internationally known hairdresser John Frieda. A woman whose family owned the loft building claimed that Frieda had moved out and was "replaced by Bryan and Wintour." When the woman, Beth Windsor, confronted them, "they froze. By this time Anna was getting her mail" from Frieda's old mailbox, "which she promptly body-slammed shut and tried to disappear into the wall. She's very small and almost got away with it. Shelby then said, 'We're only staying here for one or two days,' in a phony British accent." Then Anna and her man went out for a night on the town.

At *Vogue*, Anna had the best people working for her, the prize photographers, among them the incomparable Helmut Newton, whose erotically charged, compelling, and glamorous fashion shots had long been an asset of the magazine. He was thought of as the creator of "porno chic."

At eighty-three, Newton was still under contract and had been faxing ideas to Anna in 2003 from his home in Monte Carlo for a layout he planned to do for her in Los Angeles.

The two had a close working relationship, dating back to the late seventies when Anna was fashion editor at *Viva*.

"Over the years, we had our moments. Anna and I had *many* moments," says Newton, recalling how "tough and demanding and stubborn Anna can be. But she always knew what she was doing. She knew when to listen. It wasn't just charm that got her where she is today.

"We were at odds many, many times about her choice of my pictures. She could be very tough, but I've always respected Anna. *Vogue's* her magazine, and she knows so much about the job. Mostly she does me very proud. No one can top her. She'll be in charge of deciding what's in and out of fashion long after I'm gone."

Not long after Newton, who earned the sobriquet "King of Kink" because of his sexy portraits, arrived in the City of Angels, tragedy struck. As he was driving out of the garage of the Chateau Marmont hotel on Sunset Boulevard on January 23, 2004, he suffered an apparent heart attack, lost control, and crashed into a wall. He died in the Cedars-Sinai Medical Center. His wife and muse, June, also a photographer, shot pictures of her fatally injured husband of many years. On June 2 his ashes were laid to rest in Berlin, his birthplace.

In July, Anna was among the world's most famous fashionistas who paid homage to the great man at a memorial service held in the splendorous and baroque Theatre du Palais Royale, in Paris. Wearing a black-and-white Carolina Herrera dress, Anna spoke eloquently of her years working with Newton. "Plenty of shocking things happen at *Vogue*, but there has never been anyone so consistently scandalous as Helmut," she confided. She called him a "visionary photographer" who possessed the magic touch to turn the most boring shoot into an erotic happening. The photos he turned in to her, she said, had left her over the years "aghast, awestruck and always amazed."

Then she surprised the gathering that included Tom Ford, Marc Jacobs, Jean Paul Gaultier, Stella McCartney, and Anna's daughter, Bee, who wore one of her mother's black Prada dresses—she served as an usher at the service—by disclosing her one regret in an otherwise glamorous and very successful life. She revealed that as a young fashion editor at *Harpers & Queen*, Helmut Newton had offered to photograph her, but the shoot had never come off.

Declared Anna: "I would have loved to have been one of Helmut's women. I can't think of a greater compliment than to have been deemed worthy of Helmut's lens."

The sadness of the event for Anna, though, gave way to a feeling of elation because of wonderful news from America.

Si Newhouse informed her that the September 2004 issue would be the largest *Vogue* ever, and the biggest monthly magazine in publishing history—a whopping 832 pages. It was clear that as Anna Wintour headed toward a quarter-century as editor in chief, she had truly turned *Vogue* into the most important and successful fashion arbiter and glamour page-turner in the world.

Selected Bibliography

Bachrach, Judy. *Tina and Harry Come to America*. New York: Free Press, 2001.

Bradshaw, Jon. *Fast Company*. London: High Stakes Publishing, 2003.

Chisholm, Anne, and Michael Davie. *Lord Beaverbrook*. New York: Knopf, 1993.

Felsenthal, Carol. *Citizen Newhouse*. New York: Seven Stories Press, 1998.

Gross, Michael. *Genuine Authentic: The Real Life of Ralph Lauren*. New York: HarperCollins, 2003.

Hackett, Pat, ed. *The Andy Warhol Diaries*. New York: Warner Books, 1989.

Haden-Guest, Anthony. *The Last Party*. New York: William Morrow, 1997.

Kazanjian, Dodie, and Calvin Tomkins. *Alex: The Life of Alexander Liberman*. New York: Knopf, 1993.

Levy, Shawn. *Ready, Steady, Go!* New York: Doubleday, 2002.

Mirabella, Grace. *In and Out of Vogue: A Memoir*. New York: Doubleday, 1995.

Neville, Richard. *Hippie Hippie Shake*. London: Bloomsbury, 1995.

Schlesinger, Arthur M., Jr. *A Life in the Twentieth Century*. Boston: Houghton Mifflin, 2000.

Tilberis, Liz. *No Time to Die*. Boston: Little, Brown, 1998.

Vreeland, Diana, *D.V.* New York: Alfred A. Knopf, 1984.

Wintour, Charles. *Pressures on the Press*. London: Andre Deutsch, 1972.

Young, Toby. *How to Lose Friends and Alienate People*. New York: Da Capo, 2002.

Author's Note on Sources

Since *Front Row* is the first biography of Anna Wintour, I was faced with the enormous task of tracking down scores of knowledgeable, creditable sources—her schoolmates, friends, family members, colleagues, employees, lovers—because little was known about Anna's pre-*Vogue* life, private and professional.

Her years growing up in England, her schooling there, her first jobs in London and New York, and the Wintour family's tragedies, triumphs, and scandals were essentially unknown to the public and the media, especially in America.

It wasn't until the mideighties—a decade after Anna settled in Manhattan—that she became a subject of major news media attention and scrutiny with her appointment as creative director of *Vogue,* her first step toward being named editor in chief. News accounts beginning in that period, therefore, also were valuable sources, along with the author's first-person interviews, in the telling of Anna's story.

With all of that in mind, I would like to point out that all source quotes—people interviewed by me or my researchers—are written in the present tense ("she observes," "he notes," "they say"), and quotes from all other sources—newspaper and magazine articles both foreign and domestic, and books—are written in the past tense ("he said," "it was stated"). As I pointed out in my acknowledgments, Anna Wintour declined to cooperate with me. Therefore the quotes attributed to her throughout this book come from my sources, from news stories, or from published interviews, and those quotes are in the past tense ("Anna declared," "Anna said").

Along with my many on-the-record interviews, two books contain valuable material and intimate details about Anna's relatively brief editorship of British *Vogue* and her beginnings at American *Vogue.* They are Grace Mirabella's memoir, *In and Out of Vogue,* and Liz Tilberis's autobiography, *No Time to Die.* Quotes and thoughts attributed to them by me are from their books and from press interviews Tilberis and Mirabella gave. Tilberis had died by the time I began researching this book, and Mirabella pointed me to her own tell-all, diplomatically emphasizing that she had "no more to say on the subject of Anna Wintour."

As I have noted, reports in a number of newspapers and magazines about Anna's life and career, mostly from her *Vogue* years forward, were valuable resources. Among them are, in London, the *Guardian, The Times, The Sunday Times,* the *Daily Mail, The Mail On Sunday, The Evening Standard, The Daily Telegraph, The Independent, The Observer, Private Eye, Harpers & Queen, Tatler,* and *Time and Tide.* In the United States, the publications included *The New York Times, The Wall Street Journal,* the *New York Post,* the New York *Daily News, The New York Observer, The Houston Post, The Washington Post,* the *Los Angeles Times, Women's Wear Daily, New York* magazine, *Time* magazine, *Texas Monthly, Talk, Spy, Savvy, Viva,* and *Vogue.* A number of Web sites were also informative, among them Salon.com, BFI.Org.UK, Lookonline.com (Daily Fashion Report), Photography.About.com, Totallycool.net, Fashionweekdaily.com, Sixtiespop.com, and Hintmag.com.

Index